HARVEST C

Harvest of fear

A history of Australia's Vietnam War

John Murphy

Westview Press
Boulder & San Francisco

Published in 1993 in Australia by
Allen & Unwin
9 Atchison Street, St Leonards NSW 2065 Australia

Published in 1994 in the United States by
Westview Press
5500 Central Avenue
Boulder, Colorado 80301

Library of Congress Cataloging-in-publication
data available upon request

ISBN 0–8133–2039–9

Set in 10/11.5 pt Plantin Light by DOCUPRO, Sydney
Printed by Australian Print Group, Maryborough, Vic.

Contents

IV: Withdrawal

Acknowledgments

In the research for this book I have accumulated substantial debts. The first of these were to the archival staff who helped me find my way into the records in their care. In Canberra, the staff were unfailingly helpful in the National Library of Australia Manuscripts room and Oral History collection, in the Australian War Memorial Research Centre and Written Records section, and in the Australian Archives. In Melbourne, I am indebted to staff at the University of Melbourne Archives and the Australian Archives branch at Brighton, and in Sydney, to the staff of the Mitchell Library. In Hanoi, staff in the National Library, and in Ho Chi Minh City, in the library of the Institute of Social Sciences, were of assistance in finding materials.

A number of people helped immeasurably with comments on drafts of some or all chapters; in particular, Brian Aarons, Peter Beilharz, Lynn Buchanan, Peter Christoff, John Fitzgerald, Peter McPhee and Val Noone. For their encouragement, I would like to thank Hazel Rowley and Brian Stagoll. For help with whatever understanding I have of the Australian soldiers' experience in Phuoc Tuy, I am particularly indebted to Graham Walker. Some of the protagonists in this story, listed in the bibliography, gave me interviews and helped with their time and with recollections of particular points. Above all, Stuart Macintyre was an unstinting supervisor of the doctoral thesis on which the book is based, generous with his time and encouragement, and assiduous with comments on draft after draft. Despite all this help, at some points I have been stubborn, so the faults which remain are more than usually my own.

I am grateful to the research committee of the Department of History at the University of Melbourne for financial assistance which made it possible to travel to Vietnam for research—and to take up Tawney's recommendation that historians need to walk about the sites of their history. My colleagues in the Department of Sociology and Politics at Phillip Institute gave support for me to find the time to complete the research and writing.

For their permission to reproduce cartoons or photographs, my thanks to Bruce Petty, Les Tanner, the National Library of Australia, the Australian War Memorial, the John Fairfax Group, David Syme and Co., News Limited and the University of Melbourne Archives. I am grateful to John Romeril for permission to quote from 'The Fairy Floss Memorial', and to People for Nuclear Disarmament (NSW) for permission to use and quote from the Save Our Sons collection.

At Allen & Unwin, Mark Tredinnick, Lynne Frolich and Elizabeth Fiezkhah were patient and enthusiastic in easing the manuscript towards publication. For help with photographs, I am grateful to Ross Genat, and for maps to John Nicholson.

Translations from the French are my own; for his assistance with repairing my translations from the Vietnamese, I am indebted to Anthony Chan Nguyen.

But my greatest debt is undoubtedly to Lynn Buchanan.

Abbreviations

AA	Australian Archives
ACC	Australian Council of Churches
AFV	Australian Force Vietnam—headquartered in Saigon
AICD	Association for International Co-Operation and Disarmament (NSW)
ANL	National Library of Australia
ANZUS	Australia, New Zealand and the United States [Treaty]
APC	Australian Peace Council
ARVN	Army of the Republic of [South] Vietnam
ATF	Australian Task Force
ALP	Australian Labor Party
AWM	Australian War Memorial
CANSA	Committee Against the National Service Act
CAU	Civil Affairs Unit
CD	Commander's Diary
CICD	Congress for International Co-Operation and Disarmament (Vic)
CND	Campaign for Nuclear Disarmament
CPA	Communist Party of Australia

CPA (M-L)   Communist Party of Australia
             (Marxist-Leninist)
CRS   Commonwealth Records Series [Australian Archives]
DLP   Democratic Labor Party
DRU   Draft Resisters' Union
GVN   Government of [the Republic of South] Vietnam
HQ   Headquarters
HS   Herbicide Series [AWM records]
ILO   International Labour Office
ML   Mitchell Library—State Library of New South Wales
NLF   National Liberation Front—strictly speaking, the
             National Front for the Liberation of South Vietnam
PAVN   People's Army of [North] Vietnam
PF   Popular Forces—village-based GVN forces
PQF   Peace Quest Forum
PSDF   People's Self-Defence Forces—village-based GVN
             forces
RF   Regional Forces—province-based GVN forces
SDA   Students (later Society) for Democratic Action
SDS   Students for a Democratic Society
SEATO   South East Asia Treaty Organisation
SOS   Save Our Sons
UMA   University of Melbourne Archives
UN   United Nations
US   United States
VAC   Vietnam Action Campaign (Sydney)
VC   Viet Cong
VCC   Vietnam Co-Ordinating Committee (Melbourne)
VCND   Victorian Campaign for Nuclear Disarmament
VDC   Vietnam Day Committee (Melbourne)—later VCC
VMC   Vietnam Moratorium Campaign
VPC   Victorian Peace Council
WPC   World Peace Council
WWF   Waterside Workers' Federation
YCAC   Youth Campaign Against Conscription
YCL   Young Communist League—aligned with CPA
             (M-L)

Author's note

The French colonial division of Vietnam was reproduced in the Communist Party's administrative structure; thus the south—Nam Ky—was Cochinchina, the centre—Trung Ky—was Annam, and the north—Bac Ky—was Tonkin. With the Geneva Accords of 1954, the country was temporarily divided into the South—the Republic of Vietnam (GVN)—and the North—the Democratic Republic of Vietnam (DRV). The convention of 'South' capitalised is employed here to denote the GVN, and of 'south' to denote the old region of Nam Ky.

I have used 'Party' capitalised to refer to the Communist Parties of Australia and Vietnam, and in lower case to refer to other parties, except where spelling out their names. Similarly, 'Moratorium' capitalised has been used to refer to the Moratorium movement, and in lower case to refer to the marches by that movement.

Illustrations

Maps

Introduction

On a chilly evening in the middle of May 1954, the External Affairs minister addressed one of the heartlands of Australian conservatism. Richard Casey was speaking to an electoral meeting of some 250 people at the Peace Memorial hall in Toorak, the domain of Melbourne's old money. He was only recently back from Geneva, where an international conference on Indochina and Korea was brokering the end of French colonial rule in Vietnam—and, unwittingly, the beginning of the civil war of the next two decades. The French cause, only days before, had suffered its final setback when Viet Minh forces overran the fortress at Dien Bien Phu. It seemed another crisis point in the Cold War era, as Australians anxiously glanced at events in Asia.

Casey was a pragmatic man. An engineer by training, firmly Anglo-Australian and patrician in outlook, his mind was more attuned to his cherished light aircraft than to flights of ideological rhetoric. But he was not above 'agitating the electors', in a phrase Soviet foreign minister Molotov had used to him in Geneva. And when Casey did so, he brought considerable authority to the task. On this chilly evening, he warned his audience that Australia needed powerful friends to ensure its survival: 'With the black cloud of Communist China hanging to the north, we must make sure that our children do not end up pulling rickshaws with hammer and sickle signs on their sides.'

In a climate of uncertainty and fear, this was a powerful image to conjure, partly because it resonated through multiple layers of meaning. The vision of enslaved children was a potent one, tapping deep strains of anxiety about dispossession. But for the hammer and sickle—which gave the rickshaw its modern location in the Cold War period—the image could as easily have been invoked at any time during the previous 100 years. Since the gold rushes of the mid-nineteenth century, a substantial theme in Australian culture and policy had pivoted on the perceived '"Yellow Peril" to Caucasian civilisation, creed and politics'. The fear of Asian dispossession of a thinly-populated country ran through the labour movement's racism, the White Australia immigration policy, the experience of Japanese military aggression, and the fear of Chinese expansion after the communist victory in 1949. All touched the same vein of unease, reflecting and shaping the ways Australians thought of their geopolitical and cultural location in relation to Asia.[1]

Following the Second World War, a generation of Australian foreign policy was increasingly focused on Asia, and consisted of urging the projection of American power in the Southeast Asian region, in effect as a buffer between Asian events and Australian society. The intervention in Vietnam can be seen as part of this policy, as a pre-emptive forward defence, as an insurance premium on continued American goodwill and as an expected contribution to the American effort in Vietnam. The attempt to thwart revolution in Vietnam was part of a deeper strain of unease about Asia, but Cold War perceptions were superimposed upon this pre-existing fear. Casey's rickshaws were decorated with the hammer and sickle, suggesting the ways that the Cold War era configured and distorted understandings of Asia—indeed, although the collapse of French rule in Vietnam was his pretext in 1954, Casey's image was about China, a fusion and confusion which bedevilled conservative rhetoric for a generation.

The history of the Australian intervention in Vietnam is explicable as the outcome and then the unravelling of these Cold War patterns of thinking, which observed the decolonisation struggle in Vietnam—and the role of communism as a social movement in that struggle—as part of global Cold War confrontation. This world view systematically misread the nationalist and patriotic elements of the Vietnamese struggle, fixing instead upon the great fear of postwar policy: China. It was fear of China and, more generally, of social turmoil in Asia, that led conservatives to worry about possible American isolationism and to encourage an American role in the region. As C.P. Fitzgerald put it in 1957: 'The official Australian attitude to the New Asia can be defined as composed of one hope and two fears.' The hope was that nationalism would prosper and be anticommunist; the two fears were of communism, particularly in China, and the older fear of Japan.[2] While the latter receded, nationalism was consistently misunderstood, particularly in its Vietnamese form. China remained the constant, to be countered by the projection of American power.

The domestic aspects of the Cold War were equally significant for this history. By marginalising dissent and critical views, the Cold War contributed to an impoverishment of Australian understandings of Asian decolonisation and social movements. The impact of domestic political conflict on foreign policy debates was considerable, and frequently deleterious. When Australians caught a glimpse of events in Asia, they too frequently saw their worst fears of Cold War confrontation being played out. Within the local political sphere, they were enjoined and frequently obliged to take sides in a global struggle, between the democratic and communist blocs, which was also a struggle between West and East, and colonial and postcolonial histories. Having stifled a public sphere of informed and open dispute, the domestic Cold War polity was marked by intolerant polarisation, and this was a legacy carried well into the 1960s.

The development of an audible and critical voice on Vietnam, and of an effective movement opposing the war and conscription, depended upon breaking this mould of the Cold War. In the mid-1960s, for example, anti-Vietnam activists often still visualised themselves as marginal voices of conscience raised against a stifling conformity. As they saw it, the Cold War was not only about fear, but about new suburban forms of indifference, a sort of civic withdrawal from activism, mirrored in foreign policies which engaged only truculently with Asia. To some extent, the vision of these critics was fixed upon the past, but they touched on the ways in which the Cold War had established barriers to an active political culture.

To break the mould of the Cold War, the left had to unlearn some of what it had inherited from the experience of marginalisation in the 1950s. This depended upon a number of factors: the realignment of the left away from dogmatic Stalinism, the establishment of new constituencies in the peace movement and, to some extent, a revitalisation of the public culture. To a lesser degree did it depend on developments in the ALP. In this history, 1966 was a turning point after which the domestic legacy of the Cold War was less oppressive. One aspect of this break with the

Cold War involved the Communist Party's relinquishing—in some measure, losing—its dominant role over the peace movement, although it acted as a key strategic player in the open coalition of the Moratorium movement. Another was the development of the New Left in the late 1960s.

This is a broad canvas, and it is worth mentioning what is not considered. A third of the book is about Phuoc Tuy province, detailing the dynamics into which Australian troops were inserted, but it is neither a social history of the Australian intervention, in terms of the inner life and everyday experience of soldiers, nor an operational account of battles and strategy. The discussion of colonial and postcolonial history in Phuoc Tuy establishes the dynamics of revolution and war at a local level, against which to evaluate the 'counter-revolutionary warfare' strategy which the Australian army had developed from Cold War prescriptions.

This strategy made two presumptions: that the revolutionaries were a largely external force (for the Cold War rendered communists as outsiders) and that the local South Vietnamese government was supportable, and would be able—with assistance—to establish a popular constituency. Both presumptions proved to be wrong. Some might see in this a confirmation of the remark attributed to Georges Clemenceau, that military intelligence bears the same relation to intelligence as does military music to music. But the counter-revolutionary strategy was consistent with a Cold War pattern of thinking about revolution, social movements and legitimacy, and in fact Army intelligence developed quite realistic assessments of the intractability of local history.

One theme in the book juxtaposes Australian understandings of Vietnam with a description of colonial and postcolonial history. For example, a description of the anticolonial struggle to 1954 counterpoints conservative understandings of decolonisation, communism and nationalism; and the dynamics of revolutionary warfare in Phuoc Tuy in the late 1960s are counterposed to the metaphors of Vietnam which developed in the left and the anti-war movement. The symmetry of this exercise is necessarily imperfect, which is part of its meaning. Vietnam was both a catalyst for the New Left and a rich source of metaphors for its wider discontents. Australian debates were as much about domestic political conflicts as they were about Vietnam, as the war was drawn into the eddies of the Australian polity, taking its meaning from their currents. In focusing on the ways in which Vietnam was understood in Australia, the points of distortion and incomprehension are as significant as the points of more informed interpretation.

The intervention in Vietnam was simultaneously Australia's

longest and most contentious war, and inevitably its echoes continue. The historical memory of both the war and its opposition has become buttressed by conflicting myths—that the anti-war movement 'succeeded' in stopping the war, that the Australian government committed troops on demand as a craven satellite, that the war could have been 'won' but for the anti-war movement at home or that Australian troops were traumatised by one long atrocity in Phuoc Tuy. Each of these interpretations misses the mark, yet informs part of historical understandings of the war, played out in the present. For example, the celebrations by former anti-war activists in Melbourne of the fifteenth anniversary of the fall of Saigon met angry demonstrations from Vietnamese-Australians; a national memorial to the Australian soldiers who served in Vietnam has only recently and belatedly been established in Canberra; and every now and then right-wing columnists demand that prominent anti-war activists recant and denounce their past. These are struggles over contemporary memory, commemorating earlier social struggles.

Memorialising and mythologising are only part of the process; more importantly, recent events have dramatically reconstructed the twin pillars on which the Vietnam intervention rested. The Cold War has abruptly ended, as a global polarisation and as a pattern of thinking, and there has been a regeneration of debates about Australia's place in Asia as either a Western outpost or an integral economic and cultural part of the region. These emerging debates on Australia's place in Asia make it all the more pertinent to examine an earlier episode of the same engagement; and although hardly an edifying story, it points up the roles fear and unease have played in our inheritance. One of the most telling images that recurred in conservative rhetoric through this period was that of the frontier: the border with Asian communism was said to be moving closer. At one obvious level, this referred to the boundary between East and West, between communist dictatorship and what the conservatives called the Free World; but it was as much a boundary in the political imagination. Where did Australia end and Asia begin, and what Orientalist dreams or nightmares lay waiting in Asia's almost unknown spaces? This was a political imagery which referred both to fears of what lay beyond the frontier and to an ambiguity of Australian identity in Asia.

The end of the Cold War is often said to have removed certainties as well as constraints; regional conflicts are no longer held in thrall, if not suspension, by superpower interests, and whole institutions and intellectual patterns which were shaped by the Cold War confrontation have suddenly lost their meaning. The end of the Cold War has meant that a way of thinking and contesting domestic politics has abruptly become a thing of the past, and what is past can ebb away surprisingly quickly. If this is a release from a stultifying pattern of mind, it also means that that pattern, as it becomes more foreign, must be recaptured to make sense. The debates of this period occurred in a climate of bleak hostility, in which conservatives denied any legitimacy to communists and radicals, who often responded in kind by adopting a similar, if less triumphant dogmatism. It is this sense of the Cold War as a political culture—blighted and polarised—which most needs to be recaptured if we are to understand the period.

The significance of the Vietnam war for Australia lay in the collision of this Cold War public culture with a distinctive pattern of decolonisation in Vietnam. Australian conservatives insisted that communism was an alien and illegitimate force, yet the colonial experience had given the Communist Party in Vietnam a unique and genuine purchase on patriotic as well as revolutionary sentiment. This historical process meant that the Western search for a viable nationalist and non-communist vehicle for its hopes was futile, yet this was the rock upon which Australian policy was built.

The intervention in Vietnam represents the superimposition of these different layers of policy and meaning: the vain hope that a benign and pro-Western nationalism would triumph in postcolonial Asia, the anxiety that Asian communism was part of a global plan of expansion and conquest, and the older, more profound fear of Asian dispossession. Each of these fears was heightened by the poisoned atmosphere of the Cold War culture, which also made dissenting from their hold more difficult. When the end of the colonial order in Vietnam in 1954 prompted Casey to conjure a vision of enslaved children pulling rickshaws, his rhetoric plumbed these varying layers of meaning. But he could hardly have foretold the harvest that Australian society would reap in the next two decades.

I

The
colonial
order

1
Material life
in the
colonial world

In 1950, as the anticolonial war against the French reached its peak, the province chief of Baria, Le Thanh Tuong, published a brief history of the province. Most likely of a landlord background, as were many collaborators, he represented a class which had, since the French occupation in the early 1860s, thrown in its lot with the colonial administration, often to its considerable advantage.[1] He thus had an interest in the way he presented his history. He wrote fulsomely of the abundance of the province, with a population

> . . . peaceful and without history, because their love for their plot of land is stronger than all other preoccupations . . . the vestiges of ancient Vietnam are still visible in the province, in its mores and customs . . .

And, with apparent relief, he commented that 'extravagant modernism seems unable to take root amongst the population'.[2]

This tranquil image of a people without history, with backs turned heedlessly against modernity, was more than a little obtuse: Vietnam was in the middle of the anticolonial war and revolutionary process which sprang from its fractured history. More

3

immediately, it was only two years since Le Thanh Tuong had
survived an attempt on his life by a fifteen-year-old girl, Vo Thi
Sau. Born in a nearby village, and apparently inspired by patriotic
zeal, she had fired several shots in the crowded market place of
Dat Do, intending to break up the Bastille Day celebrations which
he had organised to mark French tradition and which were
regularly used by the revolutionary movement as an occasion to
contest the symbolism of French rule.[3]

Two years later, in 1950, Le Thanh Tuong had sufficiently
recovered his composure to assert the absence of history, and
the absence of modernity. These first two chapters explore the
ways in which this was asserting a form of amnesia in the face
of historical transformations. Nine decades of colonial rule had
triggered social upheavals in a fractured transition to modernity
which fused some parts of tradition with modern needs and
responses. Class formation was one example, where new patterns
of production coexisted and intermingled with traditional economic production. Political development was another, in which
patriotism as a sentiment of cultural and ethnic identity had been
fused with Leninism as a modern form of struggle. It is these
dynamics of colonial rule and response, rather than the tranquillity of a people without history, which explain the significance
of shots fired by a 15-year-old revolutionary on Bastille Day.

A sense of place

When Australian troops first arrived in the area in mid-1966,
they found villages which were at most three centuries old. Baria
province—renamed Phuoc Tuy in 1956—was, from the middle
of the seventeenth century, at the frontier of the southward
migration of the Vietnamese from the Red River delta in the
north to the Mekong delta in the south. Before this, the area
was largely unpopulated, described as 'a thick screen of forest'
forming a buffer zone between the Cambodians in the Mekong
delta and the Cham kingdom of central Vietnam. At the start of
the seventeenth century, the first Vietnamese immigrants arrived
near what was to be the provincial capital, Phuoc Le. These first
settlers—'outlaws, vagabonds and deserters demonstrating all the
hardy qualities of a race of pioneers'—arrived peacefully enough,
establishing villages in the relatively fertile soils of the basin
around Phuoc Le. The Khmer kings acceded to this Vietnamese
occupation because they had little use for the area themselves
and were preoccupied with the developing threat of the Thai
kingdom to their west.[4]

Despite this unchallenged annexation, the frontier remained

tense. In 1623, the trading post and citadel at Phuoc Le were ceded to the Vietnamese as part of a marriage contract between the Khmer and Vietnamese rulers, but in 1658 Phuoc Le was retaken by the Khmers. This provided a pretext for the Vietnamese to consolidate their southward expansion. Ostensibly to protect their compatriots settled in the area, the Vietnamese court in Hue dispatched a troop of 2000 soldiers to destroy the citadel, obliging the Khmers to pay regular tribute and recognise Vietnamese sovereignty. The struggle for the southern delta fluctuated for another century—the Vietnamese annexed all the former Khmer territories only in the mid-eighteenth century—but the area of Baria was under firm Vietnamese control from the mid-seventeenth century. Only a few ruins of the Khmer period remained to be pointed out to French tourists between the two world wars—an elephant bath at a Khmer temple in Long Dien and a pre-Angkor stone Buddha, found at Cape St Jacques.

From the start of the eighteenth century, as part of Vietnamese policy to populate the south, sweeps were conducted amongst 'the lower classes and vagabonds' of the central provinces, who were then transported as colonists to the south. These *colons* were at liberty to select land; having chosen a plot, they had only 'to express their intentions to the mandarin for them to become owner . . .' and for registers of the inhabitants of the new villages to be compiled.[5] As the frontier swept on across the Mekong delta, the Baria area became more established, and by the early nineteenth century its principal villages had been settled.

One of the distinctive and most important features of village life was the way in which cultural and sacred practices were tied to a sense of place. The rural social order was attached to agricultural land as livelihood, but also by the profound sense of belonging to one's native village, and by the veneration of ancestors which tied family and lineage to place. Descended from pioneers and 'vagabonds', the villagers of Baria nevertheless exhibited the same attachment to place characteristic of Vietnamese peasant culture. However, there were some differences of degree in the south. There was less insularity and more flexibility in the culture of the frontier, partly as a result of its more recent settlement. The *colons* enjoyed a relative freedom from the central government in Hue, and established looser village structures. In the north, the village was insular and autonomous, while in the south, although the village remained the administrative unit, it tended to be a less closely knit group, with a less demanding social cohesion. One consequence was that the hold of village authority and of veneration for the ancestors was less tenacious at the frontier.[6]

Despite these differences, the cultural patterns and mental
structures of Vietnamese village culture had been largely trans-
planted to the new villages of the south, particularly in terms of
belief, authority and tradition. What was true for the north was
also 'in broad outline true for all the peasants of Vietnam'. The
classic features of Vietnamese peasant culture—the importance of
the village of birth for self-identity; village cults based on the
guardian spirit of the village; ancestor worship; the ordering of
village authority on lines of age, learning and masculinity; and,
finally, the syncretic religious combination of Confucianism,
Buddhism and Taoism—are all strongly evident in a major study
of life in a southern village in the late 1950s. Even among
villagers who were not 'descendants of ancestors who have lived
in this place a thousand years, perpetuating a parochial village
world . . . the essential characteristics of the village way of life
have persisted'.[7]

The traces in published records make it clear that Baria's
villages shared the same cultural world. The French compilers
of tourist guides in the 1920s pointed out the communal houses
(*dinh*), which were the political and ritual centre of the village.
One of these—at Long Dien—was noted for its wooden columns
and framework, and its sculptured panels and inlaid furniture.
The significance of such an elaborate *dinh* was not only that it
was where decisions were made by the village notables—on
matters such as the distribution of communal land, the allocation
of the village tax burden and the dispensing of justice—but also
that it was the centre of the village cult, based on the genie of
the founding or guardian spirit of the village, on whose interces-
sion the peace and prosperity of the village were held to depend.
The people of Baria venerated the ancestors of their lineage, who
were held to exert a continuing influence. Ancestors remained
part of the family after death, their presence as spirits represented
by a tablet in the ancestral shrine within the house: 'Death is
no real departure from the family—one joins the ancestors to
exist as an unseen but nonetheless present member.'[8]

At times, the family cult of the ancestor and the village cult
of the founding or guardian spirit overlapped. In 1789, a woman
named Ria (after whom Baria was named, *Ba* being a female
honorific) migrated from central Vietnam to establish several
villages in the province, and after her death was venerated as a
cult figure in the village of Tam Phuoc. Other villages had cults
linking their village craft with cult figures. In 1865, the new
French governor made a tour of the recently conquered area of
Baria, and found in one fishing village:

A small pagoda . . . dedicated to the protective divinities of sailors

The ornate carving on the Buddhist pagoda of Long Dien village in the late 1920s reflects the significance of this market town, with a population of some 7000, as the trading hub of Baria province. (Société des Etudes Indochinoises, La Cochinchine, Saigon, 1931)

and above all to the great whales of the sea, to whom the Annamites, like the ancient Greeks, attribute the rescue of shipwrecks. A huge skeleton of one of these whales was held in the pagoda, in the midst of sacred insignia, in the place of honour normally occupied by a statue of Buddha.[9]

A local cult such as this depended on the conception that spirits moved amongst and guided the fortunes of the living, linking craft, place and spirituality.

This attachment to place is of some significance. Although eroded by some aspects of the colonial order, the *mentalité* of the village was distinctly local in the ties it made between place and cultural identity. Part of the strength of the revolutionary movement after the 1930s lay in its ability to connect this cultural identity with patriotism and national sovereignty. With a local level of organisation—the Party cells in the village—revolutionary politics redeveloped pre-existing conceptions of patriotism and identity. For patriotism was not the same as nationalism. In Vietnam, the former is a 'kinship-oriented concept with senti-mental connotations', while nationalism is a pre-eminently modern concept of the nation-state and its perceived rights to self-deter-mination and independence:

> Vietnamese patriotism harks back to the nation's physical and cultural heritage and urges fulfillment of an obligation to the community—the protection of patrimony and defense of compatriots. Vietnamese nationalism, on the other hand, relates to the nation's interests and calls for the fulfillment of its requirements of power.

Understanding the cultural power of patriotism, Vietnamese rev-olutionary elites mobilised 'patriotic traditions . . . to promote nationalist objectives'.

In the Cold War years of the 1950s and 1960s, as they viewed Vietnam with mounting alarm, conservative elites in Australia and the United States systematically underestimated the power of patriotism and the local roots of revolutionary politics. By the early 1960s, they were insisting that Vietnamese nationalism had been captured—and rendered meaningless—by the Communist Party, and that the Party had no purchase in the village other than that imposed by terror. Thus the revolution in the South could only be understood as an external act of aggression from the North. Undeniably, the Communist Party—substantially directed from the North—intended to reunify the country, but the conservative view underestimated the local level of support derived from patriotism and the ways in which this was linked to the cultural affiliation to place. Culture and patriotism were closely related through the solidifying role of ancestor worship, which emphasised the continuity of the local and ethnic community: 'there is no patriotism without *patria*; ancestor worship, in this sense, may well be the most elementary form of patriotism'.[10]

Some part of the success of the revolutionary movement in Vietnam lay in tapping the fierce peasant localism of the rural social order. The peasant world was relatively small; even at the end of the 1950s, villagers considered five kilometres a long way to travel, and knew few villagers so far away.[11] Attachment to a native place—to the village of one's birth—was crucial, as indicated by the precolonial practice of compiling registers of those born in the village. Those not registered were considered 'outsiders' and, from the point of view of the precolonial state, were non-persons, ineligible to share village communal land. Across Vietnam, the practice was to return home to one's native village for the Tet New Year and, above all, to return home to die. Until at least 1945, the cities were considered as merely a provisional place of residence. 'Urban' citizens registered the birth of their children in their village of origin, because anyone not registered in a village was considered 'an uprooted person or vagabond'.[12]

If the experience of being uprooted, with contingent ties to a social community, is more typical of modernity than of traditional societies, it is significant that the impact of colonialism was most evident amongst those who migrated for wage-labour to the southern rubber plantations established by the French. In 1931, for example, one French account explained the premodern obstacles to labour mobility in terms of village affiliation, as:

> . . . the nostalgic attachment of the Annamite to his rice field, family tombs, his small domestic altar, his deep preference for village politics, [and] his inability to conceive of a satisfying life outside the framework of this miniature city.[13]

In Baria, each of these features of the rural order as a moral and imaginative world was reinforced by the geography of settlement. At the beginning of the twentieth century, the great majority of the province population lived within a radius of ten kilometres, within the central lowlands basin. Very few lived in outlying settlements, which in part simply reflected where the fertile land lay. To the north and east of the settled area was hilly country, covered in thick forests. To the west lay marshland of bamboo and mangroves; to the south, sand dunes lined the coast. This contiguity of settlement was further reinforced by cultural attitudes: disdain for the Moi (Montagnard) tribes of the wild forest country, and fear of the malaria and tigers amongst which they lived.

All these features engraved the attachment to place into village culture. The sense of place revolved around the 'miniature city'

of the village, within a small locale. The village was, in Paul
Mus' phrase, the 'interior of the country', and it 'held the key
to the social structure of the country and to its outlook on life'.[14]
Politics in the colonial and postcolonial periods would remain
intensely local, and the strength of movements for social change
or control would revolve around their ability to hold sway over
the village.

The conquest

The colonial conquest broke in upon this village society with
some violence in Baria. The French began their military occupation of southern Vietnam with the destruction of forts built on
the coast at Vung Tau on Cape St Jacques. Overlooking the
approach to the Dong-Nai river and hence Saigon, these forts
had been established early in the nineteenth century to counter
Malay pirates. The French fleet destroyed the forts in February
1859 and went on up the river to attack Saigon, setting fire to
the rice stores and razing the citadel before withdrawing and
leaving behind a small garrison. Two years later, the assault was
renewed—with several hundred Spanish mercenaries, some cav-
alry and a number of cannon—and the Vietnamese forces,
defeated at Bien Hoa, withdrew south to Phuoc Le in Baria.
There the military mandarins attempted to reorganise a centre
of resistance of the sort which they had organised at Bien Hoa.
But they were no more successful; Phuoc Le fell to the French
in January 1862, the remainder of the Vietnamese troops were
pursued out of the province, and the leader of the Spanish
mercenaries was put in command of the province.

The French had always claimed that their intervention was
to protect Catholic missionaries and converts from persecution.
Less loftily, they had also hoped that their presence would spark
a pro-French rebellion amongst Catholic communities. With the
French conquest, some Vietnamese took their retribution. As the
citadel at Phuoc Le was taken, several hundred Christians
imprisoned there were burnt to death, and many more later died
of burns. Others were only saved by some Vietnamese who,
'touched with compassion and, contrary to the orders of their
mandarins, opened—before it was consumed by the fire—another
prison which was full of Christians, saving them from a terrible
death'.[15]

Preoccupied with rebellion in the north, the emperor in Hue
found these defeats sufficiently persuasive to enter into treaty
negotiations. In April 1863, Rear-Admiral Bonard, who had led
the French campaign, set off for Hue in a flotilla of four warships

Rear-Admiral Bonard, who successfully led the expedition to conquer Cochinchina for the expanding French Empire in the 1860s, appears the very model of imperial masculinity. The ninety years of colonial rule that followed in his wake reorganised material and political life, catalysing revolutionary change. (E. Cortambert and L. de Rosny, Tableau de la Cochinchine, Paris, 1862)

for an audience with the emperor. The latter prudently waived the usual requirement for prostration of all visitors before him, while Bonard delivered a discourse on French intentions and then waited while it was translated to the court. These preliminaries over, the emperor ceded to France the three eastern provinces of what was to be Cochinchina, with guarantees of the liberties of Christians and rights to commercial and military navigation on the Mekong river. Five years later, the western provinces of Cochinchina were also occupied.[16] Baria was thus amongst the first parts of Indochina to be annexed into the French empire.

Some effects of the conquest were immediate. The local mandarins left their administrative posts, which 'cut away, in a single stroke, one of the most powerful institutions binding the village to the centre of power at Hue'.[17] Their places were filled by a combination of French direct rule with collaboration by pro-French Vietnamese who were frequently, though not always, Catholics. The French could see that the qualities of their Vietnamese allies were variable at best. Collaborating Vietnamese were given 'a tricolour sash, in silk or in cotton depending on their rank, as a sign of the investiture which had given them the authority of France'. But this could hardly compensate for lack of education and standing, and often they had little authority amongst their compatriots, 'unless—feigning to support us—they in fact secretly fought against us'. However, local resistance was sporadic; there were small uprisings in the three eastern provinces from December 1862, which continued in an irregular fashion but—in Baria—were effectively contained by the establishment of a garrison at Phuoc Le, maintained until the 1920s. In an eloquent sign of the displacement of Vietnamese by French sovereignty, the garrison was built on the site of the residence of the former Vietnamese administrator.[18]

French rule in the village also meant a displacement of the former privileging of education and tradition. Among those Vietnamese who worked for the French as administrators, 'few acknowledged any real value in the ideals of the past'. Their interests were bound up with French power, and their ideas were more modernist. By the beginning of the twentieth century, a new class was being created by the colonial presence, based largely on land accumulated during the reshuffling of land-holdings precipitated by the French. This class most often supported the status quo and had little sympathy for nationalist or patriotic ideas.[19] Like the province chief Le Thanh Tuong, they could attain what influence the French were prepared to share with them, but were not to emerge as a class capable of articulating or controlling a postcolonial order.

The local economy

With the conquest, the French immediately set about establishing the sinews of a colonial economy. A lighthouse was built on the hills of Cape St Jacques to protect the shipping carrying colonial exports from the port of Saigon. Constructed shortly after 1865, it appeared 'like a shining symbol of France's possession'. Work also began on a telegraph line from Saigon to the Cape, which would then continue to Singapore and on to Paris.[20] These intimations of modernity symbolised the partial integration of colonial Vietnam into a world economy, through the extension of the cash economy, the rationalisation of taxation and a reorientation of some economic activity towards export production. Nine decades of colonial rule in Baria would generate new forms of material production and class formation which fused the traditional and the modern.

A description in the 1930s by the French agronomist Pierre Gourou provides some insight into the forms of material life in Baria. He pointed out that the province was more sparsely populated than the delta, but had an exceptional population density in the cluster of villages in the fertile basin settled from the seventeenth century. Three forms of production accounted for this concentration: the rice fields of the '*terres rouges*', the

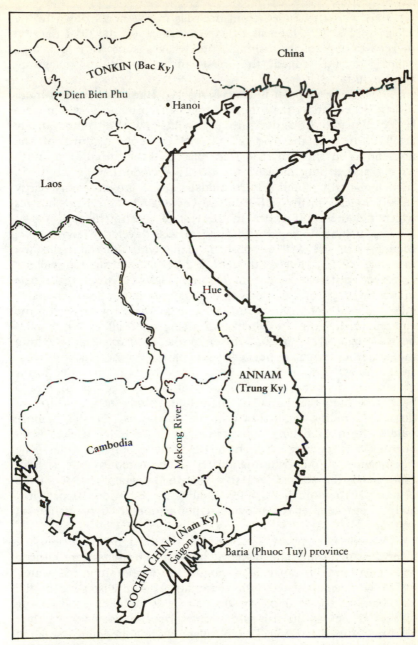

Colonial Vietnam

red soils which extended from the hills in the north down to the village of Dat Do; the salt fields established on the tidal flats on the coast; and finally, fishing from villages such as Phuoc Hai, which Gourou judged 'the most important fishing village in Cochinchina'.[21]

The fishing and salt industries marked Baria as having a more diversified economy than the Mekong delta provinces, which were largely devoted to agriculture. Agriculture was a comparatively small sector: at the end of the 1950s, only a third of the households in the province were classified as agricultural. With its salt and fishing industries, as well as modern wage labour in rubber plantations and service industries, the province only partly shared in the history of exploitative tenancy and land hunger which fed the rural unrest in the rest of Cochinchina.

The fishing industry indicated a well-developed precolonial economy. It was well established, along with the salt fields, by the start of the nineteenth century. Several substantial villages employed different modes of fishing. The first used seine nets drawn by junks, and was evidently organised along proto-capitalist lines, as one colonial account describes 'the proprietor' of the equipment dividing the catch, and giving one half to 'the coolies he has engaged'. A second form of the industry—'more within the reach of a small pocket'—was based on net fishing from smaller boats. Lower capital costs allowed more cooperative forms of labour: 'four owners of nets would join together to hire a boat, to which they attached their four fishing nets at different distances, trailing them slowly in the open seas'. Finally, a more modest form of fishing consisted of weirs built of wicker work in the shoals, trapping fish on the recess of the tide. The significance of the fishing industry is indicated by the size of Phuoc Hai, the second largest village in Baria at the turn of the century, with more than 4000 inhabitants. Between 10 per cent and 15 per cent of the provincial population lived by fishing at that time.[22]

The salt industry was located on the tidal flats between the Long Hai peninsula and Cape St Jacques. The flats were latticed with a system of canals and ponds for evaporating sea water, which was accumulated into pyramids of salt glistening in the sun. Famous for their purity, the salt fields supplied local fishing villages as well as the fish-salting enterprises on the Mekong river and in Cambodia. Long Thanh village, largely dependent on salt production, had a population of more than 1600 in 1901. Taking into account other nearby villages, a conservative estimate of 2000 people gives a proportion of 4 per cent of the provincial population involved in salt production at the turn of the century.[23]

The trade in salt, and most of the fishing catch, was

concentrated in the hands of Chinese merchants, based in the market towns of Long Dien, Dat Do and Phuoc Le. In 1901, the Chinese made up only 1 per cent of the provincial population and, in 1959, still a mere 2 per cent. But their economic presence was more substantial. In Cochinchina, the Chinese largely controlled wholesale trade, rice-milling and much of the rice export trade, and had a significant role in money-lending institutions. They had an interlocking role as middlemen in the colonial economy:

> The Chinese were convenient not only because they had their contacts in the villages and because they owned most of the junks for rice transport but also because they were at the same time usurers who lent money to the Vietnamese peasants at oppressive rates and had, therefore, forced their debtors to mortgage most of their crops to them.[24]

One consequence of the tacit official support for the dominant position of Chinese merchants was the constricted development of a Vietnamese class with a stake in a non-communist path to independence and development. This economic position helps explain the febrile character of the nationalist bourgeoisie in Vietnam and the underdevelopment of a nationalist ideology which could compete with Marxism for control of the decolonisation process. It underpinned the continuing weakness of local anticommunist forces.

These fishing and salt industries already marked the province as different from the provinces of the delta; so too did its agricultural structure. In general, colonial Cochinchina was characterised by an agricultural regime of highly concentrated Vietnamese and French land-holdings, employing between 50 per cent and 60 per cent of the rural population in exploitative tenancy arrangements. In the 1930s, in the central and western provinces, more than 65 per cent of the land was owned by less than 10 per cent of land-holders. This concentration of ownership was compounded by indebtedness; it was said that loans supported the peasant as 'a rope gives support to a hanged man'. Two out of three families were without land of their own, facing either wage labour or tenancy. In the latter, the tenant paid rent of some 40 per cent of the crop, which climbed much higher when costs—such as the rent of buffalos, seed and housing—were included. By 1935, Vietnam was the world's second-largest exporter of rice, much of it from Cochinchina, but the levels of exploitation required also produced desperate social circumstances.[25]

The provinces of east Cochinchina, including Baria, only partly conformed to this pattern, being less exclusively oriented to export rice production. In the 1920s, Fernand de Montaigut, a former colonial administrator, wrote that agriculture in the east was relatively 'backward', with few of the '. . . grand [Vietnamese] proprietors, whose fortunes, often put together by extortion and usurpation of land, are in the west [of Cochinchina] the source of demoralisation for the mass of the people'. What large proprietors there were 'belonged to families respected amongst the population'.26 It was a benign judgment which suggested a smaller and less modernised landlord class than in the delta, but it is borne out by such information as is available on Baria in the colonial period.

In the province, land concentration was less extreme, and the local economy—and with it the everyday experience of class relationships—was more diversified than in the delta. In the absence of direct contemporary evidence, we can extrapolate backwards from the pattern established by the end of the colonial period, which indicates the class formation which had been under way during the French period. Amongst the 32 per cent of households engaged in agriculture in Baria, there was a significant concentration of land. Very small holdings (less than one hectare), on the very margins of viability, made up 65 per cent of the total holdings, yet covered only 10 per cent of the total agricultural land. At the other end of the scale, the same expanse of land was owned by a small group of village landlords, on less than 200 large holdings of between 10 and 50 hectares. As no landholdings over 50 hectares were recorded, the province appears to have had no wealthy absentee landlords, who elsewhere generally preferred the comforts of Saigon and conducted their affairs through agents.

This relatively small number of village landlord families would have conducted their affairs directly with tenants and farm labourers, living in the villages, priding themselves on being staunch defenders of Confucian tradition, and often filling the local level of colonial administration. Below them, some 8 per cent of households were middle peasant families, owner–occupiers who also rented land to build a holding sufficiently large to be viable, and probably hired labourers at planting and harvest times. This gave them a certain subsistence independence, but their position was often neither secure nor prosperous, with the downward spiral to tenancy seldom out of prospect.

They were more secure, however, than the poor peasants, tenants and sharecroppers who made up three-quarters of the agricultural households. These represented roughly a quarter of the province population, a substantial number, but markedly less than the 50 to 60 per cent Gourou calculated for the delta two decades earlier. Some owned a small area of land of their own, but were compelled by circumstances to be tenants, and were most likely also to engage in wage labour.

But some two-thirds of the households of the province were classified as non-agricultural, accounted for by the fishing and salt industries and substantial groups of workers in the wage economy. Interwoven with tenant farmers were small-scale traders and wage labourers on rubber plantations, in service industries and in transport. Women figured prominently amongst the traders, making up nearly 80 per cent of those involved. Some would have been members of tenant families, supplementing family income by small-scale trade, and women were also responsible for the trade in fish before it reached the Chinese merchants. Fishing itself was a substantially male occupation, as was skilled artisanal work such as carpentry, masonry, building and mechanics. These skilled male workers figured in the early development of the revolutionary movement in the province.

Roughly a quarter of the workforce were manual labourers or wage workers such as cooks, maids, and building workers, as well as agricultural labourers. Finally, there was a small urban petty bourgeoisie in the larger villages, in occupations such as medicine, teaching and clerical work. If it conformed to the pattern of Vietnam's urban centres, this intelligentsia would have been one class most attracted to ideas of modernity, science and social change, and most disenchanted with the colonial order.[27]

The significance of these figures is twofold. First, they demonstrate a variety of material life and class in the province, quite different from the romantic image developed in the West in the anti-war movement, of Vietnam as a 'traditional' peasant society; the complex occupational pattern of Baria province, with its salt workers and artisans, village landlords and traders, represents a combination of 'traditional' and 'modern' experiences. Second, the revolutionary movement as it developed from the 1930s would find different levels of support amongst these classes. Partly, it would draw its support in the province from skilled artisans, fishermen and some of the local intelligentsia, but it would also become adept at mobilising around the particular grievances and experiences of other groups.

The French presence

The French-born population of Baria province was always small. In 1901, it numbered only 42, and in 1928, there were 228 French, still less than 0.5 per cent of the population. They were local administrators in the province and district capitals—involved in tax collection, administration and forestry control—managers of rubber plantations and timber mills, and by the late 1920s, some were involved in a burgeoning tourist industry.

As early as 1884, Cape St Jacques had been identified as an appropriate site for a sanatorium—the French settlers being exceedingly wary of malaria and other more chimerical fevers. By the turn of the century, villas stretched along the strand of the Baie des Cocotiers, where, some four decades before, the first shots had been fired in the colonial conquest. These provided 'rest and recuperation from the anaemic or wearying maladies of the tropical climate', and for holidaying Saigon officials, a chance 'to forget the cares of office, and to find the diversions and coolness which Saigon lacked'. Sixty years later, Australian soldiers on leave would visit the bars and brothels of the town—then known as Vung Tau—for a similar forgetfulness.

Overlooking the bay, on the site of a former Vietnamese fort, stood a villa of the governor-general of Indochina, prominent in white against the forest and surrounded by parklands and lawns. The resort offered its weary French guests more than villas, sea air and rest. At the lunar New Year in 1899, they held a three-day festival, with canoe, bicycle and horse races and a ball given in one of the hotels; these alternated with local entertainments—a dragon procession and theatrical troupes from nearby villages. Such distractions were said to introduce among the European population, convalescents included, 'a note of gaiety and liveliness'. It must have been a posting relished by the French soldiers guarding the lighthouse and manning the artillery at the Cape.[28]

The resort developed as a tourist destination of some note. The lighthouse was the first sight of Vietnam for the French arriving by sea from Marseille, and during the 1920s—the heyday of tourism in French Indochina—it was as inevitable a part of their itinerary as the ruins of Angkor Wat. Tourists were offered promenades, archaeological curiosities and visits to Buddhist pagodas. The more adventurous could hire a car in Saigon and drive the 120 kilometres to the Cape, stopping to investigate pagodas, climb the hills or visit rubber plantations. The hills were noted for wild bullock, stag, tigers and panthers, and hunting was part of the itinerary of the robust, just as it was part of the self-identity of many a colonialist in the domains of the European empires. One travel guide in 1930 advised its clients to carry food and wine, firearms for defence against tigers and panthers, and quinine. The indigenous people would not be hostile, and if one had an accident with a local, one should stop to help.

What the local peasants and workers made of French tourists speeding past on the roads or reposing in the villas by the sea can be surmised from observing some of the ideological baggage they carried with them. The French reassured themselves that improving the material life of the people was not 'the sole concern of a protective power', which must also '. . . be alert to the maintenance of nationalities, respect the local customs and religious ideas of the indigenous people, and finally prepare them for a future of moral and political peace'.[29]

What was articulated as 'the civilising mission' of French colonialism was premised on the assumption that the Vietnamese could one day be French; education and modernisation were quite compatible with French glory, and the appropriate Vietnamese response was considered to be cultural assimilation rather than independence. To an extent, this was more than simply a convenient rationalisation, however much tinged with cultural conceit; the theory of France's civilising mission at least muted colonial policies based on naked force and subjection, and some French people displayed a genuine ethnographic curiosity.[30] But the cultural and protective mission of colonialism was often lost on those who worked in its commercial enterprises.

In a different way, the 'civilising mission' was also frequently lost on the owners and managers of rubber plantations. Along with rice, the export of rubber underpinned the civilised leisure of Cape St Jacques. With a characteristically colonial arrogance, de Montaigut—the former French administrator—declared that any economic analysis of eastern Cochinchina was summed up in a study of the French presence, which in turn reduced to the study of rubber production.[31] Yet there was a kernel of truth in this, for the rubber plantations most clearly signalled the social and cultural transformations of colonial rule.

French settlers had little interest in directly organising the production of rice in Baria, but there were strategic and financial reasons for concentrating on rubber production. Rubber became a government priority in both colony and metropolis. In 1897, a first consignment of rubber plants for experimental planting had arrived in Saigon from Malaya. A few years later, rubber trees had been planted in Baria by the colonial administrator at Phuoc Le; by 1910, more than 61 000 hectares throughout Cochinchina had been ceded to planters, though little was yet planted. By the First World War, the planted area had almost trebled.

Rubber's strategic importance was demonstrated during the First World War when, in the face of a crisis of production, the Bank of Indochina underwrote the French planters with government-guaranteed loans. Colonial policy sought to emulate the British planters' success in Malaya and to ensure imperial self-sufficiency. In the 1930s, one writer noted

. . . the ardent desire of the colonial administration to increase the
variety of Indo-Chinese exports, and to emancipate France from
dependence upon foreign rubber. Etatism was here part and parcel
of French long-term policy aspiring to imperial self-sufficiency.

The policy was successful; although never substantial by world
standards, the production of rubber from its colonies in Indochina
had, by 1938, made the French empire self-sufficient.[32] Strong
metropolitan as well as colonial interests stood in favour of
rubber.

The immediate impact of the plantations in Baria appears to
have been minimal on the central villages; the areas cleared for
cultivation were in the hilly forest regions in the north, largely
inhabited by the Mois. Vietnamese villagers were reluctant to
leave their villages, having what de Montaigut called an 'irrational
fear' of the highlands. Consequently, it was largely Moi labour
which opened up the first plantations, clearing the bamboo forest
and planting the first trees. But the 1920s saw a substantial boom
in metropolitan investment in the plantations, responding to
increases in the price of rubber and more closely linking the
colony with the rhythms of the world economy. By 1936, the
total area conceded to rubber planters throughout Cochinchina
was more than eight times the area of 1913.[33]

The rubber plantations soon became emblematic of exploitative wage labour in Vietnam, but ironically the early period saw
an attempt to forestall the development of a rural proletariat
through a process known as *'petite colonisation'*. In the mid-1920s,
the administration allocated small plots for plantations, in Baria
and elsewhere, with preference given to Vietnamese veterans of
the First World War. The intention was said to be to prevent
the creation of 'an agricultural proletariat which would be all the
more dangerous to the colonies as it would be composed of the
illiterate, easily swayed by agitators'. But by 1929 the project—
'created in a moment of passing fever'—had failed; the small
plantations proved unviable.[34]

By the late 1930s, ownership of the rubber industry was more
concentrated in Indochina than in rival countries such as Malaya
and Indonesia, where small indigenous planters were common.
Although some small indigenous plantations in Baria survived
into the 1950s, they could not rival the two major French
holdings: the Gallia plantation at Binh Ba and the Courtenay
plantation on the northern border. Both were established before
the Depression, and were subsidiaries of two of the giants of
Indochinese rubber, the *Société des Terres Rouges* and the *Groupe
Suzannah-Anloc* respectively. The plantations, employing some 7
per cent of the provincial population at the end of the 1950s,
intricately linked the province with a world market.[35]

Rubber production was particularly labour-intensive in the milking of the mature trees, which represented three-quarters of production costs. As the industry expanded, Moi labour was seen as unviable, for the tribespeople proved reluctant to be broken to the rhythms and time-discipline of its production. The planters turned to the northern delta for contract labour. Recruitment for short-term contracts increased in the 1920s, accompanied by an escalation of exploitative practices. By 1938, the International Labour Office (ILO) described the: '. . . generally recognised existence of abuses, such as fraudulent recruiting, unhealthy conditions in the plantations, excessively long hours, the brutality of certain overseers, under-feeding, etc'.

The ILO catalogued a downward spiral of low wages, under-nourishment, malaria and low work output leading to beatings from the overseers. Among the consequences of the notoriously brutal plantation regime was an exceptionally high mortality rate—about double the rate for Cochinchina in general in 1927, and this amongst workers in the prime of life. French commentators attributed the high mortality to malaria, and argued that improvements had been made by the late 1920s, but the plantation regime continued to take its toll.[36]

A second consequence was the political mobilisation of parts of this developing working class. A campaign against recruitment spread through Tonkin in 1928, culminating in the assassination of the director of the main recruitment agency in Hanoi in February 1929. The campaign, part of a short period of revolutionary violence and official reprisal, focused the minds of the administration wonderfully. As the governor-general of Cochinchina remarked to the Association of Rubber Planters in Saigon:

> It is notorious that, as a general rule, the coolies are badly fed and suffer from malnutrition . . . Tonking will soon cease to be an inexhaustible reservoir of cheap labour if the present mistakes are not rectified.

But the reforms which resulted—regulating recruitment and setting wage and health standards—took effect as the Depression began, which drastically reduced employment, wage levels and production. The price of a pound of rubber on the New York market plunged from a postwar peak of 73c to a mere 3.5c by 1932 and was still only 19.4c in 1937. Planters suspended investment, recruitment fell dramatically, and the minimum wage was cut in 1932 and again in 1935.[37]

These events indicate one way in which part of the local economy in Baria was being integrated into the world economy; the experience of migratory labour also signified cultural changes which were underway. The ILO saw labour migration as an element in the breakup of family and village ties: contract workers lost touch with village authority, returning with a 'spirit of emancipation which is not favourable to the maintenance of village discipline'. A modern working class was being constituted 'which no longer knows the traditional social organisation of which the family and the village are the essential elements'. The ILO viewed this modernisation of class relations with concern, and significantly included the *ta dien* or tenants of Cochinchina in its diagnosis. Compounding these cultural effects, the short-term nature of the contracts dispersed such experiences as large numbers of Vietnamese rotated through the system, helping to create a common class experience.[38]

It was appropriate enough that rubber should have been the commodity most overtly involved in this destabilisation of traditional patterns of authority and culture. For rubber, as one planter eulogised it in 1936, answered '. . . the urgent need of our modern civilisation—that need for rapid transport which never rests content, and always seeks to surpass its previous performance by the winning of new records'.[39] This was an apt description of the restlessness of modernity, and the plantation economy gave some indication of the levels of exploitation and cultural destabilisation required to realise it.

The nature of the colonial upheaval in Baria can be sensed from this pattern of class relations, which had, by the end of the colonial period, shaped a local society of diverse forms of production. The traditional had been fused with the modern, and precolonial sectors such as agriculture, fishing and salt industries interlaced with modern forms of wage labour and monopolised trade. The fierce attachment to place co-existed with the experience of migratory wage labour, and the pattern of traditional village authority with new social opportunities and frustrations. This was a more complex pattern than the popular image which developed in the West in the anti-war movement, of a traditional peasant society posed against the modern industrial juggernaut of American intervention.

But it was also a social pattern different from the image of tranquillity evoked by Le Thanh Tuong, whose hope that 'extravagant modernism' would not take root amongst the people was an artifice of uneasy calm. A more portentous allusion was that of Le Myre de Vilers, the relatively liberal first civilian governor of Cochinchina, who wrote on his retirement in 1882: 'We have destroyed the past and nothing has taken its place. We are on the eve of a social revolution which began during the conquest.'[40] By the 1930s, the outlines of that social revolution could already be discerned.

2
A colonial polity

Patriotism, nationalism and communism

In late 1919, the son of a rich landowner and government administrator set out from his home in Phuoc Le, the capital of Baria, to attend the prestigious College Chasseloup-Laubat in Saigon. Duong Bach Mai was fifteen, and was stepping into a life history which would take him away from the comforts of a wealthy family in Baria and into the turbulent course of revolutionary politics in the colonial order. At the college, he became a student activist, losing his scholarship after involvement in a student strike. Although his parents were evidently wealthy enough to support him in further study, any hopes that his talents would find him a comfortable place in the colonial system were to be dashed.

He later studied at the Ecole Supérieure de Commerce in Hanoi, and then worked for a time in the publishing house of a relative in Saigon. Like many of the young intelligentsia, Duong Bach Mai then set off for France. He studied at Aix-en-Provence before working in the National Savings Bank in Paris, where he was censured for radical views. In 1929, he was in the Soviet

Union at the University of Workers of the East, and two years
later—now aged 27—returned to Saigon via Shanghai. He was
returning to a Saigon galvanised with radical politics of both
Marxist and radical nationalist forms, and during the next decade,
Duong Bach Mai would be considered 'a leading "Stalinist" ' in
the Communist Party in Cochinchina. In particular, he became
a key figure in the group *La Lutte*, which from 1933 to 1937
was a major 'united front' of Communist and Trotskyist activists
in the south. In late 1940, he was swept up in the repression
of leftists and nationalists, and imprisoned in Con Son prison.[1]

Duong Bach Mai's apprenticeship illustrates some of the
recurring features of the colonial polity: a background in the
intelligentsia which allowed him an education in the elite schools
of Saigon and Hanoi, the radicalising and internationalising
influences of Paris, Moscow and Shanghai, and the experience
of the colonial prisons, which were known as 'revolutionary
universities' or 'kilns', because they developed and hardened so
many revolutionaries. But it is perhaps equally telling that, while
Baria's landowning class had produced a leading activist, he left
the province to be a militant in groups which had little involvement in Baria. In the revolutionary politics of the colonial period,
Baria was a relative backwater.

It was not until 1934 that the first Party cell was established
in Baria, and most of the revolutionary upsurge of the early
1930s passed by the province. Before this, there appears to have
been no influence of Vietnam's radical nationalist and anticolonial
groups, whose members tended to be urban petty-bourgeois
literati, with neither the organisation nor the program to mobilise
commitment in the provinces. What movements there were in
Baria had more the character of Hobsbawm's 'primitive rebels'.
One example was a secret society which mounted a quixotic
attack on the French garrison at Cape St Jacques in 1916. This
had none of the modern, disciplined organisation of the Leninist
model; instead it emerged out of a traditionalist past, mobilising
pre-existing forms of organisation, and its activists wore amulets
which they believed would make them invulnerable to bullets. It
is difficult to know whether such groups were organised as a
direct challenge to French rule or were simply pre-existing mutual
benefit associations, which villagers regularly formed as credit
cooperatives and to make provision for burial or marriage
expenses.[2]

Certainly, the colonial authorities took them as a serious
challenge, although, in French Indochina's curious combination
of civilising and repressive outlooks any form of autonomous
association was deemed threatening. In Baria in January 1916,
the aged mother of a day-labourer—Pham Van Khoe from Long

Dien—fell ill. With her death clearly approaching, he set about making preparations for the funeral, buying a coffin which was placed in the main room of the house, and notifying relatives. According to the charges at his later trial, while his mother lingered for several weeks, Khoe 'took advantage of the situation' to hold meetings 'at his house with numerous associates'—as many as 200 on occasion—with whom he plotted an armed attack on the French.

But the plot went poorly. An armed band set out one night in early February, wearing magic amulets which had been prepared by a 'sorcerer', but they had been either betrayed or discovered: 'The police ambushed the rebels who were surprised by those whom they had hoped to surprise. Forty-nine arrests were made; the remainder dispersed into the night.' The authorities alleged that Khoe was 'the leader of a secret society of several hundred persons (for the most part vagabonds and thieves). . .' which conspired against the colonial system, but the impact and power of such a challenge was minimal.[3]

This sort of sporadic rebellion relied on pre-existing forms of association and secret societies; the communist organisation which began from the early 1930s presented a more rigorous challenge. A handful of Communist Party cadres arrived in the province from 1931 to begin to organise Party activity. The initiative came from the southern—Nam Ky—regional level of the Party, rather than arising spontaneously out of local conditions. In 1931, a carpenter and Party cadre, Ho Tri Tan, was dispatched from Quang Tri province 'to seek out patriots', and began organising in Phuoc Hai. Two years later, another three cadres joined him. During the early 1930s, the Party had a 'Special Committee for Dong-Nai', charged with the task of propaganda amongst the plantations and enterprises of eastern Cochinchina, but its influence appears to have extended no further than sending out these small groups of cadres and coordinating their activities.[4]

The revolutionary movement's beginnings were very modest. Ho Tri Tan recruited the support of two others—an ox-cart driver and a carpenter. In this early period, the few Party activists and local supporters were most often skilled workers such as carpenters, builders and artisans. By the eve of Bastille Day in 1931, Ho Tri Tan had gathered enough members to carry out the local Party's first propaganda action. A leaflet was distributed under the name of the Communist Party, demanding the repeal of poll taxes and the reduction of land taxes, condemning 'greedy officials' and appealing for the support of local workers. There was evidently no mention of land reform. During the night, hammer-and-sickle flags were hung on official buildings in the major villages of Long Dien, Dat Do and Long Tan, and a large flag was set up on the Long Hai hills, overlooking these villages.

According to a local Party history, it was the 'first time in generations' that the people had had cause for hope, their patriotism 'awakened' by the political discussion occasioned by these small provocations. The attention given these events suggests their importance as communicative actions, and their political contestation of the symbolism of Bastille Day. In the revolutionary movement, great importance was to be placed on exemplary actions as the communication of ideas—the propaganda of the sign. This meshed with a political use of locale and space; the Long Hai hills from which the flag was flown were relatively inaccessible, and it was several days before colonial officials could have the flag brought down.

If its forms of action drew on symbolism, locale and patriotism, the Party's organisation was pre-eminently modern and Leninist. In February 1934, the cadres sent by the Nam Ky regional committee established the first Party cell in the province 'to direct the movement in the two areas of Long Dien and Dat Do'. This was at the fishing village of Phuoc Hai—and was thus dubbed by the local Party history 'the red seed of Phuoc Hai'—and consisted only of the three cadres sent to Baria. The Leninist principle of admitting only disciplined and ideologically proven members apparently excluded those who had taken part with Tan in the 1931 activities.

These first Party activists began propaganda work amongst the rubber plantation workers, though without evident success. They joined local Buddhist and Cao Dai religious organisations as a legal vehicle for political discussion during which they laboured the point that injustice in the villages had material origins.[5] With these events, Baria was becoming integrated into the national political response to colonial conditions and, however marginally, becoming part of the intricate history of nationalist and communist movements in Vietnam.

In this history, three groups had been most prominent until the early 1930s. Two proto-communist groups—the Revolutionary Party of the New Vietnam (Tan Viet) and the Vietnam Revolutionary Youth Association (Thanh Nien)—had, in February 1930, been pressured by the Comintern to merge into a single Indochinese Communist Party. Non-communist nationalism was represented by the Vietnamese Nationalist Party (VNQDD), which in its brief and violent existence from 1927 to 1930 represented the vestiges of the anticolonial Confucian literati. The VNQDD's program included direct action and assassination of colonial figures, such as the director of the plantation recruiting agency in Hanoi. The colonial response to this revolutionary violence saw the VNQDD's demise in a wave of French repression in 1929 and 1930. By the end of 1930, the Nationalist Party had been crushed, its members either imprisoned or guillotined.

These events coincided with a period of intense mobilisation as the effects of the Depression exacerbated social conditions. In February 1930, Vietnamese troops at the Yen Bay garrison, directed by the VNQDD, rebelled; in the same month, plantation workers began a strike at Phu Rieng in the south. In May, in Nghe Tinh province in the north, workers and peasants established soviets and began distributing land in an uprising which was inspired, and possibly initiated, by the Communist Party. Throughout Vietnam, for a year from mid-1930, '. . . there were few days without some sort of political agitation—worker strikes, peasant demonstrations, sabotage, assassinations of government officials, and dissemination of Communist leaflets'.

The colonial response was ferocious: military repression of demonstrations, and particularly of the Nghe Tinh soviets—where demonstrations were bombed and prisoners shot—and the destruction of the communists' organisation through imprisonment. In the south, the Nam Ky regional committee was imprisoned, and one report had it that '99 per cent of our leaders were arrested during 1931 and 1932. Those who are at large are weak in theory and practice. . .'[6] Only two years after its founding, the Party apparatus was shattered.

This was the context in which the first cadre arrived in Baria in 1931, in the same year that Duong Bach Mai returned to Saigon from Moscow. Distributing leaflets and displaying flags on Bastille Day in Baria were muted forms of the more violent events occurring elsewhere. By comparison with the militancy of other areas, these were relatively timid actions, suggesting that the province had little of the same social ferment. The first Party activity only began in the province in the context that the Party, or what remained of it, was a clandestine movement recovering from the destruction of the early 1930s.

These events of revolutionary upsurge and repression had several consequences at a national level. One was that the non-communist nationalist cause was broken, never to regain an effective grasp on Vietnamese history. With the VNQDD crushed, ideological and organisational leadership of the anti-colonial movement lay with the Communist Party, which now moved to centre stage. Henceforth, the main ideological strand of the movement would emphasise social revolution alongside patriotism, and non-communist nationalism would be fragmented and marginal. Weak as it was in the 1930s, the Communist Party established an ideological hegemony which would never be

seriously challenged, and which it would cultivate through the
formation of broad alliances and mass organisations to accommodate the vestiges of the nationalist cause. An indication of the
Party's hegemony was that some members of the VNQDD who
survived the repression of the early 1930s moved across to
Communist Party adherence. There was some irony in the fact
that 'in the late 1940s, when the French were attempting to block
the Communists, they vainly sought for a nationalist alternative,
the roots of which they had already destroyed almost two decades
before'.[7]

There were other, more concrete reasons for the weakness of
non-communist nationalism. Bourgeois interests were dramatically
stunted in Vietnam, with little economic role independent of the
French; the landlord class prospered, but was usually pro-French
as a result of its cultural and economic dependence. The French
monopolised most industrial and plantation development, while
the Chinese controlled most merchant capital and trade. Those
Vietnamese with a place in the colonial administration found their
progress blocked beyond relatively lowly levels. There was only
restricted space for the development of a class with an interest
in a national independence which excluded the social revolution
the Communist Party proposed. Unable to participate in colonial
capitalism, the urban intelligentsia had little stake in it. One
oft-noted result was that the intelligentsia joined the Communist
Party and played a decisive role in the independence struggle.

Another consequence of these events of insurrection and
repression was the effective establishment of the prisons as a
system of 'revolutionary universities'. Some 10 000 activists were
incarcerated in the early 1930s, and made good use of their
sentences to develop Marxist education. One Sûreté report
ruefully noted that 'detention seems to exalt their revolutionary
spirit'. As Marr put it: 'Jails were to the Vietnamese what the
Long March was to the Chinese . . . It was as if the French
had purposefully designed laboratories to test their Vietnamese
enemies' will to struggle.' Another source of the Party's resilience
was its connection with the Comintern, which meant that, unlike
any other Vietnamese party, the Communist Party had international support when rebuilding itself after being crushed in 1931
and again after 1939. The Comintern itself, and affiliates in Siam,
France and China, provided resources, training and sanctuary,
even if this had its price. Although the Moscow-trained cadres
were regarded by some as of poor quality, and as a consequence
the Party during the 1930s was caught in a Stalinist framework
of little relevance to local conditions, the Vietnamese Party was
hardly alone in this.[8]

Yet at a local level, the Party was highly successful in

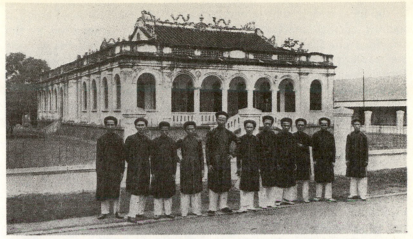

The Confucian notables of the province capital, Phuoc Le, line up outside the town's communal house in the late 1920s. Colonial rule had displaced the political authority of such notables; although they were often defenders of tradition, they also fathered a generation of anti-colonial revolutionaries. (Société des Etudes Indochinoises, La Cochinchine, *Saigon, 1931)*

developing an organisation with roots in the villages, which was able to link the material concerns of local people with the broader sentiments of national independence and patriotism. The activities of cadres in Baria up to the late 1930s are illustrative, even if they took place during a period of relative quiescence. In the village of Dat Do, Party activists organising amongst carpenters and sawmill and salt workers took up local grievances and articulated them as part of a conception of struggle in everyday life. They argued amongst the salt workers, for example, that the French monopoly on salt purchasing was the cause of low prices for the salt they produced.

An incident at Phuoc Hai in April 1938 illustrates this. The fishing village had an animated local market, trading with nearby villages and as far afield as Saigon. The women who conducted this intermediate trade held a grievance against two Indians who collected taxes on commission for the authorities, and who had—apparently with the indulgence of the local police and canton chief—been extorting taxes above the established rate and confiscating the merchandise of those who could not pay. 'Seizing on this sentiment, the party directed the women's mutual benefit association to directly organise a struggle meeting to defend the interests of the small traders.' A petition was circulated and presented to the province chief; this was followed by a three-day boycott of the market, with cadres taking some care to explain to the local people why it was closed. With one source of colonial income cut off, the tax collectors were soon reprimanded by the province chief and fined for extortion.[9] Such local-level actions were relatively insignificant, and their marginality reflected the Party's weakness in the province, but they connected immediate grievances with the independence movement and the national grievance of foreign rule, and foretold the struggle movements of the 1960s.

From the Popular Front to the French War

On 3 May, 1936, the Left overwhelmingly won national elections in France. During the Popular Front period which followed— lasting until early 1938—Vietnamese militants acted boldly in expectation of more liberal colonial policies and quickly came up against the limits of political activity in colonial society. Some early expectations were fulfilled: several thousand political prisoners were released, the governor-general was replaced and a new labour code promulgated. One effect in Nam Ky of the Popular Front was the creation in August 1936 of the Indochinese Congress, an alliance of non-communist and communist forces, the latter including the Communist Party and two Trotskyist groups which had significant support in Saigon. As part of the congress, an estimated 600 'action committees' were established in the south, holding meetings and political discussions, and building a movement demanding democratic liberalisation.

The committees grew extremely rapidly, largely at the initiative of the Party's rural network. In Saigon, *La Lutte* spelt out the rationale of the committees as relatively autonomous groups, at liberty to determine their own purposes, engaging in propaganda work and electing representatives to the Indochinese Congress, for which they would form a mass popular base. In villages throughout the south, action committees held public meetings and produced publications—tracts, brochures and posters. Their themes—described as 'simple and with immediate resonance'— were the miseries of coolies and peasants, the need to 'tear away the protective layer of silence over this exploitation', and the demand that France hear the grievances of the people. The committees were both an organised mass base and a form of political engagement for ordinary villagers.[10]

This boisterous political activity had an immediate reflection in Baria, where the Party initiated action committees in some major villages '. . . to distribute leaflets, and purchase progressive newspapers for distribution to the masses, in order to stimulate discussion about democracy, the condition of the people and to

appeal for unity in the struggle'. This represented a public form
of activism previously unknown in the colonial order. However,
it is clear that the province was relatively marginal, with less of
the vibrant activism seen elsewhere in the south. Baria was one
of a number of provinces where the movement of the congress
'hardly caught on', although there was one very active action
committee in Long Dien village.[11]

In the last months of 1936, the colonial authorities restricted
the activities of the congress, and eventually banned it, along
with all political meetings. Duong Bach Mai, the militant from
Baria who had now risen to prominence in *La Lutte*, was
dispatched to Paris to protest against this repression and to plead
the case of the congress. But he had only moderate success; the
French government was also under pressure from the colonial
administration, intent on retaining political control. Meanwhile,
the unique alliance in Saigon of Trotskyists and Communist Party
members in *La Lutte*, which had been one condition of this burst
of political activity in the south, was unravelling in acrimony.
Party members in the south were being pressed by their more
Comintern-aligned comrades in Hanoi to break off such an
unholy alliance, and by mid-1937, the Trotskyists and the
Communist Party had reverted to polemics.[12]

The congress was a brief event which illuminated the land-
scape of the colonial polity. It demonstrated the limits of political
life under the colonial regime, for the French distrusted any
semblance of democracy, viewing signs of civil life and political
independence as a threat. If the congress and its action committees had some features of a growth of public political culture,
and assumed liberal norms of the rule of law and freedoms of
speech and press, their repression indicated the necessary author-
itarianism of the colonial state. Colonial rule was not only
founded on a tiny, racially based elite, but could not survive a
test of legitimacy without the protection of repression; it was a
form of domination untenable under democratic conditions. The
colonial polity was such that Montesquieu and Rousseau were
considered subversive reading for Vietnamese, with the French
thus reduced to suppressing their own radical and democratic
traditions. But this, too, was an impossible task; as Victor Kiernan
wrote of Nguyen Vo Giap's education in Hanoi: 'France may
not have planted any tree of liberty in its colonies, but it did
plant a tree of knowledge, which bore unpredictable fruit.'[13]

The congress also illuminated the state of the anticolonial
forces. The Communist Party had, by the mid-1930s, a viable—if
fragile—network of rural cadres which could be mobilised to
organise the action committees. It was strongly committed to the
Leninist conception of the cell as a 'power technology' built upon

a small, exclusive group of disciplined cadres. This authoritarian form of organisation presumed obedience to a superior centre, connected through a command structure with the cells. The organic metaphor of the first Party cell in the province—'the red seed of Phuoc Hai'—presumes a teleology in revolutionary history, as though history is a process of producing the ineluctable. Even if this is misplaced, the first cells nevertheless were an embryonic form of Leninist organisation, which was a distinctly modern and efficacious power technology capable of seizing history and re-establishing national sovereignty.

Finally, the congress also illustrated the ways in which the Party had begun to re-appropriate a discourse of patriotism and traditional culture. In the late 1930s, the communists in Vietnam began to relearn the language of tradition, which helped promote the Party's organisation in the rural and village order. Less hostile than it had previously been to Confucian tradition and patriotic sentiments, the Party was in a position to make the most of the potential for mobilisation which lay in 'the reaffirmation of historical and national identity, in the face of imperialism, [and] the destructive effects of colonialism . . .'[14]

This was the more flexible ideological context for the strategy of broad united fronts which carried the Vietnamese Party to victories in 1945, in 1954 and finally in 1975. By May 1941, the strategy was launched in the form of the Viet Minh Front, representing the broadest possible alliance of classes and interests in mass organisations incorporating peasants, women, youth and so on, with the Communist Party retaining the central leadership role, in particular the political control of armed units. The network of cells both directed, and was shielded by, these front organisations. This strategy, which focused an alliance of interests on the principal aim of national independence, while minimising much of the divisive class character of issues such as land reform, was repeated in the Lien Viet Front (the Fatherland Front after the Party came to power in Hanoi) and the National Liberation Front in the South from 1960.[15]

But in the period after 1939, when another round of repression had dispatched Party cadres into the 'revolutionary universities', the chief focus of the Party was on rebuilding. Estimates of its strength are very imprecise; but one estimate put total membership for all of Nam Ky in 1944 as low as 200 members, with a further 600 in its affiliated front organisations. This weakness was mirrored in Baria, where the Party had been reduced by arrests and deportations after 1939, and where there was scarcely a revolutionary movement at all until 1944.[16]

During 1940 and 1941, the Japanese progressively occupied Vietnam, allowing the French a titular control. Amongst the repercussions favouring the growth of anticolonial sentiment was the spectacle of Japanese soldiers exercising power over the former colonial masters. In the villages of Phuoc Hai and Long Hai, local villagers observed Japanese officers and soldiers entering the restaurants, 'wearing long swords that touched the ground, and . . . touching the cheeks of the French women at will, to display their power over them to the people'. This power was more explicitly demonstrated in March 1945, when the Japanese carried out a *coup de force*, imprisoning some French authorities and installing a 'pseudo-independence' government. 'What impressed ordinary Vietnamese most was how the French colonial regime—after 80 years of seeming invincibility—had been shattered in a mere two days.' The French hold on the colony was slipping.[17]

By mid-August 1945, when the Japanese capitulation after Hiroshima created a political vacuum in Vietnam, the Viet Minh were able to take the north in a series of uprisings which met with little resistance. The August Revolution took a week to reach Nam Ky—where insurrections took place in Saigon and in some provincial capitals on 25 August—and it had a more tenuous foothold in the south. Events in Baria reflected those elsewhere. On the 21st, having heard of the uprisings in the north, the Party branch sent delegates to Saigon 'to meet the Regional Committee to ask for instructions'. When they returned the following day, an urgent meeting was called of cadres who then spread out to villages and plantations with instructions 'for action when the order was given'. Viet Minh leaflets were distributed, appealing for support.

During the night of the 24th, a demonstration converged on the province capital, and early in the morning, according to a local account, 'close to ten thousand people of all classes had concentrated in the capital'. A proclamation was read, denouncing fascism and calling on the provincial administration to resign; it did so early that afternoon, 'handing over power in the province to the people's committee'.[18] Although the Party had only a fragile network of cadres in Baria, their ability to contact the regional committee for instructions, and their organisational capacity to carry them out, made possible an action which was coordinated with others across the south on the same morning. For what was to be a brief interlude, the colonial epoch in Baria was over.

This bloodless takeover reflected the circumstances of the moment rather than a real balance of power. In Nam Ky, the August Revolution filled a vacuum, but the Party was not sufficiently strong to prevent a reimposition of colonial rule. That rule was re-established in the following months by British troops

under General Gracey, who had instructions to disarm and
repatriate the Japanese and maintain law and order, but who also
assumed that Vietnam was to be restored to the French.[19] Gracey,
'whom the thought of treating with upstart natives, who might
actually be communists, filled with horror', was appropriately
enough in command of mostly Indian troops: 'the British lion
was using its false teeth to the end'. He occupied Saigon in
mid-September, declaring what was in effect martial law and
rearming the French, who set about attacking the Viet Minh
headquarters in Saigon with, in the words of a British eyewitness,
'maximum ineptitude and considerable cruelty'.[20]

When it became clear that the Viet Minh would resist, as
they did over the following months, Gracey rearmed the Japanese,
who were then used with little regard to their casualties. French,
Indian and Japanese troops fought alongside each other to
reimpose the colonial regime, although there were a few instances
where isolated Japanese garrisons, including in Baria, attempted
'to do a deal with the Vietnamese'. By early 1946, the Japanese
were concentrated at Cape St Jacques, ready for repatriation, and
the British had largely withdrawn, leaving French troops to carry
the bulk of the fighting. The latter reoccupied Baria province
early in February. The First Indochinese War which followed did
not begin in full until the end of 1946—after a tense interregnum
in which the French rebuilt their strength and the Viet Minh
government in the north negotiated for time, if not for independence—but in the south small-scale guerrilla war developed
throughout that year, in the form of attacks on French posts and
convoys and assassinations of village leaders.[21]

Decolonisation

In Baria in 1945, the Viet Minh armed forces prepared for the
last act of decolonisation were pitiably weak. There were only
two small armed groups of ten to fifteen soldiers each, based in
Long Phuoc and Long Tan. Two years later, these had been
expanded to two companies, numbering between 50 and 80
soldiers each, along with some guerrillas. The company-size
groups were allocated to the districts of the province, with a
mobile battalion, designated 300, later engaged in attacking
French forces; in 1950, it ambushed a French convoy on the
road north from Phuoc Le, in thick forest near the hill of Nui
Dat, where the Australian Task Force would later be based.

Several areas in the province were regarded by the Viet Minh
as liberated during the war: the remote east of the province
around Xuyen Moc, and more importantly a section of the main

On Bastille Day in 1948, Vo Thi Sau, a fifteen-year-old local girl, attempted to assassinate the Vietnamese province chief of Baria. Four years later, she was executed by a French firing squad, only a day after being admitted into the Communist Party. Clearly fervent, she is nevertheless puzzling: what motivated her to such desperate acts—quixotic youth, revolutionary fervour, patriotism? Her mystery is an indication of the varied strands of Vietnamese anti-colonialism. (Ban Chap Hang Dang Bo, Dong Nai 30 Nam, Bien Hoa, 1986)

road running from Saigon to the Cape. Some 30 kilometres of the road were under Viet Minh control from 1947 to 1952, though it was not closed to armed French convoys. Although scarcely a populated area, it provided a base for the province Party committee, which could move from the village of Phu My on the road to the jungle area called Hat Dich immediately to the north-east. Another base area, closer to the central villages, was the Minh Dam Secret Zone, centred around the village of Long My and encompassing the Long Hai hills.[22]

Writing on the experience in the province of the anticolonial war, Frost concluded that 'control of these areas plus the two fortified villages of Long Phuoc and Long Tan . . . meant that the Viet Minh controlled almost the entire province, with the exception of the provincial capital'. The French were still able to send forces into the province on a regular basis, as well as stationing garrisons in the major villages. French troops attacked Phu My twice in mid-1946, and again in late 1949, targeting the Viet Minh armaments workshops there. Other battles took place around the Minh Dam secret zone and the Saigon road, mostly before the end of the 1940s.[23] Nevertheless, the substantial Viet Minh control of the province was not fiercely challenged by the French, and by 1948, when the guerrilla war was becoming protracted, Baria was considered amongst the major Viet Minh bases in the south. Without heavy fighting, it was an area to which—in true guerrilla fashion—Viet Minh forces could withdraw to evade the French. The latter could never spare enough forces to eradicate such enclaves 'from which the guerrillas staged their attacks and by night dominated country nominally under French rule'.[24]

Even in areas under Viet Minh control throughout most of the war, there was little land reform. Vietnamese historians working on the revolution in Baria have concluded that the amount of land redistributed was minimal. Later, when Viet Minh land reforms were reversed under the land reforms of the late 1950s—which re-established prewar tenure—the area affected in Baria was only in the hundreds of hectares.[25] This may partly reflect the nature of the local economy; there were not the great estates to be expropriated in Baria that there were in the delta. But it also reflects the delicacy with which the Party approached land reform in this period, avoiding land policies which would drive landlords into the French camp and reduce the viability of the united front. In the south, in the Party's ideology and strategy, the tension between class-based support for social revolution and a united front with a nationalist or patriotic orientation remained a constant.[26]

The Viet Minh victory at Dien Bien Phu in May 1954 marked an emphatic end to the French colonial period. It coincided with, and provided political leverage for, the negotiations which produced the Geneva Accords in July. Yet, despite the political advantage afforded by Dien Bien Phu, the Vietnamese Party agreed to a partition of the country at the seventeenth parallel, just north of Hue, with a timetable for national elections in two years to reunify the country. The Accords made much of the expectation that the partition did not indicate a new boundary between states, but the division soon became much more intractable. That the new president in the South, Ngo Dinh Diem, promptly denounced the agreements was an indication of the future.

Pending elections, the accords allowed for the regroupment of Viet Minh military forces from South to North and for the resettlement of those—principally Catholics—who wished to leave the North for the South. Baria demonstrated both demographic movements. In July 1954, the principal Viet Minh battalion left for the North, leaving behind village guerrillas and a network of political cadres. The estimates of the total number who regrouped from South to North vary from Lacouture's 20 000 to Burchett's figure of 140 000 troops and cadres. The isolated coast near Xuyen Moc in Baria was one of five assembly points designated in the accords from which Viet Minh soldiers set sail for the North; from here alone, at least 10 000 soldiers and another 5000 cadres and relatives embarked.[27]

They left in the expectation that they would be returning after the elections two years later. There is a poignant reminder of all they were leaving behind in Warner's story that all over the South there were thousands of weddings of couples who had been unable to marry during the French war: 'At worst, it seemed, the separation would be for two years.' For most, it would be at least five or six years. Across South Vietnam, between 5000 and 15 000 cadres remained behind to campaign for the coming elections. Perhaps as many as 50 Party cells remained in the province, which meant several hundred cadres. The next five years revealed the extreme vulnerability of this political network, as the temporary partition solidified, with Diem's refusal to hold the elections which all observers agreed would have seen Ho Chi Minh elected, and as the Diem government set about repressing its political opposition. For the remainder of the decade, the Party took the view that the consolidation of the North should take priority, and only realised rather late how perilously close to extinction was its network of cadres in the South.[28]

Baria also experienced the opposite movement of refugees from the North. Of some 850 000 who left the North, roughly 700 000 were Catholics fearing persecution. Some refugees settled in the province at Phuoc Tinh on the coast, and a more substantial group—some 250 families—established in 1955 a new village at Binh Gia, made up of villagers from Nghe An province led by their Catholic priest. The site of the new village was first prepared by French engineers; each family received a small block of land, some cash and building materials and a supply of food. Unlike older villages, Binh Gia was laid out on a neat grid pattern; a church was built, and by 1959 the population was close to 4000.[29]

This established a substantial village which, over the next two decades, was resolutely impervious to communist influence. There has been some suggestion that this settlement pattern was part of a strategic plan to settle Catholic, pro-Diem populations to the east of Saigon, as a demographic shield for the capital. Lacouture wrote of the new Catholic villages forming an 'iron guard' around the capital, composed of refugees who—compared to southern Catholics—were 'more ardent, more intransigent, with priests who, on the Spanish pattern, are the true community leaders'.[30] Certainly, Catholic refugees remained consistently anti-communist, and Binh Gia, during the period the Australians were in the province, was an island of militant opposition to the revolution.

Baria, then, amply demonstrates the dynamics of colonialism and the Vietnamese political response. Decolonisation had seen the Communist Party move to the fore as the only major political

force, which alone had the capacity to organise the interior of
the country through its network of cells linked with the disciplined
command system of a national Party. This dominant position
was not inevitable, but the outcome of a colonial history which
had checked the growth of non-communist nationalism. Partly as
a result, the communists could lay claim to being the party of
patriotism and nationalism. Their united front strategy successfully mobilised interests other than those committed to the Party,
and the Party's roots in the villages meant it could articulate
patriotic sentiment based on traditional and local interests. Finally,
its capacity to wage the anticolonial struggle—through the development of armed forces as the major form of Party power—meant
it could lay claim to being the party of nationalism in the sense
of articulating a modern nation-state and a postcolonial future.[31]
The communists in Vietnam had made themselves the allies of
both patriotism and modernity, of both the past and the future.

3

'A trance of uncertainty, doubt and fear': Australia and Asia in the Cold War

The events of May 1954 in Vietnam and Geneva were reported in Australia with a sense of crisis mingled with miscomprehension. During the first week of May, daily reports on the siege at Dien Bien Phu occupied the front pages alongside federal election commentary; three days after the Viet Minh victory, *The Age* headlined its editorial 'Indo-China disaster is critical for world' and wrote: 'with the fall of the French fortress of Dien Bien Phu, Asia and the Western world are again brought to a point of crisis.'

News-Weekly, the paper of the ALP's Catholic right wing, the Movement, was highly alarmed. 'Isolated and heavily outnumbered, their guns ran hot as they mowed down wave after wave of fanatical Communists, who kept coming on and on over their dead . . . On the outcome of this battle could hang the eventual safety of Australia.' The intemperate Stan Keon, the most prominent of the ALP federal parliamentarians associated with the Movement, told a public meeting in the Movement-dominated Richmond town hall: 'Today we are in danger almost as grave as the peril when the Japanese were pressing in on us.'[1]

The Age confessed to some confusion about the issues,

39

particularly with conflicting British and American policies being
argued at Geneva. The paper made a vain attempt to have Casey,
who had just returned from Geneva, illuminate matters during
the election debate: 'It would be refreshing to hear Mr. Casey's
account of his own position in this confused situation. There are
so many loose ends in the external affairs pattern, so many
problems that are vital to Australia and are yet very little
understood . . .' But Casey's interventions in the campaign were
more inflammatory than revealing; on the same evening that Keon
spoke to his constituents in Richmond, Casey was conjuring for
his Toorak audience the vision of Australian children pulling
rickshaws. On another occasion, he warned a meeting that
'International Communism could be right at Australia's northern
gateway in 18 months to two years.' Such alarming imagery was
the measure of the public discourse on Asia in the early 1950s.
Casey himself had lamented in his diary while in Djakarta in
1952 that 'We, in Australia, are living in a fool's paradise of
ignorance about the East. It is extremely difficult to get a realistic
discussion in Australia about affairs in the East . . .'[2] Yet he
was apparently not inspired to act upon this democratic impulse
and contribute to a measured debate. For the conservatives, the
political advantages of Cold War rhetoric were too attractive, and
a pattern was already established in which a gap existed between
an inflamed public sphere and the private councils of policy.

This chapter considers two major themes. The first deals with
the imagery of Asia in Australian political debate during the early
1950s, and in particular, the quality of understanding of an Asia
emerging from colonialism. That debate pivoted on the role of
nationalism and communism in decolonisation struggles. Given
the amalgam in the Vietnamese movement of nationalist, patriotic
and revolutionary strands, this was an issue of some moment,
though one poorly understood. The second theme is the ways
in which the domestic political configuration of the Cold War in
Australia coloured the perception of Asian events. Public discourse on Asia was shaped by this configuration and its tensions.

Each of the major debates which occurred on foreign affairs
in this period—in 1950 and 1954—was attended by alarming
events in Asia and fractious dispute in Australia. Thus the
parliamentary debate in March 1950, in which the recently elected
Menzies government set its stamp on foreign policy, took place
shortly after the introduction of the Communist Party Dissolution
Bill and was followed in June by the outbreak of the Korean
War. In 1954, events followed each other with bewildering speed.
In mid-April, Menzies announced the defection of Vladimir
Petrov, and the following four weeks saw the election campaign,

Key power-brokers of the Australian–American alliance in the 1950s, meeting in the White House in March 1955. Left to right *Dwight D. Eisenhower, US President, 1953–61; Sir Percy Spender, Australian ambassador to the US, 1951–58; John Foster Dulles, US Secretary of State, 1953–59; and Sir Robert Menzies, Australian prime minister, 1949–66. The four men had not agreed on Dulles's proposals for military intervention in Vietnam the year before but shared a concern to guard Southeast Asia and the Pacific against 'communist aggression'. Spender and Menzies tried to focus American regional commitments to that purpose. (National Libary of Australia, Spender papers)*

the 'fall' of Dien Bien Phu and the first spectacular sittings of the Royal Commission on Espionage in Canberra. Although Menzies cultivated the impression that he would not stoop to using the communist issue in an election, few doubted that the backdrop of domestic intrigue and international crisis helped salvage a narrow victory from what had appeared, one year before, a hopeless electoral position.

Wider forces converged in these few months in 1954. Anti-communism was a well-established discourse, fuelled as much by the bitterness between the Labor and Communist parties as it was by the Menzies government's incessant mobilisation of Cold War discourse against the left. During the first half of the 1950s, the CPA was particularly isolated, as was the peace movement associated with it. The ALP was increasingly divided by the tensions between the Catholic right and the left, and debates in and out of parliament demonstrated the incompatibility of views within the party. Just as 1954 in Vietnam was an end point for the dynamics of the colonial era, in Australia it was a point of convergence of the political dynamics of the Cold War.

Glimpses of Asia

The transition from the Labor governments of the 1940s to the conservative rule of the 1950s and 1960s marked a distinct shift in foreign policy, determined partly by the evolution of the Cold War, but as much by the local configuration of political forces. This was clear by the time Percy Spender rose to make his first statement as minister for External Affairs in March 1950. Like H.V. Evatt, Spender was a graduate of Fort Street high school and a lawyer, though he had none of the bold prominence and capricious brilliance which had taken his predecessor to the presidency of the United Nations General Assembly.

Nor did Spender have the easy social graces of his successor, Casey, who invariably took tea in high places when in London. Instead, Spender was a shy-looking man, with a nervous smile and—in childhood—a fearful stutter. The son of a locksmith, he was a dogged exemplar of the upwardly mobile conservative, with none of the patrician background which made Casey a natural part of the ruling class, but with an intense desire to be remembered by history. Yet Spender was tough in dealing with his departmental officers, he later proved to be a forthright diplomat, and his qualities had impressed Liberal Party colleagues. By early 1951, he was being mooted as a challenger to Menzies, who was seen to be failing. The challenge was forestalled when Spender accepted the post of ambassador to the United States. Yet in a short ministerial tenure of only fifteen months, he had effectively set the course for conservative foreign policy through the 1950s and beyond.

This necessarily involved breaks with the past. Evatt had always given primacy to the United Nations as the means of resolving conflicts, arguing for negotiation and the legalism of liberal rationalism. In the postwar years, this approach meshed with Labor's often vague sentiments of opposition to colonialism, sympathy for emergent nationalism and a suspicion that poverty lay at the heart of postcolonial ferment.[3] Spender, and then Casey (as minister from 1951 to 1960), brought a more oppositional vision to international affairs, as a Cold War struggle with an aggressive communist imperialism. They envisaged a lesser role for the UN, which was seen as relatively powerless, and emphasised the need to cultivate regional security alliances. They saw anticolonial nationalist forces as having roots in poverty and underdevelopment, but as unstable and too easily captured by communist influence.

But more so than Evatt, Casey or Menzies, Spender had an acute sense of social change in postwar Asia, where 'nations but recently the colonial territories of European powers' were 'involved in a perilous struggle for survival' against existing economic and political conditions. Asia, for Spender, was challenging, dynamic but not necessarily threatening; a sense of his urgency is conveyed by a powerful image recalled in 1968 of his first visit to Hong Kong:

> I shall never forget the impact that was made upon me, seeing the conditions under which people lived and how they worked, and how a ship was coaled in those days, it was almost inhuman to see these people with baskets of coal upon their back, almost like a treadmill, going up and down, throwing the coal from their baskets, going down, and being filled and going on and on, like an endless chain of human endeavour, and this was the picture which . . . throughout my life . . . strikes me.

This was a hypnotic image of the struggles of what he sometimes called 'the swarming millions of Asian peoples'.

It signified a quite different view from both the bland indifference of Menzies and the dignified amiability of Casey's Anglo-Australian ascendancy. Of the latter, Alan Watt commented: 'Casey in Asia had extraordinary dignity. Casey's attitude in the presence of a beggar on the street was identical with his attitude in the presence of the Emperor of Japan.'[4] This was less a democratic sentiment than a certain detachment from an Asia seen as timeless, whereas Spender's greater sense of urgency was a mainspring of his active interest in the region.

Nevertheless, Spender's overarching view was firmly within the parameters of the Cold War. He began his ministerial statement in 1950 with the proposition that the centre of 'potential aggression' had shifted from Europe to Asia, a reference to the Chinese revolution of the previous year. Australian policy had to meet:

> . . . new problems created in this area by the emergence of a communist China, and by the ever increasing thrust of communism, which endeavours to ally itself, in the pursuit of its ends, with the national aspirations of the millions of people of South-East Asia.

Moscow and Peking were indistinguishable in this Cold War struggle, which was now the overriding feature of global relations. The 'major responsibility' for this conflict lay with the Soviet

Union, whose 'ultimate objective' was 'a universal form of communism with Moscow as the controlling centre'; its means were 'communist infiltration in all democratic countries', including 'peace offensives' and 'industrial dislocation'.

Spender considered Vietnam only briefly, presenting it as 'the great present danger point in the South-East Asian area' and formulating a view subsequently expressed by Eisenhower in his metaphor of falling dominoes:

> Should the forces of Communism prevail and Vietnam come under the heel of Communist China, Malaya is in danger of being outflanked and it, together with Thailand, Burma and Indonesia, will become the next direct object of further Communist activities.

The suggestion that the Viet Minh was in part nationalist was brusquely dispensed with: 'It is an incontrovertible fact that their unchallenged leader, Ho Chi-minh, received his political training in Moscow.' If the Viet Minh won in Vietnam, Spender argued, their regime would be 'scarcely distinguishable from other Communist satellite Governments'. Cold War discourse worked with such universals and polar opposites that this was sufficient to close the case on Vietnamese nationalism. Finally, Spender argued for economic and military responses to these perceived threats. One of his achievements was to propose and develop a program of economic aid 'to stabilise governments' and improve living standards in Asia—a proposal which issued in the Colombo Plan. Another was his work on developing a regional defence pact with the United States, formally signed as the ANZUS alliance in July 1951.[5]

Although Evatt claimed to find considerable agreement between the government and the opposition, and argued that Spender had adopted ALP positions, he could do so only by glossing over a number of emerging fractures in foreign policy debate. The most obvious was the relative weight to be given to United Nations intervention or to regional alliances. The two were not mutually exclusive, but Evatt insisted in vain that

> . . . more emphasis should be placed upon the United Nations. That is the sole working forum today for the resolving of international disputes . . . The question is whether the solutions of international problems are to be found on a regional or a global basis.

Evatt's preference was clearly for the latter, which would make regional alliances of secondary importance, but in the relatively new climate of the Cold War he was speaking for the past. Evatt wanted the anticolonial war in Vietnam resolved by a UN monitoring body 'to keep close watch and to report periodically on any unlawful intrusion into the area or interference with it'.[6]

He apparently assumed that China controlled the conflict in Vietnam and that the UN could have a role in severing that influence. Paradoxically, Spender and Evatt both argued that Vietnam was pivotal, but had little to say about it; each assumed the real issue to be the newly emergent Communist China, which could be dealt with either by an alliance of containment (for Spender) or by UN monitoring (for Evatt).

The conservatives were notably muted on the role of the UN. Spender clearly saw only a minimal role for it in the Cold War years. Referring to the 'cloud of frustration and doubt' under which the UN worked, he argued: 'Australia lives in a dangerous world and we must look immediately to means additional to the United Nations—not necessarily to other principles—to defend our interests and exert our influence . . .' The reduction in the importance of the UN was later identified as one of the key features of Spender's change in Australian foreign policy. This was based on a scepticism best captured by Dean Acheson, addressing a luncheon in Melbourne of the conservative Australian–American Association in 1962. Truman's former secretary of state dismissed the UN as 'a nineteenth century conception founded on the belief that enthusiasm, by overlooking the obvious, could attain the unattainable'.[7]

Paul Hasluck—who followed Spender for the government side in the debate, and had only recently come into parliament after several years with the Australian UN delegation—struck an even blunter note of *realpolitik*, arguing that international relations were always a matter of the self-interest of nation-states, and the UN was simply power diplomacy carried on by the great powers. The key characteristic of power diplomacy was 'a clear intention on the part of the Soviet Union to overcome any opposition and to bring about a world dictatorship under Russian control'; such imperial expansionism refuted in action the relevance of the United Nations.[8] These arguments plainly allocated a reduced role to the UN, particularly given the Soviets' exercise of their veto power in the Security Council. Diplomacy would work not because the methods of the UN worked, but because the great powers were balanced, and for the conservatives that balance was demonstrated in Western strength and resolve.

Part of this divergence between the parties lay in the extent to which the discourse and concepts of the Cold War were accepted. Spender and Hasluck mobilised the oppositional framework of the Cold War with some enthusiasm, although the former struck a note of regret when he described the Cold War struggle as holding the world 'in a trance of uncertainty, doubt and fear'.[9] Each also accepted the possibility of coexistence with the communist bloc, though not at the expense of 'appeasement'.

Throughout the 1950s, this remained a point of difference between the conservative government and the Movement, which rejected coexistence as 'nothing more than a tactical weapon used to delude the West'.[10]

Most ALP speakers in the 1950 debate shied away from this language, though those associated with the Movement took it up with a vengeance. Evatt was anticommunist in the way of much of postwar Labor, remembering the bitter conflicts with an aggressively resurgent Communist Party in the late 1940s, fearful of the threat to the ALP's industrial base from the CPA's union strength, but cautious not to have Labor preoccupied with a debate on communism whose terms were wholly set by the conservatives. The tone adopted by Evatt, and by others such as Les Haylen, was to deplore 'the spread of Communist or other extremist influences in the region', but without adopting the confrontationist language which was becoming commonplace on the right.[11]

The interventions of Labor politicians connected with the Movement, such as John Mullens and Keon, were in harsh contrast. Mullens devoted most of his time to the 'old school tie' character of the Department of External Affairs, in an anti-intellectual speech somewhat out of character with the earnest tone of *News-Weekly* but similar to the boorish attacks of Senator Joe McCarthy in America. He confessed to being 'almost inordinately suspicious of people named Algernon, Reginald, or Percy'. And he brutally dismissed Evatt's cherished United Nations as 'ineffective': 'a babel of sound and fury, signifying nothing'. In keeping with *News-Weekly*'s policy, Mullens's preferred course was that of regional alliance with the US. But he also evinced the desperate anxiety of Cold War and Catholic panic with his vision of the coming confrontation with the 'Russian imperialists', 'a scourge in the form of a subtle expansion of an empire'. 'That empire,' he went on, '. . . the great intangible heresy of modern times . . . may one day engulf this Australia of ours.'[12] With such alarms of impending danger, the Labor right shared with the conservatives the language of confrontation and the policy solution of regional pacts. By 1950, this tension within Labor was one pointer to the later Split.

A third fracture in the debate reflects the cultural images of Asia that were current in the early 1950s. What was the relative place of nationalism and communism in the social movements arising out of Asian decolonisation? The conservatives argued that nationalist aspirations had been captured and manipulated by external influences; revolution was an alien import, reflecting Soviet expansion and subversion rather than the dynamics of colonial rule and decolonisation. Hence, part of Spender's rationale for the Colombo Plan was that Asian nationalism was '. . . a force which can be prostituted by the unscrupulous, the ambitious, and the self-seeking. . . Nationalism and the struggle for survival provided a fertile field for those whose interest it was to stir the bubbling pot of unrest and dissatisfaction.' Spender had an urgent sense of the material and political struggles of Southeast Asia. But it was a truly conservative sentiment that led him to cast revolutionary movements as 'political opportunism and disturbance'.[13]

Spender's successor used similar language, in which communist parties were the 'other', an alien force. On his first visits to Southeast Asia in 1951 and 1952, Casey wondered at the mystery of what made the Viet Minh fight, while—oblivious to the contradiction—he observed 'no noticeable patriotic spirit amongst the Vietnamese'. In 1954, he thought the quasi-independence proposed by the French was not enough to 'whip up sufficient local national Vietnam [sic] enthusiasm and fervour so that they'd flock to the colours and really set about defending their country with vigour and spirit against the Viet Minh'.[14] Even allowing for the complexities of Vietnamese colonial politics, this was distinctly muddled. Given the patriotic and anticolonial credentials Vietnamese communists had established since the 1930s, and given that they were the only major force left standing by the French, the notion of defending their country against the Viet Minh would have struck many Vietnamese as incongruous.

The conservatives' image of Asia reflected the character of intellectual conservatism in the 1950s. One useful way of describ-

Richard Casey was Australian minister for External Affairs for almost a decade, from 1951 to 1960. Part of the last generation of Anglo-Australians, he tended to think of Asia as 'the East': Alan Watt commented that he had the same attitude in Asia to a beggar on the street as to the Emperor of Japan, a reflection not of contempt but of Casey's airy goodwill and patrician demeanour. Casey saw advantages in holding Australia poised between the Americans and the British and hoped to influence both. (National Library of Australia, portrait collection)

ing this is to say that conservatism in this period was concerned less with appealing to august traditions than with preserving social stability and integration through particular interventions. The *leitmotif* was anxiety in the face of instability and change; the response was in terms of modest, pragmatic interventions of social management. The sense, then, in the 1950s of Australia as 'a part of Asia' was a sense that the two had parallel social problems. Not only was Asian revolution threatening, but its perceived problems of instability, of modernisation and of a spiritual vacuum resonated with the concerns of conservative intellectuals for their own place, and that of tradition, in postwar Australia.[15]

Glimpses of Asia as a region of social upheaval in the postcolonial order struck chords in domestic politics. For Casey, there were parallels between his description of Vietnamese communism as alien and the place of communism in Australia. As his biographer put it, Casey 'saw communism and communists as beyond the pale of normal conventions', and despite his distaste for the coarser aspects of McCarthyism, was quite ready to suspend liberal democratic norms in the pursuit of Australian leftists. If one began with the established order, those who advocated its overthrow or challenged its virtues must be outsiders. Domestically, the Cold War was a climate which marginalised dissenting views, narrowing the spectrum of acceptable opinion and attempting to place the left outside political culture. When it attempted to understand Asian revolution, the same cast of mind conjured some fundamental distortions. For Casey, nationalism was local but communism was alien: 'The local Communist party in each South-East Asian country would amount to little or nothing, if it were not stimulated and directed and aided from outside.' In the case of Vietnam, it was an underestimation of fatal proportions, as Watt recognised many years later.[16]

The official history of the Australian involvement in Malaya and Vietnam has begun to unfold these links between Asian nationalism and communism in conservative thought. When the Australian government committed active support to Malaya in 1950, it saw itself as aiding a non-communist nationalism against ethnic Chinese communists, who were presumed to be part of a global Cold War strategy. In 1955, Australian troops were added to the Commonwealth Strategic Reserve force in Malaya, and in 1965 they were made available for active service in Borneo, in the Confrontation with Indonesia. The success with which communist guerrillas were put down in Malaya during the 1950s became a sort of overture for Vietnam.

Malaya demonstrated a number of the conditions which the conservatives vainly sought in Vietnam: there was a viable form of nationalism which was ideologically, politically and even ethnically distinct from communism, this nationalism was pro-Western and welcomed foreign intervention and support, and the 'counterinsurgency' strategy was successful in crushing isolated communist guerrillas. But as an exemplary case of arranging the postcolonial transition, Malaya snared the unwary: 'Those who got Vietnam wrong did so partly because they had previously got Malaya right . . .'[17] Some reflection on Vietnamese history would have clarified that Malaya was not Vietnam. But the conservatives were locked into a conceptual framework which drew a haze over historical reflection, and within which it was difficult enough to accord legitimacy to a nationalist social movement, and harder still to distinguish the unique intertwining of nationalist, patriotic and revolutionary sentiments in Vietnamese decolonisation.

Labor groped unsuccessfully towards a more subtle understanding of social struggles in postwar Asia. Haylen—the former journalist who was now a close ally of Evatt's and prominent on the left—told parliament that 'we must learn and understand what is happening [in Asia] because every move of the resurgent peasants and socialists has a great bearing on this country'. Postcolonial social upheavals represented 'the vengeance of Asia following upon thousands of years of neglect', and Asia faced a choice, not between capitalism and communism, but between 'socialism or anarchy', as postcolonial regimes struggled to reconcile the pressures upon them.

Haylen represented a Labor view that social conditions and thwarted nationalism explained the success of communist parties. He quoted—with evident approval—Malcolm MacDonald, the son of Ramsay and the British commissioner-general in Southeast Asia. Asian people did not particularly care about communism:

> But there are two great causes they believe in passionately—national freedom and the uplift of the Asian masses. If we western democracies show that we strongly support these policies Asia will never go Communist.

For Haylen, economic growth could be a (socialist) bulwark against Asian communism, and he wanted to go further than Spender's plans for aid: 'What the East needs is a great Marshall plan for liberal spending to assist the Asian people to their feet, and to buttress the government.'[18]

In this perspective, Labor had the germ of an alternative view: emphasising local material circumstances, seeing social movements as attempts to control those circumstances and viewing nationalism with much less suspicion than the conservatives. This had more potential for understanding the decolonisation forces in Vietnam than an exclusive focus on the ideological split sundering the globe, in which Vietnam was merely a coded form of great-power tensions. Yet the theme was scarcely developed and, in the 1950s, Labor was too preoccupied or indifferent to give it much attention. Jim Cairns eventually reinvented this theme in the mid-1960s, but in the meantime, Labor lost ground and lost foreign policy debates.

Others developed their analysis of social change in Asia without being dragged into the vortex of Cold War alignments. At Melbourne University and on ABC radio, William Macmahon Ball wrote and spoke about the importance of nationalism for understanding Asian politics. For Ball, Asian revolutions were the result of three independent forces: the struggle for national independence, the social revolution against poverty and misery, and finally 'a revolt of the East against the West, a determination that the destinies of Asia shall be decided by Asians, not by Europeans . . .' With some acuity, he observed that it was easy to see each of these in Indochina, but exceptionally difficult to disentangle them. A liberal iconoclast who rejected the Cold War's polar opposites, Ball developed a coherent view of Asian nationalism, but without discernible effect on the ALP.[19]

A roughly similar view had been represented in the Department of External Affairs when John Burton was secretary from March 1947 until his departure in May 1950. Burton later drew on writers such as Paul Baran and Aneurin Bevan to argue that communism was attractive in Asia precisely because it was revolutionary. It provided, in effect, a power technology capable of drastically reshaping social and economic conditions. 'Communism . . . is better suited to the immediate and urgent needs of underdeveloped countries than is Capitalism.' In addition, 'Its spread will be all the more rapid if the existing systems of colonialism are maintained'. Consequently, exaggerated fears of communism's expansion in the West were misplaced; as ideology it could not have the same appeal in developed societies 'which have reached a high stage of economic justice'. Fundamentally, Burton appeared to agree with Bevan's argument that the solution to social upheaval was always 'social amelioration, not bombing planes and guns', but although he had a sense that fear and rearmament were diverting resources from social amelioration in both the developed and underdeveloped worlds, Burton had few specific policy alternatives to offer.[20]

Burton's replacement, Alan Watt, was more firmly in the developing Cold War tradition. Spender later presented a dispassionate synopsis of the arguments Burton put to him in 1950 against establishing a security pact with the United States. Burton had argued that an alliance devoted to containment would be seen in Asia as an alignment against social change and would restrict Australia's policy independence. But the conservatives, and especially the minister, were bent on the alliance: 'In short, I did not find myself very responsive to Burton's views. Those of Watt . . . were much closer to my own.'

With Spender's policy statement of March 1950, and Watt's appointment as secretary in the following June, a path was being set for the conservatives' foreign policy in the 1950s and into the Vietnam era. The basic features of that policy—a Cold War division of the globe, a profound mistrust of Asian nationalism and a reliance on regional defence pacts over United Nations negotiation—were all established. As Watt himself put it, Spender's statement was 'an expression of the policy which the Government was to pursue for many years to come'. To an extent, this only emerged with hindsight, as Spender and External Affairs were overshadowed in 1950 and 1951 by the Department of Defence and Menzies, with the latter skewing foreign policy towards defence of Commonwealth interests and disparaging Spender's concern with Asia. But by 1953, this phase was over, and the focus of the rest of the decade was on Southeast Asian upheavals and the protective role of America.[21] While it would be overstating the case to say that nothing changed in conservative views from 1950, subsequent debates in the next two decades were profoundly repetitive. The more dramatic shifts occurred on the Labor side of politics, and in the left beyond the Labor party.

The Cold War

Spender found a vindication of his views in the outbreak of the Korean War on June 25, 1950. Cabinet, however, when it met in July to discuss Korea, disagreed with his proposal to send troops under the United States' unified command. Spender believed a commitment would help move American opinion towards establishing the ANZUS alliance, which he had made the centre of his foreign policy; in this, he had the support of his departmental head. The public statement a month later, when Australia committed ground troops, was made at Spender's initiative—and in Menzies' absence overseas—as a result of information that the British government was on the point of making a similar announcement.[22] This was a good illustration of an emerging pattern of using troop commitments as a link in building the American alliance; the Australian government a decade later remained preoccupied with enhancing the alliance, in part because it was always uncertain of the strength of American commitment to the region.[23]

But the Korean commitment also revealed some of the dilemmas in the ALP. Labor supported the government's action, but soon *News-Weekly* was urging that the fight be taken further north into China, while the ALP mainstream was concerned to see the war limited. There was little parliamentary debate; with little difference between the parties, 'the Opposition did not want to encourage any misgivings in its ranks'. Nevertheless, the combination of the peace movement's campaign against intervention in Korea and such debate as did occur within the ALP 'had some effect in the branches and unions . . . and contributed to the rising spirit of mistrust between extremes of right and left'.

Compounding this tension was the more profound conflict in the labour movement over the Menzies government's attempts to ban the Communist Party. The Communist Party Dissolution Bill had been introduced into parliament in April, justified by the government with the claim that the CPA represented a 'fifth column' in Australia at a time of international tension approaching open warfare. Opinion polls indicated that banning the Communist Party had substantial support. The beginning of the Korean conflict two months later 'seemed to offer strong support for government arguments about the threat of communist expansion, and attitudes in the community began to harden'.

Now the prospect of a world war emerging from the Korean conflict combined with controversy within the labour movement on the attitude to take to the Bill, exacerbating the growing split between the Catholic right and the rest of the ALP. The divisions between the right-controlled Victorian executive and the federal executive opened up through 1951. On February 16, the Victorian executive censured Evatt for taking the brief of the Waterside Workers' Federation in the High Court challenge to the legislation; in September, there was public conflict between the federal and Victorian executives over reports of Keon's lack of enthusiasm for the referendum campaign; and in November the federal executive proscribed the Movement's newspaper, *News-Weekly*, in an attempt to deny the paper access to branch meetings.[24] These divisions were straws in the wind of the split of February–March 1955.

The conservatives' anticommunism, both as a domestic assault on the left and as a principle of foreign policy, was a wedge driven into the labour movement. Menzies had established the terms of a discourse which could be successfully mobilised against the ALP and the left beyond it. Evatt could claim—not without basis—that ALP governments of the 1940s had been ready to take repressive action against the CPA, and Calwell could claim that the conservatives' crusade was an extravagant diversion from social and economic issues. But with the growth of the Catholic right within the ALP since the Second World War, anticommunism became a raw nerve upon which Menzies could press at will. Each episode of pressure further discomfited the party, exacerbated the dissatisfaction of the right, and increased the unease of the left. If this was a case of poisoning one's opponents with their own malice, it also impoverished debate on Southeast Asia through the 1950s and into the Vietnam era.

However successful it was as political strategy, Cold War discourse was highly problematic. It functioned as a closed circle: all its questions were leading ones, all its conclusions foregone. Its pattern of loaded language, impugned motives and fear had the effect of foreclosing debate and the democratic questioning of policy. But if Cold War discourse was a clouding of reason, it also became its own constraint. It was not difficult to establish a public climate of fear, but having done so made it more difficult to introduce subtlety and complication. The Cold War produced a climate which limited rational policy-making, particularly by stifling informed views on Asia. As Bevan put it, 'fear is a very bad adviser'.[25]

Despite the attempts to ban the CPA, and despite the climate of innuendo and alarm, the Cold War in Australia was a more pallid version of that in America. Here there was no equivalent of the House Committee on Un-American Activities (HUAC), with its interrogations of those suspected of disloyalty. Nor was there any real parallel to 'un-American activities', a concept redolent of a more zealous patriotism than is found in the phlegmatic Australian political culture. For depth of recklessness and paranoia, there was no equivalent to McCarthy, who not only found conspiracy in the Democratic Party and the State Department but in 1954 precipitated his own downfall by accusing General George Marshall, the patriarch of the American military, of being the instrument of a Soviet conspiracy. Some Australian leftists had their livelihoods constrained or ruined, but there were not the systematic blacklists of artists, officials and 'subversive' organisations that there were in America. Although Australian communists buried their books in 1950 and 1951 and feared internment, the American Cold War went further in imprisoning Party leaders, establishing detention camps and depriving communists of liberal rights. In Australia, the Cold War domestic assault was counterbalanced by the fact that the left had real, rather than imagined, substance. Unlike the insignificant American Party, the CPA began the 1950s with appreciable political, industrial and cultural power, and the left had more substantial, if still fragmented, influence in the ALP than in the Democratic Party. Finally, there was no equal in Australia—other than the brief episode of the Petrov Commission—to the show trials of the HUAC hearings, with their public rites of denunciation and repentance.

Despite these differences of degree, the Cold War in Australia drew strict perimeters between loyalty and political deviance and, as Arthur Miller observed of America, helped to establish alienation and dissent as illicit sentiments. In drawing his parallel between the Cold War and the Salem witchcraft trials—the parallel at the core of *The Crucible*—Miller argued that, in both cases, public rites of contrition were based on 'the guilt . . . of holding illicit, suppressed feelings of alienation and hostility toward standard, daylight society as defined by its most orthodox proponents'.[26]

Australian leftists and critics found it less difficult to reject the blandishments of patriotism, but the culture of the Cold War in Australia similarly marginalised expressions of alienation from the dominant political and cultural orthodoxy. The cultural accent of the 1950s was the suppression of alienation—the marginalisation of dissent—while that of the late 1960s would be its celebration. Casey's sentiment that communists were outsiders was, in a different sense, shared by many on the left, who carried into the 1960s a self-image of dissent as the feeble voice of reason raised against crushing orthodoxy. This would have a substantial effect on the early movement in opposition to the Vietnam intervention.

Even for the conservatives, the Cold War produced a climate which limited their own rationality. Although prone to the comfortable partisanship of Cold War rhetoric, Casey felt the conservatives' self-imposed constraints. Having locked themselves into simplistic public views on Asia, the conservatives compounded the problem with indifference. Throughout the 1950s, Casey had difficulty with Cabinet's reluctance to fund Colombo Plan aid, finding its 'prejudice against the Colombo Plan . . . baffling and persistent'. This indifference extended to political understandings of Asia:

> Casey's colleagues did not really care if he waffled on about Asia, but they did react if he tried to confuse their plain thinking about communist states in Asia, and especially if he tried to complicate their thinking about China.

Having established a simplistic Cold War discourse, Cabinet was impatient with details, and was in any case constrained by a public opinion it had helped create. One persistent example was on the recognition of China, which both Casey and his department supported, but which a combination of domestic and American opposition made impossible.[27]

Despite being identified in 1950 as 'the great present danger point' in Southeast Asia, Indochina was rarely discussed in the years immediately before 1954. Japanese rearmament and Indonesian independence were more immediate concerns. Parliament did not debate Indochina: it was only mentioned once or twice per session between September 1950 and February 1954. But this was part of a wider pattern of little debate on foreign affairs. By August 1954, Labor politicians of both left and right were complaining that the government did not debate its foreign policies and did not believe in telling the public of its specific policy views. Ministerial statements were rare and debate was short.[28] Casey seemed little inclined to act on his own comments about the difficulty of finding 'a realistic discussion . . . about affairs in the East . . .'

Nevertheless, Casey's tenure saw an increased emphasis on Southeast Asia. Upon his appointment as minister, he had proposed an extended overseas tour; he felt most at ease with leaders he had met face to face. Watt was a little alarmed that Casey expected such a tour to concentrate on the Middle East, and convinced him to focus on Southeast Asia. Watt later wrote of the visit as 'a kind of water-shed in the attitude of the Australian Government towards Asia, especially Southeast Asia'. One tangible result was the expansion of diplomatic representation in the area, previously heavily dependent on British sources and advice. A legation was established in Saigon from March 1952—responsible for Vietnam, Cambodia and Laos—and upgraded to an embassy in 1959. In 1954, Watt relinquished the position of secretary in External Affairs to Arthur Tange, who would hold it until 1965. Watt took up a new post as commissioner for Southeast Asia, based in Singapore and with the task of 'viewing the area as a whole'.[29] Although these appointments meant that diplomatic interpretation of events in the region was more readily available, what insights this provided would be infrequently shared in public discussion.

The combination of a fractured ALP, a vigorous anticommunist crusade and simplistic government positions also contributed to a marked isolation of the Communist Party, and hence of the peace movement which was closely associated with it. The Cold War offensive had seen a decline of the CPA's membership and union strength from the high point at the end of the war. In 1944–45, the CPA had some 23 000 members and the allegiance of between 25 per cent and 40 per cent of the union movement; by 1952, membership was down to 6000, and in the unions the Party had experienced a 'rapid decline', particularly since the serious Industrial Group offensive which, between 1950 and 1953, reduced the CPA's union strength by half. The climate of the postwar years was clearly inhospitable, but to some extent the Party contributed to its own decline, with aggressive industrial policies, a bitter antagonism towards the ALP, and 'the bigotry of communist pronouncements concerning the Cold War . . .'[30]

The marginalisation of peace movement activity was of a piece with the Party's other deficiencies in the 1950s. The CPA was reluctant to develop policies sensitive to local conditions, relying on an internationalism which was largely subservient to Soviet interpretations of events. Consequently, although the CPA was strongly active in the peace movement, the latter remained marginal and ineffective. Both the major parties in the early 1950s dismissed the peace movement as nothing more than a communist front, further ensuring its marginalisation. In turn, the dependence of peace organisations on the CPA undermined both their public legitimacy and their ability to advocate views which did not simply mimic Soviet foreign policy.

The CPA's involvement in the peace movement can be seen as a series of concentric circles with the Party leadership at the centre. The CPA had adopted, at its 1948 congress, a policy of working through mass fronts as a means of popular mobilisation, though only the peace fronts had any limited success. Soviet vulnerability at the beginning of the Cold War meant that a major international effort was required 'to delay the threatening new war by impeding US utilisation of its military superiority'. As a direct result, communist parties established the World Peace Council, and an affiliate—the Australian Peace Council (APC)— was set up in July 1949.

But the CPA's role in the peace movement involved a series of contradictions. The problem with front activity was always one of control over those who were not Party members. On the one hand, the peace movement was a means of reaching broader masses of people without requiring membership or ideological commitment, but on the other, the Party attempted to maintain control over the pronouncements of such groups. In this, it was largely successful: until the early 1960s, a feature of CPA activity in the peace movement was its 'refusal to be party to any statement which explicitly or by implication criticised the policies of the Soviet Union, China or [any] other communist country', and its ability to have peace groups accept this view. For example, the APC remained silent on the Soviet invasion of Hungary in 1956, which the CPA vigorously defended, even against some of its own members.[31]

The clearest illustration of the CPA overshadowing the peace movement lay in the extent to which peace groups accepted the communists' own polarised vision of the Cold War. Here, the CPA mirrored conservative views, adopting the rhetoric of Andrei Zhdanov's statement in 1947 that the world was divided into two camps: the imperialist camp, led by the United States and bent on war, world domination and the destruction of democracy, and the anti-imperialist bloc led by the USSR, with the objective of undermining imperialism and strengthening democracy.[32] The significance of this rigid approach was that both sides to the Cold War contributed to its polarisation—as though two poles had established a magnetic field which rendered the middle ground virtually uninhabitable.

Nevertheless, as early as 1953, the Soviet Union was also arguing for peaceful coexistence between the communist and capitalist world systems, tempering Zhdanov's belligerence with the espousal of peace initiatives. One Australian communist who attempted to reconcile these two principles was Jack Blake, who argued in 1956 that peaceful coexistence and open economic competition would demonstrate the superiority of the Soviet system. Communists were convinced that open competition would expose to the Australian working class the flaws of capitalism and the need for a far-reaching social transformation. 'After all, when you find that ropes bound around the legs of an athlete prevent him from ever getting going in a race, the sensible thing to do is to remove the ropes from his legs so that he can begin to run properly.'[33] Sustained by hopes and illusions of the superiority of socialist production and society, CPA activists engaged in peace work in the belief that while they contributed to the defence of the Soviet Union and held off the threat of nuclear war, peaceful competition would demonstrate the necessity of socialism.

But a second concentric circle put some distance between the CPA and the peace movement. The industrial mainstream of the Party was less than fully convinced of the importance of peace fronts. Blake had been defeated in the early 1950s in a struggle which partly hinged on his argument that 'peace work' was as important as class struggle, a view condemned as unorthodox. Bill Gollan, the CPA's main activist in the Sydney peace movement from the early 1950s, reported regularly to central committee meetings, but found that peace activity was often regarded as secondary to industrial struggles. Many of the CPA's leaders found it difficult to regard 'peace work' as central to their politics, partly reflecting a continuing syndicalist streak in the CPA.

Peace activity was frequently the sphere of Party intellectuals who were incipient internal dissidents, somewhat disaffected with the dogmatism of the Party. Activists such as Ian Turner and Stephen Murray-Smith—both of whom would leave the Party after the invasion of Hungary—became prominent in the APC. Turner was its first organising secretary from 1949, and Murray-

Smith held the same position during the mid-1950s. One ironic
result was that '. . . the APC therefore remained the preserve
of a few party intellectuals and was not controlled by the party
as much as the party would have liked'.[34]

However, by no means all of the Party's peace activists were
intellectual dissidents. Gollan remained on the central committee,
although Blake was forced off it in 1954. In addition, the ties
of loyalty as much as of discipline ensured that the CPA held
its substantial control over its own activists. Turner's position at
a peace congress immediately after the outbreak of the Korean
War was a good example.

> My instinct was that the correct position for the peace movement
> to take was: 'It doesn't matter who started the war, the point is to
> stop it'. The party, in the person of Ted Hill, insisted that we
> condemn the imperialist (US-sponsored South Korean) aggressors.
> I was the lead speaker at the Town Hall. The majority of the Peace
> Council executive wanted us to take a neutral position, but I did
> what I had to do . . .

At the next meeting of the APC executive, it was clear that the
'peace parsons' were 'unhappy about what I had done, but they
stayed with us'.[35]

This last point illustrates the third circle outside the Party,
namely, the role of Christian and pacifist members in the peace
movement. The most prominent were the three Melbourne 'peace
parsons'—the Reverends Victor James, Alf Dickie and Frank
Hartley—who were members of the executive of the APC from
its inception. Regularly excoriated as 'fellow-travellers' by parliament and press, such church activists nevertheless brought into
the movement a relatively independent, if still marginal, constituency.[36] For the first half of the 1950s, the effect of the Cold
War culture's marginalisation of critique tended to increase the
alienation of dissenters, driving many of this constituency further
towards the bad faith of fellow-travelling. Thus many non-communist peace activists were drawn inevitably into the magnetic
field between the two camps and, implicitly or explicitly, endorsed
or mutely accepted the CPA's view that support for Soviet foreign
policy was the path to peace.

One fragile attempt to break from this embrace was the Peace
Quest Forum (PQF), launched in Melbourne in March 1951.
The PQF committee made much of its being constituted only
of clergymen, including the 'peace parsons'. The Forum conducted lunchtime public meetings with invited speakers, diligently
dissociating themselves from 'any other organisation . . .' It
stated its sole purpose as 'providing an opportunity for conflicting
views upon the policies that make for war or peace' to be heard

NOT FALLING FOR IT

Conservatives found it easy to dismiss the peace movement of the early 1950s as a front for international communism, with Stalin pulling the strings from the background. The Australian Peace Council had been created by the CPA and the climate of the Cold War gave non-communist activists the poor choice of either shunning the movement or living with the bad faith of fellow-travelling. (Frith, Sydney Morning Herald, 21 October 1949)

and assessed. Questions from the audience would not be controlled. The Forum was significant as an attempt to establish a public space for rational debate, a neutral middle ground which, for example, attributed responsibility for world tensions to both East and West. But such even-handedness only brought condemnation from both sides, and it was a symptom of the closed discourse of the Cold War that the PQF satisfied neither communists nor anticommunists.[37]

Such fine distinctions as the Forum was attempting to make were lost on both the major parties, which regularly condemned peace movement organisations as CPA fronts. Most significant was the hostility of the ALP towards the CPA, a hostility often returned with vigour. The ALP banned its members from involvement with individual peace groups or conferences, which isolated the peace movement—and the CPA beyond it—from substantial contact with ALP branches and unions. Thus, in May 1950, the APC was declared by Labor's federal executive to be a 'subsidiary of the Communist Party' and was officially proscribed by the federal conference in March of the following year. Similarly, in August 1953, the NSW executive directed ALP members to 'refrain from any association' with the Australian Convention on Peace and War, organised largely by the PQF.[38] The net effect of this hostility was that the peace movement was denied formal access to large numbers of ALP members and unionists.

This political configuration of the Cold War was far from conducive to reasoned debate on issues of Southeast Asian decolonisation and the role of nationalist and communist movements. Australian debates remained profoundly ignorant of Southeast Asian history and politics, and the heavy overlay of the domestic Cold War meant that public discourse on Asia was preoccupied with threats, fears and protestations of loyalty. The Australian political culture was poorly equipped to deal with the complex history of Vietnam, especially with the ways in which patriotism, nationalism, revolution and paths to modernity had been intermingled.

Instead, the conservative ruling parties had articulated a clear, pugnacious and dogmatic position, which simplified world politics and was of no small domestic political advantage. Labor was divided and uncertain, suspended before its impending split, its right moving to the positions of the conservatives, its left uneasy at the forces to both its left and right. The Communist Party was locked into polarised and dogmatic positions, unable to break out of the political and cultural isolation forced upon it by the Cold War offensive. The peace movement—marginalised, condemned and largely ineffective—was too beholden to CPA patronage to break out of its own isolation and develop a genuinely mass movement and more flexible ideas. Images of Asia were compounded by these domestic conflicts and dynamics. These were severe constraints in which to enter a debate on the significance of Dien Bien Phu and the collapse of French colonialism in Indochina.

4
1954: To the brink

United action

The first half of 1954 was experienced in Australia as a crisis. In April and early May, it became plain that Dien Bien Phu was about to fall and that the French cause was collapsing. At the end of April, the Geneva conference on Korea and Indochina opened with loud noises offstage from the American secretary of state, John Foster Dulles, threatening military intervention in Vietnam—'united action'. The international tensions of the Cold War had reached a crisis point, and Casey pondered whether they might lead to world war if not restrained.

The domestic tensions which were the obverse face of the Cold War were also reaching a crisis. In mid-April, Menzies had announced Petrov's defection, and the resulting Royal Commission on Espionage opened—in a hall more often used for Gilbert and Sullivan—on 17 May. This whirl of external and internal crises reinforced Menzies' paternal message that resolutely anti-communist government was required. One indication of the prevailing climate came in *News-Weekly*'s last issue before the election. Still putatively inside the labour movement, the paper was exhausting its reserves of self-restraint, and profiled General Giap in vitriolic terms, as 'a rabid, fanatical man . . . befouled with the vile doctrines of Marx'. In a message of some import on the eve of an election campaign, it concluded: 'Unless Australia wakes up, he may come here one day, with the same mission he carried out at Dien Bien Phu.'[1] Twelve days after the Petrov show had opened, and three weeks after the French surrendered at Dien Bien Phu, the conservatives were returned at the elections, comfortably enough, though with a reduced majority. The electoral advantages of crisis appeared to have been demonstrated again, but how much substance was there behind the public alarm? Was Dulles bluffing? There appeared a real prospect of Western military intervention in Vietnam in 1954, but the story was more complex and contradictory.

Dulles's speech to the Overseas Press Club in Washington on 29 March signalled the American attitude to the approaching Geneva conference. If the communists were to win in Indochina, Dulles argued, 'they would surely resume the same pattern of aggression against other free peoples . . .' in a region of great strategic importance for its resources and its sea lanes. America would see the 'imposition' in Southeast Asia of 'the political system of Communist Russia and its Chinese ally by whatever means' as 'a grave threat'. Striking an ominous note, he stated that 'the United States feels that that possibility should not be passively accepted but should be met by united action'.

A few days later, the implications were spelt out by the American journalist James Reston, who—although he would not say so—was known by the Australian embassy to have been briefed by Dulles. Reston reported that 'united action' was 'more ambitious than anything [Dulles] disclosed in his speech'. The objectives were to 'prepare the American people for greater sacrifices' in the war, to persuade the French not to make 'a deceptive peace with the Communists', and to 'warn the Communists that the United States will fight if necessary to keep South East Asia out of their hands'. Dulles frequently argued that 'containment' was too modest a policy, and should be replaced by more aggressive policies of the 'liberation' of communist societies. Eisenhower had come to power in the previous year, campaigning against the Democrats' 'cowardly' policies of containment, with Dulles in the van. Now, Reston described Dulles's view of Vietnam as 'a war of liberation'.[2]

Sir Winston Churchill had once characterised the secretary of state as 'a bull . . . who carries his china closet with him'. With his flair for the language of escalation and an evangelical repugnance for all things Marxist, Dulles was a formidable Cold Warrior. His apparent intention to commit troops to battle alarmed liberals in Australia. *The Age* found the proposal of 'united action' a 'rash intervention without full consideration of military and political realities'. The paper supported the more conciliatory position being taken by the British foreign secretary, Anthony Eden—and Casey—in Geneva. As Macmahon Ball commented in one of his regular talks on ABC radio, Dulles's statements seemed to frighten everybody except the Chinese, at whom they were ultimately directed; 'they certainly frightened many of America's friends and allies'.[3]

An incident in early April had demonstrated both this alarm and the ways in which Casey and the government chose to be less than candid about the complexities of events in Vietnam. Bishop Burgmann of Canberra and three ANU professors (C.P. Fitzgerald, Manning Clark and J.W. Davidson) had published a letter which pointed out the strong element of nationalist aspiration in the Viet Minh and expressed alarm at Dulles's enthusiasm for Western intervention. It was a moderate enough position, but it was an indication of the times that it should be roundly condemned in parliament. The veteran conservative William Wentworth claimed that they were presenting 'facts' which were 'so untrue that they help the Communist line'—a sentiment with which *News-Weekly* agreed. Under a headline proclaiming 'Calwell stands by friends of Indo-China Reds', the paper insisted that 'The Communist movement throughout Southeast Asia is not nationalist, but an extra-national force exploiting national sentiment.'[4]

Calwell had defended Burgmann and the professors against 'McCarthyism', while Whitlam was more direct, arguing that:

> . . . it is a fact that the Communists have been manoeuvred into the vanguard of all these movements in South East Asia, but that is largely our fault in allowing the only feasible alternative to appear to be the form of European tutelage and American protection which the new Secretary of State . . . constantly advocates.

It was not surprising that Casey singled out Whitlam in his parliamentary response, arguing that the original letter 'would lead uninformed people to the view' that the Viet Minh was nationalist and not communist—which was 'wholly and absolutely untrue'. This muddied the waters by drawing a starker distinction between nationalist and communist strains than history allowed, and Casey was simultaneously committing to his diary his exploratory thoughts on the complexity of that relationship.[5]

The controversy had touched on the core confusion of anticommunist policy on Vietnam: its failure to recognise that the French were fighting both against a communist movement and for the preservation of the colonial order, while the Viet

Minh were fighting both for social revolution and decolonisation. Colonial history had made the two inseparable, yet conservative doctrine promised national independence whilst condemning the movement which was wrenching it from the reluctant French. It was a conundrum which the conservatives—with their mistrust of Asian nationalism and their public commitment to anti-communism—chose to ignore, and with which some parts of the ALP struggled. For the CPA, there was no question. 'The vast army of patriots fighting for independence in Indo-China' were naturally led by communists: 'Communists everywhere are the staunchest defenders of their countries' independence and freedom, that is why they are the main leaders of the wars of national independence of the colonial peoples.'[6] As befitted a Cold War climate, it was a heroic simplification.

Dulles's own heroic resolution on Indochina was new-found and rather brittle. For several years, Spender had been telling Casey that there was no discernible policy in the State Department on what they both liked to call 'the Far East'. In a long cable a few days before Dulles's speech, Spender described a detailed and frank discussion with the secretary of state, with whom he got on well. Dulles was seriously worried, but 'more concerned with holding Indo-China than with seeking a settlement', since any conceivable settlement at Geneva involved the unacceptable 'loss'—immediately or eventually—of that region. 'It was, he thought, tremendously important that we should play for time.' The monsoons would soon intervene, at least delaying the French collapse. Dulles saw Vietnam as crucial to 'the total strategic balance in the world', yet was casting about for solutions. 'He was unable to see any such solution himself at the moment but if there were such a way open, he would be grateful to know it.'

Although he briefly sketched his imminent speech, Dulles did not mention the prospect of 'united action'. He may have been sounding Spender out, but the sense of a lack of clear policy was consistent with Spender's earlier impressions. Only a few days later, Dulles emerged at his most bellicose, but it was not clear whether this was bluster—intended to stall or sabotage the Geneva talks—or a genuine threat. Behind the scenes, the Eisenhower administration was divided; the use of nuclear weapons, of ground troops and of air and naval intervention were each considered, but the moderates were prevailing.[7]

A few weeks after reporting on his inconclusive discussion with Dulles, Spender wrote to Canberra in terms suggesting that 'united action' had the character more of a negotiating tactic than a strategy for military intervention. By this stage, it was clear the Geneva conference would open before Dulles could arrange the broad support and participation required by Congress and Eisenhower for intervention. The British were very unwilling and did not want to undermine the conference, the French were prideful and did not want intervention in their own affair, which they were desperate to resolve for domestic political reasons. Now Spender reported on Dulles's view that 'agreement upon united action in Indo-China, had it been capable of being reached before Geneva, would strengthen our negotiating position there as well as giving encouragement to French and Vietnamese'. This was quite different from mounting 'united action' to take up where the French were leaving off, suggesting that bellicosity was serving the purposes of diplomatic leverage.[8]

In Canberra, Dulles was taken very seriously. Tange, who had only recently replaced Watt as secretary of External Affairs, noted that while American policy had hardened to the point where they contemplated intervention 'even if the Chinese did not intervene', the French government was increasingly desperate to negotiate an early end to the war. To some extent, the Americans could go no further than the French were prepared to support, and yet the Americans were also acutely conscious of not appearing to be propping up a colonial regime. Tange advised caution: 'Australia would be unwise to agree now, even in principle, to the use of Australian Forces' in 'united action'. He proposed instead 'concerted diplomatic action' to encourage the French to hold on and to divert attention to military talks on regional collective security. In his amendments to Tange's draft, Casey accepted all this, but also called on the weather to buy time: 'Additional forces, from whatever source, could not be put into the field . . . before the monsoon starts . . .'[9] Tange's circumspection was being reinforced by Casey's, which in turn resonated with Britain's flat refusal to be involved in threats of military intervention.

Meanwhile, Spender appeared to favour intervention and was intent on supporting Dulles, while Watt—from Singapore—also urged a positive response to American resolve. On 6 April, Spender wrote to Casey, with a note of reproach: 'We cannot safely rely upon playing for time until the monsoon season comes . . .' The immediate problem was the imminent French collapse, and 'united action of some description is necessary' to prevent three evils: a communist victory, a psychological blow for other countries in the area, and 'the possible effects on United States willingness to aid us when perhaps we are more directly threatened'. After all, Spender insisted, our policy—the policy he had initiated—had been 'to achieve the acceptance by the United States of responsibility in South East Asia'. It would be too much, he implied, not to reciprocate when the Americans had at last obliged.[10]

But Casey was more circumspect, casting about for reasons to delay. He told the parliament that the fall of Indochina would threaten all of Southeast Asia, but his diary notes and diplomatic cables—which were frequently the same text—were full of caution. 'It seems to me an exaggeration,' he wrote, 'for Dulles to say that the Communist Chinese are "mighty close" to open aggression . . .' If so, 'stern warnings' to them were 'highly provocative'. 'I believe that getting into direct holts with Communist China is the most vitally important thing to avoid. Heaven knows where this would lead us, or what would be the end of it.'[11] Casey was pulling back from the brink of what he thought could be global and possibly nuclear war resulting from an intervention in Vietnam.

This accorded with the advice coming to the department of Defence from its military intelligence in Washington: there were no reports of Chinese troop movements on the Vietnamese border, and they estimated 'no direct [Chinese] Communist intervention likely unless western powers initiate united action . . .', in which case Chinese intervention was 'probable'. It was also consistent with the British view. Casey's friend Anthony Eden, sent him a personal cable saying that an American intervention 'in our view would involve the risk of war with China and possibly with the Soviet Union . . .'[12] The British were reluctant to become a nuclear target to pay for Dulles's malevolence towards communists, and had the heightened sensitivities of being what Orwell had brutally dubbed America's 'Airstrip One'. In addition, they felt no great distress at seeing the French humiliated in Indochina.

Tribune claimed in early May to have a special cable from Geneva—presumably from journalist Wilfred Burchett who was there and sending reports—showing that Casey had offered 'initially two and later six Australian battalions . . .' for 'united action'; Casey was simply the 'errand boy for John Foster Dulles . . .'[13] This was either misinformed or mischievous; it could have been part of a campaign to undermine through propaganda the frightening prospect of Dulles's policy. Casey in fact was being forced by the crisis towards a clearer definition of the Vietnam problem, and this put him at some distance from both Dulles's interpretations and from the artless formulations of foreign policy debate in Australia.

'The first thing to get straight in our minds,' Casey wrote in his diary, 'is . . . where does the menace come from in Indo-China. *My* answer is—the Viet Minh, not Communist China.' At various points, Casey observed that the Vietnamese justifiably felt little enthusiasm for the fictional independence granted by the French, that the Viet Minh would win a 'sweeping political victory' in any elections held in Vietnam, and that there could be no military, but only a political solution in Vietnam. The French and the Chinese were both unpopular in Vietnam, American aid to the former was 'very much greater' than Chinese aid to the Viet Minh, and finally, China should be recognised and take its place at the UN.[14]

Any of these views placed Casey in disagreement with Dulles, but were not conveyed to the Americans as reasons for delaying 'united action'. Instead, the approaching elections in Australia were used as a plausible pretext for inaction, and once they were over (in late May), the moment had passed; the reluctance of both the British and Congress had made it clear that Dulles's adventure was unviable. In effect, the conservatives had had two policies on 'united action': Spender's enthusiasm for standing with the Americans, reinforcing their new-found responsibility in the region, and Casey's concern to avoid the consequences of Dulles's belligerence. Both views had advocates in Cabinet, and in truth they were two facets of the same attitude.

On 6 April, Cabinet met and discussed the developing crisis. This was only a week after Dulles's first statement proposing 'united action'. Some Cabinet members thought that 'the loss of Indo-China to the free world' must lead to further losses in the region, but that 'public discussion of [Dulles's] proposal should be deferred until after the election'. The heretical view was put that it was undesirable to get involved in what was basically an anticolonial struggle, and that statements about military intervention were 'not soundly based' if there was no real certainty that they could be made good.

Cabinet was clearly not disposed to join 'united action', yet attempted to balance this with the interests of a satellite:

> It was important to Australia not to appear to the United States to be luke-warm in supporting proposals designed to ensure that communism in South East Asia was checked. The Australian government would be well advised to let others raise the difficulties associated with the proposal: there would be plenty to do that.[15]

This was the shrewd strategy which Casey followed. He expounded his doubts to Eden, Spender, Nehru and his Cabinet colleagues, while keeping them from Dulles and the Americans, and waiting for the scepticism of the British, French and Canadians to effectively veto 'united action'. This meant that even when Casey—at an ANZUS meeting held at Geneva— politely suggested to Dulles that it was 'unwise to take military action while Geneva was in progress', the secretary of state left with the impression that Australia would still participate.[16] The misunderstandings were mutual; Australia seemed unaware of the depth of Congressional reticence about 'united action', or that the American chiefs of staff were divided.

But Casey's strategy also meant that there could be no critical public debate of the proposal for intervention, which would have both alienated the Americans and lowered the suitably high temperature of domestic public rhetoric. Instead, that rhetoric gave the impression that war could well be on the way. In late April, Casey was reported as having told Menzies that the government must prepare public opinion 'for the possibility of meeting the gravest decisions which have faced Australia for 12 years'. The *Daily Telegraph* in Sydney headlined the story: 'If America comes in, we cannot be far behind: Australia may join the fight in Indo-China.'[17] By this stage, Dulles's proposal had in fact clearly faltered, and Cabinet had decided against intervention; such statements evidently had an eye more on the approaching election than on the situation in Indochina.

During May, Cabinet did not meet, with ministers concentrating on the election campaign. The attention of Australian diplomats turned to helping patch the rift in the Anglo-American relationship. Spender hoped that Australia could play a role in a rapprochement, though this seemed to take the form of convincing the British of the need for 'united action'. He had not given up all hope of intervention, and now proposed to Casey that there were 'four possible courses of military action'. They could acquiesce in the French defeat, or delay it by the use of naval and air support. Neither of these recommended itself, and he had accepted that a full-scale intervention ran too high a risk of a Chinese response.

Spender's preferred option was now to establish a military stronghold in Vietnam, not as 'a base for eventual reconquest . . . by conventional military means', but as a 'restraining influence against further possible Communist adventures', as an indication of resolve and as a base for retraining the Vietnamese. But by this time, the ambassador was out of step with Australian policy, which was seeking to divert Dulles's considerable Cold War energy into more amorphous military discussions. Casey rather smugly told Nehru that these must produce caution, because 'the very size of the forces that high level staff talks would recommend as necessary would curb American intervention ideas and stop any "blundering into war" '.[18]

These discussions between Australia, New Zealand, France, Britain and the US—the Five Power Military Conference which took place in Washington in June—eventually led to the Manila conference in early September at which the SEATO pact was negotiated and signed. SEATO was proposed as a defence arrangement for the region, to guarantee the settlement at Geneva and act as an equivalent of NATO—hopes which it would disappoint. The British saw talk of a new organisation as inappropriate before the Geneva conference had concluded; but the Americans clearly wanted if not to sabotage, then at least to maintain extreme pressure on, the conference.

Casey was relatively enthusiastic, announcing—the night before the Petrov Royal Commission began—that Australia had agreed to join the military staff talks. During late July, Australia and New Zealand were said to be the strongest advocates for the SEATO proposal, 'since it became clear that the United States might well lose interest . . . if it was long delayed'.[19] As Watt wrote to Spender on the day the Geneva settlement was signed, the conference had been 'extremely frustrating and depressing'. He worried that the settlement would be seen as grounds for 'complacency', and that there were signs of isolationism in the US: 'Now is the time for non-Communist countries to pull up their socks and get busy with the establishment of a SEATO which is effective.'[20] This was of a pattern with the ANZUS negotiations—a renewed sense of Asian threat leading to renewed efforts to secure the alliance with the US. In 1950, Spender had pursued the ANZUS pact against a background of the Chinese revolution and fears of Japanese rearmament; now, in 1954, SEATO was pursued in the context of Vietnam.

On 4 June, Cabinet met for the first time since the election. Casey had prepared a long submission on Indochina and Geneva, in which he summarised the range of his misgivings. He argued strongly against 'internationalising' the war: 'the use of American forces would involve considerable risk of Chinese intervention leading in turn to retaliatory attacks by the United States . . . and the possibility of global and atomic war'. He reported the reluctance of the British to become involved, repeating Eden's statement to him that 'it was up to the French to make the best arrangement and compromise they could', which clearly saw Vietnam more as a process of decolonisation than as an anticommunist crusade.

Casey reported that he had sided with the British against the Americans at Geneva on a number of issues—on giving the conference a chance before discussing regional collective security, and on accepting partition of Vietnam as part of the settlement, something the Americans found unacceptable. Australia could play a role in healing the Anglo-American rift: urging the British to recognise the importance of not giving the United States 'the impression that it is being deserted by its Allies', while 'holding the Americans back from rash adventures'.

Casey's reservations eventually prevailed in Cabinet, though he noted in his diary that there were 'a couple of voices that hold that the U.S.A. is our only standby in this part of the world, and that we should follow them whatever they did . . .' Yet the Cabinet minutes suggest more dispute than simply 'a couple of voices'. Some argued that, as 'little reliance could be placed on the Asian countries in resisting communism . . . it was Australia's duty to support the United States even although [sic] we might think its policy wrong . . .' When it was pointed out that many Vietnamese wanted an end to colonialism, some fell back to the eternal verities of empire—power and submission: 'The local peoples were not supporters of the French because the French were not winning. Let the military situation change and the attitude of the local people would change too.' This revealed a very truculent view of the character of decolonisation struggles.

But caution prevailed, particularly when it was pointed out that the implications of internationalising the conflict included the possibilities of nuclear and world war. Perhaps even more unthinkable, it would be a war from which the Commonwealth was 'standing aloof'. Cabinet decided, with Casey, that 'the United States appeared to be acting incautiously', and the minister was asked to help 'restrain' the Americans and 'stimulate' the British 'to put forward greater efforts' in the region.[21] Fortified with this support, Casey set off again for Geneva.

This was the end of the episode, and indeed 'united action' had been unlikely since some weeks before. But such debate as occurred had revealed some ominous shadows hanging over understandings of Vietnam. The first was the shadow of Korea, and it was frequently assumed that China might invade Vietnam just as it had northern Korea, even though there was little evidence of this likelihood. The second was the dilemma captured in the differences between Spender and Casey. A foreign policy which—through fear of Asia and distrust of its social movements—was designed to elicit American responsibility for the region, also had the effect of restricting the freedom of manoeuvre of Australian policy. As Spender had divined with 'united action', Australia could not encourage American involvement and then make a separate choice whether to join with it. In 1954, Casey had freedom of manoeuvre because the British and French held a restraining hand on American policy, but Australian policy would not usually have, or even seek, such independence.

The third shadow on foreign policy was that of Munich, and the analogy of 'appeasement' which dogged the 1950s. The parliamentary debate on Indochina, Geneva and the proposed SEATO alliance—which began on 5 August—was replete with references to Munich, to events in Europe before 1939, and to 'the greatest crisis that has confronted us since the end of World War II . . .'[22] The debate illustrated the growing disjuncture between the subtle if mendacious strategy Casey had followed on 'united action' and the quality of a public discussion which was being disfigured by domestic Cold War tensions.

Menzies' contribution to the debate was highly rhetorical, meriting Eddie Ward's description of him as a man of eloquent inaction. Menzies set out the terms of the Geneva Accords, with the division of the country pending elections; after the expected communist victory in the July 1956 elections, 'before long we may be forced to regard the Communist frontier as lying on the southern shores of Indo-China . . .' He went on to rework the Cold War into a struggle between 'confessed and clamant materialists' and 'free countries, lifted to noble issues by religious faith'. He dismissed those 'cynics' who spoke of the Cold War as 'an old-fashioned struggle for military or physical power'—as, for example, did Hasluck—introducing a relatively new religious dimension to his discourse which must have gladdened the Groupers within the ALP.

But another new note was a definite commitment to military alliance. Arguing that the West had to negotiate from strength, and that the proposed SEATO Treaty was part of 'a total world organisation for peace and security', Menzies now reasoned that we could not enter mutual arrangements 'unless we are prepared to support them with arms, with men, with ships and instruments of war, with supplies as we, in our turn, would wish them to support us'.[23] As both Evatt and *News-Weekly* were to point out, this committed Australia to supply troops, but when, where, and under what circumstances were left open questions.

It was emblematic of Labor's own crisis that it was one of the Groupers—John Mullens—who had initiated the debate. The night before Menzies was to make a statement on Geneva, Mullens asked him whether he knew of 'the almost complete unawareness in this country' of the position in Indochina, and that 'the frontier of the Red empire is now nearer to Australia, and that 1 000 000 Christians in Indo-China have been delivered into terror and tyranny?'[24] By this stage, Labor encompassed an untenable range of views, which the debate on Vietnam sharpened and irritated.

Calwell referred little to Vietnam itself, propounding instead Labor's classic—if vague—sentiment that 'hungry stomachs are easily attracted to communism, particularly in lands that have known nothing but hunger and famine for centuries'. In one of those images which disclosed how deep went his anticommunism, Calwell deplored 'the red lava flow of communism creeping ever

onward and ever southward'. What was needed was the new
world order which had been promised at the end of the Second
World War, for Asians 'certainly will not fight for the old order
. . . of repression and starvation . . .' This was part of Labor's
received wisdom, though it offered little guidance on foreign
policy.

More substantial were Calwell's comments on Malaya. If
Australian troops were to be dispatched there—as they were a
year later—it should only be 'in defence of the legitimate aims
of Malayan nationalism. They must not go in to fight in defence
of investments from the Western world.' This was a rather fine
distinction, which apparently endorsed a military intervention
against a communist movement. Calwell's anticommunism was
balanced by an instinctive sympathy for nationalism, though the
balance was unstable. As long as nationalism could feasibly be
distinguished from communist movements, as was the case in
Malaya, the balance could be maintained. But, as with government policy, the distinction was less illuminating when a communist movement was the authentic carrier of nationalist sentiments.

Ward, at this time well on the left of the party, attacked the
government for its inadequate support for nationalist self-deter-
mination; instead, it supported 'rotten regimes wherever they
exist'—in Korea, Vietnam and China. Like Calwell, he held
nationalism and communism as separate movements, and separate
moral categories, and blamed conservative policies for denying
support to legitimate nationalism, with the result that 'the Communists took advantage of the situation and moved in to support
those who were fighting for freedom'.[25] Along with others in the
ALP, Ward held the British Attlee government as the very model
of decolonisation, but his ideas on Vietnam itself were noticeably
hazy.

Ward, Calwell, Haylen, Pollard and others in the centre to
left of the party held consistent, if often vague, views. They were
inclined to see communist movements as alien but understandable
responses to social conditions and thwarted nationalism, and they
felt the beginnings of unease that Cold War policies committed
Australia to supporting insupportable regimes. Their policy prescriptions ranged from isolationism to active support for nationalist, non-communist movements, yet they were frequently supportive of the American alliance—claiming SEATO and ANZUS
as their own policies of the 1940s and only querying the extent
to which Australia was an equal partner in the alliance. The
major undertone was one of regret for the passing of that new
order, promised in the 1940s and recalled by Calwell, which was
now entirely submerged by the Cold War.

NEXT COURSE, PLEASE!

In the 1950s, there were many images used to describe the threat of Asian Communism: a Red Tide, a lava flow, clattering dominoes and spreading infection. The Catholic News-Weekly *regarded the 1954 Geneva settlement on Indochina as 'an Asian Munich': appeasement which did nothing to deter aggression. The representation of communism as a snake combined a national imagery of the bush with Catholic resonances of corruption in the Garden of Eden. (*News-Weekly, *21 July 1954)*

The Groupers within the ALP had, by 1954, explicitly rejected this reference point, and spoke with urgency of the new order of the Cold War. Keon—the most forthright and important of this group, a pugnacious and lucid speaker who was often presented by *News-Weekly* as its hope for the future—best expressed this. He argued that the old imperialist order was dead: 'Colonialism, which we have condemned and which is responsible for many of our difficulties in Asia, no longer should trouble our consciences. Our task is to save the people of Asia from the new imperialism . . .' of Soviet communism.

He went on to develop the argument which *News-Weekly* put, that the Geneva accords were an Asian Munich. 'If there is ever another generation of free white Australians—a possibility which I beg leave to doubt—they will live to revile the governments which participated in the Geneva surrender.' The crisis had illustrated the lesson which B.A. Santamaria had been starkly presenting in his paper, that—with the British abandoning their colonial interests east of Suez—only the Americans had a strategic interest in the Asian region. Australian interests lay firmly in close military and political alliance with the US. As Keon put it bluntly: 'The unfortunate fact is that Britain is in Europe and Australia is in Asia.'

But Keon now went further, displaying the headlong pugnacity which had enabled him to defeat the old John Wren machine of the Richmond ALP. He argued that the policy of containment was 'fatal and suicidal', instead urging a 'policy of liberation', which was not spelt out but which Dulles had at times advocated as a policy of taking the Cold War directly to the enemy and encouraging the overthrow of existing communist regimes.[26] In regretting that Dulles's 'united action' had come to nothing, Keon also combined Dulles's heady mix of a genuine religious animosity to Marxism with a flair for the language of escalation.

After the Split

Such parallels between a prominent member of the ALP and the right of the American Republican Party indicated the stresses within the ALP by 1954. It would strain the evidence to see the debate on Geneva as precipitating the Split of the following year, but it nevertheless acted as a focal point, concentrating the differences within the ALP. *News-Weekly*, still nominally within the labour movement, confirmed this when reporting the parliamentary debate.

Labor's true crisis, it argued, was not over leadership but 'whether all elements in the Labor Party regard Communism as being the main present danger to the security of the free world'. Santamaria indicated how close he was to a break with Evatt, who had 'failed to fulfill his responsibilities as Labor leader', was overly preoccupied with the Petrov affair, and was too little aware of the communist threat. Surveying foreign policy, Santamaria put his argument that the writ of British power now stopped at Gibraltar, and only America had an interest in Southeast Asia. But if this was the key policy shift, he now concluded that Casey—not Evatt—was the best foreign minister on offer: 'the Labor alternative is of the type calculated to send shivers down the spines of Australians with a care for the future of this land and the welfare of their children'. The only major doubt about Casey was that he might be too much the Anglophile to break with British interests.[27] This was an enthusiastic endorsement of Liberal foreign policy and a clear indication of what—only a year later—would become DLP support for the conservatives to keep Labor from office.

By the mid-1950s, a series of shifts was fragmenting the pattern of political forces of only a few years before. With these shifts, by 1957, one could see the preconditions for both the commitment to military intervention in Vietnam and the dissent from that decision. Conservative Cold War ideology had solidified, although the conservative parties were still in the early phase of almost a quarter of a century of uninterrupted rule. The only significant change in focus was towards Southeast Asia. The Korean War was over in July 1953, and East Asia receded from view. The focus on Southeast Asia was clearly marked with the commitment of troops to Malaya in April 1955. As one former diplomat wrote: '. . . after the failure of the Menzies mission to Cairo in 1956 we had no further role in the Middle East either. Communist insurgency in Southeast Asia absorbed the Department [of External Affairs] completely'.[28] The path Percy Spender had mapped out in 1950 remained largely unchanged through the 1950s, its only new embellishment being the preparedness to dispatch troops as part of 'forward defence'.

Second, Labor had split in February–March 1955, severing the increasingly fractious right wing, particularly in Victoria. Evatt's 'honeymoon' with the Movement, which had helped bring him the leadership, was over by the middle of 1954, as could be seen in the dispute over the Indochina crisis. By precipitating the Split with his statement in October of that year, Evatt salvaged his leadership by appearing to have saved Labor from an external influence. Simultaneously, Labor could move to the left, no longer required to hold off a split with the Movement. The Hobart conference in March 1955 reflected this move, calling for the recognition of China and opposing—in anticipation—the dispatch of troops to Malaya. Soon there were other indications of a new opening to the left of the ALP. After 1955, the party was less inclined to proscribe peace movement activities. Unlike its predecessors, the Australian Assembly for Peace in August 1956 was not proscribed, and a number of Labor members attended. This new rapprochement was clearest in the active defence by the ALP of the Congress for International Co-operation and Disarmament in November 1959.[29]

The Split, as the CPA recognised at the time, allowed for a rapprochement between the peace movement (and the CPA beyond it), and the mass of affiliated unionists and middle-class citizens aligned with Labor. As Blake wrote in the CPA's journal a year later, the policies adopted by the Hobart conference—on disarmament, nuclear weapons testing, Malaya and the recognition of China—meant that the ALP was 'emerging from the grip

of the Cold War and the Groupers'. This opened 'the way to
mass public peace activity by the members and adherents of the
Labour Party. It opens the way to developing united activity
between Labourites and Communists . . .'[30] These were sanguine
hopes, and much mutual hostility remained to be overcome before
they would come to anything. But the Split began a process in
which the peace movement acted as a bridge between Labor and
the CPA, much as the DLP was a bridge for some Catholics to
leave Labor for the conservatives.

But a third change was that the left itself began to open,
partly through its disintegration. Soviet leader Nikita
Khrushchev's 'secret speech' denouncing Stalin in February 1956
at the 20th Congress of the CPSU, followed by the Soviet
suppression of the Hungarian uprising in October–November of
the same year, created a turmoil of confusion, uncertainty and
dissent in the Party where before there had been monolithic
certainty. One result was that the CPA was too preoccupied to

*The Czech middle-distance champion, Emil Zatopek, being welcomed by
the 'peace parsons' at an Australian Peace Council reception during the
Olympic Games in Melbourne in November 1956. Left to right: Alison
Dickie, Rev. Alf Dickie, Dana Zatopek, an Olympic javelin champion,
Rev. Frank Hartley, Emil Zatopek, Stephen Murray-Smith, Mrs James
and Rev. Victor James. Murray-Smith, the Peace Council's secretary, was
a CPA member poised—with many other intellectuals—to leave the Party
over the Soviet invasion of Hungary only weeks before. (University of
Melbourne Archives, VPC papers)*

maintain the level of control it had previously had over the peace movement. A second was the significant number of intellectuals who left the Party, but who remained active in the left and in the peace movement. Many intellectuals had left by 1958, particularly disenchanted by the refusal of the Party to debate the implications of Khrushchev's speech and the Hungarian uprising. The leftist intelligentsia, people such as Turner and Murray-Smith, remained active in the peace movement but now had the 'ironic pleasure' of being invited by the CPA to participate in united fronts, rather than organising them.[31]

These shifts were a profound rupture of the political alignments at the peak of the Cold War. The icecap of the Cold War began to thaw, and its fragments to drift from their former, apparently immobile, positions. The ALP, no longer appeasing its right wing, could become more open to the left and the peace movement. Simultaneously, the monolithic discourse of the Cold War was losing its hegemonic power, and accusations of association with communists became less trenchant or significant. The most repressive days of the Cold War were over, though it is well to remember that the threat of communism remained a viable election issue for the conservatives through the 1960s.

These changes in turn allowed the peace movement to move closer to the mainstream of political discourse, a process which reduced its dependence on the CPA, and thus meant that the movement became more variegated and flexible and less constrained to toe a Moscow-inspired line. That new flexibility could also mean overcoming marginality, and because the movement was broader, the CPA's dominance declined further. But in 1957, these realignments of political forces were little more than embryonic, awaiting development in the 1960s. Ironically, one of the progeny of the Cold War—the DLP—kept Labor from office and thus kept the ship of foreign policy on Spender's course; another, after the Split, was the new rapprochement between the ALP and the movements to its left, which allowed for the development of movements dissenting from that policy.

II

Preparing
for war

5
Ngo Dinh Diem: 'How to revive a war', 1954–1966

When President Ngo Dinh Diem visited Australia in September 1957, he was feted as democracy's saviour in Asia. A 'striking figure in royal blue silk frock coat, long white trousers and black mandarin hat', Diem was said to be 'incorruptible and intensely patriotic'. He quickly demonstrated a capacity for playing on the limited understanding of Vietnamese history in Australia. He was head of a 'state' which in 1954 had been simply the southern zone of a country awaiting reunification in the 1956 elections—elections which Diem had then refused to proceed with for the excellent reason that the Communist Party was assured of success. By 1957, this precarious position had been transformed into speaking seriously about South Vietnam as a separate nation, sovereign and symbolic.

Clearly the Cold War precedents of apparently permanent partition in Germany and Korea in part explained this transformation, but it also required a remarkably flexible reading of the recent past. The images constructed of Diem during his visit revealed little of Vietnam, but much of political alignments in Australia. At a parliamentary luncheon on the day after his arrival, Menzies led 'enthusiastic cheering' as Diem rose to speak; the

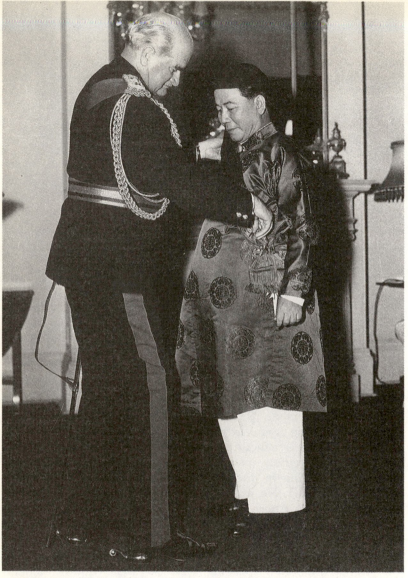

*When the president of South Vietnam, Ngo Dinh Diem, visited Australia in 1957, such 'ceremonial splendour' had not been seen since the Royal Tour of 1954. The incongruities of the visit suggested the way he was being fictionalised by Australian officials: feted as the saviour of democracy in Asia, Diem had only a tenuous and authoritarian hold on power. Most incongruously, he was made a Knight of the Order of St Michael and St George by the governor-general, Sir William Slim. (*Sydney Morning Herald, *10 September 1957)*

visitor's general argument was to draw parallels between Australia and South Vietnam, united in holding at bay international communism—the two countries were 'advanced sentinels on so vast a field'. 'Vietnam,' Diem had said on his arrival, 'is a 2000-year-old nation which has recovered its independence only to become a most threatened frontier of the free world.' Menzies fell willingly into line with this version of the past, citing Diem's 'astonishing part in the struggle of his country for independence and its resistance to Communist aggression'.[1]

These were historical interpretations of some political importance. Diem had played only a small part in the independence struggle, though his credibility as a patriot was solid. He was now made out to represent a non-communist nationalist tradition, a tradition which had once possessed some political force and presence, but was largely extinguished in the 1930s. Meanwhile the communists in Vietnam, who had led the independence struggle against the French, had come to represent an external threat to the existence of a 'nation'—South Vietnam—which itself had only very recently been a dubious concept.

At the same parliamentary reception, Evatt was quoted as saying that 'it was a miracle' that Diem's regime had proven so stable. This was no sudden religious sentiment, but more a case of Evatt's customary bluntness, and a recognition that few had expected Diem's 'state' to last long. However, *News-Weekly* took up the religious resonance, seeing in Diem a triumph of the Christian will: 'Diem just prayed and moved into action—and, one by one, the overwhelming forces against him yielded to his invincible faith and courage.' Diem's austerity, his tenacious religious conviction, and the anticommunism which arose from it all appealed to the Catholic right, which recognised its own. For the Movement, Diem represented moral and spiritual rearmament, the power of spiritual force 'against the Mammons and Molochs of materialism'. By contrast, the CPA testified to its own faith that the mark of true progress was modernisation, deriding the description of Diem as a 'miracle man'; after all, since 1954 in the South 'not a single factory has been set up, and existing factories have not been restarted'.[2]

When Casey reported to Cabinet on the Geneva agreements in July 1954, he had noted that 'the division line [of partition] is only temporary . . . It is quite possible that these elections could lead to a communist-controlled Vietnam'. Although not saying so, Casey appeared ready to accept the 'loss' of all of Vietnam, as long as the line was drawn at that point and enforced by the new SEATO alliance.[3] It was Diem's resolution and intransigence, backed by American support, which had reversed the logic of this history; by 1957, Diem had refused to hold the elections, consolidated his control over the South, broken the armed sects and begun to crush the remnants of the Viet Minh. *News-Weekly*'s image of the triumph of will and faith had some validity. But the image of Diem as a patriotic democrat, who could provide a stable postcolonial alternative to Asian revolution, was to prove eminently misplaced.

The struggle for control in the South

Evaluations of Diem's politics and place in history vary widely, from Robert Shaplen's largely sympathetic portrait of an ardent patriot devoted to the national aspirations of his people, if misunderstanding them, to Wilfred Burchett's caustic portrait of a repressive, corrupt and thoroughly authoritarian dictatorship. In Ellen Hammer's more rounded portrait, Diem emerges as an autocrat whose unwillingness to comply with American aims made him an obstacle to Cold War policy, which was directed less to ensuring South Vietnam's existence as a viable state than to guaranteeing its stability as an indigenous platform for the anticommunist offensive.[4]

There is near-consensus on Diem's mandarin disposition and on his autocratic identification of his own views with the interests of the state. This, combined with an appallingly feeble power base, helps explain the centralisation of power in the hands of Diem's family. Control was exercised through the personal appointment of administrators and through the hold by Diem's brother, the feared Ngo Dinh Nhu, over the secret police, the strategic hamlets program, and the parties and associations the regime established. Diem, while dependent on US support and material aid, displayed a fractious independence of mind which made him impervious to attempts to reform the regime in order to save it. Finally, the regime prosecuted a visceral form of anticommunism, leading to a devastating political repression of the Party's clandestine infrastructure and stimulating the development of the civil war in the South.

But before this, Diem concentrated on the other, more immediate threat to his position from the armed sects. These had risen to considerable power by 1954 with French support in the war against the Viet Minh; they represented an undoubted challenge to the fragile Diem regime. Two of the sects—the Cao Dai and the Hoa Hao—were religious in origin, though by the mid-1950s they were also substantial armed forces; the third sect—the Binh Xuyen—was the mafia of Vietnam, and controlled prostitution, gambling and the police in Saigon. By 1953, it had an armed force of some 8000 and held nine seats in the national congress. Unlike the other two sects, which had both nationalist and religious aspects, the political interests of the Binh Xuyen were clearly more in the spoils than in other fruits of independence.

In February 1953, the French had provided arms and funds to the Binh Xuyen for the task of keeping open the main road running south from Saigon through Baria province. In March 1955, Diem's troops attacked the sect in Saigon and forced them back to the Rung Sat marshes in the west of the province, where they had had their origins as river pirates. The Australian military attache in Saigon reported to Canberra: 'The three Binh Xuyen posts which were located on the Cape St Jacques road were . . . captured by the Vietnamese National Army after a very short action with no casualties.' Some 100 'scattered in the bush east of Baria'. In October, another group of the sect, which was attempting to revive its former trade of piracy in the marshes, was attacked again, and those who survived were captured or dispersed; the sect leader escaped to Paris to enjoy the riches accumulated under the French. With the defeat of the Hoa Hao and Cao Dai at the same time, this was the end of the politico-religious groups.[5]

In Baria, the remnants of the Binh Xuyen, as with the other sects elsewhere, joined the Party's secret armed forces. In 1957 they moved to the sanctuary of the Nui Thi Vai hills—the old Viet Minh base in the west of the province near the marshes— where they were melded into the Party's forces. This was the origin of the D445 battalion, the main provincial force which Australian troops would encounter in the late 1960s. Not surprisingly, local Party histories do not dwell on this connection with former river pirates, although it provides a vivid example of the reorganisation of quasi-nationalist forces under the Party's influence. The pattern was consistent with the Party's cultivation of the sects, with similar success, elsewhere in the South.[6]

Having dispatched the sects, albeit into the revolutionary camp, Diem set about a political repression of the Communist Party and former Viet Minh, in what even anticommunist writers saw as 'a tragically misguided attempt to buttress the regime in the South'.[7] The sects had never been a serious political or ideological—as distinct from military—force. The more fundamental struggle in the South from 1954 was between Diem and the Party's infrastructure, a struggle fundamentally for control of the village.

Thayer, in the most comprehensive history of the period, mapped the ebb and flow of this struggle. From 1954 until mid-1956, the Party in the South was on a 'legal' footing, relying on a defensive political strategy in preparation for the expected elections. In late 1956, it experienced a profound slump in morale. Under the pressure of Diem's refusal, the reunification strategy had failed, the Party in the North was preoccupied with consolidating the revolution there, and the thaw in Cold War relations under Khrushchev had stripped the Party of some of its international support on the reunification issue. Each of these factors made it possible for Diem to seize the initiative in a series of *To Cong* or 'Denounce Communist' campaigns, which intensified from late 1956 and peaked in early 1959. The Party in the South lost large numbers through death, imprisonment or disillusion during this period. Finally, the shift in Communist Party strategy back to an armed struggle in early 1959 regained the initiative, by stepping up its assassination campaigns in particular, and the early 1960s marked a reversal of fortunes with the newly launched NLF in the ascendancy.[8]

In the *To Cong* campaigns, the army, the police and local village authorities held public meetings to identify former Viet Minh cadres and to reassert government control over areas which had been held by the Viet Minh. The indiscriminate nature of some of these campaigns can be seen in Burchett's account, based on interviews in early 1962. Even allowing for the colouration of his own eminently populist sympathies, Burchett's reportage conveys some of the everyday experience of the Diem regime in rural areas.

> People in every town and village were forced to take part in meetings and denounce any who had taken part in the resistance . . . a few agents [were] planted in the crowd . . . Any who tried to deny 'facts' produced by such agents were arrested and often beaten up on the spot . . . During the course of these campaigns, women were forced to divorce husbands who had regrouped to the North; parents to disown their children, children to disown their regroupee parents . . .

In these meetings, the regime attempted to substitute, for what it saw as communist ideology, the official ideology of 'personalism'—a debasement of French left-wing Catholic ideas of the 1930s—emphasising collective discipline, the individual's duties to the state and traditional Christian moral and social values. But it was an attempt with few resonances in villages which were Confucian and Buddhist in their core values, with Catholics comprising only about 10 per cent of the total population.[9]

The first *To Cong* campaign was carried out in Baria in mid-1956. The local Party history recounts how 'experienced officers came down to begin *To Cong* campaigns, setting up control registers, terrorising revolutionary families and creating a state of tension amongst the masses in the hamlets'. Known cadres went underground in the old Viet Minh bases, while others remained 'to carry on among the people'. Vulnerable to exposure and restricted by Party discipline to non-violent means, they mounted a feeble response, in the form of passive resistance and disruption of the public meetings, at which

> . . . comrades instructed their relatives to bring up excuses about how difficult it was to earn a living. Or, when going to a meeting, to bring along a small child, and strike the child to make it cry loudly to upset the order of the meeting . . .

An estimated 700 Party members in the province were killed or imprisoned during the Diem period, and of the 50 cells left behind in 1954, only seven survived at the end of the decade. The Party branch in Hoa Long village declined from 60 members in 1954 to twenty in 1960, and that of Long Phuoc from 50 to three. One local history recollected mournfully: 'a sorrowful atmosphere of death covered the hamlets'. An unknown number of people who were not Party members were also caught up in the repression; increasingly after 1956, opponents of the regime were called communists. Despite such setbacks, a small though largely dormant armed force remained hiding in the forests of the Hat Dich, built around the core of the Binh Xuyen remnants; training in secret, they were reduced to cutting and selling wood to buy supplies.[10]

Both Burchett and the local Party histories present the *To Cong* campaigns as entirely external to the village; as Burchett pungently put it, 'as the military police teams swept through the provinces, they left a trail of bitterness and hostility behind . . .' But the central regime had some institutional support at the local level, and it may have been difficult for village notables to avoid at least public demonstrations of loyalty. One account of a village in Long An province at the end of the 1950s gives the impression of national campaigns and organisations projected into the village from Saigon, but taken up with varying degrees of enthusiasm, commitment and necessity by village notables and authorities. In the village, propaganda campaigns to generate loyalty to the regime and to denounce communists had been introduced

> . . . into many village celebrations. Anti-Communist slogans on banners, signs and pamphlets, and shouted from sound trucks have become part of the village scene. Support of the central government is the major theme of the National Revolutionary Movement, which is the only official political party in the village.

Most of the village leaders belonged to the official party, though from what combination of duty, zeal and obligation is unclear; the same notables also made up the Communist Denunciation

Committee, which met every Saturday evening, and at which all males over the age of eighteen were expected to be present.[11]

A general *To Cong* or denunciation meeting was held monthly in the *dinh*, usually with a speaker provided, but in Hickey's account, they were desultory affairs. 'Villagers dutifully assist at these meetings, but most do not appear particularly attentive. Some squat outside the dinh chatting in low tones while a few read newspapers.'[12] Any personal involvement in the anticolonial war, along with the consequences of being denounced, must have contributed to lingering political tension, but the atmosphere was rather impassive by the end of the 1950s.

Yet the period of greatest repression in the South was between late 1957, when Diem was being feted in Canberra, and early 1959; in these years, as many as 5000 were killed, more than 10 000 wounded and more than 183 000 arrested. One estimate was that two-thirds of the Party members in the South (estimated to number 15 000 in 1957) were lost through arrest or death up till the end of 1958, with more lost in the following year. Whatever the exact figures, it was clear that Diem's repression was highly damaging to the Party and others who had been in the resistance against the French. Military tribunals were established, with summary powers of execution and without rights of appeal. The whiff of exterminism was in the air.[13] Although they helped establish some control over the villages, such measures also alienated support amongst the populace, contributing to the mobilisation of the revolutionary movement. The repression was against a former Viet Minh seen by many as synonymous with patriotism, and which included many not in the Party. The net cast was necessarily imprecise, if not simply indiscriminate or used to settle other disputes.

The debilitating effect of this repression on the Party's infrastructure was a prime reason for the shift in Party policy in January 1959: abandoning the 'legal' political strategy and returning to the armed struggle, effectively through the creation by the Party of the National Liberation Front (NLF—strictly speaking, the National Front for the Liberation of South Vietnam). Many accounts of this decision have been shaped by judgments about the merits of Western intervention in Vietnam, polarised between those who depicted the NLF as the creature of the Hanoi-based central committee of the Party, and others who saw the NLF as an indigenous, largely independent initiative of the Southern branch. Still others, such as Burchett, presented the NLF as simply a spontaneous popular development.

In fact, a number of factors were involved in the decision to create the NLF and move back to armed struggle. There was pressure from the cadres in the South to be allowed to defend

themselves in their perilous situation, a pressure illustrated before
1959 in the cases of local action by militants in violation of the
Party's non-violence line; at the same time, the Nam Ky committee was apparently divided, attempting to exercise strict
discipline over members, though at the risk of alienating them.
Finally, the alienation of the populace in the South was creating
conditions in which the Diem regime destabilised itself, including
alienating non-communist urban intellectuals.[14] However one
strikes the balance among these different factors, there remains
some truth in Jean Lacouture's conclusion that Diem's first five
years had been an effective lesson in 'how to revive a war'.

In 1954, many had not expected the new state of South
Vietnam to survive more than a few years; by 1960, it had a
certain stability, even if its legitimacy was challenged. One part
of establishing this stability was the centralisation and militarisa-
tion of its administration, an essential precondition for the
effective repression described, and an aspect which throws some
light on the nature of the postcolonial state in South Vietnam.

By the late 1950s, holders of all positions from regional
governors down to province and district chiefs were being directly
appointed by Diem, and most appointees came from the armed
forces; from 1956, in addition, the old system of elected village
councils was abolished and replaced by nominations of the
province authorities. But Diem's administration had major deficiencies. First, officials at the provincial level, and perhaps below,
were often in effect foreigners. Because Diem frequently drew
on the support of loyal Catholics from his own base in central
Vietnam, 'to many peasants their provincial chiefs were quasi-
foreigners. When speaking to them they even have difficulty in
understanding their accents.'[15]

A second major weakness of the regime was that only a chain
of personal loyalty bound the administration together, this chain
ending with President Diem. Loyalty and security, rather than
local conditions, were the chief priority of the administration. As
the army was the only coherent social force which, however
truculently, supported Diem, increasingly these appointees were
military officers, with most province chiefs and many district
chiefs being drawn from the army. In this way, the president
was effectively dividing and ruling his own state, by playing off
the army against a militarised administration which answered
personally to him. The writers of the *Pentagon Papers* recognised
that this 'division and confusion of military authority served a
real purpose for a ruler like Diem, with no broad base of
support'; it reduced the likelihood of a coup in the short term,
though it also produced the ruling class of officers who, after

deposing Diem in the coup of 1963, went on to rule the South until 1975.[16]

These attempts to project central control into the village were a substantial challenge to the Party's clandestine rural infrastructure. As early as mid-1957, almost two years before the official shift back to armed struggle, this challenge was being met by a program of violence and assassination which apparently coexisted with the Party's official 'legal' position. It was called the *tru gian* or 'killing tyrants' program, and its prime targets were village officials, police and village guards, district and provincial officials, and cadres of Diem's party. The purpose was the same as it would be in the 1960s—to use selective terror and assassination to isolate the central regime from the rural social order.

It may be a measure of the relative success of Diem's attempt to construct a rural social base—through propaganda campaigns, through enlisting the support or compliance of village notables, and through establishing organisations such as the National Revolutionary Movement and women's and youth associations— that the Communist Party judged it needed to eliminate key officials. The number of government officials killed—roughly 430 killed or abducted in 1958, another 570 in 1959, and a definite quickening of the tempo in 1960—was relatively small compared with the numbers caught up in the government's *To Cong* campaigns. But these killings were part of the struggle for control of the rural social order, what Bernard Fall called the 'gradual "insulation" of the central authorities from direct contact with the grass roots'.[17]

Diem's system of loyalist appointments illustrates the pre-modern character of South Vietnamese administration, based on personal links rather than any sense of 'legalistic' rule in the Weberian sense; bourgeois norms of legality and democracy were substituted by religious, military and regional loyalties. But this only reflected the weakness of the regime, dependent on the support of the military and lacking both social base and coherent ideology. The only attempt to articulate an ideology to compete with Marxism and revolutionary patriotism was in the ideology of personalism, which few took seriously. Diem's regime was distinctly pre-Enlightenment, tolerating no organised dissent; as one writer put it, the president took no notice of criticism, only of organised opposition.[18] He was one of those dictators who are conscientious, but politically tone-deaf. If Diem was a nationalist, as many of his Western supporters hoped, he was a particularly premodern one, without the capacity for popular ideological mobilisation usually found in the nationalism arising out of decolonisation struggles. But these were weaknesses with their roots firmly in the soil of colonial rule.

The strategic hamlets: The struggle for the village

In the turn to a more revolutionary and violent politics from 1959, with the creation of the NLF, the revolutionary movement escalated the developing civil conflict in the South. In doing so, it clearly built upon the weaknesses of the Diem regime—its repressive nature, its dependence on US support, its centralised control and its inability to develop a coherent ideology. Each of these characteristics of the Diem period could be seen in the struggle which developed over the strategic hamlet program.

The strategic hamlets—developed during 1961 and fully implemented from early 1962—were based on the relocation experiment in Malaya; the program consisted either of relocating the rural population into a series of armed stockades, or of enclosing existing villages with guarded fences. In each case, the process was designed to sever the link between the people and the guerrillas who relied upon them for support and sustenance. Reversing Mao's dictum, they were an attempt to remove the sea from the fish. They were thus a means of intensifying the control over the rural population which had been a preoccupation of the Diem regime since the mid-1950s. Some members of the US military advisory group supported this motivation, regarding the program as an instrument of control, while others argued that this only revealed the recalcitrance of the Diem regime. They wanted the program to focus more benignly on security as a precondition for winning loyalty and popular support.[19]

The strategic hamlets had the potential for particularly dislocating effects because of the process of uprooting peasants from their land and moving them to new villages. The critical argument frequently made was that social control was bought at the price of resentment and alienation, and hence produced no control. In a peasant society, forced relocation ruptured attachments to land and village, clashed with the fierce peasant localism which traditionally regarded the centre with suspicion, and produced profound economic and cultural destabilisation. Earlier, less systematic relocation programs in 1959–1960 had generated resentment, by removing peasants from the land they worked, without land title at the new location, and by transferring people from the village dinh, the centre of the village cult. 'Removal from the dinh, as well as removal from the proximity to ancestral graves, must have been a severe blow to the peasant.'[20]

One Party member from the intelligentsia, interviewed in 1968, made the same point:

The Vietnamese peasant is very conservative when it comes to his home and the area where he was born—he hates to leave it . . .

the plan of the strategic hamlets was to take people away from their
homeland and collect them in the hamlets, while bombing everywhere
outside . . . the strategic hamlets actually created more enemies of
the government than they eliminated.

The refrain is repeated elsewhere in arguments that the strategic
hamlets were a social and cultural upheaval, threatening peasant
culture, land ties and the family system. As a result, 'patriotism
and hatred of the foreign invader . . . increasingly merged with
class interests'. Because it attempted to transform the very nucleus
of society—the village—the program can be seen as more revolutionary than anything the Viet Minh had attempted.[21]

But in Phuoc Tuy, the strategic hamlet program involved not
so much these forced relocations as the compulsory fortification
of existing settlements, with new ditches, fences and guards. In
August 1962, Phuoc Tuy was one of three provinces assigned
the highest priority for the program. At the start of the following
year, 23 strategic hamlets had been constructed, accommodating
only 14 per cent of the population, with another 83 under
construction. These were low figures compared with other provinces, though the government figures were notoriously unreliable
even by the standards of the Vietnam war, as they were subject
to false reporting.[22]

By mid-1963, a number of the main central villages had
been encircled with ditches and barbed-wire fences, with gates
guarded to control all access; in some instances parts of a village
were destroyed to relocate people in a closer settlement pattern
within their village. The general pattern was that the central
authorities provided the fencing, and the village was required to
contribute labour and other materials. This was disruptive enough
of everyday life—peasants were allowed access to their land only
outside curfew hours—but was not the destabilisation described
above. Within the newly enclosed villages, the central government
required the establishment of paramilitary organisations consisting
of all able-bodied men, who were to take guard duty in village
defence units; at the entrance to each hamlet, guards checked
the comings and goings of villagers along with all they were
carrying. But in general, the village defence units were made up
of reluctant soldiers with little or no training or motivation,
and—given that the government was unwilling to arm the
people—they were very poorly armed.[23]

If the strategic hamlets were the government's principal
strategy for social control, they also became the NLF's main
preoccupation; they were a major threat to its links with the rural
social order, isolating guerrillas from peasants, cutting off food
supplies and disrupting information channels. In Phuoc Tuy,
when the Dat Do group of villages were fortified as strategic

hamlets in May 1962, the local revolutionary forces based in the nearby Long Hai hills soon found themselves short of food; as importantly, they were starved of information about government troop movements and local political developments. Some gave themselves up, others became sick without adequate food supplies. A small example, this also illustrates the dimensions of the local revolution, in which rice and knowledge within a close locale were crucial.

The urgency of the 1962–63 period can be gauged from an internal Party journal distributed in Phuoc Tuy in late 1962. This was devoted to the strategic hamlets and the Party's counter-strategy of building what were variously called 'struggle villages', 'combat hamlets' or 'fortified hamlets' (*xa chien dau*). These were strategic hamlets in reverse: the hamlet became fortified against government troops, with tunnels, firing positions and traps. As the local Party journal put it: 'The US–Diem scheme is to fetter the people in disguised jails, so as to detach our Party, the people's armed forces from the masses.' The document repeated again and again that 'the work of setting up struggling hamlet and village [sic] is now becoming very important and is to be carried on urgently', and concluded: 'we have no other means than pushing the masses to set up struggling village [sic]'.[24] This vehemence revealed a real anxiety, for the effectiveness of the strategic hamlet program had forced the NLF onto the defensive again. This phase lasted until the assassination of the president and his brother Nhu in the coup of November 1963, when the resulting political vacuum allowed the NLF to overrun most of the strategic hamlets and led to a collapse of the political infrastructure which the regime had been slowly building.

These conflicting dynamics of the postcolonial period can be seen concentrated in the village of Long Phuoc, in central Phuoc Tuy. By 1965, Long Phuoc was mobilised as a 'struggle village'. When Australian troops entered it in late June of the following year, they found a well-established village of some 4000 people with

> . . . well constructed dwellings nestled amongst ornamental and shade trees and numerous patches of cultivations of bananas, pineapples, grain and root crops. Numerous hedgerows and fences interlaced the area . . . A stand of generally clear rubber existed to the south of the village, whilst paddi surrounded most of the remaining area.[25]

This was a diversified agricultural microeconomy, with small-scale rubber plantings, carpentry, rice fields and orchards. It was also highly politicised and, at least since the early 1960s, the village had acted as the base area for the provincial committee of the Party.

Below the ground, signifying this politicisation, was an extensive system of tunnels, some dating back to 1948 and the war against the French. These had been maintained after 1954 and then greatly expanded. By 1963 the tunnel complex included firing pits and bunkers, food and weapons storehouses, water cisterns, small hospital facilities and systems of traps for blocking off poison gas. Communicating tunnels began under the floors of houses and connected to the bunkers. After the low point of the late 1950s, when the local Party branch had been reduced from 50 to three members, the village was overtly mobilised again; at some point before 1965, it was developed as a struggle village, with the tunnel system as part of the fortifications against government troops.[26]

A sense of what this meant in the village can be gleaned from Burchett's sketch of a struggle village he visited in late 1963 or early 1964.

> The defences consist of a maze of tunnels, about 20 miles in this one hamlet . . . leading into spacious firing positions which cover every approach . . . To take even the outer perimeter of such a fortified hamlet would be a very costly affair. If attacking troops were to penetrate the tunnels, all sorts of hand-operated traps would go into action.

Thousands of work hours had gone into constructing the tunnel complexes which Burchett saw, 'built almost entirely by the young people of the villages, the older ones keeping up supplies of rice, tea and fruit while they worked often from dusk to dawn'.[27] Burchett's was a somewhat romantic vision of the whole people united in a people's war, but a struggle village such as Long Phuoc nevertheless required that the NLF have vital political roots in the rural social order. Peasants would not fortify their village against government troops as a result of coercion or lukewarm conviction; it involved too much labour and too many risks of exposure to government retaliation to be undertaken easily.

Developing a struggle village presupposed a politicising process involving a substantial proportion of the village population. The key medium of this politicisation was the struggle movement, organised by the NLF in the form of meetings, petitions and public demonstrations directed against local officials, and focused around grievances such as the shelling of villages, the imposition of strategic hamlets, American influence, military conscription and so on. One early NLF document stated: 'We must utilise the strength of the people as our great force . . . The enemy

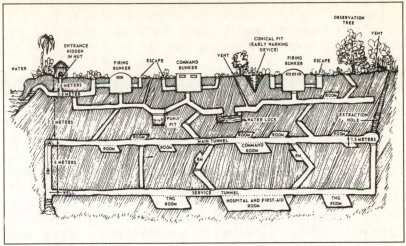

Below the surface of the struggle for the village, the Vietnamese Communist Party had developed the tunnel systems left over from the war against the French. In Phuoc Tuy, Long Phuoc village had extensive tunnelling, such as shown in this illustration. Diplomats in Saigon and officials in Canberra seemed oblivious to the roots of the revolutionary movement in the rural social order. (Australian War Memorial, Herbicide Series)

relies on its armed forces. We rely on the people . . . the people strongly bound together in the struggle movement.' Struggle movements were the political display of opposition and consolidated the gap between the peasants and the central government. One such action, against artillery shelling, occurred in Long Phuoc in December 1963—a demonstration involving 1000 people, or more than one in four of the village population.[28] In struggle villages such as Long Phuoc, mobilisation had to be all the more intense; as villages fortified against the central government, they had taken a further step which involved exposure to attack by both troops and artillery.

Several aspects of the struggle movements stand out, and suggest a continuity with the Party's activity since the 1930s. First, local grievances were used for mobilisation, as with the mobilisation already discussed in Phuoc Hai amongst the women fish traders in 1938; local issues such as the shelling of villages made powerful focal points, which in the early 1960s were combined with broader grievances such as opposition to American influence. Second, struggle movements were a principal activity of the NLF as a social movement. They focused around the exemplary actions of ordinary people, building up a conception of struggle which elevated the political significance of everyday life. This is the sense in which Pike spoke of the social movement

as constituted by communication; action provided an exemplar
of political behaviour and thought, harnessing discontent and
demonstrating ways of grappling with the rural order in transition.[29]

The conception of struggle provided a model for the seizure
of history; in the early decades of the century, the intelligentsia
had been fascinated with the idea of struggle, taking up social
Darwinism with vigour and seeing in it a Promethean image of
society as social struggle. There is a parallel here with the
revolutionary movement's emphasis on political struggle as social
action, as the mobilisation of people to control their history. Both
the local Party histories and hindsight have given the struggle
movements and the armed movement of the NLF a patina of
inevitable triumph; yet frequently, individual movements in villages were neither so triumphant nor so earnest. There were
examples of struggle movements where organisation was inadequate and where the courage of participants failed them; Burchett,
with his eye for the triumph of the people, sketched a satirical
edge to their politics. He described a 'cannon-spiking operation'
which involved subverting an artillery team about to start shelling
a village:

> . . . the village women and children raced towards the artillery team
> . . . driving pigs and buffalo ahead of them, carrying chickens under
> their arms; . . . Women and children jammed in around the guns
> and squatting on the piles of shells were wailing and shouting: 'If
> you're going to shell our village, this is the only safe place for us
> to be.'[30]

As Burchett shrewdly pointed out, such a scene would have been
impossible with the Foreign Legion during the First Indochina
war.

These were some of the political conditions in which, by the
middle of the 1960s, the NLF controlled a large part of the
countryside; after the coup in 1963, this control was deepened
in the rural social order. The official Australian and American
account in the early to mid-1960s, in which 'insurgency' arrived
from somewhere else and took over the village through a
combination of propaganda and coercion, missed most of the
point. Village history included tunnels constructed to fight the
French, the bitter experience of Diem's repression and the
alienation associated with the strategic hamlets. Increasingly, it
included villagers who had either thrown in their lot with the
NLF or lived in villages which were in any case exposed to
reprisals.

Thus, when the Australian military attache in the Saigon
embassy reported dolefully to Canberra in 1964 that: 'February

demonstrated quite clearly the Viet Cong's continuing ability to maintain the initiative and call the tune,' he nevertheless conveyed little sense of the micro-politics of the struggle for the village. The following month, he commented that, in Phuoc Tuy, government control was limited to the population centres of the south-west; 'in the remainder of the area, the VC operate almost unopposed . . .'[31] This was an accurate enough summary of the way that the initiative had swung back to the NLF after 1963, but the picture was still more complex within a struggle village such as Long Phuoc. These reports only scratched the surface of the influence of the Party and the NLF in the rural social order, and missed the crucial difference—that the government had no real network of cadres linking it to the village. They conveyed a sense neither of the tunnel systems being prepared in the more militant villages, nor of the history which lay behind them.

The Diem regime had, for almost a decade, perched atop the shifting mass of the military, held in power not so much by the support of the generals as at their increasingly truculent pleasure. Diem had attempted to construct a rural social base for the regime, through the strategic hamlets, through establishing associations and parties, and through rooting out Viet Minh cadres and sympathisers. Each was to an extent effective, in Phuoc Tuy as elsewhere, though each measure for consolidating control as often undermined it. The central weakness of the regime remained that it could not construct a nationalist, non-communist power base, and there was no major social class or political force which Diem could be said to represent.

Finally, in the November 1963 coup, the military, with direct American approval and assistance, removed its support; the generals plunged into intrigue, the administration and the armed forces were paralysed by purges, and Saigon embarked upon what became known as the 'coup season', which was only stabilised from 1965. At the beginning of 1965, General Maxwell Taylor commented that '. . . until the fall of Diem and the experience gained from the events of the following months, I doubt that anyone appreciated the magnitude of the centrifugal political forces which had been kept under control by his iron rule'. Saigon was now plagued by chronic factionalism, intrigue and mistrust, 'absence of national spirit and motivation' and a lack of experience in administration.[32]

The revolutionary movement well appreciated these centrifugal forces. As the NLF's president, Nguyen Huu Tho, described it, the coup had been a gift from heaven, and the government had been seriously weakened: '. . . the military command has been turned upside down and weakened by purges . . . the coercive

apparatus, set up over the years with great care by Diem, is
utterly shattered, specially at the base . . .' The various
organisations and parties which Diem had established, and 'which
constituted an appreciable support for the regime', had been
eliminated.[33] What remained was the rule of the generals, who
represented still less of a social base than Diem and expressed
no political creed. Their legitimacy was paltry, and did not extend
beyond repeating that they had brought an end to the Diem
regime. Yet these political weaknesses seemed hardly to matter;
the regime in the South was expected only to provide a stable
and cooperative indigenous base from which to wage the anticommunist struggle.

> Kennedy had said it best—what helps the war effort we support—and
> now the generals were ready to take over with no inconvenient ideas
> of their own about how the war should be fought—no great
> enthusiasm about fighting the war either, but the Americans did not
> know that yet.[34]

By the time that policy-makers in Canberra and Washington
determined on intervention in Vietnam in 1965, the basic political
features of the war were discernible. It was clear that the
Communist Party had a substantial claim to make as the party
of patriotism, as well as having tenacious organisational roots in
the social order of the village; the implausibility of the Saigon
regime of the generals was equally discernible, in terms of its
lack of the ideological substance to establish legitimacy, its
absence of a social base and its detachment from nationalist and
patriotic sentiment. Unhearing, the policy-makers pursued their
logic of intervention.

6
The logic of intervention: 1957–1964

The quality of knowledge

Between 1954 and 1962, Vietnam virtually disappeared from Australian public view. From being a key focal point of strategic interest at the time of Dien Bien Phu and the Geneva conference, it became a matter of some indifference. Up to September 1961, there were only a few brief periods of any substantial press coverage. The lowest points were in 1958 and 1959, when Diem's repression was at its most intense—in each of these years, the *Sydney Morning Herald* noted Vietnam only four times.[1] In the year before Diem's assassination in 1963, coverage was somewhat less desultory, but hardly amounted to a sustained public debate.

The absence of media discussion about Vietnam during the years when Diem was in the ascendancy meant that Vietnam was unintelligible when the balance swung back to the NLF in 1963 and 1964. There was little continuity between *The Age*'s enthusiasm for Diem in 1957 and its forthright condemnation of his 'hated' regime in 1963, when the paper unexpectedly revealed that 'it has long been a nagging fear of Western diplomacy that the growing unpopularity of the Diem regime, with its record of

repression and corruption, would destroy its military effort . . .'[2]
There was little in what had gone before to account for this
sudden revelation. An informed public relying on the newspapers
for its perceptions of Asian developments must have been
bemused, if not bewildered, by such shifts.

By 1963, there were rare Australian journalists based in
Southeast Asia—such as Denis Warner and Bruce Grant—who
were well versed in its politics and history. But with minimal
coverage, it was little wonder that the Australian press reported
official views dutifully, at least until 1962 or 1963 when the
Saigon press corps began to write more critically, particularly on
the Diem regime. Even as late as 1966, no Sydney daily had a
correspondent in East or Southeast Asia; *The Age* and the
Melbourne *Herald* each had a single reporter in Singapore with
the daunting brief of covering Asia from Japan to West Pakistan.
As Ball commented, a thin press coverage meant that reports on
events in Vietnam were not connected by a coherent fabric of
interpretation. Crises were reported, but remained largely inex-
plicable.[3]

One persistent feature of the Vietnam intervention was to be
the gap between official and public forms of knowledge, between
what was understood in the Cabinet and the bureaucracy and
what was conveyed to the citizenry. Yet the reports from the
Australian legation in Saigon in the late 1950s suggest the variable
quality of knowledge within the Department of External Affairs.
In the early Diem years, these reports could be positively
Panglossian in their interpretation of Vietnam. When Diem was
elected president with 98 per cent of the vote in the October
1955 elections held in the South, one report noted that this
indicated not ballot-rigging but 'the popular support that Diem
had achieved'. In 1957, the External Affairs briefing notes for
Diem's visit to Australia expressed 'satisfaction at the great
recovery made in South Viet Nam in the past three years',
glossing over Diem's political style, his repression of political
opponents and the possible consequences. In a note for the visit,
acting secretary James Plimsoll summed up the prevailing canon
in the form of points which should be conveyed to Diem:

> . . . we appreciate what he personally has done to rally Viet Nam
> . . . Indicate our understanding of the menace of international
> Communism and also of the problem of China . . . it might be
> possible to say that he and his country have taught the whole free
> world that resoluteness and patriotism with firm leadership can save
> a situation where lesser men might give up in despair.[4]

More than mere phrasemaking, this expressed the orthodox belief
within the department.

By the end of the decade, diplomats in Saigon were more guarded, though still orthodox. Early in 1958, the minister of the Legation in Saigon, F.J. Blakeney, was writing to Casey in rather bleak terms. He was concerned about the security situation, and noted that government administration was poor in the provinces; the 'Viet Minh' had 'infiltrated' most of the government's military and paramilitary forces, as well as 'all Government civil agencies—even at the national level . . .' Finally, he suggested that the recent increase in dissident activity was probably due 'not primarily to any change in communist tactics but to increasing anti-Government feeling in those regions . . .' But in September, this bleak tone had been replaced by resolution. Blakeney authoritatively spelt out his conclusions that 'the subversion threat is, in terms of its origins, fundamentally an external one', with its tempo controlled from the North; 'internal dissatisfaction . . . based on recent past history and quite distinct from external interference' was too weak to threaten the government.[5] This neatly distinguished the indistinguishable— the political claim to reunification and the local movement in the South.

As significant as the subject matter were its sources; the legation relied heavily on the US mission in Saigon, on interviews with Diem and his brother Nhu, and to a lesser extent, on discussions with French diplomats in Saigon. In the report just quoted, Blakeney canvassed the views of the French and British, which tended to emphasise that the Saigon government controlled little of the countryside, and rejected them in favour of his CIA sources. British sources, which had been used for some early reports, and which were notably more phlegmatic and sceptical about Vietnam, had dropped off.

The legation appeared to have cultivated no independent sources of information, but instead reproduced the views of government and diplomatic circles in Saigon. By 1965, the embassy could have availed itself of Burchett's excellent contacts in the Communist Party in the South—at this time, he was living in the Cambodian capital, Phnom Penh—but Burchett was anathema to the department. When Gregory Clark interviewed Burchett on the latter's return to Moscow in late 1964, after his visit to NLF areas, Clark was rebuked for seeming to endorse Burchett's views. Throughout the 1950s and 1960s, Australian diplomats in Vietnam had no real access to Communist Party or dissident thinking in Saigon, nor to events in the village. Their assessments consequently missed most of the dynamic of the struggle under way deep in the countryside.

Despite a narrow range of sources, reports from Saigon displayed some subtlety of detail, but whether such detail was

acceptable in Canberra is questionable. More often, it appears
that complicating nuances were lost amongst the traditional Cold
War metaphors. Unwelcome views could be disregarded in
Canberra. Alan Renouf, in defence of his department's inability
to seriously question, or independently assess, the trend of the
Vietnam policy, wrote that:

> Successive Prime Ministers and Ministers considered they knew
> everything about Vietnam and did not welcome objective advice. A
> public servant unable to provide confirmation got out of the way or
> lay low. Those remaining were, by character and experience, as
> conservative as their political masters.[6]

Some—such as Clark and Stephen Fitzgerald—resigned over the
developing policy in Vietnam.

A number of retired officials—with more than a little special
pleading—have implied that some in the department understood
Vietnam but were cowed into silence. Renouf and Watt both
argued that the Vietnam policy demonstrated a governmental
failure to explain policy, when it was not intentionally misleading
the public. Both laid the responsibility with their political masters.
Others have been more caustic, arguing that the department was
often ignorant, had no Vietnamese linguists, let alone specialists,
and simply combined the most optimistic of American reports
with an entrenched antagonism to China:

> In the Southeast Asian branch it was taken for granted that all
> left-wing movements in Asia were financed by Peking, that one could
> at all times and places talk indiscriminately about Chinese
> 'subversion' and 'infiltration'.

In private, some officials and ministers could be more sceptical,
but chose not to share such complications with the public. In
August 1963, the parliamentary Foreign Affairs committee—
which was still boycotted by Labor—had a briefing on Vietnam
with Keith Waller, who was about to become ambassador in
Washington. Peter Howson noted: 'We don't like Diem's policies,
but any alternative seems worse.'[7]

This is consistent with the one study available with access to
the closed archival documents. In 1963, the department was
reportedly sceptical about Diem, had few illusions and offered
only grudging support for his rule. But the official history (up
till 1965) cites no evidence that there was any sustained evaluation of Vietnam within External Affairs. There has been no
suggestion that the department opposed the policy which developed from the late 1950s, nor that there was any debate or
controversy about the nature of Vietnamese nationalist and
communist forces, nor any independent evaluation of the American analysis of 'aggression from the north'.

One mild example occurred in early 1965 when the minister, Hasluck, rebuked the ambassador in Saigon, H.D. Anderson, for being less than enthusiastic about American and Australian aims. Anderson had considerable experience in the area, having been in Saigon in the mid-1950s and then head of the Southeast Asian branch in External Affairs. But his advice was reportedly insufficiently urgent, and Hasluck may have been rallying his officials behind his view that Vietnam had to be held, rather than written off or regarded as secondary to the Confrontation between Indonesia and Malaysia. According to Whitlam, the text of Hasluck's rebuke of Anderson was circulated widely in the department 'to encourage the others'.[8]

But there was, finally, a sense in which the nuances of the view from Saigon were largely irrelevant to Australian planning in the early to mid-1960s. Australia's Vietnam policy was a policy less about Vietnam than about broader regional strategy and the perceived need to secure American involvement in the region.[9] This meant that the chief quality of knowledge about Vietnam was not so much that it was inaccessible but that it was unwelcome.

Vietnam in regional strategy

A second influence made the detail of reports from Saigon less important: Vietnam was not central to Australian strategic thinking until 1964, being largely overshadowed by the priority given to Malaysia and Indonesia. From its sudden elevation in 1954 as the touchstone of Cold War confrontation, Vietnam slipped back down the strategic agenda. Before the early 1960s, Vietnam was regarded as a trouble spot, but not one which loomed large.

In February 1956, the Defence minister—whom Maxwell Newton had once described as 'the pale and unconvincing' Sir Phillip McBride—submitted to Cabinet the most recent report of the Defence committee. It assumed the principle of forward defence, or 'defence in depth'. In effect, this stated that Australia would best be defended somewhere in Southeast Asia: this necessarily involved attracting the support and commitment of powerful allies, since Australia did not have the military capacity to arrange the affairs of the region alone. But it was notable that the Defence committee did not fix the boundary for forward defence at the 17th parallel dividing Vietnam, and defence planning at the time more often identified Malaya as being essential to forward defence.[10]

There was, however, some detailed planning for Vietnam, in the event of a possible Viet Minh attack from the North, with

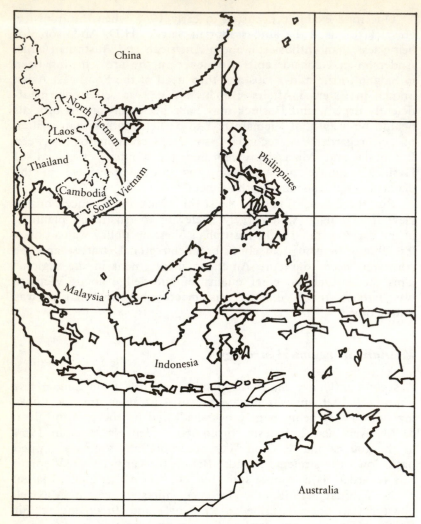

Australia and Southeast Asia in the mid-1960s.

the presumption that a breakdown in the partition arrangement would be the result of external aggression. In 1957, when he visited Canberra, Diem was expected to argue for an expansion of his armed forces in preparation for a conventional counteroffensive against the North. External Affairs advised the government that this was 'in conflict with the SEATO concept which provides, amongst other things, for an atomic attack on the Hanoi area'. SEATO's strategy was for nuclear attacks on North Vietnam, as well as 'immediate interdiction' of Viet Minh advances and the deployment of ground forces.[11] This seemingly drastic preparedness to employ nuclear weapons in a regional rather than global conflict indicated both the presumption that regional conflicts were in fact global—as part of Cold War confrontation—and the clear nuclear superiority of the United States at the time.

By the next Defence committee review, in early 1959, these plans were in need of revision. The recognition of a rough nuclear parity with the Soviet Union had altered the balance, undermining the routine expectation of the use of the American nuclear arsenal. As the committee now put it, with a notably even tone, this made the use of nuclear weapons

> . . . a most serious step; not only would it have a profound effect on world opinion, particularly in Asia, but it would greatly increase the risk of nuclear retaliation and the extension to global war.

The new nuclear balance made SEATO's plans for nuclear retaliation against North Vietnam outdated, but the Defence committee noted that SEATO had not conducted a revision of its plans. In general, the report was distinctly jaundiced about the value of SEATO, which had proved 'limited'. It had no command structure such as NATO (the model in Australian eyes), it had not persuaded any other Asian countries to join and the Asian states involved were militarily weak. 'Should SEATO prove ineffective,' the report said, 'the development of ANZUS becomes the most promising means of ensuring Australia's security.'

Nevertheless, the threats which made this security umbrella so necessary were not particularly alarming; the major concern over the next decade was expected to be the growing military capability of Indonesia, but even this was

> . . . not sufficient to pose a significant threat to the Australian mainland . . . The only circumstances in which such an attack might be contemplated would be with substantial Communist Bloc support and the belief that our major allies could not or would not interfere.

By comparison, the observation that in Vietnam, 'communist activity could reach serious proportions' over the following years, was of somewhat lesser priority. For defence planners, the situation in Vietnam was indistinguishable from the universal problem of 'expansionist communism'. 'In the event of Viet Minh aggression,' by which the Defence committee meant an attack by North Vietnam, Australian troops should be committed,

> . . . dependent on whether or not U.S. forces were similarly committed . . . South East Asia could well be lost by default in the cold war. It is therefore of paramount importance that Australia should play her full part in cold war programmes . . .[12]

This was an ominous note sounded for the future.

The Defence committee's report made two other recommendations which were significant, although neither was endorsed by Cabinet. First, it recommended the 'acquisition of a tactical nuclear capability by Australian forces', though this momentous suggestion was discreetly passed over in Senator Shane Paltridge's ministerial submission accompanying the report, and Cabinet recorded no discussion on it. Second, the Defence committee suggested that the deployment of Australian troops in Southeast Asia—other than the Malayan commitment—would usually be dependent on 'parallel United States commitment in the area', although there were circumstances where independent Australian forces would be used, such as in a conflict with Indonesia. Consequently, 'our forces should be designed primarily with the ability to act independently of allies'.[13]

It was this issue which generated the most heat in Cabinet. Ministers 'found difficulty in accepting this conclusion' and invited the chiefs of staff to attend a discussion on it. Later, in November, Cabinet returned to the question and was now more adamant; the objective of independent forces was specifically rejected.[14] The reliance on great alliances was apparently more an absolute for the Cabinet than for the Defence committee.

These principles of strategic thinking changed little into the early 1960s. There was substantial continuity with the concerns of the 1950s, focused around the growth of Indonesian military power, the presumption of forward defence and the alliances on which it depended, and the general posture of anticommunism which regarded Vietnam as of moderate concern. In 1962, when the Defence committee submitted its next 'Strategic Basis' report, the tone was 'not alarmist, but certainly sombre'. The cornerstone of strategic defence was reaffirmed as forward defence against potential threats from China and North Vietnam. 'While Southeast Asia is held,' the report stated, 'defence in depth is provided for Australia.' In this analysis, Indonesia was not just another potential domino; it was seen as a special case, given that President Sukarno was perceived as balanced between a strong Communist Party and an equally strong—and eventually triumphant—anticommunist army. The sombre tone was repeated in 1964 in a chiefs of staff minute which saw no threat to the Australian mainland, even in the event of a limited war in Southeast Asia against the Chinese. 'This sober assessment contrasts sharply with the alarmist public rhetoric of Australian leaders.'[15]

Another indication of strategic thinking in this period is in Peter Howson's summary of the briefings he had received since becoming minister for Air in June 1964. He had been told that the confrontation with Indonesia over Malaysia was 'likely to persist for many months, perhaps years' and that 'the situation in Vietnam could worsen', but he assumed that only air support would be needed. Three months later, Howson tried his hand at his own assessment of the strategic situation. In his view, global war was unlikely for the rest of the decade. China was unlikely to 'upset the present world balance', and Australia would be able to keep its bases in Malaysia, with the Americans in Thailand and the British in Malaysia in support.

'Our main threat,' he thought, 'is guerrilla action in Vietnam and/or Thailand and various threats to Malaysia, with less probable incursions into New Guinea.' Overall, 'the threat to the Australian mainland remains remote till at least 1970' but, significantly, 'we should use this period of public anxiety regarding defence to expand our defence budget'. Howson was not known as a strategic analyst, but his relatively relaxed view of the situation in Asia may indicate the tone of thinking in his department and in the government. However, a more strident influence also appeared at times, asserting that Vietnam 'is much more important than Malaysia', which may indicate the influence of Hasluck, the main proponent of the alarming argument that Vietnam was vital to Australian interests and represented an aggressive Chinese expansion southward.[16]

The logic of commitment in official circles had a certain consistency over this period, based on the three interlocking concerns of forward defence, the role of powerful allies and the presumption of a unified threat. Forward defence has already been discussed; an essential feature of this strategy was the involvement in the Pacific and Southeast Asia of Britain and the United States. Without them, forward defence was impossible, and the only alternative was a 'fortress Australia' strategy.

With the recognition that Britain was inexorably withdrawing its military involvement, the focus was increasingly on the United States, and the fear here was not so much of isolationism as of an American unwillingness to fully commit itself to the Pacific along with its other imperial interests. There was a remarkable continuity here between Spender's statement to Casey during the 1954 crisis, that his policy had been 'to achieve the acceptance by the United States of responsibility in South East Asia', and the Vietnam policy pursued in the early 1960s to ensure that the hawks in Washington prevailed, when Hasluck wrote to the ambassador in Washington that 'our stake in the preservation of United States interest in South Vietnam and South East Asia requires us to respond'.[17] Over a decade, the policy was to ensure that America acted as a superpower in the region.

The final element in strategic and foreign policy was the

presumption that regional and local threats derived from a
seamless, global design. This was more than simply the rhetoric
of anticommunism employed for public consumption. It was a
presumption of the age of nuclear parity that, with global war
less likely, conflict had shifted to 'insurgency' and 'subversion',
with local conflicts as surrogates for global war. A revolutionary
civil conflict such as that in Vietnam was global war by other
means. Thus the Defence committee in 1959 presumed that
'communist leaders, in pursuing their expansionist aims, will
continue to rely principally on cold war tactics, and are unlikely
to press to extremes policies which they calculate could lead to
global war.' They cited as an example the possible increase in
'communist activity' in South Vietnam. So pervasive was this
shift in thinking from global war to Cold War subversion, that
one historian speaks of a distinct 'Kennedy strategy' being
formed, by the end of 1961, around the notion of counterinsurgency, as opposed to the 'Dulles strategy' of containment.[18]

The presumption that insurgency was part of a larger design
had some significance. If 'insurgency' was the form the Cold
War now took, the local and historical dimensions of conflicts
tended to recede even further; Vietnam became the classic case
of this, with the struggle in the South represented as fomented
and directed by the Party in the North, itself acting under
instructions from Peking or Moscow. The kernel of truth in this
analysis was buried in a husk of exaggeration and distortion. The
NLF's historical place in the villages of the South became merely
a coded form of Cold War confrontation by other means. In
this, Cold War precepts were insufficiently parochial and regional,
recognising only the power plays of global tension. It was a train
of thought which Hasluck in particular pursued with great
enthusiasm.

Threats

Official knowledge, then, was based on relatively consistent
strategic thinking, even if some ministers found it difficult to rise
to the intellectual challenges of its complexity and relied on
blunter Cold War formulations. In turn, very little of that
complexity filtered into public discourse. An indication of the
tenor of how the government projected its strategic analysis into
public debates can be found in Menzies' speeches of the early
1960s. By this time, Menzies had acquired a reputation for
gauging the timing and temper of elections. In addition, he had
donned a paternalistic manner, asking the audience to bear with
him, hinting at dark secrets which he could not divulge but which

formed the basis of policy. *The Age* noted, in an early comment on the political uses of television, that Menzies 'takes you into his confidence . . . you and he alone are wise in a world of fools'. Menzies' rehearsed speeches were frequently benign and reassuring, but he could suddenly conjure up a world of insecurity and alarm.[19]

In September 1960, Menzies spoke to a rally of the party faithful in Melbourne on 'The Menace of Communism'. It was an opportunity outside the electoral cycle to urge his audience 'to renewed understanding and effort' against communism. His draft notes suggest that he had in mind the Crimes Act legislation which the Attorney-General Garfield Barwick had prepared for parliament, along with a need to re-establish the urgency of a domestic theme which had perhaps grown tired, having been mobilised without respite for a decade.

Despite the thaw in Cold War relations since 1956, Menzies described the Soviet Union as having 'the most concentrated and aggressive record of imperialism . . . in modern history', and its propaganda, especially under Khrushchev, as 'the most superbly organised piece of hypocrisy the world has yet seen'. These were, he conceded, grim thoughts, but 'We will either take them into account and take steps to protect our lives and ideals while we have time or the day will come when we will either live to regret it, or die without having any chance to regret it at all'.[20] Such inflated language may simply have been another of Menzies' rhetorical devices, an excess aimed at quickening a willing audience. But because maintaining a sense of urgent threat continued to have domestic political advantages, Menzies was committed to a language of escalation, in which the menace was always mounting.

A year later, Menzies opened the 1961 federal election at the Kew town hall with a solemn assurance: 'Communist threats and aggression are more violent than at any time since the War.' He spoke of 'an atmosphere of crisis and danger', and referred only to the recent resumption of Soviet nuclear tests, but his audience may also have remembered the recent confrontation over the Berlin Wall, and perhaps the more slow-burning crisis in Laos. In retrospect, these crises passed relatively calmly, but such an atmosphere had its advantages. As Howson had noted in 1964, public anxiety was an opportunity to expand the defence budget, and Menzies was adept at playing on an atmosphere of crisis to the disadvantage of the ALP, and for the cultivation of the DLP. As he put it in his final broadcast of the 1961 campaign:

> We know what side we are on . . . But in the present Labour Opposition there are influential members and aspiring Ministers who

are deeply tainted by neutralism, uncritical of the Communist aggressors, sometimes their apologists, constantly critical of our allies, by no means favourable to SEATO and ANZUS.[21]

From such a catalogue of sins there was little hope of escape; it was a feature of the Menzies era that it was always the opposition which was on trial during elections, almost invariably over what Menzies called its 'ambiguity' on defence and foreign policy.

Such a strategy was an effective counter to critical discussion of government policies, though it proved less electorally effective in 1961 when a combination of relative quiet in regional affairs and a severe credit squeeze brought the Menzies government as near as it ever came to defeat. This was the election in which the conservatives held on by a majority of one, saved only by a donkey vote which delivered it some CPA preferences. That regional conflicts were of only minor concern to the public was perhaps indicated by the offhand tone of Menzies' commentary as he showed his television audience a map:

> . . . down here in the south east of Asia in L-A-O-S, most of us call it Laos, but I believe correctly it ought to be called 'Louse', but anyhow there it is, and this country is a peaceful rural country . . . yet it is bedevilled today by civil war, by Communist pressure from the north . . . The same kind of trouble arises in relation to South Vietnam. A very gallant little country. An outpost of defence against Communism.

Curiously, there was no real attempt to explain why these countries had entered the discussion.

In fact, the crisis in Laos was more important than Menzies' homely lesson suggested. While Menzies argued that the West wanted only peace and nonalignment for Laos, the crisis there became a turning point. It was because of a perceived failure of SEATO in Laos that Vietnam came to be regarded as a test of the 'free world's' will to counter communism. In Canberra, as in Washington, 1961 demonstrated the weakness of SEATO as an anticommunist alliance. Cabinet decided in principle that it would be ready to commit forces if requested, and the crisis signalled 'a significant toughening' in attitudes towards military intervention in Asia.[22]

Immediately after the 1961 election, the government considered an American request for military assistance to Vietnam which had been passed to the ambassador, Howard Beale, during the campaign. This would lead to the first commitment of regular troops as military advisers, in May 1962, ostensibly in a non-combat role. As with the decisions on Vietnam which followed it, two considerations weighed most heavily—the advantage to be gained in Washington, and the perceived military limits on Australia's capacity to contribute. 'Demonstrable Australian support for South Vietnam,' Beale told Canberra, 'would make a very favourable impression on the US.' But the Defence committee recommended only a token contribution of military advisers, after which the initiative apparently lapsed.[23]

It was taken up again when the US secretary of state, Dean Rusk, attended an ANZUS meeting in Canberra in early May and specifically requested a group of instructors. The commitment of a Training Team of 30 Army instructors was announced by the Defence minister, Athol Townley, on 24 May 1962, in a statement which encapsulated the rationale of later commitments. The situation in Vietnam, Townley argued, was 'an urgent problem of communist infiltration and insurgency' directed by the North, whose aim was 'to take over that country by organised terrorism'. He invoked the rattle of falling dominoes. For the communists in Vietnam to succeed 'would gravely affect the security of the whole South-East Asian area and ultimately of Australia itself'. Townley went on with three statements which proved to be specious: that the advisers would not have a combat role, that their provision was in response to an invitation from the Vietnamese government, and that they were provided 'in accordance with Australia's obligations' under SEATO. Each of these claims was, at best, a half-truth. Yet it was an indication of the absence of a public debate on Vietnam that the statement passed almost without notice in the media: *The Age,* for example, simply noted the substance of the press release on its front page, without discussion.[24]

It was in 1961 and 1962 that the conflict in Vietnam came into focus in official circles in both Washington and Canberra. As Diem's regime came undone, Western policy hardened. This was to be the conflict where the line was drawn, to which Australia's forward defence was projected, and in which American imperial prestige was at stake. Yet in the Australian public sphere these decisions were communicated only in the most general terms, and there was scarcely a debate about Vietnam until after the commitment of regular troops in April 1965.

Once that debate was under way, the government had in Hasluck—the minister from April 1964—a protagonist of ideological clarity and conviction, who carried the prosecution of the war with enthusiasm until he became governor-general in February 1969. His predecessor, Barwick—minister from December 1961 till April 1964, when he became chief justice—was a more transitional figure. Certainly, Barwick was a strong advocate of the developing Vietnam policy, but in a period before the policy was being challenged.

*As External Affairs minister
1964–69, Paul Hasluck argued
forcefully that the Vietnam
conflict should be seen as a global
conflict with China: since the
1940s he had advocated a
realpolitik view of great-power
conflicts. Maxwell Newton
commented in 1965 that
government policy on defence and
foreign affairs was in the hands
of three 'hard liners': Hasluck,
Menzies and Shane Paltridge in
Defence. (National Library of
Australia, portrait collection)*

One of Barwick's tasks was to uphold the government's commitment to the Diem regime, a case which he advocated with single-minded dedication even as the Americans—despairing of Diem—withdrew their support and allowed him to fall. Immediately after the announcement of the training team, Barwick set off for a five-week tour of Asia. It was more than four years since Casey's last tour, and Menzies, the interim minister before Barwick, had shown no inclination to visit the region.

Barwick's biographer suggests he was 'won over entirely' by Diem; certainly the minister's effusive statement on returning to Australia showed not a glimmer of doubt about Diem. South Vietnam was presented as 'the focal point of Communist aggressive effort and expansion in South-East Asia'. The war was categorically 'not a civil war. It is a new form of aggression by means of subversion and insurgency directed and equipped by Communist North Viet Nam'. In a telling formulation, which he used in his Cabinet discussion but omitted from his report to parliament, Barwick argued that 'we should regard Vietnam as our present frontier'. Vietnam was thus a case study of the doctrine of Cold War waged by other means. Barwick could find no fault with Diem, and noted no popular discontent or repression. He was 'most impressed' with a model strategic hamlet he was shown at Cu Chi, unaware that this was an area noted as a revolutionary centre and honeycombed with tunnel complexes.

It may have been the 'comprehensive review' by the president which produced the more novel elements in Barwick's understanding. He exaggerated the ethnic difference of the people in the South, whom he described as 'a proud, tough and determined people . . . intensely nationalist and nearly one in every thirteen . . . a refugee from the Communist north. These are not people who will knuckle under easily to the Communists.' This made some sense in terms of the tortuous attempts of Vietnamese Catholic ideology to reinterpret the patriotic past in anticommunist terms—with Vietnam refigured as two nations and two peoples—but was less plausible outside that context.

Finally, referring to the flow of supplies and soldiers from the North to the South—which in this period still consisted largely of Viet Minh who had relocated to the North in 1954 and were returning to aid the struggle in the South—Barwick stated: 'Recruits are obtained by kidnapping and other coercive measures and sent to North Viet Nam for training and indoctrination. Later they come back to form new Viet Cong units.' This dramatised the traffic down the Ho Chi Minh trail, which amounted to a relatively modest 6000 during 1962, at a time when the South Vietnamese regular army numbered well over 100 000.[25] But the claim that these soldiers had been kidnapped was bizarre, a suggestion which, for its glancing relation to reality, could well have come from Diem. Its repetition in all seriousness illustrated something of Barwick's interest in the detail of Vietnamese history.

Marr queries why Barwick's statements on Vietnam were of such 'outstanding, orthodox simplicity . . . His much-vaunted power to look to the heart of problems had apparently deserted him'. Marr's answer was partly that External Affairs failed to provide contrary assessments, but more fundamentally, that Barwick approached the war 'as an advocate', prepared to exaggerate and simplify to make his case, which he put 'apparently without a qualm'. This is a persuasive enough argument, but may be unnecessary. Barwick was not alone in advocating without question the policy which emerged in the early 1960s, and the key ministers—Menzies, Hasluck and Paltridge—were all free of public and, as far as is known, private qualms about the course on which they were set. Striking simplifications of a complex history were a feature of official statements on Vietnam, and that they could be sustained reflected the paucity of debate about foreign policy aims in general and Vietnam in particular.

At the end of 1963, Vietnam was still not central to public political consciousness. In the election of November, in which the conservatives won back most of their majority, government support for Malaysia in its Confrontation with Indonesia was a more significant issue. Vietnam emerged only briefly with Diem's assassination and Barwick's much understated and much quoted epitaph for his rule: 'He was a sincere patriot although some of his internal policies in recent times appeared to have lost him the popular support that was necessary to the continuance of his government.' But Malaysia was the more urgent problem, and Barwick had earlier fitted it into the broader context of Australia's uneasy accommodation to postcolonial Asia when he commented that the establishment of Malaysia in September 1963 'deserves support as a major act of orderly de-colonisation'.[26]

During the election campaign, Barwick gave a brief lesson on the more disorderly aspects of decolonisation to a poorly attended meeting in the Parramatta town hall:

> Barwick had brought along coloured slides to explain his foreign policy. The lights were dimmed and up on the screen came maps of South-East Asia in red, white and blue with arrows to show the downward thrust of Chinese intentions. In the dark, with a pointer in his hand, Barwick gave a short lecture on Vietnam. When the lights came up there was a smattering of applause. The interjectors wandered away.[27]

Marr's description of this desultory event captures some of the somnolence which accompanied Cold War alarm in this period. The election was endorsing a developing policy known only in the vaguest terms.

Conscription, 1964

It was in this political climate that Menzies announced the introduction of a selective system of conscription, which specifically included liability for overseas service, on 10 November 1964. This was part of a Defence statement including a substantial increase to the small Defence budget, mostly devoted to an expansion of the army, with some modernisation of the navy and air force. Despite the later association of conscription and Vietnam, the two were not linked at the time; it was commonly thought more likely that conscripts would be sent to Malaysia.

Menzies' rationale—put to a tense, silent parliament in a speech lasting nearly an hour—was that Australia's strategic position had deteriorated dramatically in the past year. His notes for the speech were stark, itemising 'new elements in 1964' as the political crisis in South Vietnam, 'increased activities—Viet Cong', the 'N. Vietnam attack on USA destroyer' (a reference to the Gulf of Tonkin incident in August), and finally the continuing Confrontation between Malaysia and Indonesia. Menzies argued that conscription was necessary to increase the size of the army for 'a continuing requirement to make forces available for cold war and anti-insurgency tasks', a phrasing which—combined with the explicit reference to overseas postings—made it clear that conscripts were to be used for forward defence. Only the conscription part of the statement broke the silence in parliament, with government backbenchers applauding and Labor members shouting 'Shocking' and 'Oh, no'.[28]

Most commentators saw conscription with Malaysia—and Confrontation with Indonesia—in mind. Speaking in Bendigo a few days later, Calwell condemned conscription as 'a completely unwarranted, unnecessary and unacceptable scheme for service in the jungles of Malaysia and Indonesia'. Geoffrey Fairbairn, whose contacts in the defence establishment were considerable, speculated that the British were 'feeling conscious of "going it alone" ' in Malaysia, even though they were 'frankly fighting for tin and rubber'; he thought this may have led to pressure for Australia to commit troops. It does seem that Malaysia was the conflict uppermost in the mind of Cabinet, although it and Vietnam were both regarded as trouble spots which were 'deteriorating'. There was a certain amount of bureaucratic and political jostling over which of the two problems should be regarded most urgently, with Hasluck in particular arguing that the Americans must be encouraged to intervene in Vietnam. On this logic, the expansion of the Army by conscription indicated that the government hoped to entice American involvement by readying itself to offer military support.[29]

While Menzies made out his case of a strategic deterioration and the necessity of conscription, others were less convinced. The chiefs of staff had earlier in the year seen little threat to Australia and no need to expand the armed forces through conscription; in the weeks before the announcement, the minister for the Army, Dr James Forbes, made it clear that the government's military advisers did not favour conscription. The army's argument was that conscription would not provide the sorts of personnel needed—experienced officers and specialists— and would tie up skilled regular soldiers in the basic training of continuous intakes of conscripts. A week before the decision, *The Age* appeared convinced by this rationale, editorialising that conscription was expensive and would have 'unwelcome repercussions' on the labour market in a time of near full employment.

Menzies always claimed that *The Age* was his favourite newspaper, and some indication of why may have been the pliability with which the paper swung in support of his statement.

Suddenly, its editorial writer was convinced of the deteriorating strategic position, arguing that there were no alternatives to conscription and that Menzies' statement 'must command the attention and support of the nation'. The following day, criticising Calwell's opposition to conscription, the paper linked the expansion of the army to the principle of forward defence:

> The frontiers of our security extend far beyond our shores. In the current situation, where brush-fire conflicts rather than general war are the prospect, the proposed conditions of compulsory service must be accepted as reasonable.

The *Australian*, then in its first year of production, was similarly supportive; the strategic deterioration was 'undeniable', and conscription a necessity.[30]

The daily papers were disinclined to question why conscription was the only method of raising an army when little attempt had been made to increase recruitment through improving pay and conditions. *Nation* was one of the few to debate an alternative, arguing that 'before it takes away the liberty of choice of young men', the government ought to clarify its defence policy, matching this with voluntary methods of recruitment. In May 1964, Cabinet had accepted the arguments against conscription and endorsed a strategy of enlarged voluntary recruitment, chiefly by increasing pay levels. Although by the end of the same year the government was consistently arguing that the limit of voluntary recruitment had been reached, a later study confirmed that pay increases both in 1958 and in early 1964 had produced a prompt and appreciable increase.[31]

If conscription had not convinced some of the government's defence advisers, there were other divisions in ruling circles. The Liberal party room had debated conscription as early as 18 March, without conclusion. Arch-conservatives such as Wilfred Kent Hughes frequently argued for conscription, generally on the grounds of strengthening the moral fibre of the nation. In mid-1963, Howson found himself holding the line against conscription with John Gorton at the Victorian Liberal Country Party state council: 'to no avail . . . one can't sway the council by logic or facts; but they love emotion, and this is an emotional issue'. In addition, some sections of capital were also unenthusiastic; the Victorian Employers' Federation worried that, with full employment, conscription could force up the price of skilled labour.[32]

Against this background, Cabinet conducted a defence review for five days in November 1964, with conscription a major item. The *Australian* reported 'a tense struggle', with members divided over the necessity of conscription. Improving voluntary recruitment had been abandoned as a course. Security needs were now equated with conscription; the opposing arguments referred to labour shortages in the economy and the administrative complex- ities of a selective system. The Defence department was equiv- ocal. Paltridge presented arguments for and against, recommend- ing another effort at increasing voluntary enlistment while setting up the machinery for conscription, should it prove necessary. According to Howson, the department 'waited to see which way the wind was blowing before coming to a decision'.

The direction of the wind was clear enough to Howson on the first day of the review: Menzies, with his treasurer and heir presumptive, Harold Holt, wanted conscription and tailored the strategic arguments to match. Objections were simply overruled. Howson, who as a junior minister (for Air) was only coopted into Cabinet for a defence-related issue such as this, was doubtless somewhat jaundiced at finding himself on the losing side of the argument:

> PM skilfully reassessed the strategic basis to accord with the need for National Service. Harold [Holt] stated that SE Asia might fall within a few months, and that New Guinea might be attacked. Therefore we needed a large army. For the rest of the day and night he carried on, using this premise. It is a false argument. But the PM chiefly for political reasons (to win the Senate especially in NSW) wants National Service. Then he twists the military need to accord with the political need.

'It is,' Howson commented the next day, 'a terribly bad deci- sion.'[33] Ironically, Cabinet was being subjected to similar methods of persuasion as were employed in the government's public rhetoric: dramatic renderings of the strategic situation justified decisions made for other reasons. Howson's is a strong claim from within Cabinet of what the ALP and others at the time suggested: that the introduction of conscription had as much a political as a strategic rationale.

The two rationales which offer possible explanations were the advantages to be gained in Washington and those to be gained over the ALP. The first of these has been mentioned. In effect, with an expanded army, the government would be in a position to offer troops and thus match its own interventionist rhetoric under the 'Hasluck doctrine' of encouraging America into inter- vention. Menzies took the unusual step of having the ambassador in Washington pass a copy of his statement to the President, with Secretary of State Rusk expressing 'his pleasure, particularly with the new combat-ready forces conscription would establish'.[34] But while it fits the trend of policy in the early 1960s, this does not explain why the army could not be expanded by voluntary recruitment.

The second advantage of conscription was perceived to be the discomfort it would give Labor. Conscription was popular with the public at the time, and continued to be so even when conscripts were in Vietnam. Opinion poll support for conscription—in principle, though not for Vietnam—stood at or just below 70 per cent until 1969. This popularity explained Calwell's prompt, if vexed, statement that the introduction of conscription was an 'election stratagem' for the Senate election of early December, intended to create the customary atmosphere of urgency.

It was reported at the time that the government had received 'promptings from inside and out' that conscription would confuse Labor or split its ranks. When debating the issue, Cabinet was said to have had before it an assessment from Liberal strategists that conscription for overseas would be popularly supported by a small majority, and that the policy would 'provoke the Labor Party into either flat opposition or internal dissension, which the Government would be able to exploit electorally'. Labor could again be presented as 'half-hearted' on a defence issue. For its part, the ALP hoped there was a well of 'instinctive' moral opposition to conscription and that the issue might deliver back the Catholic vote they had lost to the DLP. This would prove a vain hope; the church hierarchy strongly supported the war, its antipathy to communism overriding its history of opposition to conscription in the First World War. But there was another, more amorphous factor. As *Nation* explained, while the 'resort to conscription is partly a symptom of conditions of very full employment . . . it also reflects the Government's failure to stir the people to respond otherwise'.[35] An apparent conundrum lay at the heart of the 'atmosphere of crisis and danger' of which Menzies frequently spoke, and which Barwick illustrated with maps to a lethargic audience. In the public culture of the Cold War, high alarm coexisted with deep indifference, apparent strategic threats with the most modest of armed forces, fear with somnolence. It was as though citizens and leaders covertly acknowledged an element of artifice in their fears, an artifice maintained by deference to authority.

The Senate election campaign launched nine days after Menzies' defence statement was fought as a virtual referendum on the conscription and defence issues. Once again, Menzies was able to exploit Labor's apparent vulnerability in the area of foreign policy, claiming to find ambiguities and divisions. Calwell—whose political psyche had been shaped by Labor's heritage of opposition to conscription—opposed the conservatives' policy vigorously and unambiguously. In one of his most effective speeches on conscription, which opened the debate on Menzies' parliamentary statement, Calwell argued that the case for conscription had not been made, that the selectiveness of the system would open the door for privilege and pressure, and that the ALP had no choice but to oppose it. A few days later, in one of his most telling phrases, Calwell called the conscription scheme a 'lottery of death'.

The conservatives' subsequent victory was widely seen as an endorsement of the new defence program, and especially of conscription. One Calwell supporter had to admit that: 'Opposition to conscription got us nowhere.' But in a sentiment that was pure Calwell and foreshadowed some of the period ahead, the same person continued: 'We opposed it because we thought it was wrong . . . Whether the people agreed with us or not was beside the point.'[36] This combination of the ALP's moral and unpopular opposition to conscription with a public opinion diffidently endorsing conscription as appropriate to its fears, appeared an ideal base from which the conservatives could launch their Vietnam intervention. The mould of the Cold War was not yet broken, and arguably did not break for another two years.

At the end of 1964, the conservatives were still firmly in control of the public agenda, with public indifference allowing them substantial freedom of manoeuvre. The baldest and most alarming statements on foreign policy were scarcely challenged in the media or the bureaucracy, and policy decisions were made within as closed a circle as possible, to be laid before the public as inevitabilities. These processes culminated in the commitment of a battalion to Vietnam in April 1965; the decision was made by an inner circle of senior ministers, with apparently uncritical support from External Affairs and without the agonised debate occurring in American official and public circles. This was the culmination of Spender's strategy of encouraging American power in the region and, in the first few months of 1965, key ministers and the ambassador in Washington worked hard to fortify American resolve.[37]

The atrophy of public space which characterised the Cold War began to change as movements mobilised against these two decisions on conscription and Vietnam—decisions which combined only in mid-1966, as conscripts began arriving in Phuoc Tuy. The year 1966 would be regarded as a vintage one for the conservatives, with a popular war, a divided opposition, a visit from an American president and a peace movement grasping for some purchase on public debate. The year ended with their landslide election victory. But it was the last of their vintage years for at least a decade. During 1966, ministers began to worry that they had lost control of the public debate, and with some justice. As a number of small and as yet ineffectual groups cultivated opposition to Vietnam and conscription within civil society, their activity questioned not only the specific policies but the quiet certainties and political arrangements inherited from the Cold War. In the process, they reactivated public discourse. Since these groups built upon the mainstream of a peace movement which had survived through the 1950s, it is necessary to go backwards again before going forwards.

7
The logics of dissent: 1957–1966

From the Split in 1955 to the announcement of conscription in 1964, the peace movement and the left experienced a number of shifts which diluted the ponderous influence of the CPA, began to fracture the peace movement's alignment with Cold War divisions and, to an extent, opened the movement to the participation of the ALP rank and file. Each of these changes was of degree only, but helped reduce the movement's marginality. In 1964, the movement could not be said to be influential; many of the policies of the ALP were closer to those of the conservatives than to those of the peace movement, and the stigma of association with the CPA still held some sway in the public mind. But there had been a subterranean realignment of political forces, which was a precondition for a burst of political activity in 1966.

The peace movement before 1964

One of the most important of these changes was in the relation of the CPA to the peace movement. Many at the time saw the Congress for International Co-operation and Disarmament (CICD) in Melbourne as a turning point signalling a move in

121

from the cold. Held in early November 1959, at the close of the grim decade of the 1950s, it was attended by more than 1000 delegates in a series of autonomous conferences representing scientists, artists and writers, the churches, trade unions and the more heterogeneous 'citizens' conference'. The congress attracted media attention when Casey condemned it as part of a design to advance the cause of world communism; further coverage and some embarrassment resulted when it emerged that Brigadier Spry, the head of ASIO, had taken it upon himself to discourage a Sydney academic from attending as a sponsor.

The organisers went out of their way to develop a broad constituency. The public support of the ACTU and the Victorian ALP was valued. Guest speakers included J.B. Priestley, of the resolutely non-aligned British Campaign for Nuclear Disarmament (CND); Linus Pauling, the American Nobel Prize–winner; Jim Cairns, already moderately well known in peace movement circles; and Macmahon Ball, whose commitment to a rational discourse on Asia had survived the worst of the Cold War. The Reverend Alf Dickie, the congress chairman, had stated its organising principle as being that none would be excluded; *Nation* found 'no evidence that it has been contravened'. The congress was almost entirely organised by the VPC, which remained dominated by the CPA. But as Macmahon Ball wrote—with obvious relish— so shaken had the Party been by the past decade that he could not share Casey's fears of exposure to its influence; such contact was as likely to produce 'a flow from, as a flow towards, Communist convictions'.[1]

In the event, the various sections produced uneven levels of debate and controversy. The scientists produced a declaration advocating an Australian Pugwash association, which reportedly not even the final congress found interesting; the church section argued for total disarmament to be organised through the United Nations or—failing effective agreement—through unilateral initiatives. The youth section was dominated by the CPA's Eureka Youth League, while the citizens' conference was attended by 450 delegates: 'professional men, middle-class housewives, ALP politicians, and such . . .' Their 'statement of findings' included discussion on overseas aid, Aboriginal rights, cultural exchange between countries and the recognition of China.

In a reflection of how seriously the left took cultural activity, the most acrimonious disputes occurred in the artists and writers' section, where, 'led by Judah Waten and Frank Hardy . . . a solid phalanx of communist journalists blocked every attempt to have the conference statement include a non-communist sentiment', particularly on the position of writers in Hungary. The section produced a resolution extolling 'freedom for every true artist'; only a minority supported a tame qualification recognising that 'many writers in a number of countries do not yet have this freedom'.[2]

The significance of the 1959 congress was less in its declarations, which were unremarkable, than in its break with the past. *Outlook* remarked: 'the net effect of it has been to make impossible any more of the bad old Congresses', by which it meant those overburdened by the influence of the CPA. Since its creation in 1957, the journal had represented the non-aligned and self-consciously New Left position of some who had left the CPA; looking back later on the 'stirring days' of 1959, it pointed out that the congress had reflected the state of the Party at the end of the 1950s. The rigidity of earlier peace conferences had been the direct consequence of the polarised view represented by Zhdanov's 'two camps' statement. The 1959 Congress was, by contrast, intentionally broader and more pluralist, though this reflected the views of the Party leadership more than of the rank and file. 'One occasionally had the entertaining spectacle of a leading Communist falling over backwards to allow an independent and critical viewpoint, only to have it squashed by an idiot rank and file.' A similar shift was reflected in the CICD, which was established as a continuing body after November 1959. The CPA continued to be an influential political presence, but it was less hegemonic, with less of the 'leading role' it had claimed for itself in the peace fronts of the 1950s.[3]

Another factor which diluted the CPA's influence was the growth of a small, non-aligned New Left, represented by *Outlook*, by the short-lived Socialist Forums from 1957, and by the later CND groups. *Outlook* was a key indicator of the 'revolt of the intellectuals' which had convulsed the CPA after the Soviet invasion of Hungary and the leadership's dogmatic refusal to countenance discussion. The journal's intellectual inquisitiveness also reflected the prior theoretical dominance of the CPA; outside the Party, there were few other left-wing theoretical positions, which explains *Outlook*'s quality of reinventing socialist theory.

Inevitably this was largely conducted as a discourse against the dogmatism of the CPA. *Outlook* reprinted articles on the British CND and explicitly rejected the Zhdanov doctrine, arguing that coexistence depended on building a 'set of relationships between peoples not possible within the framework of the concept that "the world is divided into two camps"—socialist and capitalist'.[4] *Outlook*'s other interests in the late 1950s reflected changes in this part of the left; 1956 was crucial in its evolution, as was an enthusiasm for the Yugoslav model and the development of a critique of the absence of political democracy in the Soviet Union. Its ideal was a socialist humanism, concerned

At the end of the desolate decade of the 1950s the peace movement was emerging from its marginality and heavy dependence on the CPA. In 1959 the Australian and New Zealand Congress for International Co-operation and Disarmament was widely seen as marking the end of an era, though it was another half-decade before the movement was galvanised by the focus on Vietnam and conscription. (The Age)

with a national and democratic path to socialism. Like the CND groups, it was close to the ALP left, though the relation between the New Left and Labor was closer in Melbourne than in Sydney or elsewhere.

Above all else, this first New Left was defined by its relationship with orthodox communism, a relationship with a number of faces. James Jupp argued that three broad groupings emerged in the New Left, the differences between which reflected their orientation to the Old Left. There were those in Melbourne, such as himself, who saw themselves as social democratic, were anticommunist and antagonistic to the CPA, CICD and, increasingly, to *Outlook* and who, within the ALP, opposed the old guard of the left. In Sydney, there was the original *Outlook* group, which—in Jupp's terms—had left the CPA in disagreement more with its methods than with its ideology. Finally, there were those in Melbourne who had left the CPA and remained 'neutralist' with regard to Marxism. All these New Left groups were to be found in the Fabian societies, in the ALP clubs of Melbourne and Sydney universities and in the CND groups. Along with subscribers to *Outlook* and *Dissent*—in Barcan's happy phrase, this was largely 'a socialism of magazines'—they perhaps numbered 900 people touched by the New Left in Melbourne and half that number in Sydney.[5] These were relatively small forces, fragmented amongst themselves, confined to an intellectual constituency, and focused upon the written word. But they represented a form of politics struggling, in different ways, to shake off the effects of the Cold War.

Inspired by the British model, the first CND group was established in Melbourne in 1960, and others followed in Sydney, Brisbane and Perth in 1962. When they held their first, and only, national congress in Sydney in 1964, they affirmed the 'importance of unilateralism and non-alignment as the two fundamental policies of the CND movement . . .'[6] One Victorian circular declared their position explicitly:

> . . . the VCND is opposed to the whole theory of nuclear deterrence, whether practiced by communists or capitalists. It is non-aligned politically, rejecting all one-sided explanations of the Cold War . . . It is not connected with the World Peace Council.

Consequently, they positioned themselves outside the superpower blocs, and argued that CICD's vision of a bipolar world was a residue of the Cold War. This candid distance from the old peace movement was illustrated when the Victorian CND committee spelt out its relation to CICD: organisationally distinct, it would cooperate with groups like CICD, but would continue to disagree on some points. In particular, the CND groups suspected that CICD was an apologist for the socialist Bomb and retained its alignment to Soviet foreign policy.[7]

The CND groups frequently overlapped with the ALP left: both Cairns and Tom Uren attended the 1964 congress, the former as a speaker. On issues such as the ALP's tortuous decision on the establishment of American bases in 1963, the CNDs campaigned against Labor policy; on other occasions, such as the ALP's support for a nuclear-free southern hemisphere, they were vocal supporters. At Calwell's policy speech in Melbourne in the 1963 election, CND supporters 'demonstrated outside the [Royale] ballroom before the meeting began, and then filed into the hall . . .' They provided 'one of the loudest bursts of applause' for the section of Calwell's speech on the nuclear-free zone.[8]

These groups were noted for their 'special subculture of defiance symbolised by the famous emblem of the drooping cross and by unconventionality in hair and dress styles'. By both their tactics—confrontation and civil disobedience—and their demeanour, they stood out as a 'fringe group' from the mainstream of the peace movement, which retained its concern for respectability. With an intellectual and often young constituency, the CND groups were small but articulate and capable of some influence. After the decision to intervene in Vietnam in 1965, they would promptly merge into the new anti-Vietnam groups and provide much of their initial impetus.

Although on the fringe, the CND groups were a more robust but integral form of the political culture of the peace movement. The high moral seriousness of that movement in the first half of the 1960s is declared in the recurrence of its themes of dissent, of moral duty and of bearing witness—and by its methods of silent protest, quiet deputations and civil disobedience. They spoke gravely of the Bomb and the Atomic Age, of militarism and West German rearmament, of SEATO and the Congo; but their goals of disarmament and peace were often posed in nebulous and distant terms.[9] Alongside its Old Left members, the peace movement had a strong strain of liberal faith in the power of reason, touched with the dissenting traditions of Protestantism; often individualist, its moral economy was one in which individuals must face their conscience and choose to dissent.

In the first half of the 1960s, these strands—directing their attention hopefully towards the ALP, to the point of 'entrism' in CND's case—coexisted with the older peace bodies still associated with the CPA. But the remnants of the peace council period were clearly in a backwater. Formerly the most dynamic of the councils, the VPC between 1960 and late 1962 evinced the tenor of the previous decade. Its financial dependence on left-wing unions was becoming more difficult to sustain, for while the Seamen's Union contributed regularly, the VPC's five volunteers—all women—found the work difficult: '. . . each ship has to be met, a speaker arranged, and literature kept moving to them'. As a result, the VPC increasingly relied on collections conducted in Melbourne's suburbs, both eastern middle-class and inner working-class suburbs.[10]

The VPC's theoretical and political qualities could be seen in a pamphlet published in 1961 in which Victor James reported on a recent trip to North Vietnam. He drew too heavily on the phraseology of his hosts to offer a credible analysis of his own. American support for Diem's 'fascist regime' derived from its desire to control Asian raw materials; but 'since 1954 the people of the South have stood up to fight the Diem regime', and 'generally speaking the entire people of the South are acclaiming the [National Liberation] front and joining it'. James came to the breathtaking conclusion that the struggle for Vietnamese independence 'has been supported by the large majority of the people of the world since 1954'.[11] The tone of the pamphlet suggested credulity, but as importantly, it suggested the propagandist character which the Peace Councils had always been accused of, in which support for a cause became its uncritical partisanship.

Early in 1960, Dorothy Gibson delivered one of her enthusiastic reports to the Peace Council executive. She had long been one of the VPC's most energetic volunteers—archly described by Murray-Smith as 'a fine, single-minded, somewhat simple-minded woman, [who] didn't worry too much about intellectual issues or Soviet labour camps or anything like that . . .' She also illustrated the ways in which the VPC remained attached to the Soviet-dominated WPC: 'The World Peace Council calls us to special action at the time of Summit Talks . . . What can we immediately do for our own independent campaign?' Quite unconsciously, this nicely captured the tension of subservience and independence, of international direction and local action, which had characterised and encumbered the peace movement of the 1950s.

The same lingering attachment was even clearer at the end of 1962, when the VPC met at Sam Goldbloom's home to discuss its future. Goldbloom had been the main organiser of the 1959 congress, and stayed on as CICD's honorary secretary. Given CICD's momentum, the VPC now decided to dissolve itself into an information centre. But should the new centre advertise its links with the WPC? Some thought it 'could be awkward' when approaching academics, but Marion Hartley—the wife of one of the peace parsons—argued successfully for an open association because 'liaison with WPC and seeking to adapt their recommendations to the Australian scene has always been an integral part of VPC activity'.[12]

Given that the new information centre went out of existence a year later, the matter was inconsequential; but it illustrated the lasting political sentiments of the 1950s. Adapting the views of the WPC to the Australian scene had always been an anachronism, though one characteristic of the movement and of Australian communism. By 1962, though, it reflected an attachment to the Soviet model which was no longer particularly persuasive amongst the CPA leadership, let alone in the New Left or groups such as CND. The VPC quietly went out of existence true to its beginnings but as a relic of its times.

CICD had taken up the task which the VPC no longer even understood, and the accusations that the new organisation—like the old—was insufficiently independent continued. Under Goldbloom's rule, CICD was a cautious organisation concerned with respectability, though it remained unwilling to offend the communist bloc. Goldbloom, commented *Outlook*, 'seems unable

to administer any sharp rebuke to the East', in contrast to his
equivalent in Sydney, where the NSW Peace Committee had
managed to cultivate a more vigorous independence: 'The Russian
tests are quite effectively condemned, and a deputation waited
on the Russian Ambassador to tell him so.'

The relative independence of the Sydney peace group partly
reflected an intentional strategy of avoiding the entanglements of
the Cold War; in 1953, Bill Gollan had proposed replacing the
NSW Peace Council with the Committee, precisely because it
shed the association with the Soviet-inspired model of Peace
Councils. One result was that a somewhat different culture was
produced, in which the NSW Peace Committee 'actively encouraged and supported independent bodies in making their contribution as and when they wish'.[13] The rationale was that a more
inclusive peace movement would attract those who might otherwise be dissuaded by Cold War allegations of communist control;
in policy, it resulted in a movement which could take independent
positions, albeit with some difficulty.

In November 1961, when the Soviet Union broke the moratorium on atmospheric nuclear testing, the NSW Peace Committee issued a statement condemning this action, though only after
agonised debate. On the executive,

> . . . two communist members debated the matter for hours with
> other (non-communist) members who insisted that there must be a
> statement . . . The debate had to continue a second night, by which
> time the two [CPA] members had convinced the CPA leadership
> that such a statement would have to be accepted or 'unity for peace'
> would suffer . . .[14]

Although the statement caused scarcely a ripple— there was some
indignation that, after such efforts, the media ignored the statement—it foreshadowed the developing independence of the CPA
itself. But the difficulty of establishing a non-aligned policy
illustrated how slowly the traditional conception of the united
front under the unequivocal 'leadership' of the CPA was dying.

The peace conference held in Sydney in late 1964—which
eventually resulted in the Association of International Co-operation and Disarmament (AICD)—was expected to reflect this
relative independence of the NSW movement. In addition, the
recent growth of CND was expected to attract a younger
constituency, further shifting the centre of gravity away from the
old peace movement. Some 1500 delegates attended, despite
government allegations that this was another CPA front; perhaps
by 1964, such allegations could be counted less relevant. The
conference, concluding just before Menzies' announcement on
conscription, scarcely mentioned Vietnam or conscription; these

issues were still beyond the horizon. Instead, its concerns were the more distant and intangible issues of disarmament, world population and third world poverty.

Turner, at this time with both CND and the ALP left, gave a paper on nuclear-free zones which considered the consequences of the Chinese nuclear weapon, first tested in that year. In his cryptic notes, he argued for a 'transition from [an] aligned to nonaligned, neutralist position—based on [the] belief that more and more areas and nations must be taken out of [the] Cold War context . . .'[15] It was a line of argument which well reflected the developments of the early 1960s, though it clearly lacked the immediacy which was shortly to be injected into foreign policy debates with the dispatch of troops to Vietnam.

The ALP and foreign policy

Immediately after the Split, the Hobart Labor conference had voted for positions which had been inconceivable with the Catholic right still within the party, in favour of the recognition of China and its admission to the UN, and against forward defence in Malaya. It was, as the right came to see it, the beginning of a 'flirtation' with non-alignment and isolationism, though one which was never followed through in a consistent fashion.

Certainly the Split allowed for a thaw in relations with the peace movement which, until 1955, the ALP had attempted to proscribe to its members. As already mentioned, the Australian Assembly for Peace in Sydney in September 1956 marked this change in relations; with the tacit support of the ALP, the conference attracted some 150 ALP members—as individuals or union delegates, rather than as party members—and Evatt, while not attending, was widely quoted in his message to the conference. Labor was even bolder in defending the 1959 congress—the next major peace conference—particularly when it became clear that the government had been embarrassed by the activities of Brigadier Spry. This thaw, however, principally affected rank-and-file members, allowing them a greater flexibility to work alongside CPA members in spheres such as the peace movement. Relations at the leadership level of the two parties remained frosty and wary, particularly as—between 1956 and 1959—the CPA leadership lurched back to its sectarian dogmatism in response to the convulsions of 1956.[16] By the early 1960s, the ALP leadership had, if anything, moved further away from the positions of the left.

In February 1960, Evatt announced his resignation from the

Labor leadership to take up the position of chief justice of NSW. As one of those who opposed him in the party uncharitably put it: 'There was a sigh of relief throughout the Parliamentary Labor Party. It was the end of a nightmare.'[17] Calwell was elected leader and Whitlam—precociously in the opinion of many—his deputy. Daly's sigh of relief was premature, as the ALP entered a period of rivalry between Calwell and Whitlam, which was overt by 1963, when Whitlam made it clear he thought his time had come, and which lasted until 1967. The leadership struggle fundamentally coloured the ways in which the ALP debated and presented its policies on Vietnam and conscription; the conflict forced Calwell, by 1965, further to the left than he was comfortable with and muddied foreign policy discussions with other tensions, such as Whitlam's plans for party reform. It meant that the ALP stumbled clumsily through the 1960s debate on Vietnam.

By 1963, the ALP had abandoned any suggestion that its 1955 decisions meant a move towards isolationism; one effect of the Cold War, and of continual electoral losses on foreign policy issues, was that the ALP substantially accepted the terms of foreign policy debate set by the conservatives. This was clearest in 1963, when two federal conferences reversed the earlier disapproval of the Malayan commitment and endorsed the principle of forward defence. At least on the right of the party, there was a basic acceptance of government principles in foreign policy development.

Labor agreed that the strategic threats in Southeast Asia had intensified and that an expansionist China was the major problem, and it argued strongly for the necessity and value of the American alliance. The belief that China menaced American security

> . . . tended to influence spokesmen such as Whitlam, Calwell, Galvin and Beazley [senior] . . . It was important to them that America should not be humiliated in Vietnam to an extent where the long term guarantees they believed were offered by the Americans were damaged.

As a result, the ALP was largely supportive of American actions in Vietnam until the large-scale military intervention in early 1965. After the Gulf of Tonkin incident in August 1964, both Calwell and Whitlam were emphatic in their support, believing that the Americans must negotiate from strength and that American intervention in the region best served Australia's regional interests.[18] In effect, until 1965, the leadership was able to dominate foreign policy debate within the ALP. The high point of this support for American and Australian government policies came in February 1965: with the intention of forcing the North Vietnamese to the negotiating table, the Americans began the

Arthur Calwell was leader of the ALP in opposition from 1960 to 1967, while his deputy, Gough Whitlam, waited with increasing impatience. The rivalry between the two coloured the ways in which the ALP presented and articulated its policy on Vietnam. Calwell was sentimentally pro-American yet his political psyche had been formed in Labor's anti-conscription tradition: Whitlam was determined that Labor should win votes on social issues rather than lose them on foreign policy. (National Library of Australia, portrait collection)

systematic bombing of North Vietnam which would later be known as 'Operation Rolling Thunder'. A statement by Labor's federal Caucus executive accepted that 'the American action of recent days' was 'based on the aim of shortening the war and achieving a negotiated settlement'. The statement went on to reject a Soviet demand for the immediate withdrawal of foreign troops, because its consequence

> . . . must be a Communist take-over of South Vietnam, snuffing out the hope of freedom and democratic independence in that country and extending the area of Communist control closer to this country.

In Caucus, Cairns's opposition to this statement was overridden and the resolution, drafted by Beazley, was endorsed. Labor's support for the bombing was based on the evident conviction that American attempts to negotiate a settlement were genuine;

the statement was welcomed by Calwell with 'unqualified delight'.[19]

Against this background, the government announced—on 29 April 1965—its decision to commit an infantry battalion to Vietnam. Five days later, the Labor Caucus was immediately united in its opposition. With a draft of his parliamentary speech in hand, Calwell sketched what his general approach would be; his argument for opposing intervention was unanimously agreed to without discussion. Yet this reversal of the drift of Labor policy is largely unexplained. What had gone before—Labor's support for troops in Malaya, its endorsement of forward defence, its support for the American bombing—would all suggest that it might agree to an intervention in Vietnam. Yet, as Graham Freudenberg put it: 'No significant member of the Labor Party ever suggested that there could be any attitude other than opposition.'

Some of Labor's sentiments account for the change. Many Labor figures had assumed in hope that the American bombing would be enough to force a negotiated settlement in Vietnam, and that it would never come to military intervention. In addition, there was a long-standing suspicion in Labor circles of sending troops overseas, and the party had, until recently, opposed the troop commitment in Malaya; as importantly, Calwell's correct prediction that conscripts must soon be in Vietnam added a dimension with deep taproots in Labor history. But to some extent Labor's unanimous opposition obscured the balance of forces inside the parliamentary party. The intensity of Calwell's opposition was unchallengable, generated from the collision of his passion for America with his hatred of conscription. There was nobody on the right strong enough to present an opposing view; the right was disorganised, seemingly unable to temper Calwell's headlong rush, which swept the Caucus along even though some had misgivings. Finally, unanimous opposition to the dispatch of troops helped obscure the marked divisions over the question of the timing and manner of their withdrawal should Labor come to office, and this was the rock upon which Labor's Vietnam policy would founder for the rest of the decade.

Labor's opposition in the parliamentary debate which followed papered over these differences. Calwell's speech—in the view of Freudenberg, who wrote it—reflected Labor's basic opposition about Vietnam but also its continuing confusion about withdrawal. Calwell made much of the implication that conscripts would soon be in Vietnam, argued that it was not in Australia's interests to have America humiliated in Asia, and now accepted that Labor's opposition would not be electorally popular. Cairns's stature on the question of Vietnam was signalled when he was appointed to follow Calwell in the debate; he was also one of two people consulted in the drafting of Calwell's speech. As he told his biographer, after reading the draft, he 'pointed out that it made no reference to withdrawing Australian troops. Calwell said, "We're not going to take that on. We'd be giving them a stick to beat us with." ' Cairns then suggested the formula used in the speech: 'Labor would work to have the decision to send troops to Vietnam reversed. Cairns penned the formula in the margin of Calwell's draft and Calwell agreed to it.'[20] Labor's position, so hastily arrived at, seemed at first glance to be unequivocal, but the stresses of the leadership struggle would open up its uncertainties during 1965 and 1966, culminating in the election defeat in 1966.

The decision to send troops had now polarised the parties and ended Labor's attempts at bipartisanship in foreign policy, which had been an attempt to defuse its complexities. Government policy on Vietnam was now clearly in the hands of 'hard-liners', as Maxwell Newton pointed out, with Paltridge in Defence, Hasluck in External Affairs and Menzies as Prime Minister: 'Australia may come to regret the lack of an alternative voice' on issues of defence and foreign affairs. Hasluck was regarded as ideologically committed, 'a proponent of the hard line, of the intransigent opposition to what he sees as the pervading threat of Chinese power in the world'. Paltridge was widely recognised as tough and equally intransigent, although he had little of Hasluck's intellectual ability; Howson, who worked under him as minister for Air, found him 'a slow worker', with whom 'every interview is pretty frustrating'.

The final planning in early 1965 for a military commitment to Vietnam was made by these three ministers, along with John McEwen (as Country Party leader), Holt (as treasurer) and McMahon (as minister for Labour and National Service). Together they formed the Foreign Affairs and Defence committee of Cabinet, which had been created in early 1963, and quickly concentrated decision-making power in a relatively few hands. Even a junior minister in the defence area, such as Howson, was excluded; the first he heard of plans to send a battalion was one week before the announcement. The decision on intervention in Vietnam was made without debate in Cabinet, let alone in the institutions of media, parliament and bureaucracy, and illustrated something of the closed nature of public debate. As Newton dryly put it: 'The Menzies style of government does not allow much room for lesser beings.'[21] Labor's sudden, if fragile, unanimity on Vietnam was important in this context in contributing to the development of that debate.

Cairns

Labor's leaders approached Vietnam from different perspectives. Calwell had the most internal conflict, being attached to a number of conflicting themes which Vietnam raised: 'the fear of China, the persecution of Catholics, racial contempt for Asians and the dream of the American century'. Only the dispatch of conscripts to Vietnam clarified things, given Calwell's truly visceral opposition to conscription.[22] Whitlam, by contrast, saw Vietnam in terms of its potential damage, strategically to America's role in Asia and electorally to the ALP. Each theme suggested caution. Cairns developed an opposition to the war which was more intellectually complex, and linked it with themes of the legacy of the Cold War and the nature of Asian revolution. As the acknowledged leader of the Labor left, especially on foreign policy, he illustrates a process in which the Labor left was negotiating its way out of the Cold War.

In the introduction to his survey of Vietnamese history, first published in 1969, Cairns sketched his developing engagement with Vietnam. In the mid-1950s, the Diem government 'appeared to me to be nationalist and effective'; when Diem visited Australia in 1957, however, Cairns was 'alarmed by his assumptions of god-like purposes'. It was not until 1963, when Diem's repression of the Buddhists attracted attention, that Cairns feared the conflict might develop into a world crisis, with America committed to 'a holy war' and with the likelihood of both Australia and China becoming involved. This was the catalyst for an early involvement in debate on Vietnam. By 1965, Cairns was well informed and active; he estimated that between 1964 and 1966 he had addressed more than 600 meetings on Vietnam.[23] During 1965, he published *Living with Asia*. For the period, it was a considerable achievement, a sophisticated attempt to link the political legacy of the Cold War in Australia with the intervention in Vietnam. In it, Cairns developed four main themes, along with a brief analysis of recent Vietnamese history.

The first and most important theme dealt with revolutionary social change in Asia. Cairns argued that the 'emergence' of Asia 'from a thousand years and more of poverty and national impotence' was an inevitable and historically necessary process. It was a social revolution that was dynamic, irreversible and demanded recognition. In this, Cairns reinvigorated Labor's sympathy for Asian postcolonial movements which—as represented by Burton and Chifley—welcomed social and economic change, though curiously Cairns did not mention this heritage. Calwell occasionally made a similar point—that Asian revolution was a

By the mid-1960s Jim Cairns was an acknowledged leader of the ALP left. He argued indefatigably that intervention in Vietnam was taking sides against Asian revolution and represented both the political conformism of the Cold War and a refusal to be part of Asia. Although later identified as the 'leader' of the Moratorium movement, Cairns was somewhat apart from that movement—a public patron standing awkwardly above the ruck of the factions. (National Library of Australia, portrait collection)

good thing, especially for Asians—but could give the theme none of Cairns's intellectual reflection, nor rid his formulations of the whiff of fear and racism.

With Cairns, there was a sense of historical dynamism, of movements engaged in a massive but comprehensible social struggle. The revolution was necessary; what was needed were policies which recaptured the dynamic of history from communist movements, changing revolutionary wars into 'peaceful social revolutions'. Policy must be directed not at

> . . . stopping all change in the name of anti-Communism, but at making all the necessary changes so that force may be taken out of the situation and the necessary national revolutions may become as peaceful as possible.

Buried here was an echo of the ALP's vain attempts in the 1950s to maintain the distinction between communist and nationalist movements, though again, Cairns scarcely considered the difference.

More curious still was his portrayal of an Asia 'emerging'

from a past which had few features; the colonial period was
much less distinct for Cairns than it had been for Chifley,
Spender or Burton. He gave little attention to the dynamics of
decolonisation as part of this 'emergence'. It was simply a struggle
out of centuries of 'poverty and ignorance to national existence,
economic strength and human dignity', with little sense of the
structuring of social relations and political movements by colonial
rule. He discussed the colonial period in Vietnam only in the
vaguest terms, as though all colonial experiences were the same.
Despite these shortcomings, the logic of Cairns's argument was
compelling. In the end, what remained most distinctive about
Living with Asia was its historical tone—a tone both Promethean
and unafraid. His conclusion on American and Australian policy
on Vietnam reflected this: that policy had set its face against
irreversible change in Asia. 'We are taking sides in history.'

In the middle of the book sat three chapters on Vietnamese
history, largely since Geneva. One focused entirely on the claims
of Northern infiltration of the South since 1959, laboriously
picking over the evidence and reflecting the centrality of 'aggression from the north' to the government's case for intervention.
Cairns's conclusions were straightforward enough, but surefooted
ahead of much Australian analysis. He argued that Vietnam's was
'a revolutionary war determined mainly by the history and
conditions of Vietnam, and influenced only marginally by arms
and men from North Vietnam and other Communist countries'.
The roots of this revolution lay, as in the rest of 'emergent' Asia,
in social needs and social structures.

Cairns's second theme followed from his embrace of Asian
social change: a policy of forward defence, designed to thwart
or make orderly this Asian 'emergence', was unjustified. At the
very least, it destroyed the necessary distinction between offence
and defence, involving the claim to station armed forces on
territory over which no sovereignty could be claimed. Such
military interventions—intended 'to check or control social
revolutions'—miscalculated the threat indigenous revolutions
involved, could not expect to be effective in 'defeating or
suppressing a national revolution', and damaged Australia's relations with Asia. Finally, forward defence involved 'a degree of
pretension beyond the capacity of a small nation to discharge'.[24]

This last point was left hanging. Cairns did not discuss the
obvious rejoinder from a proponent of forward defence, that it
was only meaningful within great-power alliances, but that as
long as these alliances were maintained, tokens had to be
forthcoming. This may have been the weakest point in the
analysis, involving what was, for Labor, the sensitive issue of the
American alliance. Labor was acutely aware of a need to avoid

the appearance of being anti-American in its opposition to the Vietnam policy. Its dilemma was always how to oppose the war without opposing America. For Calwell or Whitlam, this meant arguing that intervention in Vietnam was not in America's best interests; Cairns asserted the need for more independent policy-making while attempting to avoid the anti-Americanism of the peace movement.

His third theme sought to negotiate around these difficulties by hinting at an argument the ALP would expand throughout the 1960s. Effectively, there were two Americas, one of the military–industrial complex and the other of the continuing American Revolution. As Cairns put it in 1971, at the high tide of the left's anti-Americanism:

> The struggle for human progress is more acute in America than anywhere in the world . . . If we are to take sides in this matter we cannot take sides for or against America. We must take part in the American struggle.

In *Living with Asia*, this sentiment was less dialectical. America was referred to as the location of 'the most humane and advanced thinking anywhere in the world about international relations and economic organisation', with an 'astonishing capacity for change and adaptation'. But this effusive endorsement was not yet Cairns's later identification with radical and republican traditions in American political thought, and was not yet a plausible means of diverting protest on the war away from anti-Americanism. As Freudenberg noted, in 1965 the concept of the two Americas was 'extraordinarily difficult to sell', though after the Tet Offensive of 1968 it became more plausible.[25]

Cairns's final theme was more amorphous, dealing with the place of fear in the public culture of the Cold War. The logic of forward defence was one of fear, particularly fear of China. Cairns was here not arguing about the substance of a threat from an expansionist China, but about the debilitating effects of irrationality in political culture: 'If we are to face real dangers frankly and realistically, we must stop fearing fear.' He appeared ready to accept the need for deterrence—although he had the word in inverted commas—and only America had the military might to perform the task; but deterrence meant not 'two powerful, nuclear-armed countries glaring at one another with hatred and suspicion like scorpions in a bottle', but the capacity to negotiate and de-escalate a crisis. 'Common sense shows that the United States and China must be brought closer together and not forced further apart.' In policy, this meant recognition of China and the use of the offices of the United Nations; in social theory, it signified a rationalist notion of the uses of power.

A similar rationalism informs Cairns's scattered remarks on the role of fear in Australian public life; the 'obsessional and anachronistic view of Communism' which underlay fears of Asian revolution not only distorted perceptions of Australian interests in Asia but induced indifference and withdrawal. It was 'an attempt to contract out of responsibilities, an attempt to withdraw from something—Communism—that is treated as if it were untouchable'. Although he was far from sympathetic to the CPA, Cairns was less sympathetic to irrational anticommunism, because the mix of fear and indifference combined to produce a political climate which restricted the prospects for all radicals.

This was an incipient cultural critique of what was thought of as the 'conformism' of suburban culture after a decade of affluence and Cold War. Cairns had a sense that this involved material prosperity, the culture of the suburbs, an absence of political independence and a ruling class which derived its ideas from Britain and America. Radicalism seemed alien and out of place when everyday life was dominated by the 'mass conformity' of the suburbs.[26] Australian public culture had produced the numbing combination of fear and indifference, and this sense of paralysis pervades parts of the book, contrasting with the energy of its description of change in Asia.

The best location for this attempt to understand the public culture of the Cold War is in the contemporaneous debates on suburbia and Australian culture. A number of intellectuals in the early 1960s were discussing the cultural and political effects of the expansion of suburban patterns during the previous two decades. Amongst liberal and conservative intellectuals such as Donald Horne, Peter Coleman and Craig McGregor, suburban existence was seen as simultaneously authentic and depoliticised, both affluent and impoverished. Radical intellectuals such as Turner and Alan Ashbolt tended to see suburban life less ambiguously—as the cultural wasteland in which an Australian Legend of a vigorous and left-leaning male culture had withered away, replaced by mass culture imported from America. While the right patronisingly applauded the authenticity of suburbia, the left despaired of it. Cairns reflects this debate in his argument that the fear of Asia was part of suburban quietism, as much a form of withdrawal as genuine alarm, and others would later point to the same conundrum: intervention in Vietnam was the obverse of isolationism, because both expressed a refusal to be part of Asia.[27]

But this link should not be exaggerated, because nothing distinguished Cairns so much as his lack of explicit connections with other writers, other traditions. He took his typewriter on holidays, and it was on one such occasion that he wrote *Living with Asia.* The image of isolation and of earnestness is appropriate. Cairns did not mention writers on suburbia any more than he discussed Labor's traditions on nationalism, colonialism or the United Nations. He appeared a man without influences, the autodidact reinventing theory rather than relying on others, just as he refused to depend on others in the peace movement, a trait which his biographer characterised as an 'almost obsessive self-reliance'. McGregor's portrait captured a similar, if more grandiose quality of detachment from the movement in which he was involved.[28] It was this quality in Cairns which most unnerved conservatives when they debated him in parliament and out—his dispassionate commitment made him a relentless adversary.

The high moral seriousness which so obviously lay behind Cairns's views helps explain his authority within the movement which mobilised during 1965 and 1966. Radical earnestness had always been a part of the peace movement's self-identity. Cairns's role in the movement became that of patron and public intellectual. He was available to speak to public meetings on a seemingly inexhaustible basis, and in speaking could articulate a detailed analysis of the war rather than simply apply to it more diffuse and universal theories of imperialism or liberation or pacifism. While for many others, Vietnam took on the quality of a metaphorical archetype, Cairns could lay claim to being one of the better-read in the movement against the war, and certainly in the parliament. In speaking on Vietnam, he could also connect it with critical theories of Australian culture, 'conformism' and the Cold War, which resonated with the alienation felt by much of the peace movement and later by many in the New Left. If this remained an underdeveloped analysis and lacked a social theory to give it momentum, it nevertheless enabled Cairns to begin to link themes of foreign policy and Asian 'emergence' with an understanding of the political culture which frustrated rational and measured debate on Asia.

8
1966: The Cold War mould cracks

The politics of conscience

The mobilisation of 1965 and 1966 reflected a development of new peace groups; the difference from the movement of the 1950s was marked. Where before there had been one monolithic movement, largely directing the agenda and deciding how issues would be framed, now there were competing groups with a variety of constituencies and tactics. Their activity reanimated a public sphere which had atrophied during the Cold War; yet, as they saw it themselves, they were struggling against fear and indifference.

This proliferation of constituencies was illustrated in an open-air concert of protest against the war organised at the Myer Music Bowl in Melbourne in November 1965. The organisers estimated that between 8000 and 10 000 people attended, although neither television nor newspapers reported the event. The program consisted of folk songs interspersed with speeches from such figures as Cairns and the Rev. David Pope, the former president of VCND who was now president of the Vietnam Day Committee (VDC). The groups sponsoring the concert included

140

The Save Our Sons groups formed in mid-1965, opposing conscription and drawing on a small constituency of middle-class mothers. With embroidered sashes and silent vigils, they represented a demure but resolute use of public space. Above The Brisbane group demonstrates against the imprisonment of conscientious objector Bill White in November 1966, and below the Sydney group protests against the LBJ visit in October of the same year. These two branches were close to the established peace movement, while in Melbourne a more 'bohemian' SOS drew support from the ALP. (National Library of Australia, SOS papers)

VCND, the Victorian ALP, CICD, three groups from Melbourne University—the CND, Folk Music Club and Democratic Socialist Club—and the Youth Campaign Against Conscription (YCAC). In addition, the Melbourne Save Our Sons (SOS) group was involved.

SOS reflected the activation of a relatively new constituency— predominantly middle-class women who had generally not taken part in politics before. In Sydney, the first group was formed in May 1965, its sole focus being opposition to conscription. The tone was set by its first minuted meeting, with 'twenty mothers' present, and discussion of the need to 'preserve our reputation' from 'slanderous remarks about SOS' which had been made on radio. The meeting also touched on a confusion which the group was not to clarify until mid-1966, that 'the issue at stake is conscription and not Vietnam, but anywhere overseas at all for conscripts'. For some time, SOS members would refuse to speak on Vietnam when invited.[1]

Shortly after the first Sydney meeting, a letter arrived from Melbourne expressing interest in 'forming a branch of your SOS group . . . As we have no previous experience to guide us, we would value your suggestions as to the best way to start'. The Melbourne group, largely instigated by Jean McLean, was formed on 18 August, at a meeting held in the Assembly Hall and attended by some 50 women. They were addressed by Nola Barber, president of the Victorian ALP Women's Central Organising Committee, as well as Alan Roberts from Monash University and Glen Tomasetti, the folk singer. This established a pattern of close association between the Melbourne SOS and the Victorian ALP. Before joining SOS, only a few of its key members were politically active; by 1967, most were involved in the ALP.[2]

In Sydney, it was not the ALP but AICD which most supported SOS; the group met in a room provided in the AICD offices, for which it paid a small monthly rent, and there was some cooperation in joint activities and meetings. On occasion, AICD paid the legal expenses of conscientious objectors assisted by SOS. The other SOS groups illustrated other regional varia- tions: in Newcastle and Wollongong, the groups were quite active from late 1965, and benefited from strong local unionism, while Brisbane had a small branch which met in the Quakers' Meeting House and was closely associated with the Union of Australian Women. A Perth group held its first public meeting in March 1966 though, curiously, all its correspondents to the Sydney group were men; South Australia had a group from September 1966, though it found the fragmentation of the Adelaide peace movement difficult to contend with.

SOS represented a distinctly genteel use of public space; its members wore blue and white sashes to identify their cause, and their language was that of a faith in liberal democracy and the piercing light of rational argument. They spoke of having truth on their side and 'bearing witness' in public. Like the American group Another Mother for Peace, SOS was also mobilising conventional sentiments of women's 'caring, peace-loving and nurturing qualities' in the service of opposition to war and conscription. Its representation of women, half a decade before the growth of the women's movement, was a relatively conventional one, but its members also developed a tactical sense of maintaining an image of respectability to avoid being dismissed as militants.

Compared with the Sydney group, the Melbourne one had more of a 'bohemian' character, drawing in middle-class women from suburbs peppered with pottery and art classes. Photographs of the Sydney group show tiny clusters of women in twin-sets and sashes, resolute but terribly isolated. Their cause, but also their political tenor, struck a chord with some of the Old Left with a long opposition to conscription. The crew of the *SS Lake Torrens* was suitably archaic in its language: 'It is our opinion that the SOS movement is a valiant movement deserving of the highest commendation and most worthy support.' Support from some leftist unions for the Sydney group came, during 1966, in the form of small donations, but was never substantial.[3]

The forms of protest SOS developed were impressively decorous: the silent vigil outside army depots at the induction of conscripted youths, and deputations to members of parliament. These were very small events, particularly in the first few years; in August 1965, fifteen women took part in a vigil in Martin Place in Sydney, handing out leaflets and receiving only one inquiry as a result. In 1966, the Melbourne group planned a silent vigil and instructed its members:

> . . . we will assemble in the Treasury Gardens around our Flag. We will carry NO PLACARDS. We will wear our sashes . . . Our most orderly demonstrations have been the most effective. We will be silent, walk or stand in line, and only the spokeswoman for the day will speak to press, police or public.[4]

This mobilised an interesting symbolism, using silence to break what was seen as the silence of a public unwilling to dispute or dissent.

The political demeanour of YCAC was quite different. The Sydney group was formed as early as November 1964, after a public meeting compiled a mailing list of those willing to campaign against conscription. Its first public campaign—an advertisement in the *Australian* on 19 June 1965—objected to

conscription for overseas service and argued for peace negotiations in Vietnam. In July, YCAC was in close contact with SOS,
and the two worked together until the end of 1966. The
Melbourne YCAC was formed in August 1965 at a small meeting
of 40 people held in a Carlton coffee lounge run by the Young
Labor Association, and branches were started shortly after in
Brisbane, Perth and Canberra. These YCAC groups substantially
overlapped with the ALP, and in general identified with Calwell's
position on conscription; based particularly in the universities,
they mobilised a student constituency for the ALP. The four
office-bearers who established YCAC in Melbourne were all
members of the Young Labor Association, and five of the Sydney
executive's six members were also ALP members. The CPA's
Eureka Youth League had some small involvement and, in
Melbourne, CICD provided some administrative support, but
YCAC's basic alignment was with the ALP.

YCAC drew on the CND methods of civil disobedience,
particularly in the form of burning 'draft cards'—in fact, registration papers—and satirising government leaders. It had jazz
bands at its public meetings and rallies, whose occasional flam-
boyance at least offered some prospect of breaking into a
generally disapproving media. In March 1966, YCAC staged a
demonstration outside the Toorak home of prime minister Holt—
a keen spearfisherman—wearing snorkelling gear and carrying a
fish inscribed 'Conscript' with a placard reading: 'Stick to killing
fish, Harold.' But YCAC's strategy, and its use of civil disobedience, was limited; it involved burning 'draft cards' but then
using the available channels of conscientious objection to evade
conscription, rather than the later development of active non-
compliance with the conscription system.[5] During 1966, it
focused all its energies on assisting Labor's campaign for the
November election, and with Labor's defeat, it went into eclipse.

YCAC and SOS were both relatively new constituencies; a
third major constituency was brought into the movement by the
CND groups, which had been active since the early 1960s. These,
as might be expected from their past, developed an early critique
of the intervention in Vietnam, organising demonstrations in June
1965 and reprinting part of Cairns's pamphlet 'The Truth about
Vietnam', itself drawn from *Living with Asia*. By late 1965, the
CND groups were entirely preoccupied with Vietnam and conscription, which gave their established disarmament concerns a
sharp focus: 'The problem of the Vietnam war is the biggest
threat to today's uneasy world balance . . .' As they saw it, the
peace movement had 'in witness and frustration . . . moved into
public view'.

CND activists were the driving force behind the first com-

The Youth Campaign Against Conscription groups formed in 1964–65 and were closely allied to the ALP's Young Labor Association, with some CPA involvement. YCAC's use of humour, civil disobedience and calculated irreverence signalled a break from the established peace movement's search for respectability. Here they satirise the prime minister's passion for spearfishing. (Australian, 21 March 1966)

mittees coordinating protest on Vietnam and conscription—in Sydney, the Vietnam Action Campaign (VAC), established at a public meeting in August 1965, and shortly afterwards, in Melbourne, the Vietnam Day Committee (VDC), formed at a meeting in Assembly Hall in September. There was a substantial overlap between the executives of VDC and VCND, though the new group also had representatives from CICD, SOS, YCAC, the churches and some unions. By mid-1966, the VDC represented eighteen different organisations, although the core activists remained those of VCND.[6]

Small as they were, these groups contributed to a remarkable reactivation of the public sphere during 1966. There was a proliferation of local activities: public meetings at which government and opposition speakers put their cases, small marches and demonstrations, group discussions in lounge rooms, meetings in country towns, 'teach-in' debates at the universities, 'preach-ins' in the radical churches and public rallies in town halls. As the election approached, a new mood of buoyancy and militancy developed, and virtually unqualified support was given to the ALP, with its apparent policy of withdrawal from Vietnam. In the context of the Cold War, this activity was a significant rupture and can be taken as a marker of the end of the Cold War paralysis of public debate.

But it was still a transitional period, in which the public culture remained inhospitable to dissent. Cairns had suggested something of this in trying to explain why a radical culture was thwarted and why rational debate on Asia was so difficult. The recurrence of the themes of 'bearing witness' and of 'breaking silence' signified this difficulty. One reflection was in the way that dissent on the war was framed as an individual responsibility, as the necessity of putting loyalty to one's conscience before loyalty to the state. Early in 1965, shortly before the Vietnam intervention was announced, Goldbloom spoke of the 'barrier of silence' on Vietnam, commending a recent, critical statement of thirteen bishops as being the first to 'break through and assist in creating the necessary national debate'. 'In the face of the dangers inherent in the Vietnam situation the only treason is that of indifference and silence.'

Similarly, the CND newsletter spoke ominously of the 'generalised innuendo directed at the peace movement' and said the right to dissent was under threat. It interpreted a call from the minister for Labour and National Service, McMahon, for 'liberty marches' by supporters of the government's policy, as a possible prelude to the stifling of all public opposition; McMahon's call was more likely a sign of conservative exasperation with public dissent, and significantly, there were never substantial pro-war actions as there were in America. But *Sanity* rolled all these concerns into one grim image of the public culture.

> This then is the coming storm, with its gusts of wind snatching at shreds of evidence, its rain battering down the silent, cowered community, its lightning striking out and illuminating where there is danger of opposition. And thunder roaring to tell the world that the Australian people are 'one-hundred percent' behind the Government.[7]

Melodramatic though it was, this expressed a sentiment shared widely in the peace movement that the public culture was intolerant of dissent.

SOS encountered more prosaic but equally significant instances of the difficulty of speaking in opposition; its experience involved overcoming both the inherited culture of the Cold War and the public silence conventionally expected of women. The activists of SOS stoically overrode such difficulties, but some of their correspondents were plaintive and frightened. One woman wrote to ask for help with a debate on Vietnam which she had suggested to her school Mothers' Club: 'Having made the first move, I realise that I'm the one who has to put the whole case *against* the war in Vietnam, and I am a bit frightened of the responsibility . . .' Could a speaker come and, 'if not take over the responsibility, then support me, as I think this is a terrific opportunity and I would hate to mess it up'.

The SOS secretary congratulated her on her courage, replying: 'I and another SOS are willing to come along.' They were 'terribly busy . . . —and yet must do the usual home duties—so let me know full details . . .' Some ten days later, another letter arrived to say that the Mothers' Club discussion had been cancelled: 'The Mothers objected to the two "non-political, non sectarian" groups getting together. However I hope that something else will eventuate, perhaps a public meeting.'[8] In the everyday life of the middle classes, the decorous fear of controversy could be as repressive as the fear of communism.

In the opinion polls which attempted to plumb the political mood, the solidity of conservative sentiment was revealed. The intervention in Vietnam was popular in these years. In September 1966, 61 per cent of the population agreed with 'continuing to fight in Vietnam', an increase from 56 per cent in the previous year; 27 per cent favoured 'bringing our forces back', a slight decline from 28 per cent in 1965. By May 1967, the war was even slightly more popular. Opinion on the desirability of conscription in general was very similar, with a solid majority in favour and about a quarter of the population against. (See Appendix) On the specific issue of conscripts in Vietnam, however, there was more to cheer opponents of the war: between late 1965 and late 1967, a bare majority regularly opposed conscripts being sent to Vietnam.[9]

An emphatic public demonstration of the popularity of the war occurred in June 1966, when the 1st Battalion—which had been based in Bien Hoa since mid-1965—returned to a parade through Sydney's streets. The *Australian* claimed half a million turned out for this 'excited, emotional heroes' welcome'. Casey, as governor-general, took the salute as '. . . office workers showered the men with a stream of paper, streamers, confetti and ticker-tape . . . Children waved hundreds of Australian flags and many spectators carried banners welcoming the troops.' As the soldiers passed the town hall, several women rushed out to throw paper roses in front of them; another woman, covered

The popularity of the war was shown by a ticker-tape parade in Sydney's Martin Place welcoming home the 1st Battalion in June 1966. At this stage, some 60 per cent of the population supported the war, while a quarter favoured withdrawal. Yet the opposition movement seemed unable to claim a public presence showing this support: only one woman protested against the momentum of this massive parade, smearing some of the soldiers with red paint in an isolated protest. (Australian, 9 June 1966)

with red paint, ran amongst the soldiers to smear a few with paint. It was 'the only isolated protest'.

Charged with offensive behaviour, Nadine Jensen later told the court that her lone action was 'directed against Australian Complacency and apathy about Vietnam'. The magistrate, reprimanding her for not showing her feelings 'in a proper way', especially when aimed at gallant men returning from overseas, queried whether a psychiatric examination was in order before imposing a small fine and a good behaviour bond.[10] The isolation of this act in the midst of a ticker-tape parade—and against the dead weight of military traditions—was a good illustration of the apparent marginality of protest. The peace movement had the support of more than a quarter of the population in its opposition to both Vietnam and conscription in general, and of a bare majority in opposition to conscription for Vietnam, yet it could not claim an influence on the public agenda proportionate to this support.

A pamphlet war

Such cross-currents partly explain the irresolution of Labor's position. In May 1966, SOS reflected this uncertainty: 'In view of Mr. Calwell's latest statement on the Conscription issue, I think it would be as well for S.O.S. to write to him, asking what actually is his policy.' Irresolution arose partly from Calwell's increasingly tenuous position: besieged, his leadership under challenge from Whitlam, he found himself caught between his support for American interests and his increasing reliance on the left for support against Whitlam.[11]

In May 1966, the foreign affairs committee of the Labor Caucus adopted a resolution which formed the basis of policy for the November election. A Labor government would withdraw conscripts 'without delay, acting with full regard to the safety and security of the Australian force'. For the regular troops, Labor would—in a fine series of qualifications—'have regard to the situation in Vietnam as it exists at the time and to the importance of maintaining future cooperation with the United States'; no action would be taken without consultation, but Labor would insist on withdrawal 'as soon as practicable'. In addition, the bombing of the North should cease, and intervention be turned into a 'holding operation' while peace was negotiated, with recognition of the NLF as a party to negotiations. While appearing to clarify Labor's position, the statement brought together in one document all the ambiguities and qualifications of previous statements.[12] Labor's divisions over withdrawal continued.

The conservatives had their own anxieties during 1966, though these were born of doubts, not about the merits of the Vietnam policy, but about whether its popularity could be maintained. Howson sensed that the conservatives might be losing their dominance of public space. In mid-1965, he spoke with Sir James Plimsoll, who had recently succeeded Tange as secretary in External Affairs, about the need to counter the influence of Cairns, who was 'infecting the students'. Plimsoll agreed. Later Howson commented: 'We are holding our own, on Vietnam, on public opinion, but we can't afford to let up on the pressure . . .' This was a continuing refrain in 1965 and 1966, as the government engaged in a political struggle to justify its policy and hold the public debate. Ministers spoke at public meetings on Vietnam, often with Cairns or Senator John Wheeldon as their adversary, and the Liberal party room discussed the problem: 'We are meeting much opposition in the electorates; we must plan for a bigger public relations campaign . . .'[13]

In late 1966, the wavering within conservative ranks produced the breakaway Liberal Reform Group, which campaigned in the election on its opposition to the Vietnam intervention. Some dismissed the rebels as the product of mere pique—one of their leading lights, Gordon Barton, had been thwarted in an attempt to break in upon the two-airlines policy—and certainly their opposition to Vietnam had more the quality of disquiet than dissent. Nevertheless, the peace movement welcomed them with enthusiasm and relief.

The Reform Group—which claimed to stand 'For a Strong Right Arm and a Helping Hand'—published a pamphlet on Vietnam, arguing that if blame for the war must be apportioned, it lay with the refusal by Diem and the Americans to allow the reunification elections in the mid-1950s. The pamphlet quibbled over the legality of American intervention and hinted that the NLF was not entirely controlled from Hanoi. But it shrank from condemning the intervention, arguing only that inhumane means were a poor advertisement for democracy, and that the policy of 'containing communism at all costs' was producing deep domestic stresses: 'Confidence in official veracity has been shaken and national division created . . . The effects of this are disguised and will not be fully evident for some years.'[14] While the prediction was accurate, the Liberal Reform Group's opposition to the Vietnam intervention was primarily a case of fretting at the loss of the sterile consensus of the Cold War.

These were sufficient cracks in the monolith of foreign policy to warrant attention. One result was a rash of pamphlets during

Prime minister Holt was said to be anxious during 1966 that the public mood might swing against the intervention in Vietnam: the Liberal party room resolved to work harder on its 'public relations campaign'. Holt visited the troops of the 1st Battalion based at Bien Hoa, in April 1966. Left to right: Lt Col A.V. Preece, Corporal B. Battersby and Harold Holt. (Australian War Memorial, CUN/66/340/VN)

1965 and 1966, in which the conservatives justified their views on Vietnam in a tone of belligerent and uncompromising certainty. The ministers most responsible for government policy, especially those who made up the Foreign Affairs and Defence committee of Cabinet, presented a solid phalanx marked by their commitment to what one critic called 'a doctrine of considerable rigidity'.[15] One pamphlet outlining that doctrine posed apparently thorny questions ('what right do we have to interfere in the domestic affairs of Viet Nam . . .'), which were then answered with consummate ease. The pamphlet suggested the novel interpretation that during the French war there had been two distinct Vietnamese paths, the Viet Minh and another, nationalist path, and that these had regrouped after 1954 to the North and South respectively. At one stroke, this was reviving the fortunes of non-communist nationalism, though giving it a greater role than its fragile shoulders could bear. The pamphlet asserted that Australia's intervention was a direct response to an appeal from South Vietnam 'for help in defending itself against external aggression', a deception which was not exposed until the publication of the *Pentagon Papers* in 1971. The war, the pamphlet went on, 'is not a civil war . . . but a war in which one state is trying to subdue another . . .' The NLF was 'an instrumentality' of Hanoi, which had 'not attracted any well-known South Vietnamese nationalists to its ranks'. And finally, standing behind Vietnam was Chinese aggression, the 'central feature of post-war history in this region'.[16]

The Chinese role in Vietnam was the major plank of conservative policy, and the war in Vietnam was effectively presented as a surrogate for confrontation with China. Menzies had stated this plainly at the original commitment of a battalion in April 1965: 'The takeover of South Viet Nam . . . must be seen as part of a thrust by Communist China between the Indian and Pacific Oceans.' Hasluck spelt out the same rationale with more subtlety but no less ideology. Détente with the Soviet Union had only been possible after its aggression had been successfully blocked; the same would be true for China. As he told the Action Assembly for Moral Rearmament in Melbourne in 1967, in Vietnam '. . . we Australians are . . . in large part defending ourselves, blocking aggression and ensuring our survival . . . we cannot neglect to do anything about the threat, for it must be checked'.

In this view, Vietnam was only a part of the containment of China, and the war's own dynamics and history must be rewritten in the light of superpower confrontation. As Whitlam delighted in pointing out, the government frequently went further than the Americans, in both the vigour of its rhetoric and the implications of its policy.

> The Government does not want negotiations which would possibly lead to an American withdrawal . . . It wants to ring China with fire until the Chinese revolution normalises . . . The Prime Minister's real slogan is not: 'All the way with LBJ', but: 'Further than LBJ'.[17]

In spite of such criticism, Australia's official attitude to China hardened in these years. In June 1966, it was announced that an embasssy would be established in Taipei, completing—rather belatedly—the refusal to recognise the Chinese Revolution, or as the communiqué quaintly put it: 'the movement of the Chinese capital from the mainland'. Editorials chided the government, and External Affairs was thought to have been overridden; the decision was seen as a victory for the backbench 'China lobby', led by old warhorses such as Kent Hughes.[18]

The insistence that Chinese imperialism was the explanation for Vietnam was pursued with more energy by Australia than by its American ally, as the latter moved towards the more subtle relations which would issue in Nixon's rapprochement in 1971–

72. When, in early 1965, the State Department released its document *Aggression from the North*—which sought to establish that the war in Vietnam was entirely the result of Northern aggression and infiltration—it included no allegations of Chinese responsibility. But for Australian conservatives, the real villain was Peking, even more than Hanoi. The Liberal Party published a pamphlet which plagiarised—without attribution—large parts of the State Department document, and then added the Chinese dimension the Americans seemed to have missed.

> The war fits into the pattern proclaimed by Peking that the real focus of revolutionary struggle is now in the under-developed areas of the world and that the real leader of this struggle is the Chinese Communist Party.

Vietnam must be seen 'not as a kind of local civil war, but in terms of the power drive of Chinese Communism and the security of the whole Pacific area . . .'

The chief quality of these conservative arguments was their exaggeration. One unconscious illustration of this propensity was a government misquotation of Mao: 'Everything grows out of the barrel of a gun', when Mao had been more modest, only speaking of power. The government's pamphlets tended to baldly overstate their case: Vietnam was not a civil war, but an assault on a sovereign people by a neighbouring state. The intentions of the Chinese were imperialist and their influence over Hanoi complete, as was that of Hanoi over the NLF.[19]

Each assertion took a kernel of truth and buried it in a husk of alarmist ideology. The North had undoubtedly assisted the communists in the South, but then the Party saw Vietnam as one, rather than two, sovereign states. The NLF was substantially driven by its (Southern) Party members, though it also had grouped around it other patriotic forces in the South. China's rhetorical support for wars of national liberation was undoubtedly belligerent, but not evidence that such wars were the product of Chinese design, and the Vietnamese Party was decidedly wary of the old empire to its north with its new claims of ideological hegemony. But having set the same course for a decade and a half, Australian conservatives had no intention of allowing historical complexities to muddy the waters; in the end, they would be overtaken by historical change, as the Americans dismantled their containment of China.

In what may have been Australia's last controversy using the pamphlet form, these official arguments were challenged or sustained by similar broadsides from opponents and supporters of the intervention. Some bore the marks of the polarised culture of the Cold War. The CPA published direct replies to the two government pamphlets cited. These also at times overstated the case: arguing that the NLF was not entirely communist and was quite independent of Peking, the CPA glossed over how autonomous the Front was from the Vietnamese Party. It insisted that the NLF was only formed as a result of American aggression—in the form of advisers and military aid—neatly reversing the notion of Northern aggression. In the CPA's view, 'the groups which dictate Johnson's policy' were the financiers and industrialists who profited from expenditure on the war.

Elsewhere, the CPA argued that the NLF represented 'what patriots have always done' in a situation of dictatorship—which was to fight—and detailed the argument that the Front was largely Southern in inspiration. It was understandable that Vietnamese patriots refused, after the early Diem years, to accept a partition which 'had never been accepted in 1000 years of her history', an odd formulation given that the South was relatively recently settled. The CPA also adopted the Vietnamese Party's view that the American presence was a direct continuation of colonial rule: it was a 'colonial war' which must end by 'the exit of the colonial occupying power . . . whether early or late'.[20] Some of these glosses must have meant little to general readers, though the CPA's interventions represented direct contradictions of conservative policy.

Other contributions were issued at the same time. *News-Weekly*, in a long and sophisticated analysis, denied that there was a civil war in Vietnam, advancing the proposition that the war was part of the dislocations of modernisation. Despite their attractions as a path to modernity, communist ideology and methods should have no part of this process, and the paper now adopted Walt Rostow's bitter phrase, calling the Chinese communists 'the scavengers of the modernization process'. The Democratic Socialist Club at Melbourne University produced a reasoned argument for withdrawal and negotiations, and dismissed the domino theory as nonsense. Labor produced a few pamphlets—one written, and the other clearly inspired, by Cairns—and although they successfully contested some of the conservatives' historical interpretations, they were inevitably lame when it came to policy proposals.[21]

This debate in 1965 and 1966 represented a revival of the art of the pamphlet, and circulated arguments about Vietnam in the public sphere. Much of it may have been a dialogue of the deaf—with contending interpretations of a Vietnamese history which must have been alien to many readers—and it may not have greatly enlarged public understanding. But it signalled a public contestation over government policy which, significantly, was carried on largely by forces outside the Labor opposition, and to which newspapers contributed very little. A quite vigorous dispute occurred in the years immediately after the commitment to Vietnam in April 1965, even though the peace movement continued to believe its efforts were in vain.

Along with the growth of new groups opposing the war or conscription in the same years, this flurry of pamphlets was perhaps more important for its existence than its quality. It signalled a revival of public debate, whose energy was channelled into the election campaign of November 1966. One commentator argued as early as mid-1966 that, with its rigid doctrines of foreign policy, the government had 'lost its hold first on informed opinion and then on public opinion generally'.[22] The judgment was premature: informed opinion was divided, if uneasy, and public opinion continued to support the war until 1969. But even if it was premature, something had shifted during 1966, and the conservatives never again captured that tone of confidence mixed with belligerence and alarm found in their pamphlets of 1965 and 1966.

'Better to be right than to be Prime Minister'

The conservatives' unease that the Vietnam and conscription policies were being challenged with some success grew as the election approached. Conscription, in particular, was regarded as a volatile issue, and although it was known that conscription for Vietnam was unpopular, nobody knew the size of the anti-conscription vote. Jim Killen later wrote that, during 1966, Holt 'was worried about the way the war was faring. It showed on his face whenever he was asked a question about it'. To add to these problems, Holt had disappointed his party since finally taking the long-promised succession when Menzies retired in January 1966. His parliamentary performances had been desultory, and his visit to America in early June, when he made his 'All the way with LBJ' speech, was regarded even by some conservatives as cutting too servile a figure. Whitlam, in particular, delighted in drawing out the comical aspects of Holt's performance, suggesting that Holt was ready to replace President Johnson's beagle, which had recently died.[23]

Johnson reciprocated these attentions by visiting Australia one month before the election, while in the region for the Manila conference on Vietnam; announcing the visit, Holt was, as the American embassy reported back to Washington, 'obviously elated'. Another commentator at the same press conference described him as 'exultant and rather childish'. Holt's statement that ' "this is the biggest fish I ever speared!" . . . spoke

volumes'. Despite Holt's enthusiasm, there were others who
doubted whether the President's visit would be an electoral
advantage, and worried that the Vietnam debate, which they
hoped had quietened, might flare again. Ever the rural lobbyist,
the Country Party leader, McEwen, had his mind on more venal
matters, and was expected to lobby Johnson for the contract to
provide lamb for the huge market of Americans in Vietnam.

The ALP had no doubts that the visit was an electoral ploy,
but the American embassy, reporting local reaction, remarked
that Calwell had repudiated those opposing it in the ALP and
would welcome the visit while criticising the Vietnam policy.
Some demonstrations were expected, but the 'left-wing anti-Vietnam fringe' carried 'little weight politically', and the embassy was
confident that 'voices of dissent here will be drowned out by [a]
great surge of pro-American sentiment'.[24]

Two aspects stand out from Johnson's visit during the election
campaign. First, it highlighted the dilemmas within the ALP; for
the right in particular, it was the combination of political forces
they most dreaded, exposing the ALP to being depicted as
anti-American, while the left of the party explicitly called for
demonstrations. Wheeldon, from the left, at a VDC meeting in
Melbourne argued the case for showing Johnson that there was
a mass of sentiment against American foreign policy. In his
speech welcoming Johnson, Calwell negotiated these dilemmas by
lauding the American Revolution and the dream of the American
century which he associated with it. After arguing his disagreement with the Vietnam policy, he concluded by reciting the
Gettysburg Address from memory: 'The situation was so charged
with nostalgia that his voice quavered and broke, which testified
to the feeling that lay behind it.'[25]

This extraordinary performance also testified to the conflicting
forces which Calwell was attempting to balance. He was condemning the Vietnam war and appealing to his support on the
left while trying to avoid its anti-Americanism; he was campaigning with progressively less moderation against conscription while
knowing that conscription in general was popular; he was arguing
for withdrawal from Vietnam while knowing that the right of his
party was highly equivocal about the circumstances for that
withdrawal.

As the election progressed after LBJ's curtain-raiser, Calwell
abandoned all caution, focusing on conscription and suggesting
Labor had a policy of complete and unconditional withdrawal.
Increasingly, he tapped the tribal memory of Labor's opposition
to conscription, conjuring images of 'The Blood Vote' of 1916:
at one rally, days before the election, he shouted at a heckler:
'You are beyond military age. I will not allow you or Holt or

Menzies or anyone to plunge your arthritic hands wrist deep in the blood of Australian youth.' Calwell's campaign was seen by many as the last stand of a distinctive Labor style—impassioned, traditionalist, Irish Catholic—and certainly, conscription was his most appropriate cause.

In connecting 1966 with the conscription referenda of 1916 and 1917, and with the struggle against Curtin's proposals of 1942–43 (when he had helped reduce Curtin to despair), Calwell drew upon an anti-conscription legend. But his style and passion meant that young uncommitted voters in 1966 were as likely to regard him as an anachronistic echo from the past as to endorse his principles. Similarly, when the Seamen's Union, in the 1969 election, reproduced the famous anti-conscription cartoon and poem 'The Blood Vote', it had a distinctly archaic look about it. It was no longer clear whether the anti-conscription legend had a widely endorsed meaning, though it undoubtedly had for Calwell. Importantly, it enabled him to avoid the tortured ambiguity of Labor's policy on withdrawal from the war. His release from ambiguity disconcerted Whitlam amongst others; Calwell was seen as the old warhorse, sniffing the air for a last campaign, but it was a situation as unpredictable as it was sentimental.[26]

Calwell had been given his head, which worried many; but it won him support on the left and meant that the peace movement mobilised behind Labor. The VDC had for some time been impressed with Calwell's willingness to attend rallies, and the CPA's journal in September was cautiously pleased with Calwell's position, while noting that Labor's right remained basically committed to government policies. In Melbourne particularly, the peace movement campaigned for Labor; a 'Vote No Conscription Campaign' was organised from late September, with the aim of turning the election into a referendum on conscription. 'We need only to persuade 10% of Liberal voters, mainly women, that their vote means life or death to hundreds of young men—and conscription will be defeated.' Coordinated by SOS, the campaign involved television, radio and press advertising, and public events such as a vigil by candlelight, a theatre revue and leaflets at polling booths.

This campaign made little specific reference to Vietnam, concentrating—as Calwell was attempting to—on conscription. Its television advertisement, prepared by an advertising agency, featured 'a flag—at half mast—the sound of a bugle sounding the last post and the words "Should not conscripts be asked if they want to go all the way?"' In an image encapsulating the cultural alienation of the peace movement, with a dash of Marx, one writer in *Sanity* commented: 'I cannot wait for this spectre to haunt suburbia . . .'[27]

The divisions which haunted Labor came to a head within a week of the election, when Whitlam interpreted the ALP's policy on withdrawal from Vietnam in his own terms. The May position had been for immediate withdrawal of conscripts and the withdrawal of regular troops after consultation with the Americans, but with Labor insisting on withdrawal. As the campaign went on, Calwell increasingly shifted to the left of this position, giving the impression that it meant immediate and unconditional withdrawal; Whitlam was to the right of it, placing greater stress on the consultations and suggesting these could result in regular troops remaining. When he repeated this position to the press, Calwell repudiated him. The differences illustrated the struggle within the ALP, and were taken as graphic proof of disunity. Whitlam, wrote *The Age*, had 'ripped the wallpaper off its shaky facade of policy . . . Like all armies under divided orders, the party can hope for nothing but a humiliating defeat'.[28]

The second aspect of the LBJ visit was the new edge of violence in the demonstrations against the visit; whether this sprang from a more desperate political climate or from greater police brutality depended on one's political position. But it was evident that the tenor of political conflict had intensified. Although the embassy had been correct to predict substantial demonstrations in support of the President's visit, it also met violent opposition. On 21 October, LBJ's motorcade sped past demonstrators outside Government House in Melbourne. Shortly after, as police attempted to disperse the crowd, scuffles and arguments broke out and the police—uniformed and plain clothed, along with American security guards—moved in with heavy-handed action. This intensity carried into the election campaign. Some public meetings at the end of the campaign were fiery: 'fending off punches aimed at the Prime Minister, policemen three deep almost carried him through a wild crowd shouting anti-conscription slogans outside the Rockdale town hall'. As Holt entered the hall, 'a deafening roar went up with supporters and opponents shouting, clapping, cheering and jeering'; Holt had difficulty making himself heard as he spoke on defence and conscription. It was, wrote *The Age* a little primly, 'the wildest scene of his election campaign'.

At another 'rowdy' meeting in Brisbane, Killen was again impressed that Vietnam was troubling Holt:

> He was given a question about his war service . . . Harold leapt at his interrogator with the ferocity of a wolf . . . [Later] Harold said: 'Jim, I think it is all right. They are with us on Vietnam. My fear is that we will win the election too well.'

In the Melbourne Club a few days before the election, the

conservatives were expected to win with a slightly reduced majority. In the event, Holt's intelligence was more accurate. The conservatives had a landslide victory, increasing their majority in the House from 22 to 40; Labor's share of the primary vote dropped by more than 5 per cent. At the time, the result was seen as a substantial vindication of the intervention in Vietnam. Many said that Vietnam was the only policy which had been endorsed.[29]

Identifying the cause of Labor's defeat led to a flurry of political debate both inside and outside the ALP. Variously, the blame fell upon Calwell's passion, leadership disunity, the opposition to Vietnam and a general lack of policy coherence. For Calwell, nearing the end of his public life, the root cause was still the 'fear of communism', focused upon the Vietnam issue; he regarded Whitlam's actions as the next primary factor. But ever since his first speech against the commitment to Vietnam, Calwell had presented opposition as an unpopular cause, an obligation vindicated by calumny and defeat. In a perfect statement of the righteous culture of defeatism with which the Cold War had marked Labor, Calwell wrote that he could not back down in the leadership struggles of 1966 because he had begun a campaign against the Vietnam war. This campaign had to be fought to the end: '. . . a leader who deserts betrays his cause. I also felt that it was better to be right than to be Prime Minister'.[30]

For the peace movement, which had thrown all its resources into the campaign and invested great hopes in the change of policy which would result from a Labor victory, 1966 was a demoralising blow. It left some at a loss as to what to do next. The YCAC groups faded away and their student constituency began a process of radicalisation; the parliamentary left would, to some extent, abandon the parliamentary sphere to work more closely with the peace movement.

But immediately after 1966, there was something of a hiatus. The demoralisation which characterised the period was illustrated by Turner in an open letter to Douglas Brass in May the following year. In April 1965, Brass had written the editorial in the *Australian* which—alone amongst the dailies—condemned military intervention as 'a reckless decision on Vietnam which this nation may live to regret . . .' More recently he had written of a popular callousness on Vietnam. Turner commented that he himself had been inactive for the past six months, because

> I don't know what to do . . . Last year, for a while, we thought we had a chance. The Opposition was opposing the Government on Vietnam . . . people went into [the campaign] with a passion and a hope that had not been seen in Australian politics for a very

long time, people, young people, who had not been involved in this personal way before. And we lost.[31]

At the end of 1966, the balance of political forces in Australia appeared to be with the conservatives, though this proved to be deceptive. They had won the election but were losing their unchallenged dominance over public discourse. Although opposition to the war had suffered a setback, the campaign during 1966 had stimulated a debate on Vietnam which made the traditional conservative strategy of marginalising dissent less effective. The conservatives never recaptured the assured tone of their pamphlets of 1965 and 1966. More fundamentally, it became increasingly clear that the prosecution of the war was in other hands—in Washington and in Vietnam—which meant that the government parties spoke with progressively less authority. Over the remainder of the decade, the consequences of 1966 would be played out, culminating in the disintegration of the conservatives' Vietnam policy. Nevertheless, the conservatives ended the year—their last vintage year—on a peak.

The peace movement had lost most of its battles and, despite a major effort which had succeeded in generating a public discourse during the year, it was now disoriented. Those who opposed intervention in Vietnam seemed unable to translate public support into political influence; the peace movement clearly did not have an influence proportionate to the levels of support for its positions. Of the 1950s it was sometimes said that the CPA had more influence in civil society and public discourse than its actual size warranted; in the mid-1960s, this situation was reversed, with the left and the peace movement more marginal than expected.

Thus Nadine Jensen staged her lone protest at the ticker-tape parade in Sydney, and saw it in terms of breaking 'Australian Complacency and apathy about Vietnam'; yet, in 1966, at least a quarter of the population opposed the military commitment to the war in Vietnam. The members of Save Our Sons saw themselves as breaking a silence and stood as often solitary figures; yet in their opposition to conscripts being sent to Vietnam, they represented a majority. The conundrums here reveal something of the puzzling and transitional character of public debate in this second decade of the Cold War. Was the peace movement acting on the basis of the past, presuming inaccurately that it was isolated and embattled? Did its support in opinion polls come from a silent majority, unable to be converted to social activism? Did the Cold War stigma of the peace movement as a communist front still hang heavily, isolating the movement from its potential support? Or had the movement simply erred strategically, placing all its eggs in the parliamentary basket, so that when Labor lost, the peace movement was also lost?

Two months after the election defeat, the Rev. David Pope gave a talk to a Sydney meeting of anti-Vietnam groups; he spoke of a 'vast, latent subterranean sea of disquiet and disenchantment' on the Vietnam policy, which the movement must encourage 'to add their voices, but in a society where a tepid mediocrity prevails, and where critical discussion is not encouraged, this is very difficult'. This was the same problem which Cairns had tried to grapple with, and to which the SOS member at the Mothers' Club had apparently succumbed. In an image which captured the movement's alienation from the political culture, Pope compared Australia to 'a beleaguered city, tucked away behind high walls, into which an occasional courier enters . . . with news as to what it really feels like outside'.[32] It was an apt image for the first, and unsuccessful, phase of the movement against the war. That Pope was at a loss to offer any strategies for breaking out of this 'beleaguered city' was perhaps equally apt.

III

Intervention

9
Counter-revolution and the village: 1966–1969

'Counter-revolutionary warfare'

Some six months before the election which endorsed Australia's Vietnam policy, Australian soldiers began moving into Phuoc Tuy, establishing a base in a small rubber plantation at Nui Dat to the north of the settled basin. After a year attached to American forces at Bien Hoa, the army now constituted a largely independent task force (ATF) with primary responsibility for the province. This was an opportunity, for the following six years, to apply the principles of 'counter-revolutionary warfare', developed from the experience in Malaya since 1955 and reflecting the early 1960s conception of global Cold War being conducted through 'insurgency'.

In Phuoc Tuy, army intelligence officers began reconstructing the history of the province, attempting to understand their adversary. The complexities of Vietnamese history dawned as they discerned the levels of local support for the NLF, and as it became evident that the republican government in the South (GVN) had limited popular support in the province. Many ordinary soldiers arrived with a naivety reflecting their society; some had little idea of where Vietnam was to be found on a map. It is unclear how many were entirely convinced by the Cold War truisms expressed in a pocket-book distributed to each soldier, which presented the conflict as one of external aggression. The Vietnamese, it suggested, 'are prepared to welcome you officially and unofficially . . .' The Australian intervention was 'helping the people of this proud nation repulse the aggression of the Communist Viet Cong . . .' The pocket-book went on to insist that the conflict was not a civil war, before giving a potted history of the country and descriptions of its culture and customs.[1]

Australian soldiers arrived with little sense of the contradictory history into which they were being inserted. One of the more poignant images in some memoirs is of Australians being ignored by the local people, who look away, eyes downcast, as though this foreign force could be made to disappear. Some had expected welcome—though few had illusions of being liberators—and some anticipated antagonism, but this aloofness was chastening. They called the local people 'noggies', a derogatory though hardly vicious term; but for many soldiers the villagers remained an unknown. Many came to regard the GVN's armed forces with disdain and some mistrust, while their respect for the determination of the local NLF was considerable. One young soldier joked to his commanding officer: ' "There are only two lots of good soldiers in Vietnam . . . Us and the Viet Cong . . . let's get together and do the rest over". . . it was a joke that illuminated a very serious issue.'[2] It was also a common sentiment.

Most Australian soldiers had little direct contact with villagers, but one sphere of involvement was through 'civic action': the political aspect of 'counter-revolutionary warfare'. This reflected an acute insight, that 'defeat of an insurgency movement is fundamentally a political problem as the ultimate cure is the removal of the causes of unrest and dissatisfaction on which the movement is based'.[3] The strategy had two parts. The guerrillas would be sought out in their bases and, even if they avoided battle, would be harassed and weakened through the jungle patrolling on which the army prided itself. Second, the guerrillas would be isolated from their support in the villages, choking off vital supplies of food and information. It was intended to reverse Mao's metaphor of the guerrilla as a fish in the sea of the people. Free of intimidation, the local people would be won over to support the South Vietnamese government.

Civic action—in projects such as medical aid, construction work and agricultural assistance—was first conducted by a small team within the ATF, and then by a distinct Civil Affairs Unit which arrived in mid-1967. This unit saw its purpose as winning 'the support of the people for the GVN with the secondary aim of establishing goodwill towards the Australian forces'. One early plan argued that although villages such as Hoa Long had a revolutionary past, 'if the village can be offered effective security and government administration it should be practicable to persuade a majority of the people to transfer their allegiance *back* to the government'. This presumed that a political allegiance could be reconstructed where it had never existed.

The earliest forms of civic action consisted primarily of largesse in the form of charitable and relief activities. Medical aid was distributed, children were taken for helicopter rides and sides of bacon were given to orphanages. In 1967, it was hoped that the political effects would develop through three phases. In the first, contact was made with unfriendly or semi-friendly villages and 'the villagers are assured that the Task Force is there to help them . . .'; then, attention was 'directed at winning the confidence of the local population . . . by overt acts of help'—short-term projects such as digging wells and repairing roads.

In a final stage, described significantly as 'complete community rehabilitation', more extensive projects would 'develop and educate the local population and lead them to a better way of life'. Although there was some recognition that credit should be attributed as much as possible to the Vietnamese civil administration, the general framework was a paternalistic and rather naive conception of development aid.[4] Civic action had resonances here with the 1950s conception of 'civics' as the inculcation of orderly, community-minded citizenship, and with development ideas of 'nation-building' as the construction of a stable, pro-Western polity. But the key tension was quickly identified: how to coordinate projects with the GVN in such a way that they did not overshadow that regime. In 1968, one evaluation suggested that civic action had had little discernible effect on the proportion of the population actively supporting the GVN, which was thought to have remained static at some 30 per cent. Part of the problem was that where the local authorities were inert, corrupt or simply ineffective, it was all too easy to overshadow the regime.

One response was to develop projects jointly with Vietnamese authorities, through programs of village self-development or revolutionary development. In the small hamlet of Ong Trinh in late 1969, one project consisted of building a school, a task allocated to the 5th Infantry Battalion (5RAR). The village contributed a third of the funds, with the task force providing the rest:

5RAR were to manage the project and provide most of the labour,

but the village had agreed to help. This was 5RAR's first major . . .
project, and although not enthusiastic, the unit set about it in a very
businesslike manner . . . the people of the hamlet worked very well
alongside the 5RAR team, mixing cement, assisting with bricks,
joinery, painting and so on. After one or two weeks the team became
accepted by the villagers . . .

Good relations were further developed through medical aid and
volleyball, and

. . . the team began to help out the people in many other small
and simple ways—new culverts, new hamlet gate posts, concrete slabs
for drying rice and so on. By the end of the eight weeks . . .
relations were excellent. The people gave the team an elaborate
formal pre-Christmas lunch.[5]

This sort of contact built goodwill towards the Australian army,
but there was little reason why this should in turn reflect well
on the GVN, itself conspicuously absent from village welfare.

The dilemma of overshadowing the GVN remained, and by
the end of the decade, civil affairs activity was often unpopular
among the province officials. The Civil Affairs Unit seemed
resigned to the contradiction: 'Care is being taken to ensure that
the Province Agricultural Service is not overshadowed by our
efforts. This is a difficult aspect and will always be with us.'[6]
Developing a popular base for the GVN—by building its authority and legitimacy—was a more intractable endeavour than the
army had anticipated. Ironically, it was still more difficult when
Australians were fulfilling some of the GVN's own state functions,
in welfare and development roles. Projects might win some
goodwill—though the good discipline of Australian soldiers in the
villages was the key element in maintaining a modicum of
goodwill—but did not necessarily reflect well on the GVN.

These contradictions reflected some of the political relations
between the Australian army and the GVN, which were substantially coloured by distrust, inertia and the effects of petty
corruption. The texture of everyday life was interwoven with
local corruption, in which officials extracted prosaic though
significant sums from the villagers. Village chiefs charged fees
before they would issue passes which the ATF required, and
developed inventive taxes to be paid before they would fulfil their
normal duties. There were cases of village officials being voted
out of office but being kept in place by the provincial administration; other officials were simply reluctant to act, such as the
official decribed as 'an elderly man of mandarin origin who
deplores menial activity' and whose cooperation had been alienated years before.

There were effective local administrators, but they were

themselves overshadowed. A report in 1967 noted 'the problem of corruption, inefficiency and plain disinterest on the part of too many officials . . .' and the refrain was rarely broken thereafter. Such problems were compounded by other factors. The NLF made effective local officials a target for assassination, which made the recruitment of local officials more difficult as their tasks became less attractive or lucrative, reinforcing a vicious circle.[7] All of these cross-currents made the role of civil affairs, in building a village constituency for the GVN, the more impossible.

The venality of local officials reflected, on a prosaic level, the corruption and extortion on which the South Vietnamese regime was based; local officials were poorly paid, and effectively survived by living off the land through petty forms of extortion. In the upper echelons of government, corruption was seen as the cement which held the state together, with the elite calculating that only loyalty to the president would ensure access to the spoils of office.[8] The strategy of counter-revolutionary warfare depended on there being a reasonably viable regime which would be supported militarily while it re-established popular support; the very language of the strategy assumed the legitimacy of established government. Yet this was what was begging in the South. The politico-military elite was too corrupt to be popular, and too dependent on external support to be an authentic ruling class. This again reflected patterns of class and political development inherited from the colonial era; marginalisation in the past and extortion in the present were not a stable foundation for a ruling class.

Long Phuoc

Within a small triangle of thirteen by twelve by nine kilometres in the centre of Phuoc Tuy lay three villages—Long Phuoc, Hoa Long and Ap Suoi Nghe—and two army base areas—the Australian base at Nui Dat and the NLF bases in the Nui Dinh hills. This small area also encompassed the social order of the village and its relationship to the space around it, and provides a glimpse, at the level of the village, of the experience of counter-revolutionary warfare and of the complex relations binding the NLF, the villagers, the GVN and the Australian forces.

From June 1966, Long Phuoc existed only as a trace on the map and as the memory of an earlier Party strategy. The strategy has been examined earlier. In the early 1960s, the village had been mobilised as a 'struggle village', fortified against the GVN, honeycombed with tunnels and serving as the headquarters for

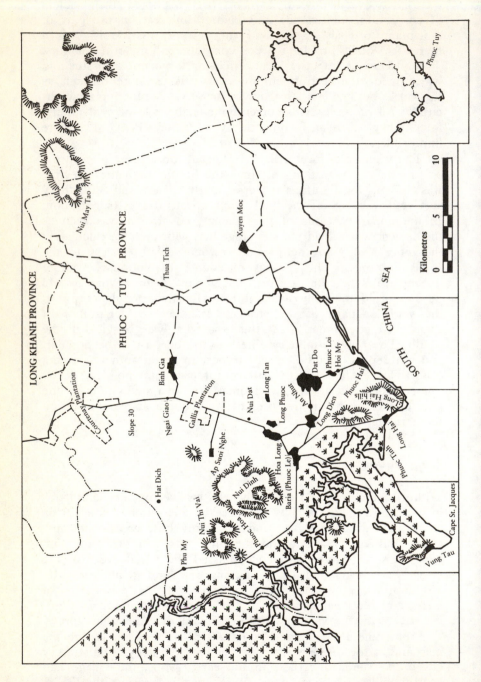

Phuoc Tuy (Baria) province

Long Phuoc, the headquarters of the province Party committee and honeycombed with tunnels since the 1940s, was destroyed by Australian forces shortly after their arrival at nearby Nui Dat in June 1966. After moving the villagers to Hoa Long, the village was burnt and bulldozed, but remained a trace on local memory and a continuing cause for resentment. Here a soldier waits while the village burns. (Australian War Memorial, CUN/66/521/VN)

the Party committee in the province. With Western military intervention in mid-1965, such 'struggle villages'—overtly defying the Saigon regime—were acutely exposed. Long Phuoc was also unfortunate enough to be only some three kilometres from Nui Dat. To 'secure' the area for the arrival of the Task Force, the village was destroyed and its population relocated.

The Australian journalist Pat Burgess visited the village in 1965, and later described its 'deep cool wells . . . fishponds shaded with flowering shrubs' and tiled roofs. 'In almost every yard there were wood shavings. It was a village of craftsmen who made their own furniture . . .' As one soldier recalled, its brick houses were quite unlike the grass-hut villages they had

expected to find. In May 1966, a joint American and Army of
the Republic of Vietnam (ARVN) force had met fierce fighting
in the village. This was followed by artillery bombardments and
air strikes over the following month. At the end of June, the
Australian army arrived in the village, having determined to raze
it lest it always be a base—too close to their own—from which
the NLF would oppose them. It was a strategic rather than an
indiscriminate action, though the distinction would have been lost
on its occupants. There was no resistance, the Party committee
having moved to a safer place, apparently abandoning the village.
Houses and wells were destroyed using acetylene gas explosions
and bulldozers, caches of food and weapons were found and
concrete bunkers blown up; 537 houses were demolished, and
below them some 500 escape tunnels and air-raid shelters.

Burgess noticed a young 'baby-faced' Australian soldier sitting
in the doorway of one house: 'Behind him in the dining room
. . . there was a pile of crockery in a white and blue pattern.
Plastic fruit on the mantelpiece was a flash of colour before the
family altar of Buddha.' When another soldier reached to souvenir
the fruit, the first told him to leave it: 'It belongs to some
bastard.' Later, when the time came to burn the ruins of the
village, the young soldier smashed the crockery, pushed the
furniture into a pyre and 'Buddha's plastic fruit . . . flared, then
ran like a votive candle.' With its resonances of belonging,
innocence and loss, Burgess's story evoked the complexities which
a young soldier had inherited.

Most of the villagers were moved to Hoa Long, a neighbouring
village a kilometre away. In the following years, the destruction
of Long Phuoc remained a continuing grievance, and Hoa Long
as a slum offshoot remained inhospitable to Australian soldiers.
This resentment was only slowly recognised: a month after its
destruction, one report ingenuously described the people from
Long Phuoc as 'previously "neutral" villagers and refugees who
are anti-government and anti the allied forces as a result of the
recent resettlement and curfew restrictions'. Under the curfew
restrictions, former Long Phuoc residents were denied access to
their land, but the writer seemed unaware that the village had
been a revolutionary centre.

For several years, a dispute continued over access to Long
Phuoc, which was both poignant and an example of the NLF's
ability to use local issues in political struggles. As one peasant
put it: '[The] people are forbidden to go working in the ricefield.
What do we live off? Now my family is only depending on some
mango trees . . .' At first, the army refused permission to return
to the land, but by late 1966 it was allowing access twice a week
to tend crops and orchards. When Burgess returned to the ruins

in 1971, they were overgrown with bamboo and bougainvillea. A woman was stacking unbroken roof tiles. 'She didn't look up.'[9]

The army was in a dilemma; to refuse access only exacerbated the grievance of land dispossession but, if allowed access, the peasants could not be prevented from resupplying the guerrillas. Towards the end of the war, there was a sense of defeat in the face of this dilemma and doubtless in the face of the vexations of being petitioned by peasants. In early 1970, a report noted gloomily that many of those from the ruins of Long Phuoc 'have relatives in the VC and must therefore be considered as pro-VC. Many people still go to Long Phuoc by day to work their orchards'. The peasants had evidently won a minor victory.

The ruins of the village also served as a reminder and may have taken on a mythic role in local Party ideology. Long Phuoc recurs in the diary of one local guerrilla, though it was the American bombing which preceded the Australian action that he condemned, describing it as a 'blood debt':

> The warrior . . . remembers the sad scenes of bombing in Long Phuoc . . . The imperialists have committed so many abominable crimes . . . Oh! Warriors of the four corners! Revenge Long Phuoc from its devastated scenery . . .[10]

Continuing as a vexing grievance and as a trace on local memory, the village may also have served as an animating cause.

Hoa Long

During 1966 and 1967, the task force pursued a strategy of concentrating the province population into villages which the army hoped it could control. Small outlying hamlets and isolated settlements were destroyed, as were some substantial central villages—Long Phuoc, Long Tan and Phuoc Hien—which were noted for their revolutionary pasts and were close to the new base at Nui Dat. Enforced demographic change was intended to help withdraw the sea from the fish, but generated new grievances over land and cultural location.

In 1966, Hoa Long was one of three villages to which the inhabitants of other villages were to be resettled, the others being Binh Gia and Binh Ba. Its 'pacification' was consequently a major priority in the first few years of the task force. In the mid-1960s, Hoa Long had a population of some 3000: Burgess saw it as a 'dusty dog-leg street and huddle of shacks . . .' By the end of the decade, the village population had swollen to more than 5000 as a result of refugees created by the war. With some 1000 houses in 1970, it covered an area five kilometres square including its surrounding agricultural lands, on which were raised rice, herds of cattle and some pigs. There were working rubber trees in small plantations on the west of the village. To the south lay flat rice paddies, beyond an earthen embankment which surrounded the village; by late 1966, it was also surrounded by a more ominous wire fence.

The village had ten stores, a cafe, a small sawmill and a rice mill, as well as two small dispensaries and five schools. It also had an active political history. In the mid-1950s, it had been controlled 'day and night' by the Viet Minh, and was another central area of support for the NLF during the Australian period. When, in September 1971, the local newspapers announced the final Australian withdrawal, 'jubilation' was reported in Hoa Long.[11]

But in 1966, there had been sanguine hopes that Hoa Long would be a showcase of Australian–Vietnamese cooperation. It became an object of Civil Affairs attention; a new market and dispensaries were built, wells and roads repaired and dental and medical care provided. Gifts were distributed, even if this was occasionally at times when all but richer peasants were in the fields working. The Australians felt they were making a good impression and recounted stories of improving relations; one old man told of how, during a joint Australian–ARVN search of the village:

> . . . after having rummaged [in his house], one VN [Vietnamese] soldier took away my beautiful cane (I usually use this cane when I attend any traditional ceremonies organised in the village)—One Australian saw it, he had the VN soldier return it to me and beg my pardon.

By the end of 1966, the reports were flushed with optimism; the people were reported to have a greater degree of confidence in their village administration and a more friendly attitude towards Australian troops.

In this atmosphere the new marketplace was opened by two lieutenants-colonel—one an Australian battalion commander and the other the Vietnamese province chief. In celebration, a scroll was presented which read in part:

> The Australian Government in cooperation with Free World forces and your National Government in Saigon, respectfully presents this market place to you, the citizens of Hoa Long, with the belief and hope that in a free and open market place, truth will prevail and where truth prevails, men will know themselves and their neighbours.

Such grandiloquent terms suggested high hopes of the enlightening power of rationality, but the same market soon figured in a more grisly symbol of the war. In March 1967, an American report was discouraging the 'regular' practice of '. . . public exhibition of the dead bodies of VCs killed in military operations by the Australian Task Force or the ARVN . . . The displays are made either at the market-place or before the village office . . .' The report canvassed the intended objectives: the identification of the dead, uncovering NLF supporters by observing 'the reactions of the viewers', and propaganda functions. The practice was said to be counterproductive, as the villagers considered it inhumane and uncivilised. A covering note testily insisted that the practice was neither 'regular' nor official policy; nonetheless, it recurred in 1968 in allegations of Australian atrocities. More often, though, the guerrillas—who went to extraordinary lengths to retrieve the bodies of their dead in battle—noted with relief that the Australians treated NLF dead with a modicum of dignity.

In the Hoa Long incidents in 1967, more attention was given to the politicisation of burial of the bodies displayed. The village chief claimed there were no funds for burial, and was forced to call upon the *Dao-Tuy*, a local mutual aid association formed in the late 1950s to provide funerals for members. In one case, the body of an NLF cadre—a rubber plantation worker from Long Phuoc—had been left by Australian troops before the village office and later buried at some expense: 'The Long Phuoc folks contributed funds to give the corpse a good burial . . . although the *Dao-Tuy* chairman did not give any contribution he was personally present during the last rites for the dead Viet Cong.'

This contrasted with the treatment of a *hoi chanh* (an NLF soldier who had defected or 'returned' to the government side, and who was killed by the NLF in reprisal). His family was prevented from hiring a vehicle to bring the body to the cemetery; nor would the *Dao-Tuy* assist with funds, with the chairman claiming ignorance of the death of his neighbour.[12] Although custom placed a high value on the family's dead taking their proper place as ancestors, burial was here an allegory for civil conflict, as the village divided on the fault lines of political allegiance. An element of vindictiveness ensured that, in the case of the *hoi chanh*, the dead could not rest easy.

Throughout the late 1960s, a substantial section of the Hoa Long population continued to give essential support to the guerrillas and to NLF cadres within the village; there was said to be some form of guerrilla activity virtually every night. The village was assigned by the province Party committee the responsibility for supplying food to the NLF's Chau Duc district Company, who came at night across the five kilometres of footpaths connecting the village to their bases in the Nui Dinh hills. As late as April 1970, when the Task Force cordoned off the village with nightly ambushes to prevent this resupply, the most that could be claimed was that 'the VC were unable to penetrate Hoa Long albeit only for three nights'. The political infrastructure within the village had proven resilient enough to survive the various trials of war—including a rapid expansion of population, increased surveillance and economic dislocation.[13]

Suoi Nghe

A hamlet to the north of the province, Suoi Nghe, illustrates some of the same themes but in a more artificial manner. It too was the result of resettlement to deny guerrillas access to the people, though in this case an entire hamlet was created on newly cleared land. And it too was, in the minds of Australian planners, the object of exaggerated hopes before a more realistic and brutal awareness developed.

During September 1967, the task force destroyed a number of small settlements and hamlets straddling the road running north through the province. Inelegantly called 'Slope 30', this was an area between the village of Ngai Giao and the rubber plantation on the province's northern border. During the French war, convoys using the road had been regularly attacked; though sparsely populated, the area's significance lay in its location between two major NLF bases: the Hat Dich forest (in the north-west) and the Nui May Tao mountains (in the north-east). Tracks and trade routes between these two bases crossed the area.

The operation involved the relocation of more than 1000 people, with a swath of land 200 metres wide cleared along each side of the main road, destroying houses, extensive bunker and trench systems, crops and—one report meticulously noted—a coffee grinder and two bicycles. The villagers were medically examined and found to be suffering from skin diseases, malaria, hookworm and a few cases of tuberculosis. Many had never received any form of medical treatment. By the end of September, all had been moved to the new, model hamlet, closer to the Nui Dat base but on previously unused land, and a dramatically miscalculated social experiment began.

At the new site, land had been cleared, roads and prefabricated houses constructed, stock pens built and water tanks erected. The design—planned by the civil engineer commanding Civil Affairs—was ramrod straight, a rectangle of right-angled streets which could hardly be more different from the organic growth of older villages. An army press release announcing the new village was at once exaggerated and revealing:

At La Van, a tiny hamlet to the north of the 'model village' of Suoi Nghe, Civil Affairs engineers assemble a windmill to establish a water supply. Civil Affairs distributed supplies and undertook development projects, but could not win popular support for the South Vietnamese government. (Australian War Memorial, HIN/68/936/VN)

In appearance the model village . . . is not unlike a neat Australian housing sub-division. Compared with other villages and hamlets in Phuoc Tuy province its streets are straighter and wider, houses roomier and amenities areas bigger . . . we believe more families living in remote areas around the Province will come in from the jungle as the word spreads.[14]

Suoi Nghe represented a cultural image of a model Asia, similar to a suburban subdivision, modernised and leaving the past behind.

There was an echo here of Spender's project in the Colombo Plan, in which a modernised and developmentalist nationalism would be a counter to the ideological attractions of communism. Yet one key flaw in the Suoi Nghe project—apart from the practical problem, which only subsequently emerged, that there was no water to be found—was its implicit erasure of the past. This became clear when the province chief passed on a request to the Task Force from some peasants who wanted to return to their land to harvest crops. In reply, Brigadier Hughes, the ATF commander, pointed out that the area was now prohibited and, in any case, the crops had been defoliated. He wrote pointedly 'I believe it is important . . . to do what we can to help the people forget the past and allow them to think fully in terms of developing their new area . . .'15 While this might accord with strategic needs, it was inadequate in such a tenaciously historical milieu.

Over the following two years, Suoi Nghe was treated as a showpiece, with a brief, obligatory visit by Australian politicians touring Vietnam: Whitlam as opposition leader in early 1968, Phillip Lynch as minister for the Army, and Sir Henry Bland as secretary for the Department of Defence all toured the hamlet. More importantly, the village was also a development experiment, though one which went awry. There were persistent problems with the distribution of land to the peasants, with the GVN exceedingly slow in its allocation. A range of projects was attempted, including pig and chicken farming, but came to little. Genuine, if culturally incongruous, efforts included a sewing centre established as part of 'a vocational training scheme', and training in 'basic animal husbandry', which may have seemed unnecessary to a peasant culture of long standing.

Some of the problems suggest a wry hand of fate. The first crops were accidentally killed by defoliation, the village was off the main road and was unable to participate in local trade, and it was clear by late 1970 that there was no water to be found. The windmills were dismantled and plans were considered for pumping in water from outside the village, but the model village was in decline. The peasants, unable to grow viable crops in weak soil without water, were reduced to dependence on charcoal burning, one of the lowliest and most impoverished occupations in the province.

Some residents of Suoi Nghe actively supported the NLF: in 1970 it was noted that the village regularly helped to resupply D440, one of the local force battalions in the province, and that political meetings were occasionally held in the village. But the impression from the documents is of a village languishing with little economic or political coherence. NLF interest seems to have been less in building a base in the village than in ensuring its failure as a counter-revolutionary project. One night, during the Tet Offensive, the hamlet chief, his secretary and another official were killed by a small group of NLF soldiers, the former being knifed and the others shot. In August, their replacements were decapitated in a similar manner: 'The weather was very wild and the murder squad of 15–20 entered the hamlet, did their work and departed undetected.'[16]

This targeted use of terror was an exercise in undermining local government links with the village. As one old woodcutter said: 'Now nobody dares to be a hamlet chief. If I was forced to be hamlet chief, I would move my house away. Nobody would dare to do it even if he had three heads and six hands.' Assassinations had a clear political purpose. They ensured that the GVN's local officials remained disconnected from the social order of the village, leaving the ground free to the NLF. Despite provision for the election of hamlet and village officials, those in both Hoa Long and Suoi Nghe were appointed by the provincial government and generally lived outside the village they represented. This was the case in 1967 with the Hoa Long village officials, who returned to the province capital every night, and in 1969 with the hamlet chief in Suoi Nghe, who was a native of Binh Gia and lived there.

This enforced distance between local government and the people also helps account for the continuing incidents of petty corruption displayed by many, though not all, officials. In Suoi Nghe, after the accidental defoliation of the first crops, forms had to be filled in to claim compensation. The hamlet deputy chief required a bribe of $VN100—the wage for roughly a day's unskilled labour—from each villager. The hamlet chief ordered the money returned, while his deputy claimed innocence; ironically, both were assassinated in the incident mentioned above and the money was deemed lost.[17] Such petty corruption and venality in the fabric of everyday life signified the absence of vital links between the GVN and the village. While the Party had a complex local organisation from the district down to the village level, and worked to defend and nurture it, the GVN had little real basis in the rural social order.

In April 1971, an Australian army research team spent four days in Suoi Nghe and came away disconsolate. The water was dubious and the villagers poor, with 80 per cent living by producing charcoal. Rice had to be brought in from the province capital, local officials seemed uninterested and there was 'a lack of solidarity amongst the people'. The report concluded: 'The attempt to move people to a "western" type hamlet structure is depressing for those who visit Suoi Nghe. It is virtually a hamlet without a soul.'[18]

These three villages represented different facets of the local experience of war in Phuoc Tuy. Similarly, they were different aspects of the Australian army's rendering of Phuoc Tuy: its representation of Asia and its interpretation of what it was attempting to do in the villages. The first village, Long Phuoc, continued to exist as a trace on the map and in the memory; the second, Hoa Long, began as civil improvement (the market) but reasserted a radical history; while the third, Suoi Nghe, intended as the implantation of a new order, made a more piteous transition from suburban subdivision to 'a hamlet without a soul'.

If war is the continuation of politics by other means, the doctrine of 'counter-revolutionary warfare' understood this. It recognised that the task was to cut the links between guerrillas and peasantry and to construct a popular constituency for the GVN. This was an attempt to drain one sea and replenish another—and the metaphor reveals something of the futility of the exercise. With experience, the Australian army began to realise, with some dismay and frustration, that the government which it was its task to support was insupportable.

It is striking how much these examples refer to local history. Civic action foundered not so much because its rationale was flawed but because it depended on a viable political order, which the inherited weaknesses of the ruling elite made impossible. The villages also illustrated the tenacity of the past. The army could hardly avoid rupturing the sense of place in the village and disturbing the cultural affiliations of land, community and history. Both Suoi Nghe and Long Phuoc—as forced resettlements which displaced people and asked them to forget their past—suggest that the past was the Australian army's weakness, its blind spot. In turn, the past was the NLF's most precious asset, with its widely accepted claim to be the continuation of the anticolonial struggle and its evocation of local events such as the destruction of Long Phuoc. Patriotism and nationalism trade heavily in the currency of the past, and peasants experience the past as a sense of place, as locale. All this reinforced the NLF's place in the social history of the village. War may be politics carried on by other means but, in Phuoc Tuy, it was also the past continued by other means.

10
Rice, place and revolution

'Dual power'

In Phuoc Tuy, as elsewhere in the South, the political cadres of the Party and NLF formed the local level of a parallel state, challenging the legitimacy, and capacity to govern, of the GVN. One level of this political struggle was linguistic. The revolution-ary forces frequently referred to the GVN as *dich*, 'the enemy', and more pointedly as *nguy quyen*, usually translated as 'the puppet government', but literally meaning 'the false authority'.[1] For their part, the GVN and the task force referred to 'insurgents' and 'terrorists', seeking to give the impression that these were a minor, largely external force.

If the state is, as Max Weber said, that body which can successfully claim both to rule a certain territory and to assert a monopoly of legitimate violence, there was no state in the South in this period, or more exactly, there was an interregnum while two political movements laid claim to the state. Both forces acted as though they had legitimacy, and both made claims to govern which they could only partially fulfil. Each had its taxation system, its economy of production and trade, its armed forces and conscription of youth, and each asserted its right to use

181

violence and enforce its laws. One of the Party's strengths was its capacity not only to establish a provisional government but to develop a parallel state and economy reaching into the village, matching the 'nation-building' claims made for the GVN. The Party sought not only to build its power base but to establish a 'dual power' as contestation in practice.

An indication of this in the province was the way in which space was divided and claimed. The Party had its own administrative division into districts, with different names and boundaries from those on GVN maps; the NLF province of Ba Long comprised both Phuoc Tuy and most of the province to its north. Geographically, the GVN and the Party had political and armed concentrations which were complementary. The former was based in the provincial capital of Phuoc Le, with district centres in the villages of Dat Do, Xuyen Moc, Long Dien and Duc Thanh— each on a main road and close to population centres. The Party had its provincial headquarters at Long Phuoc until its destruction in 1966, when it moved to a base in the Nui May Tao hills; in 1970, this province committee was estimated to have a staff of some 300. District committees of the Party operated from relatively safe bases—'secret zones'—closer to the population centres, in the Long Hai hills (the Long Dat district) and the Nui Dinh hills (the Chau Duc district). There was a certain geographical complementarity in this interrelation of GVN and Party territory. At night, the distinctions were more blurred. Cadres and guerrillas had almost unchallenged access to the villages, with the local-level GVN armed forces—the Regional Forces (RF) and Popular Forces (PF)—being notoriously reluctant to emerge from their posts.

The complementarity between these two powers was demonstrated in everyday exchanges between the soldiers and supporters of each side. The most vivid demonstration of this 'war without frontiers' was in the many families with members in both the NLF and ARVN forces. This was explicable in terms of the complicated history of the South since 1954, but contradicted ideological descriptions of the 'insurgents' as a largely external agency terrorising the population. Particularly in those villages which had long supported the Party, families were caught in cross-currents of loyalty. One of the commanders of the Australian force later put it:

> The majority of the families in Dat Do had at some stage members [in] 445 battalion. Long Dien [was] the same . . . absolutely infested with VC sympathisers. The [RVN] soldiers . . . in these hamlets . . . had mothers, brothers, uncles involved [in the NLF]. Hoa Long was the same . . .

Family relations between supposed enemies were partly the product of Vietnamese history, but were also a result of the NLF's deliberate policy of infiltrating its opponent. During 1969, the Xuan Loc district committee of the Party dispatched some members to join the ARVN and some women members to marry ARVN soldiers.[2]

The extensive infiltration of NLF supporters and spies into the GVN's administration and army was widely recognised. The Australian task force routinely showed its reluctance to share information with even the highest levels of the South Vietnamese government. In late 1969, GVN district and province officials were given details of an Australian plan, and a security leak occurred shortly after; the conclusion drawn by the Task Force was hardly complimentary to its ally: 'A strict "need to know" basis must be maintained at all times—especially with South Vietnamese officials.' One sure sign of an impending NLF attack was the disappearance of GVN officials and civilians, forewarned by relatives in the opposing forces. The province chief in 1969 was 'said to be honest (unlike his deputy)' but 'does not trust his staff, apparently with reason from what we heard about "leaks" . . .' Such examples were unexceptional—the South Vietnamese state was extraordinarily porous and had few secrets, not because its members were careless of security but because it was impossible to know where an individual's loyalties lay. The province illustrated in miniature the character of the Saigon government, which was also infiltrated at the highest levels by NLF agents.[3]

Finally, everyday exchanges occurred as part of the NLF's propaganda activities to undermine the political will, such as it was, of the local levels of the GVN armed forces, which were mostly based in their village of origin. One NLF document reported an encounter with the People's Self-Defence Forces (PSDF):

> . . . during the night we caught 6 PSDF in Hoi An hamlet, and after a warning let them go on the spot . . . we . . . talked with [the families of three others] . . . gave them the instruction [a warning] from [the] District [Committee] and told them to pass it on to the PSDF. During this phase we made a big impression, generally speaking the PSDF is afraid.

This prosaic level of contact between protagonists—often no strangers to each other—illustrated what Burchett wrote of as 'living integrated with the enemy'. In effect, the GVN was honeycombed with its own revolution.

The interdependence of political and military strategies was a constant refrain in NLF activity. The small guerrilla groups which entered villages at night had multiple purposes: they were collecting supplies and information, maintaining their links with political cadres, recruiting and sometimes conscripting the young, and often engaging in political meetings and discussions. One captured NLF soldier recounted:

> He was told his [battalion] was to go on a proselytising mission to Binh Ba. After entering the village, the unit divided into cells to work with the local VC in the people's houses . . .[4]

The organisational charts which Australian intelligence officers painstakingly compiled of the NLF's local infrastructure demonstrated the importance of this political activism, with their sections devoted to proselytising, propaganda and struggle movements, as well as associations of interest groups such as farmers, women and youth.

The political cadres at hamlet, village and district levels were crucial in maintaining this integration of political and military actions. Their roles included arranging supplies for the guerrillas, collecting taxes, organising political meetings, passing on intelligence and implementing the instructions of higher levels of the Party. District-level cadres tended to operate from the relatively safe base areas in the hills, and in 1970 it was estimated that the Long Dat and Chau Duc district committees had staffs of 190 and 160 respectively. Lower-level cadres were, where possible, still in the villages. The activities of these political and support cadres represented the administrative roots of 'dual power' in the village. It was in recognition of the critical importance of these political cadres that the CIA, shortly after the Tet Offensive, initiated the Phoenix program to coordinate intelligence to 'target' political cadres ('Viet Cong Infrastructure') for assassination or arrest.[5]

The Party's parallel administration in turn organised and supported its military forces. Crucial as it was, an emphasis on the village gives the misleading impression that the military struggle in the South was largely waged by local guerrillas, a citizen-soldiery poor in military strength but rich in political spirit. For many on the left in the West, this was part of the romance of the NLF—it was one enduring image from Burchett's books of the early 1960s, for which period it was quite accurate. But by the second half of the 1960s, village guerrillas were the lowest level of armed forces which were increasingly complex, professional and militarily orthodox as one went up the tiers.

Each level effectively corresponded to an administrative level of the Party. In Phuoc Tuy, the small groups of village guerrillas were directed by their village Party committee, while the district committees controlled district concentrated companies, the largest

In Phuoc Tuy, soldiers of the infantry battalions spent much of their one-year tour searching for NLF military units: by the end of the 1960s these efforts had forced most larger military units out of the province, though local level NLF forces survived with continuing popular support. Here, Australian soldiers are shown on a 'search and destroy' sweep in June 1966. (Australian War Memorial, SHA/66/6/VN)

being the 60- to 90-strong Long Dat company. The province Party committee commanded local or mobile force battalions; one of these, the most consistent adversary of Australian troops—known as D445—was more than 300 strong in 1967. Largely recruited from the Dat Do group of villages, its history could be traced back to the Binh Xuyen river pirates brought into the Party's forces in the late 1950s; a decade later, it was described as 'well armed, well led and well motivated' with 'expert local knowledge'. Together, these district and province forces were 'local forces', operating almost exclusively within the province.

By contrast, 'main force' elements, which might be based in the province, were under the direct control of higher echelons of the Party, usually the Central Office for South Vietnam (COSVN), the Party's committee for the South. The main force groups were more often composed of a mix of locally recruited and North Vietnamese soldiers, the latter having made the arduous march south along the Ho Chi Minh trail. As the war went on, and particularly after the appalling attrition of the Tet

Offensive, the relative importance of Northern soldiers in the
South increased. In Phuoc Tuy, however, the balance if anything
shifted the other way, as the relative military successes of the
task force pushed all large forces northwards out of the province,
beyond the reach of Australian patrols. The main adversaries of
the task force remained locally recruited NLF, in D445 battalion,
the district companies and the small groups of village guerrillas.[6]
The latter—in populist imagery the peasants who put down the
hoe to take up the rifle—were relatively marginal in military terms
after the mid-1960s, although the political infrastructure in the
rural social order remained critical.

Illustrations of the ways in which the Party was engaged in
a political as much as military struggle can be seen in its practical
assertions of authority and legitimacy. One example was taxation:
the NLF established rates for regular fund-raising, duplicating
the GVN's taxation system. In March 1967, the NLF taxation
rates in Phuoc Tuy were based on the size of the land-holding
and paid as a percentage of the value of farm produce. Other
forms of production were also taxed: to add to the miseries of
the charcoal burners of Suoi Nghe, the NLF levied a tax on
those who owned kilns, its rate depending on whether the
charcoal was carted by ox-cart or tractor.

The rubber plantations also provided a ready source of tax
income. Workers on the plantation near Binh Ba were paying an
annual tax of $VN300 in 1970, which amounted to about five
days' pay. Tax gathering amongst plantation workers was frequently mentioned in army intelligence, reflecting both their
regular incomes and perhaps a long-standing support for the
Party. In addition, the French owners and managers of the major
plantations were understood to have reached an accommodation
with the NLF, paying taxes to both sides in order to remain in
operation. One NLF document in 1971 reported: 'The French
owners [of the Xuan Son plantation] have requested our permission to resume work. We have agreed and cleared the mined
areas so that they can begin.'[7]

Amongst the Australian soldiers, stories circulated of the
differences between NLF and government tax collectors. The
latter would arrive, accept a drink, and then accept a bribe to
undervalue the plantation output, reducing the tax paid; the NLF
collectors would refuse a drink, already know the output of the
plantation and expect the appropriate tax to be paid. Apocryphal
or not, this account was consistent with the moral and political
styles of these parallel powers. For the NLF, rubber plantations
were valuable as a source of taxation and as a locale of political
support; in addition, their dense foliage provided excellent ave-
nues for guerrilla troop movements, and the plantation settlements

provided 'an important manpower pool, food supplies, machine shops, medical facilities and vehicles for transportation'. With a nice symmetry, the former emblem of modernised colonial exploitation now sustained the revolutionary forces; it also provided sustenance of a different sort for some Australian task force commanders, who occasionally made social calls on the French owners and managers, availing themselves of the tennis courts.[8]

Taxation was a clear means of asserting legitimacy and authority and raising funds to purchase food, arms and other supplies. Another notable form of the same assertion revolved around violence. It has already been suggested that the use of terror was selective and discriminating, with the political intention of isolating the GVN by ensuring that it was unable to establish roots in the rural social order. Assassination was frequently claimed by the NLF as a legitimate exercise of retributive justice; often the NLF was scrupulous in explaining its terror, establishing for it a gloss of popular justice. Notices left on the bodies of assassinated officials declared their guilt and their sentence. One, found on the body of a hamlet official in 1971, read in part:

> Nguyen Van Bong has been a henchman for the enemy since 1962. Until 1969, he has been the security assistant of [the] Nhon Tri hamlet chief—the subject has captured, beaten and terrorised people . . . He has received three warning letters from [the] People's Liberation [Committee]. But he did not repent. 1. Bong was judged by his many atrocities. 2. The subject had been warned many times. 3. The subject was judged by the will of the people.[9]

The leaflet was signed by the People's Liberation Committee of Xuyen Moc. Despite the defensive tone, this was too common an occurrence to be special pleading. It was also a political claim to the legitimacy of retribution based not on procedural criteria but on a populist and patriotic claim to represent the general will.

The shadow economy and 'rice denial'

Armed forces and taxation, an administrative network and a claim to retributive justice were all important aspects of the 'dual power' established by the NLF. In turn, they were underpinned by a trade network of supply routes, procurement in the villages and agricultural production which effectively constituted a shadow economy in the province. Counter-revolutionary warfare recognised the importance of cutting this supply, under the candid title of 'rice denial'.

Inevitably, the supply routes developed by the revolutionary forces focused on the more populated centre of the province, particularly its trading hub of Dat Do and Long Dien. One intelligence report stated in early 1967 that the strong NLF presence in the Dat Do area, and the 'completely ineffective' GVN forces there, gave the NLF

> . . . access to the main population centres of Phuoc Tuy, and to the rice, fish, salt and fruit producing region. It also gives them free access to the town's market where they are able to purchase unlimited quantities of medical supplies, cloth, batteries and other supplies . . .

A major supply route ran from these central villages along the coast to the east, and then north by trails to the major base—and a substantial field hospital—in the Nui May Tao mountains.

Another supply route ran across the north of the province, connecting the base in the west with the Nui May Tao base. These main trade routes were supplemented by smaller paths linking villages with the Long Hai and Nui Dinh hill bases. When the presence of Australian or GVN troops made access to the village markets too dangerous, intermediaries were often used to buy rice. On occasion, daring was enough:

> In one case five VC entered a village, purchased food, and hired a Lambretta [a small three-wheeled taxi] to transport the food. One of the VC was dressed in a police uniform, enabling them to pass through the checkpoint as they left town . . .

Finally, the NLF had also established supply routes by sea; local supplies could be bought in Vung Tau and Long Hai and brought ashore on the isolated beaches to the east, around Loc An, to the south of Xuyen Moc.

This was not only local trade. In 1962, the Party in the South had established a sea route between the main Northern port of Haiphong and Loc An on the coast of Phuoc Tuy. From September 1963, supply ships sailed south, taking two months for the journey and bringing weapons for use throughout the south-east provinces. This sea route was presumably increasingly tenuous after the escalation of the war, and would have been largely replaced by the main supply route of the Ho Chi Minh trail. However, the beaches around Loc An were still a landfall in 1967 for small expensive items such as radios and possibly some arms, and for transporting high-level Party cadres.[10]

Supplementing these supply lines—the trading routes of the parallel state in Phuoc Tuy—were areas where the guerrillas grew their own rice and vegetables in isolated regions near NLF bases. From 1968, this production of crops by NLF forces and their defoliation by Australian forces followed a continuous seesaw. As the task force established greater control over the province, making the movement of major supplies more difficult, gardens and rice fields were established on the northern reaches of the Song Rai river and around Xuyen Moc, as well as near the Nui May Tao base. As regularly as they were established, they were defoliated with herbicides by aerial spraying.

By 1969, despite the political advantage of waiting for the Western withdrawal to gather pace, there were indications that the local NLF was in a parlous state. By the end of that year, the province committee was thought to be desperately short of supplies, relying on bush bananas, dried vegetables and discarded American rations. In May 1970, the province committee issued an instruction that agricultural production was 'of paramount importance this year . . . it requires the efforts of all party members, the entire army and all the people to divert the threat of starvation'. One NLF soldier wrote in his diary in 1969 of:

> . . . a difficult situation which does not suit our ideology. My eyes are staring up somewhere while my stomach is really empty—(I'm starving) and my hands are shaking . . . It is late at night, the more I think of my [military] unit the more I feel my heart bleeding, relating to very sad stories of the war.

Below this entry, an officer, mentor or political cadre wrote— rather unhelpfully perhaps—'in a difficult situation we must stick to our ideology and overcome obstacles'.[11]

Despite such travails, the trade routes which existed in 1967 were still operating in 1969 and 1970, though less busily. The problem appeared to be less critical at village and district level, where the guerrillas had easier access to the villages from their bases and were able to collect supplies at night. The relative ease of this resupply signalled the ineffectiveness of the GVN forces at a village level and the cross-currents of political loyalties in which they were caught. As Brigadier Weir put it later:

> Some of these RF companies were so idle, so corrupt, so poor. There were cases where they tried to kill our advisers—where they were infiltrated by VC—[where] our fellows were ambushed . . . It was terrifying . . . in some cases—not in all cases but in sufficient to make it a worry.

These inadequacies of the local GVN forces continued into 1970 despite Australian government statements that the army could be withdrawn due to the success of 'Vietnamisation'.[12] With such reluctant soldiers 'guarding' villages against the NLF, and with a viable political network in many major villages, local guerrilla forces continued to be resupplied.

These patterns of supply lines were the background to the construction of a minefield to prevent NLF access to the rice harvests in Phuoc Tuy. The rationale—as spelt out in early 1967—was to build an impassable barrier preventing guerrilla access to the villages and cutting the guerrillas off from the rice basket and markets of the province. A fortified position was established on a hill to the north of Dat Do; for the twelve kilometres to the sea, a swath was cleared through trees and rice fields. Two-metre fences were constructed, with as many as 30 000 mines laid in between. To the south lay the sea, to the north the task force would be free to patrol. The minefield was to be a labour-saving device in the project of 'rice denial'.

This strategy was based on two assumptions: that the NLF were fundamentally outsiders who could be kept out by a barrier, and that the local GVN forces were reliable enough to patrol the fence. Each proved to be a political misconception, and the minefield became 'probably the worst error of the Task Force during its presence in Phuoc Tuy'. Because it was presumed that the NLF were outsiders, it was expected that, freed of their influence or pressure, the villagers would be more ready to develop a political allegiance to the GVN, whose authority and

Soldiers of 7RAR walking through the prosperous fishing village of Phuoc Hai, as part of a 'cordon and search' operation in late 1967. A cordon of soldiers was set up around the village, and the inhabitants were searched for revolutionary sympathisers, draft dodgers and so on. The networks connecting villages with the guerrillas tended to be re-established as soon as the cordon was removed. (Australian War Memorial, COL/67/759/VN)

popular appeal would be consolidated with civic action programs. More fundamentally, the minefield strategy assumed constant vigilance by GVN troops, a task in which—for a variety of reasons—they failed.

It is an axiom of military logic that a minefield is only a barrier if continually observed and covered by fire; otherwise it is easily picked through and at worst becomes an arsenal. The worst happened with the Dat Do minefield. Some 5000 mines were dug up by the NLF and re-used to protect their own bases against Australian troops. It was later estimated that, from mid-1968 to the early 1970s, 50 per cent of Australian casualties were from mines from this source.

As the fence was being constructed in early 1967, one soldier wrote to his parents:

> Just now we are laying our Fence past a village, and right by us are women in the padi and children picking melons. All this goes on side by side with the ceaseless traffic of helicopters, Armoured Personnel Carriers and working infantry. It's a funny life.

There were some early and optimistic evaluations that the fence was providing 'a strong barrier to the VC domination of the area'. Rather prematurely, this strongly NLF supporting area was now considered 'secure'.[13]

However, it was soon evident that the fence was being inadequately guarded. When, two years later, the issue became a political controversy in Australia—after media comment that Australian troops were being killed with their own mines—the major-general at Australian Headquarters in Saigon cabled back to Canberra:

> Agree ARVN/RF/PF protection since the minefield was laid in May 67 has been ineffective. For example, a *hoi chanh* who rallied in Jan. 68 reported that more than 2000 mines were lifted from the minefield in the period Jun.–Aug. 67.

By November 1967, only six months after the minefield was completed, the commander of the task force wrote to the province chief in frustration. There had been 'repeated verbal requests' to have breaches in the fence repaired, 'but with no result'. Through one of these breaches, he had discerned 'a definite small cart track', and concluded that the guerrillas were 'enjoying unrestricted passage through the fence'. As early as March of the following year, there were reports of mines being lifted and replanted to the east of the fence.

The minefield became entangled with the political difficulty of knowing whom to trust. To repair the fence, a senior ARVN officer had asked for a map of the minefield, but who could be

entrusted with such knowledge? An American adviser acknowledged the problem; the map 'would not necessarily need to be
handed over to the Vietnamese'. The inertia of the Vietnamese
authorities dragged on through the paperwork. The repairs could
be done once certain supplies were provided; a plan was developed and then postponed, while Australian officers awaited a
'breakthrough'.

By the end of 1967 still nothing had been done; the following
April, the task force decided to abandon the minefield as a
mistake and began the laborious task of clearing the mines. Over
the next two years, there was effectively a race between Australian
mine-clearing teams and the NLF to claim the mines. In the
Party histories, these events are remembered with triumph,
though lifting the mines was dangerous work; cadres from the
local villages competed with each other in an 'emulation
movement' to claim the most mines. As one Long Dat guerrilla
reported to the district committee in 1969:

> . . . some personnel have been mobilised by the [Hoi My] Village
> [Committee] to lift close to 100 mines, and place them in minefields
> along the jungle areas as defence . . . Anyone going in there who
> has no business there could, from now on, come to grief.[14]

In the political struggle to control territory, the mines were now
used to protect the Minh Dam secret zone.

The minefield barrier had been conceived as a politico-military
means of denying the use of space by severing supply routes.
With grim humour, it became popularly known among Australian
soldiers as 'Graham's mistake', after the Brigadier who had
conceived the idea. But the mistake was consistent with the high
expectations of the first years in the province, when the viability
of the GVN army and administration was overestimated, and the
cross-currents of historical and political loyalties in which it was
caught were obscured.

The Tet Offensive

These dilemmas of the American and Australian position in
Vietnam were not enough, however, to resolve the war. As early
as the end of 1967, both the Vietnamese Party and some in the
American administration viewed the war as a stalemate. The
former could not lose politically, though the enormous military
might brought against it had rendered some of its active supporters passive or exhausted, and ensured that it could not win
in conventional military terms. The Western forces could do little
to salvage the political credibility of the GVN, but nor could the

rapid military escalation since 1965 bring military victory against an antagonist which refused to be drawn and which was intent on conserving its forces. It was this stalemate which formed the context of the Tet Offensive in February 1968.

The contemporary Vietnamese account of the rationale of the offensive is that it was intended to confront the American administration with the limits of its options. The Party had analysed the American options as an invasion of North Vietnam, the bombing of the south of China or the introduction of nuclear weapons; at least the last two options involved the possibility of drawing the USSR and China into the conflict, and the Party believed that the Americans had not the will for this nor for extending the war to the North. On this reasoning, the Americans had reached the limits of 'limited war', and could not continue escalating. It was hoped that the political impact in Saigon and Washington of an offensive would at least shorten the war, and although the offensive was presented to the troops as the final effort, the subtext was of a radical tilting of the balance of forces, without the promise of finality. The Party's orders for the offensive, distributed to its military forces, spoke of moving 'forward to achieve final victory', and went on: 'This will be the greatest battle ever fought in the history of our country. It will bring forth worldwide change but will also require many sacrifices. It will decide the fate and survival of our Fatherland . . .'

During mid-1967, the Party in Hanoi conducted seminars to discuss its options. Three courses had been rejected; the first, initiating large battles, would be too uncertain and severe in terms of losses; a second option, mounting a rural uprising, would have little echo in the West, and it was intended that the offensive have a political impact in Washington and on American public opinion; finally, large-scale attacks on the cities were seen as beyond the capacity of the Party in the South. The strategy adopted involved coordinated small-scale specialist attacks on the cities, using mostly local forces (except in Hue) and anticipating urban uprisings if the GVN collapsed. Main-force units would be waiting nearby to capitalise on any uprisings which occurred, but the Party was uncertain about the strength of its political infrastructure in the cities.[15]

Attacks began across the South on 31 January and continued over the following few days. Troops entered Saigon, where the American embassy was attacked by a small but spectacular group, and Hue, where a regiment of the North's People's Army of Vietnam (PAVN) occupied the old imperial citadel and massacred many government sympathisers and officials. Attacks were made on 36 of the 44 provincial capitals and 64 of the 242 district towns. In Phuoc Tuy, the pattern was similar, using local forces

who threw themselves into desperate attacks on the capital, Phuoc
Le, and Long Dien. Early on the morning of 1 February, the
D445 Battalion began an attack on the province capital, and by
the afternoon had taken the hospital and electricity supply station.
Australian infantry and armoured vehicles were dispatched from
Nui Dat and there was street-to-street fighting in the town;
sporadic fighting was still going on a week later. Elsewhere in
the province, there were minor actions as part of the offensive.
Trees were felled across some roads to prevent the movement
of reinforcements, the army posts were attacked in major villages
such as Xuyen Moc and Hoa Long, and the officials in Suoi
Nghe were assassinated.

Some of the fiercest fighting took place in Dat Do and Long
Dien, where the Long Dat district company occupied the Long
Dien market, beginning its attack on the morning of the 2nd.
By the afternoon, the NLF was in control of the Long Dien
police post, power generator and communications buildings, and
the GVN forces there had either fled or retreated to the military
barracks. The fighting continued for seven days, and was joined
by an Australian infantry company which arrived in the town's
market early on the 4th. The southern part of the village was
almost completely destroyed by artillery and air strikes called in
to dislodge the NLF. Finally, on the evening of the 8th, the
NLF district command decided to withdraw and carry the
wounded to Minh Dam base.

These attacks, as throughout the South, were repulsed and
had little immediate military impact; but they had a galvanising
effect in the West, demonstrating a capacity for coordinated
military action which refuted calm assertions that the war was
under control. Within Vietnam, they precisely exposed the balance of political forces. The armed forces of the GVN were, in
Phuoc Tuy as elsewhere, frequently conspicuous by their absence,
reluctance or ineffectiveness. According to one later report, an
ARVN battalion in Long Dien displayed 'open cowardice . . .
observed by the civilian population'. In the same town, the
Australian Civil Affairs unit had established a temporary camp
for those whose homes had been destroyed. An ARVN battalion
was left to protect it overnight, but it failed to do so and the
camp was burnt down. Worse were the sins of commission. In
both Long Dien and the province capital, once the fighting had
subsided, ARVN troops set to looting houses and shops. If the
GVN troops acquitted themselves like soldiers with nothing at
stake, nor was there the anticipated uprising in the towns and
cities. In the province capital, many citizens temporarily left to
escape the fighting; in Long Dien, while there was some active
support for the NLF, others left to avoid the destruction.[16]

A popular uprising clearly did not occur during Tet, in Phuoc Tuy or elsewhere; the Party knew that its infrastructure in the urban areas was weak, but had expected to mobilise 'a substantially greater number of people than actually responded'. The political and military conditions for a successful uprising did not exist, with the Western military presence too strong and pervasive, and with many of the Party's less zealous supporters simply standing back, exhausted or cautious. According to one CIA report at the end of the hectic month of February, 'the Viet Cong received virtually no popular support, but neither was there a rallying to the government side . . . further military defeats could cause a sudden swing away from the government . . .'

The offensive nonetheless achieved a minimal victory. Tet eventually forced an American de-escalation of the war, a bombing pause and the opening of peace negotiations. In the immediate short term, it forced the American and GVN forces to a more defensive position to protect the urban areas, releasing some of the pressure on the countryside, where the Party's political strength lay. But the offensive and its aftermath—the added offensives of May and August—cost the Party substantial losses, and during 1968 and 1969 the revolutionary forces were weakened by these losses. In addition, the 'targeting' of the Phoenix program, which killed or captured many experienced village cadres, did further damage over the following few years. Ironically, the Americans thought the program was unsuccessful because it swept up few high-ranking officials, when more crucial was its impact on the rural infrastructure.[17]

But if the Party was weakened by Tet, so were its antagonists. This is the origin of the somewhat misplaced interpretation that Tet was a military defeat turned into a political victory. The argument was that the Party and NLF lost a military battle but were able to manipulate American democratic institutions—the uncensored public sphere of television coverage and opinion formation—to turn opinion against the war. Thus the political dissent of an 'open' society was a weakness in dealing with a closed, 'autocratic' society. General William Westmoreland later told one reporter that Vietnam was the first war in history lost on the front page of the *New York Times*.[18] Certainly, the opposition to the war was galvanised by Tet, and more so than the Vietnamese Party had expected, but the Westmoreland argument rests on several flawed assumptions.

First, it assumes that the war was in some meaningful sense winnable for the Americans, and that—but for political dissent and the weakening of political will—the course of the war could have been radically different. But once one discounts the option of continued occupation, this assumption relies on a collapse of the Vietnamese Party's willingness to continue, which was unlikely, and a dramatically improved capacity of the GVN to establish its rule. The latter proposition was already seen as dubious among some American policy advisers.

The second assumption is that it was political dissent and the anti-war movement which made the difference; that, in effect, a growing anti-war movement broke the American will to continue. Yet Kolko argues convincingly that American policy changed after Tet because the American establishment confronted its own crisis. This sense of a crisis involved a range of factors: a dollar crisis brought on by the budget deficits incurred by the war, a political recognition that the war was draining resources away from dealing with domestic social and racial tensions in the cities, a strategic alarm that Vietnam was absorbing military power at the expense of other strategic interests (such as NATO and Korea), and finally, the growing unpopularity of the war in the opinion polls and among the ruling elite. Thus 'the Tet Offensive's most decisive effect was to articulate clearly the fact that the United States was now confronting a potentially grave crisis'.

While the Tet Offensive helped to reverse public opinion in America and, after some delay, in Australia, the impact was broader and more complex than a simple opposition between military and political imperatives, or in Westmoreland's terms, a military victory undermined by media distortion. In the months immediately after Tet, the Pentagon, the CIA and the State department all argued that further escalation was futile, and began to consolidate their scepticism about the war. By the beginning of 1969, these three agencies were entirely pessimistic about continuing with the war, while even the optimists—primarily in the armed forces—agreed that the GVN could not survive either a political or a military contest with the revolutionary forces. As importantly, immediately after Tet, the ruling elites in American business, law and the media began to articulate their doubts and to view the war as an economic and political liability in which American interests were hopelessly bogged.[19] In these senses, Tet forced a recognition of the limits of the American imperium, as the Vietnamese Party had hoped it would; it was the turning point of the war because it revealed the limits of American power and the fragility of the South Vietnamese ruling elite upon which it had built its hopes.

11
Morbid symptoms: Australia, 1967–1969

The three-year period from the election of 1966 to the Moratorium mobilisation which began at the end of 1969 has all the features of a pause. The anti-war movement began the period demoralised, while the government became progressively more disoriented, and the ALP struggled to contain its divisions. It was also a confused interim period between the hegemony of Cold War support for intervention in Vietnam and the clear disintegration of this perspective in the early 1970s. As Gramsci put it, in such times, when the old is dying and the new has not yet formed, morbid symptoms appear.

In this process, the Tet Offensive acted as the pivot point. For each of the different political forces in Australia, Tet was crucial in different ways. For the conservatives, it signified the crumbling of their postwar policy, though this was only clear after the implications of Tet for American policy had emerged. Within the ALP, the left felt Tet vindicated its view that the Vietnam War was unwinnable as well as immoral, while the right was convinced that the party's policy of withdrawal was now in the interests of the Americans themselves. For the radical left developing within the universities, Tet reinforced the romantic, millennial idea that 1968 was the beginning of the end for

capitalism, and encouraged the argument for an NLF victory
over an imperialist venture. And finally, although within the peace
movement Tet was little commented upon, it set in train a decline
in the popularity of the war and a growing assumption that the
war was coming to an end. But this, ironically, made it more
difficult to mobilise support for the movement.

The impact of Tet

Editorial reaction to the Tet Offensive was dramatic. It had
abruptly punctured confident assurances that the war against the
NLF was being won. *The Age* was representative of considered
opinion when it asked in an editorial entitled 'What went wrong?':
'When the crunch is over and the dead have been counted, are
we to return to "normal" war with the methods which have been
ineffective . . . ?' Now the paper spoke gloomily of its 'looming
doubts whether [the war] is being won'.

> Confidence in American power has been shaken, since [the offensive]
> proved that it could not even protect its own embassy in Saigon.
> Confidence in American tactics and strategy has been undermined
> by evidence that it is ineffectual in practice and mistaken in theory.
> As for the new Thieu–Ky Government, its administrative facade has
> been exposed as paper-thin.

This quickly became the conventional wisdom about the Tet
Offensive: as Creighton Burns put it, the psychological impact
was 'shattering'. But Burns, who now regularly reported the war
as a staff reporter based in Singapore, drew a wider conclusion.
Tet also demonstrated that 'the political and social conditions for
military success have been seriously neglected', in the sense that
the social roots of the revolution were still strong. The 'tinsel
achievement' of maintaining the regime in the South, in spite of
its corruption and unpopularity, had produced a 'false
confidence'. The Americans might win military victories, but they
were losing the political struggle.

    The Tet Offensive also suggested that the war could not be
further escalated. This had been part of the Vietnamese Party's
strategy: to reveal to the Americans that they had reached the
limit of their power and, short of an escalation into nuclear war
and a possible Chinese intervention, had to find a negotiated
way out. The Australian government was in the same position,
being unwilling to increase its commitment, though for more
prosaic reasons. On 3 February the new prime minister, John
Gorton, revealed this in one of those off-the-cuff remarks which
so disconcerted his party. Asked at a press conference whether
there would be any increase in the force to Vietnam, he replied:

"We ARE winning their hearts and minds — Yesterday seventeen Viet Cong presented themselves at the U.S. Embassy."

The Tet Offensive of early 1968 punctured American and Australian assurances that the war was 'going well'. One of its most dramatic episodes was played out before TV cameras at the American Embassy in Saigon, when a small group attacked the compound. The year 1968 was a turning point, and one of the signs of this was a growing scepticism that language and evidence were being distorted to maintain the official version of the war. (Tanner, The Age, 1 February 1968)

'Australia won't increase its commitment.' There had been no American request to do so, and 'as far as I'm concerned that's a permanent statement'.[1]

Coming as it did in the midst of the Tet Offensive, this appeared to indicate a flagging will to proceed with the war, but in fact revealed a local imperative. During the second half of 1967, both Cabinet and its military advisers had concluded that the commitment to Vietnam had stretched Australia's military capabilities to their very modest limits. In August 1967, the Foreign Affairs and Defence committee of Cabinet had met to discuss a possible further expansion. Howson reported that the advice of both Treasury and the military was to keep the increased assistance as limited as possible.

The decision to increase the Task Force from two to three battalions was made in principle in early September and announced on 17 October 1967. This brought the total troop commitment to a mere 8500, but was made in the teeth of some reluctance, a reluctance which was pragmatic and fiscal rather than reflecting doubts about the policy of intervention. Holt, apparently impressed by President Johnson's persuasive powers, had to overcome the opposition of McMahon, Hasluck and Allen

Fairhall—his Treasurer, and ministers for External Affairs and Defence respectively—to sway Cabinet to commit a third battalion. Holt was disposed to send as much aid as possible, citing possible advantages in the form of trade negotiations.

That the prime minister felt it necessary to overrule such senior ministers indicated a compelling motivation. Shortly after, when McMahon was in Washington—the decision to expand the Task Force not yet having been conveyed to the Americans—he came under extremely strong pressure for more troops. According to Freudenberg, Holt was being 'bullied' by Johnson, and this explained the stress Holt was manifestly under during the latter part of 1967, before his disappearance in December. Nevertheless, despite these pressures, the reluctance of some senior ministers to expand the Task Force was shared by the Defence committee, which insisted during December 1967 that further military commitments were impossible; Cabinet reportedly accepted this view.[2]

Another tension associated with the escalation to a third battalion soon became evident. An opinion poll taken during November revealed that 46 per cent of the electorate disapproved of the decision, with 37 per cent in favour and 17 per cent undecided; this was the first time that more had opposed than approved an increase in the commitment. One government response to intimations that the tide of opinion was turning was the issuing in late 1967 of a pamphlet, in which the conservatives seemed to tone down their intransigent justification for intervention and endeavoured to show that they and the Americans had always sought peace, while Hanoi and Peking had refused to negotiate in good faith.[3]

By the end of 1967, then, the line had been drawn at the existing level of troop commitments, though this decision had not been made public. Gorton's statement during Tet that the Task Force would not be increased was consistent with this view in Cabinet and in the Defence committee. But, occurring while the shock of the Tet Offensive was front-page news, it conveyed other messages. As 'the first discordant note in the carefully orchestrated rhetoric of the past six years', it suggested an erosion of the will to continue, a less than fulsome view of the American alliance and a pre-emptive approach to policy-making. Finally, it alienated, and would not be forgotten by, the DLP. Santamaria commented that Gorton's 'unfortunate statement made Australia seem to weaken, even before the United States actually did weaken . . .'[4] For the right, the incident sowed the seeds of distrust and would be a symbol of Gorton's responsibility for all that was going wrong.

The conservatives were prisoners of the rhetoric of their past, yet had little control over decisions on the future. Some two months after Tet, President Johnson announced that he would not renominate for the presidential elections, and made an offer to open peace talks, accompanied by the suspension of bombing raids over most of North Vietnam. Widely interpreted as a response to Tet and to the demoralisation of the American ruling class which it triggered, the announcement was described by one Australian commentator as 'momentous', with the Gorton government 'decidedly embarrassed'. According to Renouf, Johnson's announcement was met with consternation in Canberra, where no one had divined what was happening in Washington, and no one had been consulted; when Gorton protested to the Americans, they replied that they had intended him to be told at the same time as the media.

Howson heard the news in the Melbourne Club, and the following day lunched with Alan Watt. They agreed that the announcement brought

> . . . a feeling of some apprehension. To my mind, it's the first step of the Americans moving out of South-east Asia . . . within a few years . . . there'll be no white faces on the Asian mainland . . . from now on, and to a much greater extent, we shall be isolated and on our own.[5]

This Kiplingesque response—the 'white faces on the Asian mainland' was a nice touch of Howson's Anglo-Australian vision—nevertheless divined the drift of American policy.

Since 1949, conservative foreign policy had been founded on anxiety at the British withdrawal from Asia, fear of China and the need for its containment, and concern to encourage American 'responsibility' in the region. The enthusiasm for intervention in Vietnam had been an outcome of that policy. But over the few years following Tet, the postwar American policies of containment and superpower confrontation began to be dismantled. In late 1968, Johnson called a halt to the bombing and recognised the NLF as a party to peace talks; in May and June 1969 the new president, Richard Nixon, announced the first withdrawal from Vietnam and the 'Nixon doctrine', which envisaged a less directly interventionist role in the future; and in mid-1971 it was announced that Nixon would visit Peking. With Tet, the Americans had begun to recognise their limits, shifting from containment to rapprochement. In Australia, a generation of conservative foreign policy—dependent on encouraging the expansion of American power—was disintegrating.

During 1968 and 1969, the conservatives were becalmed, unable to reassert their old policy, which the Americans were undermining, and unable to consider its replacement. This was widely noted at the time. The CPA, Labor, the DLP and commentators in the *Australian Quarterly* all noted the indecision, paralysis and division within conservative ranks. While *News-Weekly* fulminated against the loss of direction, the CPA clearly took some satisfaction in describing Johnson's announcement as 'an admission of defeat, personal as well as national', as a consequence of which 'Australian foreign policy is in ruins'.

> Like Saigon, Canberra is disoriented, confused and most unhappy . . . Like the Bourbons, the right has learnt nothing from the collapse of the Vietnam policy . . . The present Government is unable to produce any new ideas, and so it sticks to the old, even when they have failed.

As importantly, the *Tribune* editorial predicted that the conservatives would shift towards more repressive domestic policies in a desperate attempt to stem the tide of events. It suggested that the proposed amendments to the National Service Act, which increased penalties for non-compliance, were a straw in the wind. But a more repressive policy towards dissent was internally contradictory: 'It widens the front of the struggle against conscription, the Vietnam war, government policy, by introducing new elements of democratic rights.'[6] Much of this was prescient, both the early recognition of Tet as a turning point and the diagnosis that a more repressive policy on enforcing conscription would draw wider social forces into the movement against the war.

The paralysis in conservative thinking in this period was marked. In June 1968, Gorton announced that the Defence committee had been instructed to prepare a new strategic assessment. Completed by the end of August, its consideration by Cabinet was delayed, partly 'because the Prime Minister, reluctant to make up his own mind, put off discussions'. Cabinet came to the issue in November, but no major announcements were expected until after Gorton visited Washington in March. Everything was in suspense pending the outcome of the Paris talks on Vietnam and the still unclear direction of American policy under Nixon.

In February 1969, Hasluck left the ministry to take up the position of governor-general, and the conservatives lost a committed ideologue or, as Howson put it, 'a real pillar of the government'. Santamaria worried out loud in *News-Weekly* that this was the end of an era during which foreign policy had been 'clear and purposeful, even if the purpose was limited'. Now 'clarity and purpose have vanished', and defence policy was 'non-existent'. Howson, too, was worried that 'possibly this will indicate a change in Australia's foreign policy'. But nothing so decisive was to occur. One legacy of the stability of conservative foreign policy over the previous two decades was that there were no mechanisms within the Liberal Party for rethinking policy. Decisions had been centralised in a few hands and reflected the indolent consensus amongst the conservatives. It was only after McMahon became minister at the end of 1969 that External Affairs set up a policy unit responsible for considering the future. During 1968 and 1969, the conservatives waited for Gorton to articulate a policy, even though this promised to be a long wait. Howson reported 'a growing fear that Gorton does not really know where he's leading us in foreign affairs', and *News-Weekly*, always quick to articulate such fears, had earlier noted Gorton's 'fatal indecision on the matter of defence'.[7]

But the focus on their leader belied deeper divisions amongst the conservatives, in which the dispute on defence issues became a coded reference for a leadership struggle. Gorton had a number of qualities which made a significant section of the Liberal Party regret they had elected him on Holt's death: he was an avowed centralist in a party which had always claimed it was otherwise, and a populist in a party habituated to patrician leaders. He was insufficiently reverential to the certainties of the conservatives' own past, and had a disconcerting willingness to answer any question put to him, which led to off-the-cuff policy statements. Finally, and most incautiously, he had alienated the DLP, whose support Menzies had always assiduously cultivated.

Perhaps above all, Gorton cared little for forward defence or for the precedence which foreign policy took over national issues amongst the conservatives. Although it was never clearly articulated, he was moving towards a policy of 'fortress Australia', which envisaged troops being posted overseas only for specific purposes, rather than permanently stationed in forward defence positions and inevitably drawn into local and regional conflicts. Like Menzies in the 1950s, Gorton appeared to view national economic development as a higher priority than military capability; he hinted at an 'Israeli-type defence force', by which was meant trained personnel in civilian occupations capable of ready mobilisation. In all this, there were intimations of self-reliance, though Santamaria could point out with some justice that the 'fortress' appeared to have few defences, with no evident intention of increased defence spending.[8]

To the limited extent that these views were articulated, they were bitterly opposed by some within the Liberal Party. As early as May 1968, there were reports of the distress caused when Gorton had challenged the forward defence policies 'so dear to the hearts of the old guard on his back bench'. When, in August, the Liberal party room debated foreign policy, the result was a

split between 'fortress Australia' and forward defence views. 'Not
an extremely satisfactory debate', Howson noted in his diary, but
'it does indicate to us that there is no policy on external affairs
at present . . .'[9]

The opposition to a rethinking of foreign affairs and defence
issues was more than simply backbench opinion. Influential
ministers such as Hasluck and Fairhall were strong public advocates of forward defence and resisted change, while the manifest
ambition of McMahon guaranteed that he opposed Gorton on
this, as on most other issues. The paralysis of the conservatives
was being compounded by their internal divisions, and it was
telling that these should have focused on foreign affairs and
Vietnam. It was small wonder that in this period the peace
movement had difficulty finding government members prepared
to speak at public meetings and 'teach-ins' on the war. The
enthusiasm to publicly argue the case, evident in 1965 and 1966,
had evaporated by the late 1960s; the secretary of CICD
recollected that 'gradually it was just impossible to get people to
participate from the conservatives'. When Malcolm Fraser, the
new minister for Defence, spelt out his views in February 1970,
his speech was considered 'the first substantial defence of the
Government's Vietnam policy for many months'.[10]

If the conservatives' policy paralysis was compounded by
internal division and the leadership struggle, the DLP provided
another obstacle to reformulating policy. While the government
vacillated, the DLP valiantly resisted change. When Santamaria
met Gorton shortly after the latter became prime minister, he
was alarmed at what he saw as Gorton's casual disregard for the
problems of defence and foreign affairs. The right's concern that
Gorton's attachment to forward defence was less than reverential
was further increased by the appointment of Gordon Freeth to
replace Hasluck. Freeth was junior and inexperienced, particularly
compared to the powerful men who had held the portfolio since
1949; Santamaria wondered aloud whether Gorton wanted to be
his own External Affairs minister, 'with Freeth as his mouthpiece'.

Freeth's statement the following August that the Soviet naval
presence in the Indian Ocean posed no real threat to Australia,
while consistent enough with the new atmosphere of détente,
placed the right in high alarm. Increasingly, the conservatives
were vulnerable to attack from the ALP for being more hawkish
than the Americans, and from the DLP for being less hawkish
than the Americans had been in the golden age of Dulles. In
the election of October 1969, the DLP campaigned against
Freeth, and the minister for External Affairs lost his seat. It was
ironic that one of the DLP's last hurrahs should be directed
against the conservatives; it was appropriate that it should be in

And his ghost may be heard as you pass by the billabong . . .

In June 1969 US President Nixon announced the first unilateral withdrawal of troops. The Australian government appeared to have been caught unawares, though in fact prime minister Gorton had recently returned from Washington dropping broad hints that the Americans might begin withdrawal. While in Washington, Gorton had promised to go 'Waltzing Matilda' with Nixon; his government seemed caught in a state of paralysis, unable to rethink its policy and internally divided over Gorton's leadership. (Collette, Australian, *11 June 1969)*

defence of the Cold War past against the present.[11] The conservative government was in a genuine dilemma. Contrary to what many on the left supposed, the decision to intervene in Vietnam had been made in Canberra, rather than dictated by Washington, and was based on a web of strategic fears and presumptions. But now that policy was being unmade in Vietnam and in Washington, with the government and the Department of External Affairs seemingly unable to anticipate the turn of events.

When he returned from Washington in May 1969, Gorton presented a reassuring face, reporting to parliament that Nixon had 'authorised' him to say that the US would 'continue to participate in the Pacific and to strengthen the "forces of freedom and progress" in Asia'. This apparent continuity with the past was rudely contradicted some three weeks later, when Nixon announced the first unilateral withdrawal of 25 000 troops, accompanied by the now-standard platitudes about the increasing strength of the South Vietnamese forces—platitudes which *News-Weekly* brusquely dismissed as 'humbug'. Gorton stated that there were no plans for a similar Australian withdrawal, as it would be 'militarily quite ridiculous' to withdraw parts of a 'self contained' force.[12]

Informed opinion was that the government had been caught unawares again, unable to recognise the American shift from escalation to de-escalation. In *The Age*, Bruce Grant commented: 'The Government maintains the public position that nothing has changed, a position so fanciful that it is impossible to contest seriously.' Cartoonists depicted Gorton bogged in the quagmire of Vietnam, singing 'Waltzing Matilda' while Nixon passed him by. However, Gorton's report to parliament on his return from Washington, when he dwelt at great length on what Australia would do if the Americans should announce a unilateral withdrawal, contained veiled hints at events to come. But these were no more than an undercurrent, and did not dispel the more dominant impression of a government unaware of policy shifts in its major ally, an impression reinforced in July when Nixon announced his 'Nixon doctrine', which established the basis for an American disengagement of ground forces and for the 'Vietnamisation' of the war. Momentous as they were, these decisions were not accommodated in Australian foreign policy. A perfect statement of the disarray in conservative ranks came from Fairhall when he told a meeting of Liberal Party candidates that the war was 'inevitably moving towards an unpredictable end at an indefinite date'.[13]

Labor: After the debacle

The disintegration of the conservatives' position provided excellent conditions for the ALP to minimise its own dilemmas on Vietnam. Tet was again a turning point. As the consequences became more obvious, the official ALP position became more electorally acceptable. The right could argue that retrieving American prestige was now the highest priority and required withdrawal from the war; the ALP's policy was thus made consistent with support for the American alliance. The left could feel that their opposition to the war had been vindicated by events. In this, ALP leaders were often better informed of the drift of opinion in America, particularly within Congress. In 1968 and 1969, Labor could present itself as aligned with an emergent American policy, and the conservatives as out of step, if not obstinately outdated.

When he became Labor leader in February 1967, Whitlam

had moved quickly to defuse the issue of Vietnam both within the party and electorally. As he wrote with hindsight, his task was 'to ensure that foreign issues were no longer turned to the ALP's disadvantage'. His prime concern was to 'de-escalate' the debate in the party. A number of factors were involved here. First, there was a widespread acceptance within the party that the 1966 debacle had resulted from both the substance and the handling of the issues of Vietnam and conscription. In this period, opposition to Vietnam was an electoral liability. About half of ALP supporters were in favour of a continued involvement in Vietnam, while some 70 per cent of conservative supporters favoured the war; this meant that—on the single issue of Vietnam—the ALP, by opposing the war and arguing for withdrawal, would lose more of its own support than it could hope to gain from the conservatives.[14] Not until August 1969 would it become electorally popular to oppose the war, though the enthusiasm for escalating the war had clearly waned by the end of 1967. In diluting Labor's stance on Vietnam, Whitlam sought to bring the policy more into line with a conservative public opinion.

Second, Whitlam and his circle were concerned that the ALP should gain votes on domestic matters rather than lose them on foreign policy. In the detailed account of a Whitlam insider such as Freudenberg, it is telling how modestly Vietnam figures by comparison with the preoccupation with reform of the party machine and the development of urban, social and health policies. Disputes over Vietnam were frequently entangled with other issues—particularly with the struggle to shift the balance of power from the administrative to the parliamentary wing—but those in Whitlam's circle were predominantly concerned with developing policies, winning government and implementing those policies. Vietnam was seen as an issue that could only damage and poison the party. They did not intend to allow it to stand in the way.

The third feature was that the party, especially the Caucus, allowed Whitlam and his deputy, Lance Barnard—as shadow spokesmen for External Affairs and Defence respectively—greater autonomy in the public articulation of policy than had recently been the case. Partly this was a recognition of the need to deal with the debacle of 1966, and partly it reflected a growing conviction on the left that an extra-parliamentary movement was a more effective means of changing government policy. Whitlam and Barnard had a virtual monopoly on foreign policy, and Caucus allowed them a relatively free hand while the left pursued its independent line. There has been some suggestion that this was an implicitly agreed *modus operandi*. The leadership had substantial licence to articulate policy, which it intended to keep vague, and this in turn gave the left similar room for manoeuvre: 'Whitlam and Barnard indicated clearly that they were the authoritative spokesmen. Alternative viewpoints, notably those held by Cairns and others on the left, appeared the expression of minority attitudes.'[15]

Each of these factors reduced some of the tension within the ALP, though Vietnam remained, with other issues, a source of factional dispute. After 1966, Labor was perceived to be moving to the right on Vietnam. In late February 1967, in his first test on the issue as leader, Whitlam told an ABC interviewer that it was 'academic' to discuss withdrawing troops until there was a settlement or armistice, and that this settlement was Labor's major focus. The executive, Caucus and party chieftains outside the parliament remained silent, and it seemed that Whitlam had been allowed a free hand, without rebuke, to make Labor's position on Vietnam appear more moderate.

When the ALP's federal conference met in Adelaide in August, it was presented with a motion from the foreign affairs committee which gave the leadership a good deal of latitude, stating simply that the ALP opposed the war and would work to end it and Australian participation. But this was too much for the conference, which passed a resolution that an ALP government would 'consider that it had no alternative but to withdraw forces' if the Americans did not agree to three conditions: a halt to the bombing of the North, the recognition of the NLF as a negotiating party and a transformation of the war into a 'holding operation'. This signalled that there were limits on Whitlam's freedom of manoeuvre, but a less equivocal amendment put by the veteran power-broker of the left, 'Joe' Chamberlain, was defeated, illustrating the shift in the balance of power since 1966. The successful resolution had been drafted by Cairns and Whitlam, and signalled the new flexibility which both left and right accorded each other. Compared with Calwell's unequivocal and emotive opposition, ALP policy was now seen as more flexible and less electorally damaging.[16]

If Labor was defusing an electoral liability, this nevertheless lost the party some support on its left, particularly in the peace movement. The rapprochement of the 1966 campaign was clearly over. Some parts of the peace movement were alienated by what they saw as a betrayal of the Vietnam policy, while Labor's right just as actively sought to dissociate itself from the movement. The NSW branch was the most aggressive in this. Early in 1967, William Colbourne, the right-wing secretary of the NSW branch, accused some ALP members of aligning themselves with communists by taking part in the LBJ demonstrations and thus providing 'the television and Press with the type of propaganda they wanted to support their claims that the ALP was anti-American'. A few weeks later, the NSW executive banned ALP members from activity in AICD, ostensibly on the grounds that AICD had supported some non-Labor candidates in the 1966 election but more bluntly, as the executive put it, because 'association of members of the ALP with the AICD has been and now is damaging to the political image and electoral prospects of the ALP'. As the increasingly radical Vietnam Action Campaign commented, these were some of the first indications of a 'campaign to change A.L.P. and Peace Movement policies on Vietnam . . .' Although Labor's federal executive had, at the last minute, overruled the NSW branch, 'attacks of this kind . . . are bound to increase in the near future'.[17] In NSW, the disenchantment was clearly mutual. In Victoria, because Labor leaned more to the left, there was less of a breach.

The dilution of Labor's opposition on Vietnam continued in early 1968, when Whitlam returned from a ten-day tour of Vietnam just as the Tet Offensive exploded. Wisely, he begged off giving interviews until he had acquainted himself with local political reactions to the offensive. At a press conference the following day, Whitlam argued that 'the allies are pursuing basically the wrong method in dealing with the war', and 'the emphasis should be switched from attacking North Vietnam to clearing, holding and building'. He criticised the South Vietnamese government as corrupt and ineffective; the Americans, he argued, could not be defeated militarily, but their objectives needed to be more limited if hostilities were to be concluded. While this was sceptical, it was more about how the Americans could avoid failure in Vietnam than about withdrawing from the war.

Later in the same month, Whitlam again illustrated his licence to interpret policy when he stated that the 1967 policy meant withdrawal 'only if no notice was taken' by the Americans of the changes Labor wanted in the conduct of the war, which left open to interpretation what constituted 'taking notice'. By early 1969, one by no means unsympathetic writer was referring to 'the ambiguities and shiftiness of A.L.P. policy on Vietnam'; others were more critical and catalogued Whitlam's evasions as betrayal.[18] Only so much can be learnt by detailing these changes in position, precisely because their basic feature was a concern to avoid an explicit position. By presenting a moving target, the right hoped to defuse the issue, thus avoiding the divisions in Labor's ranks and within its electoral support; in this, some on the left complied, recognising the liabilities involved in their own opposition.

These gaps between the peace movement and the ALP

disclosed another dynamic in the politics of the war: in the late 1960s, Labor was seen less and less as a hopeful medium for dissent from the war. Although the efforts of some Labor leaders to dissociate the party from overt opposition to the war had little impact on the peace movement participation of rank-and-file ALP members, they reduced Labor's capacity to represent and channel opposition to the war. Before 1966, the dissent against the war had primarily taken place outside official political processes, being voiced in journals, universities, pulpits, meeting halls and in the streets. After the 1966 defeat, the party system was increasingly unable to contain opposition, and failed to channel and respond to the increasingly radical cultural momentum of the movement. The resulting frustration fuelled the radicalisation of the movement and took its centre further beyond Labor's concerns, to the satisfaction of many radicals. It was only in the early 1970s that Labor succeeded in recapturing the momentum of the movement, and by then its creative and cultural powers had dispersed to other sites such as the women's and anti-apartheid movements. The volatility and creativity of the movement in the late 1960s were well beyond Labor's control, and to an extent the centre of political gravity had moved outside the parliamentary system into a more amorphous social movement. The conservative parties were unable to argue their rationale for the war, and Labor had only limited capacity to define alternative policies.

Nevertheless, after Tet, Labor increasingly had the upper hand in party political struggles. By 1969, both the direction of American policy and the tide of Australian public opinion were running Labor's way. In August 1969 an opinion poll found, for the first time, a majority in favour of withdrawal: 55 per cent now favoured this course, up from 40 per cent in May. It was presumably significant that Nixon's first announcement of a withdrawal fell between the two dates. As importantly, a large majority of Labor voters (72 per cent) were in favour of withdrawal. Of conservative voters, a bare majority wanted to continue and 41 per cent wanted withdrawal. It had taken this long for public support for the war to erode.

Whitlam had bought time, even if this won him no friends on the left. By mid-1969, Labor had the good fortune that the course of the war had fallen into line with its policy: the Americans had recognised the NLF, instituted bombing pauses and announced the first withdrawals. Whitlam was able to go into the election in October pledging the withdrawal of Australian forces by June 1970, and arguing that

> The greatest assistance . . . Australia can now render the United
> States in its tragic dilemma in Vietnam is to stop impeding the

liquidation of this war which the American people and the American nation so desperately seek.

Gorton, by contrast, reaffirmed his commitment to an unpopular war, attempting to hold the resentful allegiance of those to his right. Labor would reap the harvest of these shifts in the election of 1969, providing the basis for 1972. As Bevan once wrote, the essence of genius was to align oneself with the inevitable. Whitlam was right, if for the wrong reasons, when he stated in 1968 that 'the Labor Party will emerge stronger than ever from the agony of Vietnam'.[19]

Conscription: From conscience to non-compliance

One immediate effect of the 1966 election on the anti-Vietnam and anti-conscription movement was the disintegration of the ALP-aligned YCAC groups. As disenchantment with Labor grew during 1967 and 1968, a number of other effects emerged: the peace movement began to split along the fault lines of strategy and constituency, the anti-conscription movement moved from conscientious objection to a more active non-compliance with the system, and finally there was an accelerated radicalisation of student politics. After the concentration on parliamentary politics in 1966, the anti-war movement fragmented in a search for effective strategies, and would not reunite until the Moratorium campaign of 1970. The sense of demoralisation after 1966 was acute, though more among the left-liberal parts of the movement—YCAC, SOS, the church groups—while the established left, such as the CPA, had a more dogged approach which had never relied greatly on Labor's fortunes.

The splits opening in the peace movement were evident in the demonstrations against the GVN prime minister, Air Vice-Marshal Nguyen Cao Ky, in January 1967. Older hands in the peace movement were worried by a new militant turn of events illustrated when a demonstration in Sydney marched to the prime minister's residence, Kirribilli House, and was stopped by police barricades. Some of the demonstrators, primarily with the 'ultra-left' VAC, argued for moving against the police. Tom Uren, long a voice of the Labor left in the Sydney peace movement, urged them to disperse, and the confrontation was avoided.[20]

In a sense, the Ky visit was a godsend for the peace movement. Demoralised after the election, it now had a focal point around which to reorganise. As one SOS activist in Sydney put it: 'We were just wondering how we could get going again . . . and here they did it for us by inviting Ky out.' Ky was ideally suited for the role. After training in a French military

academy near Hanoi, he had served in the French air force after
1954; with his tailored black flying suit, lavender scarf and
pearl-handled pistol, he was familiarly known as 'The Cowboy'
on the Saigon nightclub circuit. By June 1965, as the leader of
the 'Young Turks' in the armed forces, Ky had emerged as prime
minister, one of a zealously anti-communist duumvirate with
General Nguyen Van Thieu as president. Ky's theatricality did
not obscure the qualities with which he had successfully risen
through the military ruling class during the dangerous 'coup
season' after Diem's assassination. Much was made during his
visit of an earlier statement of his regard for Hitler, who 'pulled
his country together when it was in a terrible state in the thirties
. . . We need four or five Hitlers in Vietnam . . .'[21]

Howson, delegated to accompany Ky on the visit, found
nothing objectionable in him, and decided that his guest was
'incorruptible, a patriot, tough and a quick learner'. It was true
that Ky was comparatively free of corruption, though the CIA
had wondered whether this might prove a weakness in the
patronage politics of Saigon once his supporters realised 'he does
not have a great deal of money to hand out to them'.[22] But it
was all part of Ky's 'elan', along with his barely restrained zeal
for prosecuting the war by an invasion of the North. Howson
believed that Ky had been a resistance fighter in the war against
the French, though his sole recorded experience of an anticolonial
war had been on the French side in Algeria. The credulity
suggests something of the ways in which, in conservative circles,
Ky was fictionalised as Diem had been. The mould first developed for Diem in 1957—'incorruptible and intensely patriotic',
with excusable dictatorial traits—was still serviceable a decade
later. But where Diem had passed almost unnoticed, Ky became
a focus of heated protests.

Calwell, in particular, threw himself into the demonstrations
with the passion of one with nothing to lose. His intemperate
attacks on Ky reflected the bitterness of the recent electoral loss,
with more than a touch of racism. He called Ky 'a little Asian
butcher' and 'a little quisling gangster'. The wild language
contrasted with the wariness of many of Labor's politicians; as
one commentator put it archly: 'So many Labor MPs proved to
be unavailable . . . on holidays, or out of town, or fishing, or
doing constituency work, that Dr Cairns ticked them off publicly
for avoiding "their active political duty".'

Overstated though it was, Calwell was touching on a view,
held by many in the peace movement, that Ky illustrated the
sort of 'freedom' being defended in South Vietnam. There was
a new civil libertarian element to the protests, along with its
established peace movement dimensions. This democratic element

was not usually identified with any great precision, though the Monash University academic Max Teichmann illustrated it at one Melbourne protest when he queried whether Ky's visit was 'perhaps to condition us to an Asia run by military dictators . . . [by] the professional anti-Democrat . . .' This aspect he linked with repressive policies in Australia:

> . . . forcing people out onto the streets to demonstrate; . . . forcing our domestic police force to take on the role of a semi-political force . . . and forcing our courts to try what are in essence political offences.[23]

The protests against Ky were neither well-attended nor effective in upsetting the tour, which the conservatives regarded, with relief, as a success. With Howson's coaching, Ky had charmed journalists and had made no inflammatory statements.

But the protests illustrated both the developing division within the peace movement over militant versus established strategies, and the widening of the front of opposition as the parameters of legitimate democratic dissent were extended. As protest became more militant during 1968 and 1969, the role of the state, and particularly the police, became more interventionist, in breaking up demonstrations and in political surveillance of leftist activities. One element in these developments was the growth of the student New Left, dealt with in the following chapter. Another, closely related, was the shift to more active and defiant forms of non-compliance with conscription, which pulled the anti-conscription groups outside the universities to the left and linked up with themes of the legitimacy of dissent against actions of the state.

During 1967 and 1968, conscientious objection to conscription on the grounds of pacifism was not enough for many. Michael Hamel-Green expressed this existentially: 'The letter telling me of my conscription was like a harpoon barb that I suddenly discovered sticking in *me*,' and considered his choices: escape overseas meant leaving loved ones; joining the army was 'complicity with genocide'; refusing to comply with the procedures meant two years in prison. Finally,

> conscientious objection procedures were not open to me: at first because I was a particular war objector, later because . . . it became obvious to me that the conscientious objection procedures were simply a means of legitimising, 'whitewashing' the whole system by allowing exemption to a predictably small number of absolute pacifists.[24]

Many outside the universities approached these choices in isolation, and many did not come to the last conclusions; in the first years after 1965, many wrote to Save Our Sons, asking advice about the grounds for conscientious objection. But by 1968 there had been a shift from the politics of conscience to those of non-compliance.

This involved some telling differences between situations less than three years apart. In the 1966 election campaign, the *cause célèbre* had been that of Bill White, a school teacher who had registered under the National Service Act and then argued for conscientious objection. His grounds were judged 'insincere' by a magistrate, and court appeals failed. White refused to report for military duty, and aroused much public sympathy and press attention as he waited at his parents' home for the army to act. Only days before the election, in the full glare of media attention, he was forcibly taken by police to the army. For his subsequent refusal to comply with army commands, he was placed in military prison; it was only after later allegations of brutal treatment under this system that the Act was amended, in 1968, to replace indefinite military detention with two years civil imprisonment. Further legal moves had White brought before a different magistrate, who judged his objections sincere, and 'much to the relief of White and his family, and, it may be supposed, the Army' he was exempted.

This tended to be the path taken until early 1967, though the degree of media attention in White's case was unusual. The only legal grounds for exemption were complete pacificism, rather than objection to the Vietnam war in particular, and many of the groups assisting conscientious objectors did so less on the basis of their views on Vietnam than on the more liberal grounds of the right to conscience. The Bill White Defence Committee, for example, spoke entirely in terms of liberal conscience and the defence of rights, rather than in the later terms of challenging the legitimacy of conscription and the war.[25]

During 1967, there was a marked shift from this position. In March, SOS in Sydney agreed to help fund a series of court challenges arguing conscientious objection to Vietnam in particular; in Melbourne, the Peace Quest Forum, which had reassembled in the early 1960s, was discussing broader measures than simply assisting with conscientious objection cases, such as a public statement of non-compliance with conscription. Early in 1968, a Melbourne group called Conscientious Objectors (Non-Pacifist), of which Teichmann was the Chairman, was organising a test case to establish the right to object in conscience to military service on grounds other than pacifist ones, namely of objection to Vietnam; this group was, a few months later, collecting for the legal appeal of John Zarb, jailed for non-compliance in October 1968. At the same time, the Australian Council of Churches began to argue that the National Service Act should be amended to allow for objection to service in Vietnam alone.[26]

In mid-1968 the movement against conscription mobilised the imagery of the American civil rights movement, with a Freedom Ride to Holsworthy Military Prison drawing attention to the imprisonment of conscientious objector Denis O'Donnell. Here, Fran Newell and Michael Hamel-Green prepare to set out from Melbourne. The Freedom Ride mobilised sentiments of conscience and civil disobedience, a strategy paralleled by the more vigorous resistance of groups such as the Draft Resistance Movement which promised in 1968 not to oppose but to 'wreck' conscription. (University of Melbourne Archives, CICD papers)

But these concerted attempts to liberalise the grounds for legal exemption came to nothing. Amendments to the Act in May 1968 contained no such provision. Shortly after, in August, the High Court ruled unequivocally that only a total pacifism was grounds for exemption. Barwick—as chief justice—delivered the majority judgment on the legal meaning of the National Service Act. He interpreted it in the most constrictive terms possible:

> To my mind, the section calls for the existence of a present compulsive and complete conscientious aversion to military service of any kind including non-combatant service at any time and in any circumstances, even in the country's defence in the direst circumstances.[27]

Slamming the door shut on attempts to liberalise the law through the courts, Barwick had given an unambiguous directive to magistrates hearing conscientious objectors' cases.

With this course closed, one result was a move towards more active defiance of the conscription system. In Sydney in late 1968, the Committee Against the National Service Act (CANSA) was formed, with aims including the encouraging of 'non-cooperation with the Act'—an illegal activity under the Crimes Act. The strategy was endorsed by a range of groups, including not only radical forces such as the University of NSW Labor and ALP clubs, the CPA and Resistance, but also groups which had previously confined themselves to a liberal approach, including the Bill White Defence Committee, Save Our Sons and the Federal Pacifist Council. Thus the new strategy of encouraging non-compliance and civil disobedience had emerged by late 1968 amongst pacifist, peace and leftist groups, in parallel with the radicalisation of student politics. In a signal of the declining legitimacy of the conscription scheme, dissent had also begun to turn to mockery. The Melbourne SOS amongst others organised 'fill in a falsie' parties, with wine and bundles of registration forms to fill in: 'Clifton Pugh's wombat's marble was once pulled out of the barrel, people's cats were called up, and a few Liberal politicians.'

During the same period, a small number of individuals began the grinding process of active non-compliance; at the end of 1969, the Federal Pacifist Council published a list of 43 young men in various stages of non-compliance, from refusal to register (which involved a fine), or failure to attend a medical examination (a mandatory seven-day prison sentence), to refusal to obey a call-up notice (two years civil imprisonment). Almost all were intentionally defying the conscription laws, although some had first exhausted their legal options by attempting to argue conscientious objection. Some had already been jailed for two years, while one—John Zarb—had been released after ten months on 'compassionate grounds'. His case had galvanised civil libertarians, some unions and many who simply felt that two years in jail for obeying one's conscience was illegitimate or unduly harsh punishment. In addition, by late 1969, a total of '60 liable young men had publicly declared their resistance in the form of declarations and letters to the government and press'.[28]

In 1967, non-compliance still had much of the isolated character of the earlier period. As Hamel-Green put it, they 'must have felt like someone entering a tunnel of darkness—hoping that others are behind but haunted by the sense that . . . they are now quite alone'. By the end of 1969 the tunnel was more crowded, and non-compliance was a less isolated act as it took on the broader political dimensions of civil disobedience. For parallel with this was developing the strategy which CANSA had first signalled, of organised civil disobedience in defiance of the Crimes Act.

In June 1969, when it appeared that the government might take action against three Sydney academics who had publicly urged young men not to register, a similar statement of incitement was signed by more than 500 academics in support. In the following month, the Committee in Defiance of the National Service Act, with strong support from AICD, launched a 'Statement of Defiance' which urged against registration, and by November had 8000 signatures.[29] The government was increasingly in a bind—to prosecute would only widen the front of opposition, while to allow defiance to pass unnoticed undermined the legitimacy of the conscription system.

The statistics of the conscription scheme illustrate that the strategy of resistance was relatively thinly spread. More than 800 000 young men complied with the registration requirements, and of these fewer than 30 per cent were balloted in through the lottery in which their birth dates were selected out of a barrel—Calwell's 'lottery of death'. Of those balloted in, about a quarter were then selected and enlisted into the army. Only a tiny fraction—some 3500—were allowed exemption on conscientious objection grounds. Some 12 000 young men refused to register with the system, and between 1965 and 1972 were in one form or another of open defiance of the system, though an average of only 202 a year were prosecuted. The proportions actually sent to Vietnam were small: fewer than one-third of those who were conscripted. A young man who registered had about a one in twelve chance of being conscripted, a one in 40 chance of being sent to Vietnam, and a one in 4000 chance of being killed there.[30]

While these statistics might suggest that the odds were favourable in 'the lottery of death', Calwell's phrase was about justice rather than chance. Figures do not account for the swirl of political forces in which the conscripted men were caught. Similarly, the numbers defying the National Service Act were relatively small, but the public nature of that defiance, like the death of an unwilling conscript, had become invested with a political significance beyond statistics.

Finally, there was the dispersed effect of universal registration for conscription amongst the general citizenry. Some came to see the drift in opinion against the war as predominantly the result of an accumulating opposition to conscription. The proportion actually conscripted was small, but the families of that much greater number whose fate hinged on a ballot had to face the prospect of losing loved ones in a war whose urgency was diminishing. Although there was always a majority in favour of conscription itself, opinion polls in 1966 and 1967 had shown small majorities against sending conscripts to Vietnam, even when the intervention was at its most popular. While the political views and motives of activists were legion, this widespread exposure to conscription may have been 'the hinge of whatever support the anti-war movement commanded in the more passive community at large'.[31]

By the end of the 1960s, before the mass mobilisation of the Moratorium, the movement against conscription had taken on a more defiant nature, raising the issue to a level of controversy and contributing to focusing this more passive support. Public defiance of conscription had been added to the conservatives' other woes—the disarray of their policy and the developing opinion against the war. To these must also be added the revitalisation of forces on the left.

12
The left revived

The New Left

In understanding what drove the New Left of the late 1960s,
Alan Ashbolt commented, it was a decided advantage never to
have belonged to the Old Left. The point was a shrewd one.
The New Left was of a different generation, was little preoccupied with orthodox communism and was mostly critical of
'actually existing socialism'. In this, it differed from the 'first'
New Left of a decade before—'the socialism of magazines'—
which had been primarily a fragment broken from the communist
bloc, defining itself in opposition to that bloc's past.

The student New Left—also called at the time the 'new
radicals' or the 'student revolutionary left'—developed in an
antagonistic dialogue with the Old Left, which it helped to
transform. Similarly, the New Left's mobilisation, in which
Vietnam and conscription were essential catalysts, was a departure
from the analysis and strategy of the established peace and
anti-conscription movements. In surveys of its development in
Australia, 1966 recurs as the crucial break. The failure of 1966
was seen as revealing the inadequacy of electoral and protest
politics, and of the cautious analysis of society which underpinned

them. Instead, the new student politics which developed between 1967 and 1970 was characterised by a more activist orientation and by social theories which attempted to connect opposition to the war with a broader social critique.

By the end of 1968, the rough outlines of organisational development were clear; on many campuses, the ALP clubs or old Labor clubs—the latter as often aligned with the CPA as with the ALP—had been either superseded or radicalised, or had split. There were marked variations in origins and in political theory, for the trajectories of student politics were remarkably autonomous. In Brisbane, civil libertarian issues were the basis for the formation of Students (later Society) for Democratic Action (SDA) before 1966, and without any pre-existing leftist groups; in Adelaide, the SDA developed out of the Labor Club during 1968, and took a similar path to that in Brisbane, organising originally around civil liberties issues. At Melbourne University, Students for a Democratic Society (SDS) emerged from the old, CPA-aligned Labor Club in 1968, and took on a radical democratic and libertarian politics, with an emphasis on decentralised and participatory forms of organisation. At Sydney University, SDS developed directly out of the ALP Club in the aftermath of the 1966 election and Labor's shift to the right under Whitlam, while the Labor Club was contested between the Trotskyist group, Resistance, and young members of the CPA.

Finally, the *bête noire* of the conservatives, the Monash Labor Club, had by 1968 completed a transition from the ALP right to the Maoism of the Communist Party of Australia (Marxist-Leninist) (CPA (M–L)). Monash students had been active in YCAC, and the 1966 election was the final blow for this strategy; the void thus created was gradually filled by Maoism. Although there was a branch of the CPA (M–L) at the core of the Labor Club, it was only in 1969 that Maoism became the dominant force. The club was propelled to the vanguard of student activism by the heavy-handed response to its campaign, launched in July 1967 by non-Maoist members, to raise money for the NLF. With the government legislating to make this illegal, the university authorities attempting to ban collections and the media fuming, the club was galvanised in more radical and utopian directions.[1]

With these accelerated developments, the New Left represented a substantial revival of radical social forces, but carried with it three weaknesses. First, it was highly fragmented, being much more a series of localised cliques than a social movement. This was widely recognised at the time. The radical student groups developed independently and autonomously, and were markedly uneven in their levels of sophistication and theoretical development. Reinforcing this localism was the fact that the different groups often depended on the leadership of key individuals, whose personal leadership was frequently unable to be channelled into organisational forms. National coordination was sporadic, and localised competition more the pattern. Nonetheless, during 1968, several unsuccessful attempts were made to form a national organisation. In June, the Brisbane SDA instigated the formation of a Socialist Students Alliance as a potential equivalent to the nationally based SDS in America, but it had broken up a year later. At the end of 1968, an attempt to establish a Sydney-based Revolutionary Socialist Alliance also foundered on the disunity of competing local groups.[2] The New Left remained fragmented.

A second weakness lay in the inability to radicalise a broader student constituency. Despite media impressions that the mass of students was in revolt, the student New Left tended to remain a small elite of radicalised groups. They were able to 'detonate' broader action and undoubtedly the campuses became a radicalising milieu, but the numbers actively organised and committed were relatively small. In mid-1968, seven student leaders noted phlegmatically that the core of active radicals on their campuses was very small, even if they had greater influence than numbers would indicate. The Monash Labor Club, one of the most visible and radical groups, had a core of some 100 students, forming a tight social network and dominated by Albert Langer, along with a more amorphous group of student activists. In all, the 'movement' at Monash was perhaps 600 strong. These were substantial numbers of activists, but it was increasingly noted by 1970 that the New Left groups had—even at Monash—failed to engage large numbers of students in regular political activity.[3]

Many of the broader mass of students were doubtless bewildered by the minutiae of the militants' ideological disputes, which related to a third deficiency of the New Left—the fractured and underdeveloped character of its social theory. In Australia, the New Left—unlike the American SDS for a brief period in the middle of the decade—did not develop a coherent critique of society and an accepted set of counterfactual values around which a movement could cohere. The New Left had, instead, an embarrassment of theoretical riches. Liberationist and humanist ideas, derived from Marcuse amongst others, jostled with the classically Leninist revivals of Maoism and Trotskyism; pacifist civil disobedience sat awkwardly alongside aggressive revolutionary postures. Theories of participatory democracy and the revolt against bureaucracy coexisted with countercultural ideas of a generational change in lifestyle and sexuality. Feminist theory was noticeably absent and, in the late 1960s, women had more voice in debates in the CPA than in those of the student New Left.

To add to the imprecision of what the New Left represented, the resurgence of radical politics was riding the wave of a more amorphous 'youth movement' of cultural change, reflected in music, sexuality and political challenge. Bob Dylan, one of many expressing the view that times were changing, celebrated a form of alienation from the material aspirations, cultural conformism and stultified politics of the Cold War generation.

In this, the New Left represented a remarkable growth of radical discourses. In the middle of the 1960s, the dominant social metaphor available to non-communist leftist intellectuals was suburbia, and radical action was seen as a form of dissent against stifling conformity. It held out little hope, but was a moral duty, as 'bearing witness'. By the end of the decade, the metaphors were legion. The most persuasive examples were the revival of Western Marxist debates on alienation and the dehumanisation of capitalist society, theories of the 'repressive tolerance' engendered by material prosperity and controlled democracy, and arguments about postindustrialism and 'countercultural' values.

With such a range of metaphors in social theory, critique had the potential to be more fluid and creative. But the problem in Australia was not so much that these various social theories were incompatible with each other—though some were—but that the New Left was disinclined to engage in theoretical and political debate. By the end of the decade, sympathetic critics were observing that theoretical discussion took the form of the controversy of 'lines' rather than critical and open debate. Some groups self-consciously avoided theory, equating it with 'ideology', and more attention was given to national liberation movements and American imperialism than to the development of a coherent critique of Australian society and culture. At the end of the decade, one of the young intellectuals attracted to the CPA commented tellingly that there was 'more intensive discussion and open-ness in sections of the Communist Party, in the last few years, than amongst even the most "intellectual" student radicals'.[4]

These weaknesses suggested that the accelerated development of the New Left had, by the end of the decade, brought it to the verge of either a breakthrough or an implosion. The lack of theoretical debate meant that it had not moved from general theoretical frameworks to radicalising the broader mass of students by being able to articulate their concerns and experiences, much less those of wider social forces. The New Left was in some danger of isolation.

After 1966, some in the student left had adopted militant tactics, which had the effect of breaking the pattern of protest

politics. But their premature adoption of revolutionary stances—
particularly after the events of 1968 in Paris and Vietnam had
reinforced the romance of insurrection—was driving a wedge
between radicals and the larger group of unmobilised students.
With repetition, militancy was in danger of being ritualised as
'"the politics of display": a tendency to posture as the most
radical radicals . . .' One of the more volatile aspects of the
student left was this development of radical nihilism, a 'retreat
from reason' into an enthusiasm for 'unbridled activism' rather
than the less romantic work of social change.[5]

The potential for 'infantile leftism' was by no means confined
to Australia. Nor did it go unchallenged—there were discussions
of these issues in the pages of *Tribune*, *Australian Left Review*
and *Arena*, which reflected both the self-consciousness of parts
of the New Left, and the CPA's attempts to come to terms with
developments. If, by the end of the 1960s, the New Left had
developed extraordinary momentum—radicalising the anti-conscription movement and contributing a new militancy to the
protests against the war—channelling this momentum into the
coalition of the Moratorium would be a major challenge.

The most revolutionary groups—the 'ultra-left'—were the
Maoists at Monash and later La Trobe universities, and the
Trotskyists in Sydney. The latter force, in the VAC, had tapped
the new mood of militancy since 1966, and in 1968 had evolved
into Resistance, which was particularly vocal in the Sydney
University Labor Club. Both Maoists and Trotkyists had an
external origin in existing leftist groups projecting their influence
into the campuses; both were also distinctly orthodox Leninist
groups. Although they tapped the radical temper of the times,
their leaders did not share the rest of the New Left's enthusiasm
for radical democracy and liberation; if one key theme of the
New Left was a discourse against power, the 'ultra-left' was
predominantly concerned with a discourse against imperialism,
holding—like Mao—great respect for power.

Maoism had had the fortuitous advantage of a coincidence
of cultural change in the West with the anti-authoritarian rhetoric
and militant practice of the Chinese Cultural Revolution after
1966. Dylan's lyrics found their way, incongruously, into the
pages of the *Peking Review* as Mao urged all and sundry to
question and rebel. The stridency of the Cultural Revolution,
along with Chinese encouragement to Third World national
liberation struggles, gave Maoism in Melbourne its edge of
militancy and visceral anti-Americanism. Capturing the spirit of
youth rebellion, it emerged as an attractive alternative to what
was seen as the more old-fashioned communism of the CPA, a
development of some concern to the CPA leadership.[6]

Some within the New Left—particularly in the SDS groups—noted these contradictions in the 'ultra-left' between rebellion and orthodoxy. At a Melbourne conference in 1968 organised by the Vietnam Co-ordinating Committee (VCC), Hamel-Green argued that advocates of violent confrontation tended to adopt an 'impotent revolutionary posture or romantically identify with Third World revolutionaries'; such confrontation 'excites people temporarily but doesn't make them more committed'. The 'ultra-leftists' were also criticised for their tendency towards secretive and elite forms of organisation, which arose both from their Leninist traditions and from their attachment to tactics of confrontation and guerrilla action. Against this, the SDS groups tended to assert participatory democracy as the core value of the New Left, as 'an anti-bureaucratic, spontaneous and highly participatory atmosphere in which differences can be argued in a genuine spirit of democracy'; such sentiments were far from those of a vanguard party, and explain this key division within the New Left.[7]

But it was the CPA which developed the most vigorous critique of the 'ultra-left'; to understand Maoism, in a reversal of Ashbolt's aphorism, it was a decided advantage to be of the Old Left. Inevitably, the disputes between Maoists and the CPA were focused in Melbourne. It was in the Victorian branch that the developing Sino-Soviet split most reverberated through the Party, marked by the defeat in the early 1960s of the pro-Chinese leadership of the branch under Ted Hill. Just as Peking had been the *éminence grise* of Asian politics for a generation of Australian conservatives, it had been a beacon for the CPA. Middle-ranking cadres began to go to Peking for training from 1951 and, particularly in Victoria, the Party was strongly influenced by enthusiasm for China.

The dispute between Peking and Moscow had become obvious by 1959—as the Chinese criticised the policy of 'peaceful coexistence' and began to stake out their claim to leadership of Third World liberation. By 1962 the CPA had, in effect, chosen Moscow and loyalty to international unity, over Peking and loyalty to world revolution and the unsullied memory of Stalin. Then in March 1964, the Party had split, with Hill forming the CPA (M–L)—a 'back to Lenin party', as Davidson put it—while the majority of the CPA continued their slow march to eurocommunism and the break with Soviet influence, demonstrated when the Party condemned the Soviet invasion of Czechoslovakia in 1968.

The influence of the CPA (M–L) in the student left, and its contest by the CPA, was an echo of this history. As its Victorian leaders became more concerned that they were being left behind by events, and that Maoism was becoming the dominant strain of radicalism, the CPA also attempted to channel the momentum of the student movement. In Sydney, the pattern of political forces was different: the challenge of the 'ultra-left' was neither as coherent nor as organised, and the CPA was more influential in student politics.[8]

This contest was more than just an attempt to win influence and control; it also reflected theoretical and strategic differences, and images of political action. At Monash, the Young Communist League (YCL)—a CPA (M–L) offshoot—starkly illustrated these differences in 1970; the YCL believed 'the working class has to violently overthrow the dictatorship of the monopoly capitalist ruling class in order to establish socialism and the dictatorship of the proletariat'. Such stern and absolutely orthodox sentiments were combined with what may have been a rare flash of sardonic humour as the league conceded that 'the bourgeoisie will not welcome or encourage this prospect'. But the implication was deadly serious. Revolutionaries must 'prepare for future (and present) repression. For this reason we are not a public organization with an open membership'. This envisaged political action as carried out by an elite and romantic underground, and reflected the obsessive secrecy of the Maoists' parent party.

The Maoist analysis of the Vietnam war was equally dogmatic and unambiguous. As Langer articulated it, the war was the outcome of the imperialist nature of American capitalism, and Australia's role was that of a dependent satellite. Any advocacy of compromise or negotiation in Vietnam was 'a betrayal of the Vietnamese people', and the opposition to the war in Australia was 'part of the general struggle to end American domination'. It was part of a worldwide offensive against American power. The outline of this analysis was widely accepted in the New Left and in the CPA, though none pursued it with such zeal as the Maoists.

Nor could all accept the implications drawn about the nature of Australian society and its political forces. In a social theory of imperious simplicity, the YCL argued that 'there are two sides—the side of the ruling class who make profits out of wars of aggression and the side of the people, the masses . . .' This division 'exists wherever there is imperialism and oppression', which, inevitably, was everywhere: in America, in Australia and at Monash. Those who did not take sides were 'irrelevant' to the struggle. Those who were cautious about the anti-war movement springing to anti-imperialist postures, such as 'the "C"PA–Pacifist coalition in the CICD', were 'revisionists'.

The political implications of this position were substantial. The 'ultra-left' worked from a coercive rather than a consensual theory of authority and power, with no place for the conceptions

of hegemonic rule which were becoming more widely accepted
in the CPA, and which explained the relative conformism of
Australian society as a coherent world view which sprang from
everyday existence. For the CPA, radical action meant gradually
eroding the coherence of hegemonic understandings of society;
for the Maoists, it meant provoking confrontation with police in
order to expose the state's 'true' coercive character. This was an
early step on the path which led towards armed terrorism, though
not one pursued in Australia. The 'ultra-left' ignored hegemony,
trusting to the socialist instincts of the masses. Angry and
romantic at the same time, its arguments on Vietnam largely fell
outside the framework of the Australian polity, because it saw
no need to challenge hegemonic understandings.[9]

The consequence of this view was that, while the 'ultra-left'
endorsed a 'broad united front against imperialism', it could
hardly hope to form an alliance with all the political forces which
opposed the war without being stridently anti-imperialist—for 'the
masses' were composed of left-liberals and humanists, of libertarians and pacifists, of ALP members and churchgoers, and of
many others who, for reasons hard to plumb, were turning against
the war. The task of reassembling the peace movement was to
be more difficult than the 'ultra-left' imagined.

Re-formation

It was a symptom of how much the strategies of the peace
movement were diverging that, while many in the New Left
experienced 1968 and 1969 as years of escalation, for the
established peace movement it was a period of decline and
increased difficulties. The new groups would argue that this was
because groups such as CICD and AICD had lost the initiative
and no longer tapped the energies of the anti-war movement,
and there was some truth in this.

Increasingly, the strategy of the established peace movement
was disparaged as the politics of 'the lowest common
denominator'—in which effectiveness was sacrificed in the pursuit
of respectability, and radicalism in the name of unity. This
'defencist' position, developed by the CPA during the inhospitable
years of the Cold War, had made historical sense. Struggling
against marginality, the peace movement had sought legitimacy
through respectability, by attempting to win the endorsement of
pillars of society. As Alec Robertson, a former national secretary
of the APC and editor of *Tribune,* argued, it may have been
politically impoverished but it had often been the highest common
denominator possible. But after 1965, the CPA itself—more than

the peace groups it had helped establish—was aware that 'defencism' was now an unnecessary legacy of caution.

But the militants were in a hurry. By 1968, the old peace groups were being consistently criticised as too heavily reliant on electoral strategies, were derided as 'peaceaucrats' and were challenged with strategies based on the rupturing of consensus rather than the building of broad support. As Mike Jones, the chairman of Sydney SDS, put it—with all the disarming precocity of a 20-year-old—they were 'sick and tired of being involved in united front organisations with the communists', and were 'disenchanted' with the ALP. Henceforth, 'we regard ourselves . . . as the conscience of the peace movement—fighting the nine-to-five-big-business attitude within it'.

This divergence was evident in Sydney, where the VAC advocated protests on Friday afternoons and derided AICD's strategy of weekend rallies as too cautious. In Melbourne, it was clearest in the transformation of the July 4 demonstrations. For some years, VCND and CICD had held small vigils outside the American consulate on Independence Day. The 1967 demonstration began similarly, as a 24-hour candle-lit vigil. Monash Labor Club activists attempted to transform the demonstration into a denunciation of imperialist aggression in Vietnam, and intended burning an American flag, but were held in check by CICD organisers.[10] Just as the Vietnamese Party had focused anticolonial sentiment on Bastille Day, American Independence Day became a potent symbol for anti-American sentiment.

The following year, the demonstration became more confrontationist, with media reports of a 'wild city riot' and allegations of police violence. Afterwards, the organisers—the student-based Vietnam Withdrawal Campaign—claimed that the demonstration had 'introduced a new and more militant high into the anti-war campaign and thrown into relief the serious stresses within the peace movement'. For its part, CICD was clearly dismayed by these stresses. The executive discussed the turn of events and urged its members not to take part in 'unannounced activities'. Early in 1969, it resolved to issue a statement supporting the VCC's plans for the coming July 4 demonstration and encouraging people not to react to external or internal provocation.[11]

This rude shift from candle-lit vigils to a 'wild city riot' was emblematic of how much CICD had lost the initiative. The ALP had lost much of its capacity to channel opposition to the war, as that opposition became more radical; now, the established peace movement was being left behind by events and was at a loss how to respond. In September 1969, Goldbloom suggested some measures to overcome the failure to attract 'people of a much wider political and social diversity . . .', noting that

'Sydney's experience [in AICD] in this regard is much better
. . .' They should spend more time on evaluating political
situations and trends, the newsletter should be made more
'professional', and they should consider a draft-resistance coun-
selling service, with the evident aim of recapturing some of the
momentum of the anti-conscription struggle.

There were other signs of lost momentum. Union involvement—so much the lifeblood of CICD's predecessor—had
declined, and although the leadership of some leftist unions
remained actively supportive, the rank and file were less so. CICD
proposed factory meetings to renew the links. But more critical
was a palpable sense that public debate had withered. In August
1969, the CICD secretary, John Lloyd, commented:

> Whilst the Vietnam War and the Peace Talks drag on, public interest
> in the issue of Vietnam has faded significantly . . . It is obvious
> that the US will slowly phase out. The question is 'how slowly'?
> The fact that there is no longer any debate about Vietnam is
> disturbing.[12]

The view that the war was winding down after Tet and the first
American announcement of withdrawal meant that the established
peace movement was in a trough in the years immediately before

*By 1970 and 1971, draft resistance had become overt: defying the law,
evading capture and challenging the power of the state to enforce its laws.
In September 1971, four underground resisters—including Tony Dalton,
second from right with others who were declaring their intent to resist
conscription—surfaced at the University of Melbourne, which students had
declared a 'sanctuary'. Behind them staircases were barricaded with piles
of furniture which held up the 150 Commonwealth police who raided the
Union building at 5 a.m. The resisters were not found. (University of
Melbourne Archives, CICD papers)*

the Moratorium mobilisation, which began in December 1969. There was little synchronisation between the war and the movement opposing it. At a time when the New Left and the draft-resistance movements were mobilising excitedly, the broader movement was in a lull, unable to regenerate debate. This was not simply a case of being out of touch with the militants and, in fact, CICD had a number of student leaders on its committee; it was more a case of being more in touch with middle Australia, where the war seemed less important an issue.

The announcements for the first Moratorium attempted to confront this sense of decline:

> Unfortunately, many of those active in the anti-war movement have allowed themselves to be deceived by the bland sophisms of Washington and Canberra. The level of involvement has fallen and interest has been diverted . . .[13]

Public opinion had turned against the war by August 1969; the American withdrawal was publicly known, and it seemed that all that held up an Australian announcement was inertia. Against this background, the remarkable mobilisation of the first Moratorium, which astonished even the organisers, requires some explanation. By early 1970, the political culture had seemingly moved again, from ennui to mobilisation.

One incident in this turn was the exposure, early in November 1969, of the My Lai massacre. The murders themselves had taken place in March 1968, in the aftermath of the Tet Offensive. My Lai became a focus of revulsion against the routinisation of the war, and contributed to atrocities' becoming the dominant metaphor of the war—at least after 1968. It was a powerful metaphor, simultaneously encapsulating the grotesque imbalance of technologies available to the two sides and the slaughter of innocents in Vietnam.

In response to the My Lai massacre, the *Australian* now turned unambiguously against the war. Long the most sceptical of the major newspapers—though it had endorsed Gorton in the recent October election—the paper now editorialised: 'There is no longer any political justification for the Vietnam war. Morality is now paramount and morality . . . demands that the war stop.' Quoting witnesses to the murder of children at My Lai, it continued with a note of moral urgency:

> . . . where, in Australia now, does one hear the anguished voice that is heard in all America . . . the whole moral basis of our military presence in Vietnam . . . is now shown by unspeakable deeds to be in ruins.[14]

In demanding the withdrawal of Australian troops, the paper was the first to reflect the majority position of the opinion polls. Simultaneously, it demonstrated that My Lai was a moral crisis for those who were concluding that the issue in the war was not so much imperialism as barbarism.

The My Lai revelations also contributed to a mobilisation of the union movement at the end of 1969. Some leftist unions— such as the Seamen's, Waterside Workers and Engineering unions—had been prominent in the anti-war movement in the past, though when the Seamen's Union banned work on the *Jeparit* supply ship a number of times after early 1967, it was isolated and exposed. The union movement was fundamentally split on Vietnam, in ways which replicated divisions arising from the struggles of the early 1950s. In November 1969, waterside workers refused to unload the *Jeparit* when it next returned from Vung Tau, in defiance of both ACTU and WWF policy. In part, this was in reponse to My Lai, and this time the ban received wider support amongst other unions. In the following month, a meeting of the Victorian 'rebel' leftist unions urged their support for non-compliance with conscription.[15] But while these were straws in the wind, they only partly explain the extraordinary mobilisation of 1970.

Although the established peace movement might have felt itself to be in a trough, the late 1960s had seen a decided quickening of the pulse of the left, which was a major factor in the Moratorium mobilisation. For all its precocity and vanguardism, the New Left represented a development of radical thought which had contributed to the vitality of the left, and the CPA in particular made efforts to tap this new energy and fervour. This was more than simply the pursuit of new blood. In one sense, the leaders of the Party—around Laurie Aarons and Bernie Taft—were attempting to free themselves of the conceptual legacy of their past, which weighed heavily indeed. As Davidson put it, by the late 1960s the leadership was subject to 'a sort of schizophrenia'. Its members had been formed by a Stalinist and sectarian past yet were committed to a national path to socialism, which entailed a genuine commitment to democratic liberties, a final acceptance of the reality of the ALP, and a strategy of counter-hegemonic struggle. The Party's membership also reflected this mix of old and new ties: in the discussion journals issued before the CPA's 1967 congress, members debated draft proposals and revealed a range of views, from feminist and youth concerns to nostalgia for the past.

One step on the national path was the adoption at the 1967 congress of the strategy of a 'coalition of the left'. In discussion before the congress, many members presumed that this was a rerun of former ideas—the People's Front and the unity of working people against monopoly capitalism. There was only a faint recognition that it would involve a pluralist and democratic conception of a coalition in which the CPA would finally abdicate the 'leading role' it had expected to play in fronts of the past. Aarons's report to the congress reflected the conundrum involved. At times, the 'coalition of the left' seemed to be a socialist government-in-waiting, with the coalition as an alliance of various classes and social forces whose objective interests were opposed to those of monopoly capital. The Party had always had a strong streak of populism, with its vision of the people opposed to monopoly capital. Yet there were also glimmers of a more modest conception, that the 'coalition of the left' was a new political process, involving qualitative changes and democratic advances which gradually chipped away at hegemonic power, and embracing different movements and issues: 'within these broad, democratic movements around a particular peace, democratic or national aim there will be some who come to see the need for basic social change . . .'

In the event, and partly by default, it was the latter conception on which the CPA came to operate, intent on building a pluralist coalition around particular struggles, abdicating pretensions to a 'leading role', and recognising the ALP for what it was. This was significant because it involved the acceptance for the first time of the legitimacy of other leftist, radical movements, which were also entitled to shape the future.[16] The best example of this coalition—though a short-lived one—would be the Moratorium campaign.

It was in this context that the Party in 1968 and 1969 cultivated its links with the New Left. This had the effect of opening the Party to more radical, often more democratic influences, while tapping the momentum of these developments. CPA publications gave extensive space to New Left and student views, commissioning articles on student power, worker–student alliances and views of the connections between opposition to the war and wider social criticism.

E.A. Bacon, the Queensland state secretary of the CPA, captured some of the dynamic of this relationship when he wrote that:

> We communists, working to improve our party, can learn from the students and we can teach them something, for they are not anti-Communist, but they are justly impatient with old-style dogmatism and undue caution.

Noting the variety of views in the New Left, he isolated one of its most 'healthy' features—at least in Brisbane—as its tolerance of diversity.[17]

The Left Action Conference, held in Sydney over Easter in
1969, was part of the same dialogue. Organised principally by
the CPA, it was attended by some 850 representatives of most
of the New Left groups, including the Sydney 'ultra-left' VAC,
but apparently excluding the Melbourne Maoist groups. The
conference was intended for exchanging opinion rather than
deliberating on strategy, and reflected a new tone of unity, despite
continuing differences. Given that fragmentation was one of the
New Left's major weaknesses, it was of some significance.

But as natural as divisions were continuing suspicions of the
CPA's motives. Some claimed that the conference had a manip-
ulative intent, and that the Party had not clearly stated that it
was part of the organisational program of building a leftist
coalition; yet only this motive explained the exclusion of some
political forces. But others, outside the Party, defended its role
and commented that, if anything, the leadership was bending too
far in its enthusiasm for accommodating all views.

News-Weekly took the view that the CPA was attempting to
re-establish its 'slipping grip on the reins of an increasingly
uncontrollable extreme Left'. But while it was true that no one
group could control the cultural momentum of the New Left,
the conference signalled the new possibilities of coalition and also
the CPA's declining capacity or claim to take the leading role.
In the context of the continuing struggle with the old guard of
Moscow-liners in the Party, the conference amounted to an
attempt

> . . . to revitalise the Party by exposing its activities to radical thinking
> clearly revolutionary in intent but extremely critical of the Party and
> particularly of its legacy of Stalinism.[18]

The conference was a conscious attempt to develop links between
the CPA and the student left; the ability to work together was
one precondition which suggested that an open coalition such as
the Moratorium was becoming possible.

Images of Vietnam

What did Vietnam mean to the various forces which would make
up this coalition? The metaphor of the atrocity has aleady been
mentioned, but there were other, less immediate metaphors, which
connected protest against the war with radical social theories. To
the reader of the mass of pamphlets, articles and records of the
movement in the late 1960s and early 1970s, a conundrum
emerges. Here was a movement which passionately opposed the
war yet did not analyse it in detail. Australian involvement was

the key event around which radicals mobilised from 1966, yet there was very little discussion of what was happening in Phuoc Tuy. Vietnam was the animating issue, yet there was no clear and widely accepted interpretation of what it meant.

The answer to this conundrum partly lies in the nature of the war as a metaphor in public discourse. During the 1950s, conservatives had projected into Asia their anxieties about social stability, and now, for the left in the late 1960s, Vietnam became a metaphor for other discontents. As Jack Lindsay wrote in a poem for an anti-war anthology:

> Vietnam was once a name
> without an echo . . .
> . . . Now everywhere,
> its dangerous shadow falls,
> its moment of choice we share,
> bare in stark judgment-light.
> Vietnam is everywhere.[19]

For the diverse groups opposing the war, Vietnam was a talisman of dissent, capable of conjuring passionate commitment because it condensed other meanings arising from social critiques. Such a process abhors precision, thriving on ambiguity. As a social movement, the opposition to the war had become an energetic cultural force, tapping widely dispersed sentiments of protest and critique; yet this cultural diversity was also a political weakness. Part of the strength of the Moratorium was that it drew on this ambiguity, representing dispersed radical sentiments without demanding a precise commitment to any one interpretation of the war. But its weakness was that only briefly could it hold together cultural force and political focus.

After the first Moratorium, Cairns published a commemorative volume. He briefly rehearsed Vietnamese history, arguing that Australian policy had turned its back on Asian history. His text ranged across a number of themes: atrocities such as My Lai were magnified a hundredfold by the dehumanised technology of the electronic battlefield; sustaining the Saigon regime was part of a pattern of supporting reaction in the Third World; the war was fundamentally one-sided. Yet what was most striking was the impression that the war was open to a plurality of interpretations.

The book was also a photo-essay, and many of the captions expressed this imprecision: 'They know there is violence in Vietnam, and they are against violence' (with a photograph of women in the Moratorium march); ' "They were obviously all of one ilk"—Sir Henry Bolte' (students, a schoolboy and an elderly war veteran); 'Technologically the Vietnam war has been

Harvest of fear

a great success' (a Vietnamese women grieving for her dead child); and 'Another village is "pacified" ' (a village in flames).[20] The heaviness of the irony made some of the meanings of these captions obvious. But more often an unspecified interpretation was being set against the dominant discourse, which raised the question: if the village was manifestly not 'pacified', how was its destruction to be understood? A range of answers coexisted within the movement by the end of the 1960s.

Although the anti-war movement expended more effort on interpretation than on description of the war, it did so against a background of extensive media coverage. While television provided some of the war's most riveting images, newspapers conveyed a flood of information, mostly of American origin. In Australia, though, it is striking how limited a role newspapers played in the evaluation of government policy. Apart from the *Australian* and a few critics such as Bruce Grant at *The Age*, newspapers were relatively uncritical of the reportage they provided and—if they passed judgment—erred on the side of caution and government policy. In addition, they were generally unsympathetic to protest against the war.[21] Newspapers were a key part of the public sphere in the 1960s, but as purveyors more of information than of opinion; they did not provide the interpretations of those opposing the war.

As a consequence, a major focus of the diverse groups in the movement lay in interpreting the meaning of the information circulating in society, producing a number of critical metaphors. The metaphor of Vietnam as an atrocity had strong resonances with the left-liberal humanist tenor of the peace movement of the early 1960s. The war was seen as barbaric and its atrocities inevitable and routinised. Moral revulsion arose less from an explicitly pacifist impulse than from a rejection of the use of a disproportionate and dehumanised technology. A failure to act would involve the guilt of complicity. The atrocity metaphor thus had links with the culture of dissent of the early to mid-1960s with its sense of a duty to bear witness, now modernised by the New Left's theme of dehumanising capitalist technology.

This view often included a presumption that the Australian experience of the war was the same as that of American soldiers. So—in the most prominent example—when Alex Carey published a pamphlet in 1968, he laboured to demonstrate that Australians were involved in atrocities as frequently and routinely as Americans. He cited a case of water torture, several accounts of the shooting of wounded prisoners, the handing over of prisoners to the GVN in the knowledge that they would be tortured, the destruction of villages and finally the display of bodies at Hoa Long. But the general argument was that the war itself was the atrocity, as an indiscriminate application of firepower and as a genocidal strategy. This allowed Carey to draw his extravagant conclusion that 'we have totted up a record in Vietnam that no 8000 among Hitler's storm troopers would have been ashamed to own'. This both derived from and reinforced the metaphor of the war as an atrocity, but had little to do with the Australian experience in Phuoc Tuy.[22]

This perspective overlapped with that of those in the New Left who saw the war as a metaphor for the bureaucratic instrumentalism which Marcuse had described; Vietnam's peasants were the victims of a technocratic rationality which made human values and reason increasingly precarious. In this view, the war expressed the end point of dehumanisation. While for Marxists in the CPA and the Leninist ultra-left, history was still a positive value of potential progress, for many in the culture of the New Left, Vietnam captured a sense of nihilism and despair. One poet conjured up an image of Vietnam in the year 2001, 'smooth and flat as the pavement':

> adrift in the pacific
> bombed free of the asian sub-continent
> it drifts treeless and peopleless and silent
> the final solution.[23]

Alienation, dehumanisation, technology, despair and revolt were a heady mix in the New Left. The war condensed a range of themes, adding both volatility and energy to the older peace movement's vision of it as an occasion of moral complicity, or—for the Old Left—of imperialism. The war dramatised a rupture in society which was generational and cultural as much as it was political.

Finally, the New Left's positive identification with anti-imperialist struggles marked a more widely shared enthusiasm for Third World revolution. Discussion of the old issue of nationalism was notably absent from debates in the late 1960s, replaced by a romantic ardour for 'national liberation'. In this, some on the New Left were prepared to accept—or more often ignore—forms of revolutionary 'ethics' and authoritarian rule which they roundly condemned in the Stalinism of the Old Left. As the American intellectual Irving Howe wondered after meeting some American SDS leaders, if they were such libertarians, why did they insist on admiring Castro's Cuba ?

The Third World and liberation encapsulated several themes. Peasants were Marcusian marginals, possible agents of history who had not been incorporated as had the working class of post-scarcity capitalism. In addition, Maoism had latched upon national liberation struggles as the means of demonstrating the fragility of the imperialist world order. Finally, the peasant represented a premodern world which was standing up to the juggernaut of modernity, a theme which gave the Vietnam struggle an aspect of 'David and Goliath' which was attractive to the New Left and liberals alike. The populist image of the Vietnamese revolution as a spontaneous revolt of 'the people', rather than a highly organised, disciplined and often ruthless movement, was the strongest and most urgent example of this romance of the Third World.

If Vietnam was its political form, the beatification of Che Guevara was the cultural version of the same desire. Guevara was both cultural icon and commodity, exemplar and 'star'. His brief life was perfectly formed for the New Left's image of the Third World. A minister in Castro's post-revolutionary government, he had—'in an existential gesture irresistibly appealing to the New Left'—given up his post to lead a guerrilla band in Bolivia, intent on exporting revolution under his slogan 'Create two, three, many Vietnams in Latin America.' When he was shot by the Bolivian military in October 1967, his image 'flashed around the world . . . [and] the younger generation had its supreme martyr, its Jesus . . . Posters of Che plastered the walls of a generation.'

Guevara was the quintessence of the cult of the heroic guerrilla who had given up his bureaucratic job and achieved authenticity amongst the people; that he did so with arms, and in the service of a distinctly Old Left ideology, was lost on many of those for whom he was the perfect icon of the Third World, with an undertone of oedipal revolt. Some in America and elsewhere had taken the call to arms seriously by the end of the 1960s, though not in Australia, where the left never resorted to armed violence. Instead, the enthusiasm for Third World revolt had a more romantic and even nostalgic tenor, of authenticity in contrast to the artificiality of the modern. When Denis Freney and friends were establishing a shop and anti-war centre in Sydney in 1969—and paying the rent through the lucrative trade in posters of Guevara, Dylan and Jimi Hendrix—they considered possible names: Revolution, Che, Solidarity, Liberation. In a haze of cannabis smoke, they settled for Liberation.[24]

By the end of the 1960s, the war had entered—via a range of metaphors—the cross-currents of Australian political and cultural change. As an animating cause, it was caught up in the dynamics of domestic political developments on the left, which linked only tenuously and disjointedly with the dynamics of the war. It was technocratic irrationality and the inevitable atrocity, it was a Maoist struggle and a Third World romance. These interpretations of Vietnam were certainly not about Phuoc Tuy and the Australian role there, which was reported very little with the result that both critics and supporters of the war knew little of the concrete Australian experience in Phuoc Tuy. In different ways, both opponents and supporters tended to see the war through American eyes and American camera lenses. For the right, it was refracted through their concern for the alliance; for the left, the war was interpreted through symbols often derived from American critical social theories.

Journalists' access was restricted in Phuoc Tuy, and by at least 1968 the Australian Army had forbidden its soldiers to speak to the press without authorisation; the Task Force had none of the American enthusiasm for waging the war in an open, transparent manner. In addition, most Australian reporters focused on the larger war, regarding Phuoc Tuy as a relative backwater. There was some sense in this, but it meant that, for opponents of the war, the visible features of the American war—the indiscriminate use of technology, the collapse of army discipline and the resulting atrocities, the routine use of napalm and bombing—were mistakenly presumed to be equally features of Phuoc Tuy. This was a misconception carried into the Moratorium.

In the few years immediately before the Moratorium, the political rhythms of Australian society had altered considerably. If 1966 was the year which broke the mould of the Cold War by regenerating public debate, the three years that followed were strangely ambiguous—hence their morbid symptoms. They were years of some stasis, as public debate appeared to freeze over again. The ALP leadership withdrew as much as possible from specific commitments on Vietnam, while the conservatives paused, apparently transfixed, as their postwar strategy unwound.

Yet at the same time, the preconditions for the Moratorium mobilisation had developed. Groups on the left had grown dramatically, exerting some influence on the character of the peace movement, the CPA and the anti-conscription movement. Each of these was—to different degrees—pulled to the left, with some enthusiasm in the case of the latter two. Some groundwork had been laid for a re-formation of the scattered parts of the peace movement, to be organised no longer in the monolithic unity of a front but in the pluralism of a coalition. Finally, public opinion had turned against the war. So if, after 1966, the surface of the public sphere had appeared to freeze over again, the currents below were of greater importance.

IV

Withdrawal

13
The
Moratorium

The Moratorium campaign

Initiated in late October 1969 and culminating in May the following year, the Moratorium campaign's rapid growth suggested it was not only timely, but an essential development of the political realignments of the previous years. Ten days after the first and biggest Moratorium, the AICD committee met and, in the midst of congratulations, agreed that 'the campaign swept the movement out of a trough of frustration and stagnation and engendered a new sense of purpose and relevance'. After the protracted slump of 1968 and 1969, the peace movement had mobilised precisely the coalition of forces to which it had always aspired.

That the Moratorium was constructed upon the base of the longstanding institutions of the peace movement is clear. But this was also a source of fractious dispute, with the militant left arguing that the CICD/AICD groups were attempting to control its course and character. It was a matter of some satisfaction to CICD that it had taken the initiative. In mid-October 1969, Lloyd had met in the CICD offices with Norman Rothfield, one of the organisation's vice-presidents, and Bevan Ramsden. Inspired by news from America, where the first Moratorium march had recently been held, they discussed the possibility of a similar mobilisation. On 22 October, the executive endorsed the idea—though only after the initial caution of Dickie and Hartley had been overridden—and gave Lloyd the authority to initiate an interstate consultation. The resulting national consultation took place in Canberra on 25 November, and was attended by 36 representatives, primarily of the established peace groups. Student and militant groups would later argue that they had not been invited.[1]

In the meantime, events had moved quickly in America; in mid-November, the My Lai story had been taken up by the major American dailies, further undermining the credibility of the pro-war position. Two days later, the second Moratorium march had been held, the first having occurred in mid-October. One of the largest demonstrations in American history, the November march in Washington was variously estimated as numbering between 400 000 and 800 000 people. The Moratorium was conceived as a continuing process to disrupt 'business as usual', for some activists in order to force reflection on the war, and for others to bring the social system to a halt. These first marches effectively punctured the Nixon administration's efforts to convey the message that—with the troop withdrawals announced in July and September—the war was all but over.[2]

Any hopes the Australian government had that its own announcement of withdrawal would silence its critics were similarly dashed. After the indecision, paralysis and leadership conflicts of the previous two years, Gorton finally conceded—on 16 December 1969—that an unspecified number of Australians would be withdrawn to coincide with the next American withdrawal. Appearing on television, Gorton sat 'dressed in black . . . with folded arms and reading his announcement . . .' The posture was somewhat begrudging, the policy more so.

Gorton's insistence that 'we will not abandon the objectives for which we entered the Vietnam war' was a suitable face-saving device. The immediate objective—to preserve an anti-communist regime—was being abandoned behind the shaky facade of 'Vietnamisation'; the more implicit objectives of Australian intervention—to commit the Americans to a regional role and to maintain their goodwill—were becoming increasingly elusive. The withdrawal itself was hedged about with ambiguities, with Gorton telling his audience that he knew of no timetable for American withdrawals, and that it had not been decided which Australian units would be withdrawn, nor when they would return.

According to one report, Cabinet had discussed the decision in the previous week, with a joint submission from the departments of Defence and External Affairs arguing that partial withdrawal was feasible. In a telling reminder of the paralysis in government and bureaucracy, this was thought to be 'the first major review of the Vietnam conflict for more than a year . . .' Indeed, when McMahon had replaced the hapless Freeth as External Affairs minister the month before, he was disconcerted to find little forward planning in the department. On the Sunday after Cabinet's discussion, McMahon phoned Howson, with whom he regularly plotted Gorton's fall: 'He, Gorton and McEwen spent most of the day deciding on a new policy for Vietnam . . . at last Gorton has got the message that he has to face up to the problem and make some decisions.'[3] Despite leadership tensions, and the enmity between these three, a decision had finally been made.

McMahon and Howson were pleased that Gorton's perfunctory manner in making the announcement was poorly received. For Gorton, though, there was little that could be salvaged in announcing the disintegration of a generation of foreign policy. *The Age* commented that the decision would not satisfy those who wanted immediate withdrawal, but that it at least showed the government had 'come to terms publicly with the new situation in Vietnam'. This was 'a turning-point and . . . no less noteworthy for having been inevitable'. The *Australian* was unforgiving. Less than two weeks after demanding an immediate withdrawal in the wake of the My Lai revelations, the time for qualifications had passed; any conditions on withdrawal only served 'to prolong the war and all it has come to mean'. The government's ambiguities indicated it 'still shows no sign of recognising that this is the position it has reached'. Urged from one side to withdraw faster, the government was also being criticised from its right, with *News-Weekly* writing that the decision was 'a political blunder of the first magnitude. It represents a concession—quite unnecessary in Australia—to the power of the streets'.[4]

Unwittingly, this touched on an important point. Before the Moratorium, the government had decided on a gradual and reluctant withdrawal, though not as a result of 'the power of the streets'—the peace movement was still in a trough and the debate had stilled. The shift in public opinion may have been one consideration, but principally the conservatives were responding to pressure not from the streets but from the Americans, who were plainly—and unilaterally—changing the basis of foreign policy. The later statement, on 22 April 1970, that a battalion would be withdrawn in November, gave substance to Gorton's earlier ambiguities. It, too, predated the Moratorium, though the timing—some two weeks before the first march—may have been a pre-emptive response to it. The conservatives had begun their retreat in the face of the inevitable just as the Moratorium mobilisation began.

In that mobilisation, the established peace groups provided a crucial organisational core. In Queensland, Victoria and NSW, CICD and its equivalents provided the delegates to the Canberra consultation, as well as the subsequent provisional convenors of the Vietnam Moratorium Campaign (VMC) committees established in each state—Geoff Anderson from AICD, John Lloyd from CICD and Norma Chalmers from the Queensland Peace Committee for ICD in Brisbane. Similarly, the three members of the national coordinating committee established at the Canberra consultation were all from AICD. When delegates dispersed to their home states to call together VMC committees, it was hardly surprising that the first conflicts were between those of moderate tendencies and militants over who would control the new mobilisation.

In Sydney, the first meeting of sponsors repudiated the Canberra consultation as unrepresentative, and later insisted that the VMC have an office independent of AICD. The Resistance group was one voice in this, though a largely spent force by 1970; others were the SDS and other student groups. In Melbourne, meanwhile, CICD presented its proposal on 9 December to the first VMC meeting of some 120 people, held in a city restaurant. CICD suggested that it would financially underwrite the campaign and administer its funds, and that the VMC executive should consist of the seven-member CICD executive, with seven others from affiliated groups. The proposal was loudly rejected as an attempt by CICD to control the developing campaign. As Lloyd later recognised, while it partly arose from an underestimation of how large the Moratorium would be, it did nothing to assuage the suspicions of the left.

On 1 February 1970, at the first of the large and volatile mass meetings held in the Richmond town hall, a more open and accommodating structure—proposed by the CPA's Laurie Carmichael—was adopted. All affiliated organisations would have the right to send one delegate to the executive, which in turn elected office-bearers. A similar structure was developed in NSW, where sponsors' meetings were the equivalent of the Richmond town hall meetings; in NSW, sponsors sent representatives to the VMC committee, which elected a secretariat. By late 1970, some 150 organisations were affiliated in Victoria, while the NSW VMC had some 70 supporting organisations in April, and more than 1000 sponsors.[5]

The breadth of this support attested to a new unity of various forces, old and new. But the balance of these forces varied. In

Sydney, where the 'ultra-left' did not have an extensive base and the ALP left was weak, AICD could expect substantially more support to its right than opposition to its left. In Melbourne, the CPA (M–L) and its offshoots provided a greater influence towards the 'ultra-left', which was counterbalanced by an alliance between the CPA and the ALP left. These balances, along with administrative resources, meant that the moderates largely controlled the course of the campaign. Nevertheless, in Melbourne, the militants began strongly. At the first VMC mass meeting, Goldbloom successfully proposed Cairns as chairman, but later in the afternoon, the militants carried proposals for a token occupation of the city streets on Moratorium Day, for the removal of a clause declaring that the Moratorium would be non-violent and for declarations of overt support for the NLF in the struggle against American imperialism.[6] Each of these was a sentiment which CICD felt could alienate the broad constituency it had always sought.

Once the organisational work began, however, CICD—like its counterparts in NSW and Queensland—exercised substantial influence over the course of the campaign, in particular over how its slogans were presented. These were not simply disputes over organisational position or political credit. They were recognised as struggles over the strategy of the campaign, reflecting differing interpretations of the coalition and conflicting views about militancy as against broad-based support. To a large extent, the success of the first moratorium reflected the strategy which the moderate left, particularly the CPA, developed in pursuit of public presence and influence—an open and inclusive coalition placing breadth of participation before coherence of ideology.

In the event, on 8 May 1970, between 120 000 and 150 000 people demonstrated in cities and towns around the country, in what the chief historian of the Moratorium called 'the greatest single demonstration of strength that the peace movement in Australia had ever achieved'.[7] The largest—numbering at least 70 000, and perhaps as many as 100 000—was in Melbourne. The violence which conservative politicians and the media had predicted and even appeared to be threatening, was avoided. Even disapproving papers such as *The Age* were impressed:

> Seventy thousand citizens took to Melbourne streets yesterday, shouting, 'Peace', 'Stop the war!' A thousand police, many armed with pistols and shotguns, waited. But hardly a punch was thrown. The riots did not happen.

Another journalist described the spectacle in Bourke Street:

> . . . the great mass coming from Spring Street . . . rivets

everybody's attention. Banners and placards high, moving like some
great outback river in flood down the grey deserted watercourse of
Bourke Street. As they get to the intersection . . . and meet their
fellows coming from the opposite direction, there is this great roaring
chant that echoes off the canyons of the city: Stop the War! Stop
the War! Stop the War! . . . All the way up to Spring Street is this
vast crowd and like a slow ripple they all begin to sit down in the
street. It is impossible for those at the back to see those in the
front . . .[8]

The Moratorium, like the war itself, had different meanings for
the different fractions of society involved. For some, it expressed
a weariness with a war which had focused public attention for
five years and had recently escalated again with the American
invasion of Cambodia. For others, it was a moral protest, in
which the My Lai massacre had become a powerful metaphor.
For many on the left, it represented a major blow against the
conservatives which might yet be turned in more radical directions.

Ian Turner stood watching the march go by for half an hour
before joining in. He commented that nine out of ten of those
marching were young—'the counter-culture on the march'—and
that Vietnam was only a symbol of a deeper cultural shift. He
saw this as primarily a demand for more participatory forms of
politics, and slightly misquoted Bob Dylan: 'There's something
going on, but you don't know what it is, do you, Mr Jones? It
was good to see.' It was a sentiment Turner clearly relished and
had quoted before. For those such as himself who had long
struggled in the peace movement for a legitimate voice, the
Moratorium completed a process of prising open public space:

. . . for the old demonstrators, it was an experience of a new kind:
no longer that part-embarrassed, part-defiant feeling of parading
one's beliefs in isolation before a hostile, mocking or indifferent
public.

Now there was an unfamiliar legitimacy to the use of public
space: 'For a whole afternoon the city returned to one of its
traditional functions—a place where pedestrians could define their
own needs and purposes . . .'[9] In the mid-1960s, the peace
movement had thought of itself as the voice of reason and moral
duty raised against a storm of intimidation. The intellectual left
had despaired of suburban conformism, and Cairns had
attempted, with only modest success, to explain political apathy
in its relationship to the fears governing foreign policy. By 1970,
after the New Left's proliferation of critical social theories and
of militant action, it was possible to be more assertive in claiming
the legitimacy of autonomous political action.

At a press conference announcing the Moratorium, Cairns

Between 70 000 and 100 000 demonstrated in Bourke Street, Melbourne, in May 1970 at the same time as large demonstrations in other capitals. After a slump in the movement in 1969, the crowd exceeded the expectations of organisers and reflected the breadth of the Moratorium coalition. The Moratorium came after the start of the de-escalation of the war, but represented the cultural shifts which had made a Cold War pattern of politics obsolete.

drew the wrath of conservative politicians and editorial writers
by suggesting that citizens had a right to occupy the streets for
political purposes. The *Herald* found this 'a strange and disturbing call'. Cairns simultaneously ensured free publicity for the
campaign and articulated a democratic, rather than revolutionary,
justification for action. As the public face of the mobilisation, he
formed a bridge between the mid-1960s ideas of dissent and
morality and New Left ideas of participatory democracy.

This aspect made his parliamentary speech defending the
Moratorium a 'manifesto of dissent'; for many in the peace
movement, Cairns offered a vindication for action and articulated
beliefs that were not explicitly spelt out in the formal aims of
the Moratorium.[10] In parliament in the month before the first
march, he had defended its aims:

> Some . . . think that democracy is just Parliament . . . But times
> are changing. A whole generation is not prepared to accept this
> complacent, conservative theory. Parliament is not democracy. It is
> one of the manifestations of democracy . . . Democracy is govern-
> ment by the people, and government by the people demands action
> by the people. It demands effective ways of showing what the
> interests and needs of the people really are. It demands action in
> public places all around the land . . .

When challenged, Cairns declared himself to be within 'the great
American tradition of radicalism', in an echo of his argument of
'two Americas'—the military–industrial complex and the continuing American revolution.[11] His identification of the assertive use
of public space with democracy harked back to the concerns of
the old peace dissenters while being radical enough to have some
relevance to those in the New Left interested in participatory
democracy.

This was inevitably a conception of democracy to which the
right was hostile. Howson made clear how much such a conception of politics distressed those who had benefited from the Cold
War closure of public discourse. For him, the first moratorium
illustrated that 'popular opinion can be mobilised to interfere
with government policy', which nicely captured the conservative
view of the proper balance between authority and citizenship.
Such forms of protest had been discussed at the seminars Howson
attended at the ANU, where 'the CIA representative forecast that
this would be the sort of problem with which democracies would
have to deal in the next decade . . .' On the day before the first
moratorium, the minister for Labour and National Service, Billy
Snedden, had joined the attack on the VMC organisers,
characterising them as 'political bikies who pack rape
democracy'.[12]

Others on the Catholic right continued the theme of 'the

power of the streets'. One pamphlet, partly reprinted from *News-Weekly*, argued that Cairns had become a 'totalitarian' by organising the Moratorium as a form of 'mob rule' which displaced the institutions of representative democracy. But finding parallels as it did with Hitler and Lenin was drawing a long bow, and the author seemed more comfortable with his other, more orthodox argument, that the Moratorium was the creation of a CPA front.[13] In effect, conservatives were asserting the decorum of a representative and constitutional form of democracy against what they saw as the unpredictability of participation and 'mob rule'.

This democratic element in the first moratorium suggests its character as a vindication of the past. Particularly for those who had long been involved in the peace movement, the Moratorium was the broad front they had always aimed for, and it vindicated their attempts to break into the public culture during the Cold War. Given that the campaign had little effect on the conservatives' Vietnam policy—the logic of withdrawal, if not its speed, was now inevitable—the political significance of the Moratorium was more in its prehistory than in its subsequent effects.[14] The Moratorium was as much about the political culture as about the war. It marked the end of the Cold War epoch which had produced the Vietnam intervention and made opposition to that intervention so difficult. It finally reclaimed the political use of the public sphere against a Cold War which had tended to silence it; in this sense, the Moratorium, significant as it was for its participants, was historically an ending rather than a beginning.

The open coalition

The Moratorium campaign was the most successful form of a leftist political alliance since the Second World War. It established an open, flexible, but ultimately short-lived coalition between the left of the ALP, the range of established peace and anti-conscription groups, some Old Left unions, some church groups, the New Left, a still-small women's movement and a revitalised CPA. The vigour of this coalition—along with the erosion of the pro-war position which had now made participation less ideologically challenging for the middle class—contributed to the exceptional mobilisation of May 1970.

Four features help to account for this early succes: the administrative resources of the established peace groups, the role of the ALP, the strategy of a 'coalition of the left' argued out by the CPA, and finally, the decentralised aspects of the cam-

A common theme of conservative attacks on the Moratorium was that it represented 'mob rule' in the streets; but for many the claim sounded shrill. By 1969, one of Whitlam's more telling promises was to represent the country in international forums with a more assertive and lucid voice. (Petty, Australian, *8 May 1970*

paign which built support in middle Australia. Yet this first of the three moratoriums was the broadest and most successful, reflecting a peak of support for the campaign beyond which it could not substantially build.[15] After May, the campaign did not grow, and after September it would dissipate.

The struggles over who would control the campaign continued. Throughout the Moratorium campaign, the established groups such as AICD and CICD positioned themselves at the administrative core of the movement, frequently defending themselves against accusations of control with the riposte that it was they alone who did the actual day-to-day work. There was a good deal of truth in this: the New Left often appeared to have the view that labour had been superseded by the illumination of radical action. During 1970 and 1971, both AICD and CICD devoted themselves almost exclusively to the Moratorium. As Lloyd put it in one report:

> The Congress [CICD] provided the bulk of the administrative work for the Moratorium in Victoria. We catered for all the official mailings, organised the official public meetings, executive meetings

and secretariat meetings. The office was used as a centre for the sale of Moratorium goods.

In addition, CICD coordinated suburban groups, distributed hundreds of thousands of leaflets, arranged public speakers and provided secretarial staff to the Moratorium. The volatile meetings of activists in the Richmond town hall claimed the right to make authoritative decisions, but it was more often CICD staff who did the actual work of the campaign.[16]

In Sydney, AICD occupied an equivalent position at the administrative centre. The VMC secretariat included Anderson, AICD's secretary of many years, and Ken McLeod, also from AICD and the Moratorium secretary in NSW. Other AICD staff worked on the campaign at AICD's expense until mid-1970, after which one salary was paid by the VMC. From mid-1970, the VMC rented an office in AICD's building and, by design or default, AICD largely ran the campaign. When AICD was accused—by Resistance amongst others—of taking over the campaign, it replied that it was AICD staff who did the mundane but essential work, adding with a note of resentment that 'no one has challenged this and no other organisation has offered to assist'. Late in 1971, McLeod wrote that 'AICD can justifiably claim to have been largely responsible for the initiative and development of the Moratorium campaign in this state', although it had paid a heavy price for 'this leading role' in terms of a reduction of the capacity to develop its own initiatives.[17]

Although this centrality of the established peace groups was attacked as control, it provided an organisational framework rather than ideological or strategic leadership. It allowed them to mute the more radical demands of the 'ultra-left' and gave an often cautious tenor to the campaign, although the broad outlines of strategy and aims were set by larger meetings. The established peace groups were important as the bureaucratic sinews of the campaign, for the Moratorium was as much an organisational as a political phenomenon.

With Cairns's prominence in the Victorian campaign, the impression developed that Labor stood at its centre. Freudenberg later wrote that 'the leadership of the anti-war movement beyond the official Party remained with Cairns' in 1970. But Cairns's position was both more complex and more detached. He was a figurehead and patron, standing awkwardly above the ruck of the factions. As a public intellectual, the media identified him as the movement's personification and he provided inspiration for many, but the 'ultra-left' disparaged him as an incurable reformist: 'Mr Peace'. Cairns often chaired the Richmond meetings, but he was never a strategist or organiser. Ormonde captured the relationship between Cairns and the movement when he wrote that Cairns rarely organised anything. Cairns focused a critique of the war and spoke indefatigably at public meetings, but 'his role was inspirational rather than organisational'. Seeing himself as a servant of the movement, he yet remained aloof.[18]

The part played by the ALP varied in different states, but outside Victoria, the party's official response to the campaign was at best ambivalent. A number of Labor's leaders remained cautious about both the policies and the politics of the moratorium and both the Victorian leader, Clyde Holding, and Whitlam distanced themselves from the first Moratorium. In Tasmania and NSW, Labor was largely hostile, and AICD noted with some satisfaction that its success was achieved without—and even in spite of—the NSW branch. The major exception was Uren, who held open a path for Labor members to join the movement. In Queensland, South Australia and Western Australia, the party was little more than nominally supportive. In each state, however, there were prominent ALP identities who lent their prestige and help, but in general the party itself was immobile. Only in Victoria was Labor's organisation mobilised for the campaign, with suburban branches functioning as active networks for the Moratorium. But even in Victoria, the organisational impetus remained with CICD.

Whitlam's position gave a guide to Labor's caution, just as Cairns's involvement gave legitimacy to the left. In December 1969, Whitlam was involved in a frequently quoted exchange with his perennial adversary, the ALP federal secretary 'Joe' Chamberlain, who had asked Whitlam to place himself at the head of the campaign. In explaining his position, Whitlam argued:

> We maximise our opposition to the Vietnam war by maximising support for our Party. I do not believe that I should single out any one of half a dozen major issues for my exclusive attention.

He believed it was inadvisable for him to be associated with actions representing 'a less than complete view than our Caucus or Conference or presenting a different emphasis . . .'

Whitlam was arguing that if Labor had little or no control over the direction and temper of the campaign, it was better for the party to remain dissociated from it. Consequently, he took a markedly different position from Cairns on the question of the extra-parliamentary movement.

> Members of the Party should not give the false and damaging impression that under a Labor Government foreign policy would be determined at mass meetings or by public petitions. For this reason I concentrate my own actions in Party and Parliamentary channels.[19]

The contrast in approach contained within the ALP by 1970 could hardly be more stark. Whitlam's studied distance from the peace movement jealously guarded Labor's freedom of manoeuvre and his own sense of parliament's prerogative as the forum of democracy. Cairns's enthusiasm for political activism—chairing the Richmond town hall meetings at which fiery rhetoric crackled through the air—was an endorsement of a social movement which for a time dwarfed parliamentary politics.

By 1970, Labor was able to accommodate its divisions over Vietnam. The Moratorium did not damage the party, producing none of the acrimony of 1966. Now Labor was in step with American policy and with a majority public opinion favouring withdrawal. The October 1969 election had encouraged Labor to expect government at the next election and vindicated the appeal of Whitlam's modernised labourism. Consequently, Labor's flexibility meant that even within the national leadership there was little difficulty in accommodating perspectives as different as those of Whitlam and Cairns.

The ALP, however, was in no position to argue the merits of a broad coalition. Nor were the established peace groups, which, for all their organisational skills, consciously avoided ideological self-definition, suspecting that this would inevitably exclude potential support. For them, unity was everything, their primary political impulse being to keep escaping the isolation of the past. The criticism from the left since 1966 had forced some minor recasting of this view, and to some extent they had been affected by critical theories on the left. But when pressed, both AICD and CICD restated their traditional positions. AICD defined itself as 'a broadly based organisation embracing quite divergent political tendencies'. This was its established self-identity as an inclusive group, particularly when under attack from the right as a CPA front. Ironically, it was now being argued against 'ultra-left' accusations that AICD was 'politically aligned'—by which was meant CPA-aligned.

In Melbourne, CICD rejected invitations to adopt an explicitly anti-imperialist position:

> The role of CICD is to give a broad cross section of people an opportunity to participate in specific anti-war campaigns. Such people may hold contrasting political views of [sic] ideologies, or no ideology at all.

Any exclusive position might preclude reaching the non-committed middle ground, and with their focus fixed firmly on this middle ground, the established peace groups reasoned that 'many of those who remain uninvolved do so because we have failed to reach them'. Although increasingly prepared to agree that their

For a brief period in 1970 and into 1971 the Moratorium campaign mobilised a coalition of forces and sentiments in a social movement which dwarfed the parliamentary forms of politics. Here a crowd gathers outside the Victorian parliament in the first moratorium, May 1970. (Australian War Memorial, P671/14/04)

past practice of simply—often piously—arguing for peace was insufficient, they were acutely aware that 'the overwhelming majority of the community have not yet taken the first simple steps of protest'.[20]

The effect of these views, shaped by their history, was that the established peace groups had little capacity to formulate a common strategy for an open coalition encompassing liberals, churches, radicals and moderates. The role of arguing for this coalition was more often taken up by the CPA. Since 1967, the Party had at least the strategy of a 'coalition of the left', in which it would be one influence amongst others. This, along with the CPA's cultivation of links with the New Left, had placed it in a good position to articulate the nature of the Moratorium.

Consequently, the CPA leadership was prominent in arguing for the Moratorium campaign as an open, non-exclusive coalition. Disputes centred around the aims and slogans of the movement— which the 'ultra-left' wanted to push to more radical levels—but underlying them were different conceptions of the coalition. Bernie Taft was the CPA's main representative in the Victorian campaign and one of the VMC's three vice-chairmen, the others being Jean McLean of SOS, and Harry van Moorst of the Draft

Resisters' Union. Noting that it had become a truism that the campaign was diverse, Taft argued that its

> . . . common factor is the opposition to the war in Vietnam. It includes both supporters and opponents of the present social system. It includes revolutionaries, reformists, pacifists, humanitarians, liberals and a lot of people who don't fit into any of these categories.

While the 'ultra-left' argued that these differences were no reason why the leadership and political tone should not be revolutionary, the CPA had a keener sense of the Moratorium as 'a voluntary coalition', its various elements organised in a 'democratic and genuinely non-exclusive movement'.

The key issue was not diversity but how it was to be encompassed. CPA leaders argued that plurality should be encouraged and, in effect, that the movement be seen as counter-hegemonic. An element of the CPA's coalition theory had always been that through involvement citizens would come to more radical views. As Taft put it, to impose anti-imperialist aims and slogans on the movement would

> . . . restrict its ability to grow and attract new forces . . . It would in fact demand of people that they should understand *before they join the movement,* that the war in Vietnam is a product of imperialism—instead of teaching them when they are in the movement.[21]

In this view, the role of radicals was didactic rather than incendiary.

For the 'ultra-left', the concern with broad unity risked diluting radical sentiments. Langer, the most articulate in putting this position, argued that the movement had radicalised over the past five years because

> . . . the tactics of militant direct action, defiance and sharp, clear-cut propaganda have built up a far more successful and dynamic movement than the vacillations of the right wing . . . policies that were 'infantile disorders' only a few years ago [are] the 'conventional wisdom' of today.

Although it was true that the bounds of the possible had expanded since 1965, this claimed too much credit for building the Moratorium and assumed a unity of purpose and politics which the movement manifestly did not possess. The contribution of the 'ultra-left' was decisive action and a brutally forceful analysis, but what came after the sit-in and the police retaliation? With neither a mass base, a coalition strategy nor a recognition of the importance of hegemony, the 'ultra-left' soon came up against the limits of radical posturing.

Ultimately, these were judgments about how radical the centre of gravity of the movement was. The established peace groups

were still concerned that they had not reached the safety of the
middle ground. The CPA was concerned that the coalition not
be jeopardised by prematurely militant postures—and went out
of its way to quote Lenin on the point. The 'ultra-left' was
convinced that the mass movement was part of the worldwide
struggle against imperialism, which was being retarded only by
the caution and reformism of the leadership. To push this
development, 'our slogans must be clear cut, and must lift the
tone to an anti-imperialist level'. Langer brutally reversed the
logic of the open coalition: 'Struggle is absolute while unity is
only temporary and conditional'.[22] This had the virtue of honesty.
The coalition was an expedient, and there was no other, intrinsic
value to democratic pluralism.

In the event, it was generally the CPA which acted as the
broker, holding together this unlikely coalition and restraining the
ultra-left's militancy while still legitimating 'advanced' actions to
the more cautious groups in the coalition. The VMC in each
capital city had differing configurations of forces, but in the two
major centres of Sydney and Melbourne the CPA played a leading
role in steering the course which it judged appropriate to the
political temper of the movement, and which preserved its
didactic effect.

And in practice, if the CPA could not win the argument with
the 'ultra-left', it could win the votes. The argument was largely
a dialogue of the deaf, but was worth making to convince the
unconvinced. But given that Maoism was the least democratic of
the strains in the Moratorium, moderating its influence involved
a dilemma. Pluralism required that all those involved accepted
common democratic norms. In the absence of this condition,
CPA activists in effect reverted to ensuring they had the numbers
as well as arguing their case.

In the Richmond town hall meetings which—as a forum of
direct democracy—claimed the right to determine VMC policy,
the Maoists could muster substantial numbers. But they were
usually defeated by the CPA's leadership and supporters, which
aligned with Cairns's less identifiable but appreciable constituency
of Labor members, established peace groups, Save Our Sons,
church groups and others. Taft and Cairns would regularly
consult before the meetings, working out joint motions which
would draw broad support while offering some concessions to
the 'ultra-left'.[23] The coalition of the left, based on pluralism and
open democratic contest, was being tempered by the more
traditional techniques of 'stacking' meetings, techniques in which
both the CPA and the ALP had some experience.

A final important element of the Moratorium, which kept the
moderate left sensitive to the limits of mobilisation, was its

decentralised organisation in the suburbs. Local activities were seen as the first stage of the campaign, publicising the marches, making the arguments for opposition to the war and raising funds. In Sydney and Melbourne, the movement built upon existing networks within civil society, in the form of workplace groups, neighbourhood meetings and Saturday morning activities in shopping centres. In these two cities, activities organised by local groups outnumbered those organised by the central committees; in the other states, the campaign was more centralised.

Developed in early 1970, these networks were one precondition for successful mobilisation, and kept the established peace movement attuned to the middle ground. The 'ultra-left', largely out of touch with middle Australia, felt no such constraints upon its hopes, seeing suburban actions as a right-wing attempt to dilute the movement's radicalism. In NSW, 20 local Moratorium committees were established by the end of March, and much emphasis was placed on their importance for local mobilisation through small meetings. A month later, the number had grown to more than 30, along with regional groups in Newcastle, Wollongong, Canberra and Armidale. These networks were in addition to the sponsorship of the Moratorium by existing groups with their own roots in civil society, such as individual unions, Christian groups, the Humanist Society and the Rationalist Association.[24]

In Melbourne, the suburban network built substantially upon ALP local branches. By April, at least 29 branches were represented on the VMC executive, and ALP women's and Young Labor groups acted as sponsors. Some branches were active in the suburban mobilisation, organising functions, films and public meetings and distributing literature. Alongside this ALP network, some 20 suburban Moratorium groups were established in Melbourne by April, coordinated by CICD, which asked them to distribute a VMC broadsheet and undertake door-knocking and small Saturday morning demonstrations. The old VPC and then CICD had always had a network of local peace groups, which were now being duplicated, although 'the Moratorium groups invariably involve more and younger people than the long-standing peace groups'. The established peace movement was cultivating the younger constituency it sought, though the local groups were to be short-lived.

The work of these dispersed local groups was crucial in building the mobilisation which distinguished the first moratorium. In neighbourhood meetings and suburban actions, they built momentum and helped politicise a broad constituency. The range of their activities involved

> . . . talks to and debates at public meetings, teach-ins at universities
> and colleges, talks to students at secondary schools, discussions in
> churches, film evenings, motorcades around shopping centres, door-
> knocks in the suburbs, silent vigils in public places, factory-gate and
> shop-floor meetings, and even luncheons, barbeques and dances.[25]

Overshadowed by the spectacle of the major marches, this
suburban mobilisation was important in politicising Goldbloom's
'middle ground'. It was a flowering of public activities which had
not been seen since the 1966 election campaign.

If the key features of the moratorium of May 1970 were its
size and apparent unity, these reflected less the fiery vision of
the 'ultra-left' than the more prosaic strategy of the moderates.
The organisational framework provided by the established peace
groups, and the more accommodating stance of the ALP, were
both important elements in the mobilisation. But more essential
were the dextrous balancing act performed by the CPA in holding
together the coalition and the extensive roots which the campaign
had developed in the suburbs.

The public mobilisation in the first months of 1970 avoided
strong ideological statements and detailed analysis of Vietnam,
preferring simply to focus the sense of moral opposition to and
disenchantment with the war. That it should succeed—well
beyond the expectations of its organisers—reflected the collapse
of a conservative hegemony which had constrained civil society
and militated against vital public discourse. Hence the importance
in the Moratorium of the themes of dissent and participatory
democracy. The first moratorium reflected a sea-change in political attitudes, in which middle Australia was no longer enthralled
by the fears which had paralysed political debate since the Cold
War began. With the Moratorium, the Cold War was finally
shrugged off, suggesting less a mobilisation for the future than
a shedding of the past.

14

Things fall apart

The failure of counter-revolution in Phuoc Tuy

The successive announcements of Australian withdrawals from Phuoc Tuy were invariably accompanied by platitudes about the success of Vietnamisation. On 22 April 1970, Gorton told parliament that the 8th Battalion would not be replaced when its tour ended in November. This meant a reduction of some 900 from the ceiling of 8500. He expressed relief that the situation allowed this first withdrawal to be made: ' "I will be yet happier when all Australian forces can be withdrawn provided that our objective is not in danger." . . . Because of the progress of Vietnamisation in Phuoc Tuy, Australia was changing the shape of its contribution.'[1]

The decision overrode the vocal objections of the DLP, whose federal leader, Senator Vince Gair, pointedly told a press conference immediately before Gorton's statement that Australian troops should not yet be withdrawn. The government's dilemma was a real one. It depended—though more than it seemed aware—on the forces to its right, within both the DLP and the governing parties, which intransigently defended the verities of Cold War foreign policy. Yet this dependence restricted its ability

259

to face the situation in Vietnam and reverse its policy.
Vietnamisation attempted to balance these demands. Ostensibly,
it meant that the GVN's armed forces were capable of taking
over the role previously filled by Australian and American forces;
its subtext was the assurance that the regime in the South would
not immediately collapse with the removal of Western support.
The prospect of the South Vietnamese army winning the civil
war was scarcely considered.

But if Vietnamisation was the last major deception of the war,
it was significant that so few gave it credence. In Phuoc Tuy,
Task Force assessments were decidedly phlegmatic. During 1970
and 1971, a series of reports doubted that the GVN's army had
sufficiently improved to hold its own, or that the regime itself
had won popular support. Yet these had been the ingredients of
'counter-revolutionary warfare': the provision of an armed shield
behind which the people were freed from contact with 'terrorists'
while the army was reconstructed, the government won popular
support and the revolution withered.

By 1970 and 1971, the revolutionary forces in Phuoc Tuy
had clearly not withered; their activities were curtailed and they
had sustained substantial losses, but they were still viable, above
all as a political force. In early 1970, the emphasis of NLF units
was judged to be more political than military. Avoiding military
risks, they concentrated on assisting village-based cadres to
organise political meetings. The pattern described earlier—of
village propaganda meetings combined with procuring supplies—
continued. One captured guerrilla described the process to his
interrogators:

> . . . upon arrival the soldiers hand over empty sacks to the cadre
> and on departure the sacks are returned full of supplies. As far as
> he knows, no attempt has been made on any occasion by local
> authorities to prevent or disrupt these meetings.

Despite five years of counter-revolutionary warfare, the Vietnamese Communist Party's political infrastructure continued to func-
tion, the inaction of local authorities contrasting with the dogged
survival of the revolutionary forces.

The Australian army's reports on the effectiveness of the
South Vietnamese army ranged from cautious to deprecatory. In
early 1971, the Joint Intelligence Organisation in the Defence
department in Canberra was preparing a report on the progress
of Vietnamisation, and sent a draft to the military attache in the
Saigon embassy for his comments. ARVN, it judged, had progressed from being on the point of defeat in 1965 to an army
which 'can now operate effectively as it has in Cambodia and
Laos, even though it is still uneven in quality . . . and suffers

from defects in leadership'. The RF and PF—numbering some half a million—suffered a 'chronic shortage of competent leaders', and were 'patchy in performance, but have the potential to improve'. The revolutionary forces were 'not yet ready to test the process of Vietnamisation', but as withdrawals continued the balance would become 'even more delicate'. In his comments, the attache noted that the armed forces were 'absorbing the pace' of Vietnamisation well enough, but would 'certainly have more problems in doing so in 1972'.[2]

These assessments of the balance of forces were cautious enough. Those of army officials in Phuoc Tuy and Saigon were more pessimistic. They noted the 'ineffectiveness of local security and intelligence sources', which were unable or unwilling to detect movements of the NLF in the province. The local GVN forces had not improved: 'weakness in command, planning, co-ordination, leadership and logistics, which have been the subject of earlier reports, still exist'. The situation 'does not bode well for the time when the protective shields of the two 1ATF battalions are withdrawn'. As a later assessment succinctly put it:

> The grip of the cadres on the population was never really broken, ensuring a continuing flow of recruits, supplies and intelligence to the VC units . . . By contrast, the government forces, particularly the RF and PF, were inept with no stomach for the fight . . .[3]

The continuing viability of the revolutionary forces, along with these manifest weaknesses of the GVN's forces, made it plain that Vietnamisation was a face-saving device behind which disengagement could proceed.

The final aspect of counter-revolutionary warfare—the construction of a political constituency for the GVN—was equally flawed. The Psychological Operations Unit was perhaps the most attuned to popular attitudes in Phuoc Tuy, involved as it was in 'marketing' the South Vietnamese regime to its people. The summary reports of the province senior advisers in this area were markedly pessimistic, if not jaundiced. 'The people of Phuoc Tuy', one report concluded,

> . . . are definitely not pro-GVN . . . The psyops community can only sell and exploit effective programs to the people, who are not fools and see enough evidence of inefficiency and failures in many of the GVN systems. Graft and corruption (in unacceptable levels even for an Asian society) is [sic] ever present.

A year later, things had not changed:

> The population of Phuoc Tuy tends to be suspicious of GVN policies no matter how much effort is put into selling them by the psyop [sic] community. They see corruption at all levels. They see nepotism and inefficiency. Then they are asked to believe the official

organizations which speak for the government. It is no wonder that
they remain sceptical and it is to the Psyop community's credit that
the game is drawn and not lost.[4]

The project of Psychological Operations—common to both the
Australian and American efforts—was always implausible: to
apply advertising techniques, in the middle of a civil war, to
building a political constituency for a military elite with few
patriotic credentials and fewer local roots. The jaundiced tone of
these reports is in part a reflection of the failure of this project.
But it also plumbed the disenchantment amongst the local
population in Phuoc Tuy, where very few had been convinced
to support the GVN, and enough continued to actively or tacitly
sustain the NLF for its forces to remain viable.

It was in these circumstances that the Australian government
withdrew its intervening force. On 18 August 1971—the fifth
anniversary of the battle at Long Tan—prime minister McMahon
announced that the remainder of the Task Force would be
withdrawn by the end of the year. He had laid the groundwork
a month earlier with another statement about the 'courage and
determination of the South Vietnamese forces [who] have steadily
taken over the combat role', which meant that Australians could
'look forward to the withdrawal of all our combat forces'. In
Phuoc Tuy, the reaction of the villagers to the August announcement was reported to vary 'from jubilation in Hoa Long [the
NLF stronghold] to apprehension in Binh Gia [the Catholic
refugee village established in the mid-1950s]'.[5] The apprehension
of the latter was well founded.

By the end of 1971, all that remained was a small Australian
force providing training. Since the first troops in the training
team had begun arriving in Vietnam in August 1962, some 504
Australians had been killed, about 200 of them conscripts; more
than 3000 soldiers had been wounded or injured. A decade later,
in April and May 1972, NLF and NVA forces launched a
long-expected offensive throughout the South and quickly
exposed the weaknesses of the ARVN troops. In Phuoc Tuy, the
province capital and Dat Do were isolated, the latter virtually
destroyed in a nine-day battle that brought upon it American
bombing. As the offensive continued across the South, and as
the Americans responded with massive bombing of the North,
the peace talks in Paris stalled again and, in the words of one
commentator, 'Australians could only stand back and consider
the stark awesome ruins of American policy in Indo-China, to
which we have contributed for seven years and more.'[6]

The strategy of counter-revolutionary warfare, which had been
intended to reverse the postcolonial momentum of the Vietnamese

The last Australian troops leave the base at Nui Dat in November 1971 on their way to Vung Tau for embarkation. Nine years of military intervention had cost some 500 Australian lives, without success for the strategy of counter-revolution. (Australian War Memorial, CUN/71/539/VN)

revolution, lay amidst these ruins. Perhaps a residual meaning of Vietnamisation remained: that western disengagement would finally leave the contending political forces in Vietnam to battle it out amongst themselves. Interventionist policies since 1962 had not profoundly altered the fate of those forces, despite the terrible cost. The weaknesses of non-communist nationalism had never been remedied, and the Communist Party continued to articulate patriotic aspirations—attracting sufficient support for a front strategy under its leadership and control. If anything, massive Western intervention had undermined non-communist forces, which were increasingly dependent on, and associated with, American occupation and its destructive social effects.

In 1972, one officer who had been with the Task Force when it took over Phuoc Tuy in 1966 was in the province again. Observing the balance of forces, he made a comment full of poignancy and futility which could well stand as a judgment on the counter-revolutionary policy of postwar conservatism: 'It was for all the world to see as it had been in 1966 at the very beginning . . . as if we had never really been there.'[7]

The end of the open coalition

In the euphoria after the first moratorium, it was not yet clear
that the movement had already passed its peak. For eighteen
months after May 1970, the movement was a forum for fractious
dispute within the left, and the coalition was under severe stress.
The second set of marches, in September, were perhaps as large
as those in May, but—particularly in Sydney and Adelaide—were
broken up by concerted police action. The third moratorium, a
two-month mobilisation culminating at the end of June 1971, was
by its nature more widely dispersed.

By mid-1971, the movement had radicalised its stated aims
and its methods, but had failed to build public support beyond
the levels of the first mass action. Numbers had declined and
enthusiasm waned. Rather than building into a mass movement
for broader social change, the Moratorium ebbed away. The most
obvious reason for this decline was that the movement's most
emphasised demand—the withdrawal of Australian troops—was
being met, even if not in response to the movement and at a
slower pace than it demanded. The Moratorium had peaked after
the announcement of the first withdrawal and ebbed before
McMahon's announcement of the final withdrawal in mid-August
1971. Partly this was because its dynamics had as much to do
with the political and cultural tides of the Australian polity as
they did with responses to the Vietnam intervention.

Immediately after the first moratorium, a national consultation
of state VMC committees was held in Melbourne. It was
dominated by the moderate left—such as CPA activists—who saw
some potential for the movement to be radicalised without losing
broad public support. To some extent, this faction was opposed
by a small minority of 'conservatives'—the more cautious of the
old peace activists—who wanted only that the second moratorium
repeat the form and success of the first, and by the radical
student activists and the 'ultra-left'—who believed that the Moratorium should have condemned imperialism and endorsed the
NLF, and who remained dissatisfied that it was a movement for
peace rather than for revolution.

With this balance of forces, the moderates remained in control
and largely regulated the pace of the movement's shift to the
left. The national consultation registered a cautious step towards
more radical demands and methods. The earlier demand of
'withdrawal of Australian and all other foreign troops from
Vietnam' was stiffened to 'immediate, total and unconditional
withdrawal . . .', with removal of all support for Saigon. The
earlier aim of the 'repeal of the National Service Act'—which

had received surprisingly little emphasis in early 1970—became
the 'immediate abolition of conscription in any form'. More
importantly, the consultation recommended that all state VMCs
consider occupying the city streets 'for a considerable period' in
the next march. This explicitly adopted the tactic of mass civil
disobedience which had been successful in Melbourne in May,
but put the Moratorium campaign on a collision course with a
government bent on enforcing 'law and order'. In hindsight, these
shifts were relatively minor, but reflected a radicalisation of the
campaign, in response to the continual pressure from the 'ultra-
left', though largely at the discretion of the moderates.[8]

Internal and external pressures on the coalition were building.
Internally, the disputes between the 'ultra-left' and the CPA
remained fractious. In Sydney, they took a curious turn when
Bob Gould's Resistance group opposed the total abolition of
conscription, and aligned itself with the Australia Party to defend,
unsuccessfully, the more moderate aim of repeal of the NSA.
Gould's rationale was that in a future workers' state, conscription
might be necessary and desirable, though it was promptly pointed
out that this made the unhappy presumption that the workers
would not voluntarily defend their state. In Sydney, Melbourne
and Brisbane, the 'ultra-left' continued bitter disputes with the
CPA, which they regarded as standing between them and the
radical masses. In Brisbane, the Revolutionary Students' Socialist
Alliance was led by Brian Laver, who had been considered close
to the CPA in 1968 but now loudly condemned the CPA's role
in the first moratorium, demanded more radical actions and
informed all who would listen that they had been 'dupes of the
communists'.

Such disputes between Maoists, Trotskyists, communists and
others had little effect on the balance of forces in the movement,
but may have wearied those with little interest in sectarian
division and factional alliance. Doctrinal disputes are an acquired
taste, and they alienated or bewildered some who identified with
the movement for general political and cultural reasons but were
not closely attached to ideology. For some, it seemed 'a total
waste of time arguing about purist positions and engaging in
endless in-fights and bun-fights'.[9]

More serious was the campaign conducted by the conservatives during the winter of 1970, denouncing the Moratorium as
a threat to 'law and order'. Ministers adopted with enthusiasm
the DLP's characterisation of the movement as 'the power of
the streets', and attempted to associate Labor with a decline into
lawlessness. The government appeared to adopt a tougher
approach to those defying the conscription laws, threatened
legislation to prevent demonstrators invading commonwealth

premises, and churlishly refused a visa to the American enter-
tainer and anti-war activist Dick Gregory, who was to have been
a guest speaker at the September moratorium.

These measures—widely seen as a deliberate campaign to
discredit and possibly intimidate the Moratorium movement—also
served to fortify the conservatives, who were otherwise in disarray. The intransigent right, particularly those on the government's
backbench who watched unhappily as foreign policy came
undone, seemed gratified with these displays of authority resolute
in the face of lawlessness. Backbenchers 'practically mobbed'
Philip Lynch, the minister for Immigration, after a fierce speech
against Gregory, 'their frantic behaviour disclos[ing] some of the
forces behind the government's law and order campaign'.[10]

By representing the Moratorium as a dangerous and lawless
assembly, the 'law and order' campaign sought to draw strict
bounds around the definition of political decorum. Government
and the media conjured nineteenth-century images of 'the mob',
of dissenters and youth as the new 'dangerous classes'. Undoubtedly, there was in the movement an 'ultra-left' minority which
espoused cathartic confrontations with the state, but its presence
was a narrow foundation on which to construct the public myth
of the Moratorium as a danger to public order. In general, the
movement was carefully managed, its rhetoric and its tactics
calibrated to what the moderates judged was the prevailing
political temper. In its debates, there were always strong voices
in favour of non-violence and concerned that radical action not
take the movement beyond the reach of public understanding.
Nevertheless, the representation of the Moratorium as 'the mob'—
part policy and part panic—helped undermine its public support,
and drove an effective wedge between the movement and the
ALP in all states but Victoria. Although the moderates remained
in control, the public perception was that the coalition was more
militant than it was.

The 'law and order' campaign was then adopted by some
state governments as a cue for police suppression of the second
moratorium, which took place on 18 September 1970 in an
atmosphere of extreme tension. Violence had occurred the week
before in Melbourne, when police broke up demonstrators from
La Trobe University. On the day, both police and marchers were
wary and restrained. Between 50 000 and 75 000 people participated in a 30-minute occupation of the city, after which Cairns
led the bulk of the march away from police barricades, much to
the chagrin of the militants. In Sydney, deliberate police attacks
prevented separate marches from converging and, although perhaps as many attended as had done in May, the march itself
was a shambles. More than 170 people were arrested, and even

the conservative press queried whether the police had overstepped the bounds of legitimate state violence. In Adelaide, the recently elected Labor government withdrew its support, police and marchers met violently and the movement subsequently split; in Brisbane, the belligerent tone of the state government resulted in less support for the march, although in the end it passed without confrontation.[11]

The popular support for the Moratorium had declined from its peak shortly after May 1970, with the violence of the second set of marches leaving an unfavourable image, reinforced by media hostility. After September, the movement increasingly succumbed to its centrifugal forces. McLeod informed the AICD committee that the different state movements appeared to be going their own ways. By the following April, the news was more grim. The coalition in NSW was 'not in a very healthy situation'; some organisations had withdrawn and the Moratorium was dependent on AICD's facilities and staff, without which the coalition would collapse. Despite having worked for years towards the sort of coalition that was expressed in the Moratorium, AICD—like CICD—found that the burden of servicing the coalition threatened its own viability. As serious was a growing recognition that the early enthusiasm for the Moratorium had waned, partly because it was built on ephemeral and diverse foundations. Many of those who had been involved were motivated by 'little more than sentiment'. There was a need for educative activity and more rigorous analysis of the war lest they be lost to the movement, but the moment might have already passed.[12]

These were some of the reasons why the third and final moratorium was planned as a two-month mobilisation, culminating on 30 June 1971. The mobilisation was dispersed in local activities, with small rallies, workplace meetings, and a concerted effort to build union support. Yet this could not recapture the local mobilisation of the first moratorium, which had tapped more profound changes. The local groups were less vital, the mobilisation suffered from harassment by local authorities, and in Victoria, Queensland and South Australia, intense dispute among the factions absorbed much of the movement's energy.

By September 1971, the movement was disoriented and indecisive about its next steps. The emphasis of its demands had always been on the withdrawal of troops, and McMahon had already announced that the remainder of the Task Force would be home by Christmas. The 'sentiment' of opposition to the war, which had brought many into the movement, was defused if not satisfied. Conscription—the other main issue of the movement, though one it had never emphasised as much—remained, though the period of service required had recently been reduced from 24 to 18 months. More importantly, conscripts would no longer be in Vietnam, and that most emotive and politically volatile nexus had been broken.

In these debilitating circumstances, activists sought ways to revitalise popular support and to extend the life of the movement. 'To keep our support,' wrote one of the activist groups in Melbourne, 'we have to show people not only that the war hasn't finished, but that there is every reason for us to continue fighting.' It was proposed to focus on conscription (in itself, as a denial of rights, and as the supposed preparation for further imperialist ventures) and on the American alliance (particularly on war profiteering and the American bases in Australia). Other proposals focused on the defence budget, apartheid in South Africa and New Guinean independence. The movement attempted to recapture its momentum by broadening its concerns, but it had lost the sharp focus of intervention in Vietnam. While decidedly more radical, it was drifting back towards the often remote generalities of the peace movement of the early 1960s.

The underlying disintegration of the coalition was finally spelt out by the Victorian VMC Executive in early 1972. Nationally, the movement was 'virtually non-existent'; 'Sydney and Canberra [had] officially and publicly terminated their Moratorium organization . . .' and most other states were tacitly in the same position. Local groups had 'declined in activity and enthusiasm'. The war continued, but activists and general public alike viewed it as 'winding down', with Australia's withdrawal complete and a perception that 'it has now reverted to being the *US war*'. The coalition had lost its rationale. Putting a brave face on things, the VMC noted that the more radical groups, in particular, 'feel it is now time to launch into other programmes, and to build upon the good that the Moratorium has achieved'.[13]

This obliquely acknowledged that the coalition had disintegrated, two years after its formation. Its development had reflected the variety of political changes in the years before 1970, when the coalition had drawn together the diverse strands of the New Left, the anti-conscription movement, the established peace groups and many with a less tangible and articulate disenchantment with the war. The coalition focused these various forces on the Vietnam policy, though after that policy had been reversed, and while leaving the coalition's own interpretation of Vietnam equivocal.

Although it had made its mark on radical politics, the movement proved to be short-lived, able to hold neither the commitment of the 'ultra-left' nor the attention of the uncommitted. The CPA had always hoped that a coalition of the left

would be a step towards socialism, eroding hegemonic understandings and radicalising a wider constituency; instead, the
coalition concentrated around the animating causes of Vietnam
and conscription and, with the removal of only one of these, its
tide ebbed. The diverse cultural energies which the movement
had tapped fuelled its progress, but could only briefly be focused
on a precise political cause. Those who had attempted to regulate
and direct the Moratorium were drawing on forces they could
not control, because its centrifugal forces were those of the
disintegration of the Cold War political culture.

The death of a foreign policy

The conservatives had their own account with the Cold War,
though it was to be settled for them in humiliating circumstances.
McMahon's first policy statement as minister for External Affairs
made it clear that the government was as anti-communist as ever,
that Freeth's indiscretion on the Russian fleet (that the Soviet
naval presence in the Indian Ocean posed no real threat to
Australia) was behind it, and that no change could be expected.
These aspects, one commentator found, were 'a depressing
reminder of an earlier period in Australian foreign policy'.[14] One
year later, in March 1971, McMahon's ambition to be prime
minister had finally been realised when he deposed Gorton, who
promptly returned—to the astonishment of observers—as minister
for Defence. After being becalmed in 1968 and 1969, it appeared
that the ship of state had returned to its habitual course in
external affairs, though its masters seemed unaware that they
were in uncharted waters.

'Fear,' wrote Macmahon Ball in 1967, 'has always been the
taproot of our interest in Asia.' Since the revolution of 1949,
that fear had focused primarily on China. While Macmahon Ball
doubted China's intention or ability to enslave Southeast Asia,
to a generation of conservatives the danger was an article of
faith. It was China which Spender spoke of in sombre tones in
1950, and Chinese rickshaws which Casey envisioned Australian
children pulling in 1954. It was China which Menzies declared
in 1965 was bent on a thrust between the Pacific and Indian
oceans, and China which Hasluck was convinced lay behind the
intentions of Hanoi. China was the touchstone, the presence
behind Asian revolution, the threat which required containment
and which Spender, Casey and Hasluck had hoped to block by
interposing an American presence in the region. Communist
China was not officially recognised, though this rejection was
tempered by the pragmatic aspirations of the wheat lobby, which

For a generation, Australia's Asian policy had focused on the containment and denial of Communist China. In July 1971 prime minister McMahon denounced the ALP—who favoured recognition of China—as 'pawns of the giant Communist power in our region'. Days later Nixon announced that he would visit Peking, ending the policy of containment and leaving Australian conservatives in his wake. It was the final indignity of the Vietnam intervention.
(Petty, Australian, *17 July 1971*)

placed its scruples behind its commercial instincts. But as Freudenberg put it, since the Revolution, 'the "true patriot" had been judged by his soundness on the "China question" '.[15] So it was appropriate that it should be on China that Cold War foreign policy finally disintegrated in 1971.

By June that year, there had been a rush of European powers to recognise China, and even the intransigent stance of the United States appeared to be softening. Britain, France, Canada, Italy and the Netherlands had all recently taken the step, and at the United Nations, the Americans were no longer emphasising Peking's sins but only arguing that Taiwan must not be abandoned. At the beginning of 1971, one commentator saw Canberra as awaiting a lead from Washington: 'It seems almost inevitable that the United States will change its position on the China question. It would be heartening if just this once Australia could anticipate the American move.'

But the conservatives seemed firmly held by the dead hand of the past, even against the better judgment of some. Early in June, the federal council of the Liberal Party had debated and rejected a proposal to recognise China; McMahon had told the council that the government was establishing a dialogue with Peking but closely guarding the national interest. *The Age* was scathing: if McMahon's political antennae were working, he must know when to 'discard the cliches which have fallen out of fashion'. The government must not be the last in a queue of nations recognising China, and must note

. . . the darkening prospects of our export markets for primary products . . . the message should be clear to a Government which is not frozen in obsolete attitudes . . . Political fright should be replaced by political realism.

Finally, the paper commented that the ALP's 'daring' proposal to send a delegation to Peking had 'jolted' McMahon's thinking into the 1970s.[16]

But from as long ago as Casey's attempt to recognise China, the conservatives were captives of their own rhetoric, playing to, and succumbing to, the politics of fright. While the government now made timorous attempts to open a dialogue with Peking, Whitlam led a delegation—with great fanfare—to meet Chou En-Lai. Their arrival in China was front-page news. As Allan Barnes reported excitedly from Canton: 'To the amplified strains of The East is Red and sipping mugs of instant tea, the first Australian political delegation to visit mainland China since the communist revolution' had begun its twelve-day visit. The conservatives could not resist the opportunity to condemn Whitlam, playing down the significance of their own overtures to Peking and falling further out of step with history. The DLP's Senator Gair reported that he 'felt sickened' to see Whitlam 'fawn, praise and flatter' the Chinese prime minister, though most observers had thought Whitlam handled the meeting well. With a fine disregard for consequentiality, Gair commented that this was 'the first time an Australian political leader has been pre-selected by a Chinese totalitarian Prime Minister'. Santamaria pursued a similar theme: Whitlam was 'the Chinese candidate' for prime minister.[17]

Labor had favoured recognising China since 1955, and Whitlam since even earlier. The latter's policy was now to adopt the Canadian formulation, which recognised Peking as the legitimate government, merely 'noting' its territorial claim to Taiwan. On the evening of 12 July in Melbourne, McMahon spoke against this view to a Young Liberals rally, complete with 'flag waving, banners, whistles, streamers, trumpet blasts and a pop band . . .'

Amid the commotion, McMahon drew upon the certainties of the 1950s, directing his speech against Whitlam. Recognition of China would be dangerous, and would isolate Australia from its allies:

> This policy must be disowned. We must not become pawns of the giant Communist power in our region. I find it incredible that at a time when Australian soldiers are still engaged in Vietnam, the leader of the Labor Party is becoming a spokesman for those against whom we are fighting.[18]

With this, McMahon appeared finally to have declared war on China. Perhaps the commotion of trumpet blasts had put him off, but his slip of the tongue, which amalgamated Vietnam and China in one Asian threat, revealed the conservative psyche in the Cold War.

At the time, there were comments that the debate on China had returned to the 1950s, which was both 'tragic and dangerous'. An element of this was that the government was playing to the more xenophobic elements in its own ranks, sensing an opportunity to attack Labor for being 'soft' on communism. These were political reflexes which had worked well and debased rational debate for a generation. As McMahon reportedly told a meeting in Tasmania shortly after the trumpet blasts of the Young Liberals, 'China has always served the Liberals well politically and will continue to do so.'

Only days later, Nixon announced that he would be visiting China. It was the end of the Dulles policy of containment which had underpinned the Cold War and had been the rock upon which Australian policy was based. *The Age* editorialised portentously: 'At last the ice has cracked, and with a bang which has been heard all over the world.' At a tense press conference, McMahon appeared shaken, allowed no questions, and was reduced to claiming that this had been his policy all along. *The Age* was unforgiving:

> After his short spell in the Foreign Affairs Department he should have learned enough to recognise the changed climate of the world and to abandon the worn-out cliches which served previous Prime Ministers.

Labor was exultant. Whitlam's first reaction was said to have been a triumphant: 'They're finished.'[19]

Three days later, Howson had dinner with McMahon at the Lodge. The latter was, as so frequently, anxious to talk about his problems, and considered the recent events as one of only two failures since he had become prime minister. But the fault was Nixon's, 'particularly as he didn't tell us'. McMahon later told Freudenberg that he had shown the rough outlines of his embarrassing speech for the Young Liberals to the American embassy—'we thought we were being helpful'—but had not been alerted to Nixon's impending announcement.[20]

The debacle was a demeaning commentary on that 'habitual closeness' with the Americans which the conservatives had cultivated to the point of losing all initiative. But more than this, it revealed the extent to which the conservatives were captives of their past and of the successful formulae of the past. As the *Australian* wrote, employing a nautical metaphor:

> The sight of Mr. McMahon running from one end of the boat to the other as the realities of the China question overtake his policies (such as they are) will cause some people to gloat and others to excuse him. To be fair to him, the Prime Minister is a prisoner—albeit a willing one—of years of cynical misuse of China for domestic political reasons.[21]

By 1971, the conservatives resembled a once-great family in which none of the heirs had lived up to the shadow cast by the patriarch. Querulously, they repeated the formulae which had once brought success but now, unaccountably, appeared to bring only humiliation. They seemed not to have noticed that the debasement of rational debate which had served them so well in the golden days of the Cold War now looked shrill and self-serving. They appeared condemned to the recitation of what had once been tragedy, now repeated as farce.

Conclusion

Australia's Vietnam intervention was fundamentally a form of intervention in Asian history, deriving from the fears triggered by Asian decolonisation. Cairns had argued that it was taking sides in history, but it was also colliding with a colonial and postcolonial history. By the end of the colonial period in 1954, the Communist Party in Vietnam had achieved a distinct status as the party of patriotism as well as of social revolution. No other social force could challenge its village network, while it adroitly cultivated its links in the rural social order and its patriotic credentials. Yet this historical outcome was anathema to the Cold War view of what Barwick had called 'orderly de-colonisation'. Perhaps the origins of the tragedy played out in Vietnam lay in this collision of a unique process of decolonisation with the political temper of the Cold War in America and Australia. For the latter required that communism be an external, unwelcome force, inserting itself into history illegitimately and by terror. Rostow's characterisation of Communist China as a scavenger on the modernisation process captured this premise perfectly.

Cold War perceptions meant that a generation of Australian policy on Vietnam was built on great expectations of just the force that was most weakened by the history of colonialism and decolonisation: a bourgeoisie with a coherent non-communist nationalism. It was symptomatic of this that the West had to place its faith in Diem—an autocratic but fractiously independent Catholic in a Buddhist culture—and then in the armed forces. Neither represented a viable ruling class or a viable stream of nationalist ideology. This implausibility of the non-communist forces in Vietnam was one of the rocks on which the Australian army's doctrine of 'counter-revolutionary warfare' foundered.

The Cold War tended to make policy-makers not so much blind to complexities as silent about them. Casey in 1954 had pragmatically noted some of the complexities of Vietnamese history, and so was privately sceptical about 'united action' to intervene in Vietnam. But the crisis in that year also revealed the substratum of Australia's Vietnam policy—that it was a policy about the containment of China and the encouragement of America's regional role. Spender's readiness to respond to Dulles's bellicosity had indicated this, though it was not the only element in foreign policy. But by the late 1950s and early 1960s, as Pemberton in particular has shown, this strand of policy had become dominant, and resulted in the readiness to commit troops to Vietnam.

One domestic aspect of the Cold War was also illustrated in 1954. In such strongly ideological times, the gap between public rhetoric and private knowledge widened. There were too many electoral advantages in Cold War alarm for more reasoned policy debate to be joined. Casey's doubts about 'united action' were not voiced publicly until the crisis had passed, and in the meantime he had to ensure that Cabinet did not take the public rhetoric too literally. Similarly, the conservatives locked themselves into an inflexible opposition to the recognition of China, which they maintained for over two decades despite Casey and External Affairs—and even Spender—being willing to explore recognition. The language of escalating threats which rolled sonorously from the tongue of Sir Robert Menzies was a continuation of this public rhetoric, alarming the voters, comforting the DLP and confounding Labor.

Amid the bleak inheritance of the 1950s was the cultural and political marginalisation of dissent. Casey viewed communists as simply beyond the pale, and in this he was far from alone. Dissenters, too, came to see themselves as outsiders. The connection Cairns had drawn in the mid-1960s between fear and indifference, between high alarm and civic withdrawal, was one barrier which the anti-war movement had to overcome. But its members had also to overcome themselves, to relinquish the habits of mind and of political organisation that had seemed

appropriate in the hostile climate of the 1950s. It was this that
the New Left was most impatient with, demanding a more activist
approach and a more urgent social theory. The dynamism of the
Moratorium perhaps derived most from the tension between these
two political forces. The established movement was frequently
too cautious, but it also had a keen sense of the limits of what
was acceptable to the broad base which came briefly into the
movement. Meanwhile, the New Left pushed the movement to
those boundaries, attempting to extend them in more radical
directions. If the Cold War political culture had involved a
flattening-out of alternatives, a repression of expressions of
alienation, the New Left now celebrated alienation, because for
it, life was only authentic on the margins of a repressive culture.

It was the Communist Party, rather than Labor, which proved
most adept at balancing these conflicting intentions, part facing
the past and part the future. And Turner—an ex-communist—
best captured this, perhaps because he had spanned the gamut
of the left from the dogmatism of the CPA in the early 1950s
to an enthusiasm for the 'counter-culture' and eventually the
mainstream of the Labor Party. Consequently, he located the
Moratorium as the end point of the domestic Cold War inheritance, and in the first march no longer felt that 'part-embarrassed,
part-defiant' sense of being isolated before 'a hostile, mocking or
indifferent public'. The public sphere had been reclaimed from
the Cold War.

But such a triumphal posture obscured the marked dis-
continuities in the Australian experience of Vietnam. The popular
image that the Moratorium was the result of an unbroken
maturing of opposition which finally ended the war by demanding
withdrawal is an attractive myth. It resonates with a vision of
enlightenment inexorably overcoming irrationality.[1] In practice,
the process was more difficult and uneven. In the few years
before 1970, the movement had been through a pronounced
slump, and the turning point of the war—from escalation to
de-escalation—had been passed in 1968. But myths, like metaphors, are important. Vietnam had been, during the 1960s, a
chronic catalyst for social division, ferment and the mobilisation
of new constituencies. This helps explain both why the movement
developed so unevenly and why the meanings ascribed to the
war varied and the movement, tacitly at least, skirted the divisive
issue of what the war meant. It was not only that the 'ultra-left'
demand to 'smash imperialism' was an imprecise guide to action,
but that it was meaningless to many for whom the war meant
a dehumanised technical rationality, or a barbaric series of
atrocities, or simply a disquieting erosion of cherished social
cohesion. As a catalyst for social mobilisation, there was not one

Vietnam, but many Vietnams, refracting different aspects of the political culture.

This was not a process unique to opponents of the war. Since the 1950s, Vietnam and Asia in general had been rendered meaningful in the light of domestic concerns. For many Australian soldiers in Phuoc Tuy, Vietnam was a vacant place into which little was projected; for the army's planners it was a locale for employing doctrines of counter-revolutionary warfare, but as importantly for futile attempts to erase the past and reconstruct a model Asia in planned village developments. Similarly, events in the war were being drawn into the currents of the Australian polity, as the crisis of Dien Bien Phu in 1954 had been refracted through the Cold War alignments of local conflict, and as when Diem and Ky visited Australia, they were figures of fiction and of conservative hopes as much as concrete political forces.

These attitudes to Asia shared a form of 'orientalism', the way the West has frequently imagined and culturally colonised the East. For example, many Australian conservative intellectuals in the 1950s sought an 'essence' of Asia, and some Vietnam veterans' narratives romanticise Vietnamese culture while patronising it.[2] Much of the cultural imagery of Vietnam in the 1950s and 1960s was projected into what was, for want of enquiry or knowledge, an oriental void. One of the most striking images in conservative rhetoric was that of the frontier between Australia and Asia as an imagined boundary between West and East, between the democracies and threatening communism. The concern seemed to be less with what lay within the oriental void as with where it began. Menzies in 1954 spoke of the frontier lying on the southern shores of Indochina, while Mullens expressed the Movement's worry that the 'frontier of the Red Empire' was coming closer. Diem, when he visited in 1957, called his 'nation' the frontier of the free world. And later, in 1962, Barwick was urging his Cabinet colleagues to consider Vietnam 'our present frontier'. In 1971, McMahon's gaffe in equating China and Vietnam as one enemy best captured the sense that beyond the frontier lay *terra incognita*, full of unknown threats. The metaphor of the frontier had several implications: it marked out the field into which forward defence would be projected, and it evoked the threat of Chinese communist advance. But above all, it evoked the continuing unease about Australia's geopolitical place in an Asia in the throes of decolonisation and independence.

Australian veterans found themselves shouldering the consequences of these historic burdens of fear, incomprehension and confrontation. During 1966, they had returned to a ticker-tape parade in Sydney, but therafter were greeted with contestation, hostility or sullenness, especially after the My Lai revelations of late 1969. Some still marched through city streets on their return. When the 9th battalion returned in November 1969, it marched through Adelaide, greeted by a 'moderate crowd', but also by a group of demonstrators. One veteran recalled: 'A large placard expressed support for the NLF. They had turned up to our march to condemn us.' Later, he was confronted with the cruel challenge: 'Did you kill any babies?'[3] The hostility of some, and the indifference or awkwardness of others, became a common sentiment of veterans' narratives. Denial had always been a key accent of the Cold War: the denial of China, the denial of Asian nationalism, the ostracism of dissent and the retreat to civic indifference. It was the final, and saddest, irony of the Vietnam intervention that its veterans were denied even the simple dignity and solace of the returning soldier. That they should feel their experience shunned was one wound too many.

Appendix

Opinion polls on the war and conscription

**Figure 1   Do you think we should continue to fight in Vietnam or
bring our forces back to Australia?**

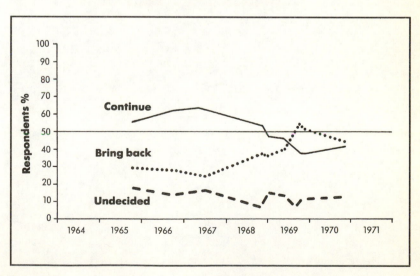

Source: Goot and Tiffen, in King, P. (ed.) *Australia's Vietnam*, p. 135

Figure 2   Various questions relating to the conscription scheme, but not specifically relating to overseas service

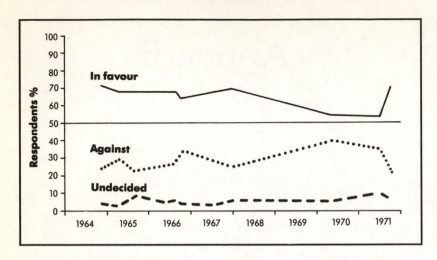

Sources: Michael Hamel-Green 'Conscription and Legitimacy, 1964–1972' *Melbourne Journal of Politics* no. 7, 1974–75, p. 6 and Forward, in Forward, R. and Reece, B. (eds) *Conscription in Australia*, p. 128

Notes

Introduction

1 Molotov's comment is in T.B. Millar (ed), *Australian Foreign Minister: The Diaries of R.G. Casey, 1951–60*, Collins, London, 1972, p. 151, Casey quote from *The Age*, 13 May 1954, and Deakin's 'Yellow Peril' statement, from 1909, in D. Jaensch and M. Teichmann (eds), *The Macmillan Dictionary of Australian Politics*, Macmillan, South Melbourne, 1979, p. 248.

2 C.P. Fitzgerald, 'Australia and Asia', in G. Greenwood and D. Harper (eds), *Australia in World Affairs, 1950–55*, Cheshire, Melbourne, 1957, pp. 200–242, at p. 201.

Chapter 1

1 The term 'collaborator' is a harsh one, but it is frequently used in work on the colonial period. See David Marr, *Vietnamese Tradition on Trial: 1920–1945*, University of California Press, Berkeley, 1981, and Huynh Kim Khanh, *Vietnamese Communism: 1925–1945*, Cornell University Press, Ithaca, 1982. On the intricate patterns of collaboration, see Milton Osborne, *The French Presence in Cochinchina and Cambodia: Rule and Response (1859–1905)*, Cornell University Press, Ithaca, 1969.

2 Le Thanh Tuong, *Monographie de la province de Ba Ria*, Publiée par Le Thanh Tuong—Chef de la Province [1950]. Introduction.

3 Phan Ngoc Danh & Tran Quang Toai, *Lich Su Dau Tranh Cach Mang cua Huyen Long Dat*, [History of the Revolutionary Struggle in Long Dat District], Nha Xuat Ban Dong Nai [Bien Hoa], 1986, pp. 64–65.

4 'Thick screen', Le Thanh Tuong, *Monographie*, p. 11, and 'outlaws', Le Thanh Khoi, *Le Vietnam: Histoire et Civilisation*, Les Editions de Minuit, Paris, 1955, pp. 264–266.

5 G. Aubaret, *Histoire et description de la Basse Cochinchine*, Imprimerie Impériale, Paris, 1863, pp. 2, 18; Le Thanh Khoi, *Le Vietnam*, pp. 265–273, 508; and Guides Madrolle, *Indochine du Sud: De Marseille à Saigon*, Librairie Hachette, Paris, 1928, pp. 15–16.

6 Osborne, *French Presence*, p. 14, and Michael G. Cotter, 'Towards a social history of the Vietnamese southward movement', *Journal of Southeast Asian History*, vol. 9, no. 1, March 1968, pp. 12–24.

7 'Descendants', Gerald Hickey, *Village in Vietnam*, Yale University Press, New Haven, 1964, p. 285, and 'in broad outline', Dinh Van Trung, 'La psychologie du paysan du delta: Etude sur la culture vietnamienne', Thèse présentée devant l'Université de Paris V, Paris, 1974, p. 3.

8 Hickey, *Village*, p. 99 and chapters 3 & 8; Guides Madrolle, *Indochine*, p. 15, and Leopold Cadiere, 'La famille et la religion au Viet-Nam', *France-Asie*, vol. 15, no. 145, 1958, pp. 260–271.

9 Paulin Vial, *Les premières années de la Cochinchine, colonie française*, Challamel Aimé, Paris, 1874, p. 12.

10 This discussion of patriotism and nationalism is drawn and quoted from Huynh Kim Khanh, *Vietnamese Communism*, pp. 27, 31.

11 David Hunt, *Villagers at War: The National Liberation Front in My Tho, 1965–1967*, Special Issue of *Radical America*, vol. 8, nos. 1–2, January–April, 1974, pp. 5–9, and Hickey, *Village*, p. 278.

12 Dinh Van Trung, 'La psychologie', p. 514, and A. Schreiner, *Les institutions annamites en Basse Cochinchine avant la conquête française*, Claude & Cie, Saigon, Tome II, 1901, pp. 17–20.

13 J. Loubet & G. Taboulet, *L'Indochine française*, Librairie Hachette, Paris, 1931, p. 42.

14 Paul Mus, 'The role of the village in Vietnamese politics', *Pacific Affairs*, no. 22, 1949, pp. 265–272, at p. 265.

15 Vial, *Premières années*, p. 131; also based on Société des Etudes Indo-Chinoises, *Monographie de la province de Ba-Ria et de la ville du Cap Saint-Jacques*, Imprimerie L. Ménard, Saigon, 1902, Le Thanh Khoi, *Le Vietnam*, and E. Cortambert & L. de Rosny, *Tableau de la Cochinchine: Rédigé sous les auspices de la Société d'Ethnographie*, Armand le Chevalier, Paris, 1862.

16 Auguste Thomazi, *La conquête de l'Indochine*, Payot, Paris, 1934, pp. 75 ff, and Thomas E. Ennis, *French Policy and Development in Indochina*, University of Chicago Press, Chicago, 1936, p. 41 and passim.

17 Osborne, *French Presence*, p. 263.

18 Thomazi, *La conquête*, p. 67; see also Vial, *Premières années*, pp. 120, 133, and Société des Etudes, *Monographie*, p. 61.

19 Osborne, *French Presence*, pp. 264–268.

20 Vial, *Premières années*, pp. 290, 132.

21 Pierre Gourou, *L'utilisation du sol en Indochine française*, Centre d'Etudes de Politique Etrangère, Paris, 1939, p. 135.

22 Société des Etudes, *Monographie*, pp. 52, 13–15; see also John White, *A Voyage to Cochinchina*, Oxford University Press, London, 1972, pp. 54, 211.

23 Société des Etudes, *Monographie*, pp. 57, 64.

24 Ngo Vinh Long, *Before the Revolution: The Vietnamese Peasants under the French*, MIT Press, Cambridge, 1973, p. 118, note 18. See also Société des Etudes, *Monographie*, p. 14–15; Le Van Hoang & Truong Nhu Hien, 'La stratification et la mobilité sociale au Viet-Nam', *East Asian Cultural Studies*, vol. 4, March 1965, pp. 205–226, and Pham Cao Duong, *Vietnamese Peasants under French Domination: 1861–1945*, University Press of America, Lanham, 1985, at pp. 114–115.

25 Ngo Vinh Long, *Before the Revolution*, pp. 88, 103–104; see also Gourou, *L'utilisation*, pp. 275, 282–3.

26 Fernand de Montaigut, *La colonisation française dans l'Est de Cochinchine*, Imprimerie de Perette, Limoges, 1929, p. 29.

27 These figures are based on two Vietnamese surveys: République du Viet-Nam, *Recensement pilote de la province de Phuoc-Tuy*, Institut National de la Statistique, Saigon [1960], and Republic of Vietnam, *Report on the Agricultural Census of Viet-Nam, 1960–1961*, Department of Rural Affairs, Cholon, 1962. The difficulties of these sources are discussed in Appendix 1 of my thesis 'The Australian Intervention in the Vietnam War', PhD, University of Melbourne, History, 1992. Comments on the likely character of these classes are based on Marr's typology in *Vietnamese Tradition*, p. 28.

28 Société des Etudes, *Monographie*, 19–24, and Guides Madrolle, *Indochine*, p. xvii.

29 Guides Madrolle, *Indochine*, p. xiv, also pp. 327, 15, and Georges Nores, *Itinéraires Automobiles en Indochine; Guide du Touriste: II. Cochinchine, Cambodge*, Imprimerie d'Extreme-Orient, Hanoi, 1930, p. 12.

30 Osborne, *French Presence*, p. 266 and *passim*.

31 de Montaigut, *La colonisation*, p. 15.

32 Helmut Callis, *Foreign Capital in Southeast Asia*, AMS Press, New York, 1978, p. 80. See also Charles Robequain, *The Economic Development of French Indo-China*, Oxford University Press, London, 1944, p. 201–206, de Montaigut, *La colonisation*, pp. 19–21, and Octave Homberg, 'Rubber in Indo-China', *The Asiatic Review*, July 1936, vol. 32, pp. 583–588.

33 de Montaigut, *La colonisation*, p. 33; Callis, *Foreign Capital*, p. 78, Joseph Buttinger, *Vietnam: A Political History*, Andre Deutsch, London, 1969, p. 166, and Gourou, *L'utilisation*, p. 136.

34 de Montaigut, *La colonisation*, pp. 73, 106–110.

35 Robequain, *Economic Development*, pp. 207–208; de Montaigut, *La colonisation*, pp. 100–103, and Republic of Viet-Nam, *Report*, pp. 93, 120.

36 International Labour Office, *Labour Conditions in Indo-China*, ILO, Geneva, 1938, pp. 262, 92; Robequain, *Economic Development*,

pp. 215–217, and Ngo Vinh Long, *Before the Revolution*, pp. 113–115.

37	ILO, *Labour Conditions*, pp. 53, 59, 291; see also Huynh Kim Khanh, *Vietnamese Communism*, pp. 94–95.

38	ILO, p. 275; and see Buttinger, *Vietnam*, p. 171, and Pierre Brocheux, 'Le prolétariat des plantations d'hévéas au Vietnam méridional: Aspects sociaux et politiques (1927–1937)', *Le mouvement social*, Janvier–Mars, 1975, no. 90, pp. 55–86.

39	Homberg, 'Rubber', p. 588.

40	Quoted in Ennis, *French Policy*, p. 63, note 23.

Chapter 2

1	See the profile in Daniel Hémery, *Révolutionnaires vietnamiens et pouvoir colonial en Indochine: Communistes, trotskystes, nationalistes à Saigon de 1932 à 1937*, Maspero, Paris, 1975, p. 443; and Huynh Kim Khanh, *Vietnamese Communism*, p. 198, n. 11 and p. 254, n. 49.

2	David G. Marr, *Vietnamese Anti-colonialism, 1885–1925*, University of California Press, Berkeley, 1971, for a detailed description of this form of anticolonial politics; and see Ngo Vinh Long, *Before the Revolution*, chapter 4.

3	Georges Coulet, *Les sociétés secrètes en terre d'Annam*, Imprimerie Commerciale, C. Ardin, Saigon, 1926, pp. 31, 281, 338.

4	Phan Ngoc Danh, *Lich Su*, pp. 17–21; Gouvernement Général de l'Indochine, *Contribution à l'histoire des mouvements politiques de l'Indochine française*, Direction des Affaires Politiques et de la Sûreté Générale, Hanoi, 1933, vol. IV, pp. 40–41, 122–128.

5	Based on Phan Ngoc Danh, *Lich Su*, pp. 17–21.

6	Quotations from Huynh Kim Khanh, *Vietnamese Communism*, pp. 152, 161; see also chapter 2, and John T. McAlister, *Viet Nam: The Origins of Revolution*, Alfred Knopf, New York, 1970, chapter 3.

7	'In the late 1940s', McAlister, *Viet Nam*, p. 91, and chapter 3 *passim*; also Huynh Kim Khanh, *Vietnamese Communism*, chapter 2, and Buttinger, *Vietnam*, chapter 9.

8	Marr, *Vietnamese Tradition*, p. 308, and see pp. 308–315 on the effects of prison. The Sûreté quote is from Huynh Kim Khanh, *Vietnamese Communism*, p. 163, and see chapters 3 and 4 on the Stalinism of the Vietnamese Party.

9	Phan Ngoc Danh, *Lich Su*, pp. 22 and 27–28.

10	Hemery, *Révolutionnaires*, p. 319, and see pp. 281–321; also Huynh Kim Khanh, *Vietnamese Communism*, pp. 212, and see 205–215 in general.

11	Description of activities, Phan Ngoc Danh, *Lich Su*, p. 23; and on Baria being marginal, Hemery, *Révolutionnaires*, p. 320.

12	Hemery, *Révolutionnaires*, pp. 377–394, and Huynh Kim Khanh, *Vietnamese Communism*, pp. 225–228.

13	V.G. Kiernan, *From Conquest to Collapse: European Empires from 1815 to 1960*, Pantheon, New York, 1982, p. 214. On French writers, see Buttinger, *Vietnam*, p. 122.

14 Pierre Rousset, *Communisme et nationalisme vietnamien: Le Vietnam entre les deux guerres mondiales*, Editions Galilée, Paris, 1978, p. 243.

15 Based on Huynh Kim Khanh, *Vietnamese Communism*, pp. 256–289, and more generally David G. Marr, 'World War II and the Vietnamese Revolution', in A. McCoy (ed), *Southeast Asia under Japanese Occupation*, Yale Southeast Asia Council, New Haven, 1980. Strictly speaking, the Viet Minh Front was replaced by the Lien Viet Front in 1946, but historians conventionally refer to the Viet Minh throughout the period to 1954.

16 McAlister, *Viet Nam*, p. 132. On Baria, Van Tao, Thanh The Vy & Nguyen Cong Binh, *Cach Mang Thang Tam* [The August Revolution], vol. II, NXB Su Hoc, Hanoi, 1960, p. 238.

17 Marr, 'World War II', p. 145; 'wearing', Phan Ngoc Danh, *Lich Su*, p. 30.

18 Quotations from Phan Ngoc Danh, *Lich Su*, pp. 32–35; see also Van Tao *et al*, *Cach Mang*, p. 241.

19 George Rosie, *The British in Vietnam: How the Twenty-five Year War Began*, Panther, London, 1970, p. 11, and McAlister, *Viet Nam*.

20 'Maximum', Rosie, *British in Vietnam*, p. 61; on Gracey and the British lion, Kiernan, *Conquest to Collapse*, p. 214.

21 McAlister, *Viet Nam*, chapter 23, and on the Japanese in Baria, Rosie, *British in Vietnam*, pp. 92–93.

22 Based on interviews with Col. Nguyen Van Kiem, Long Hai, 23 February 1988, and Phan Ngoc Danh, Bien Hoa, 22 February 1988.

23 Frank Frost, *Australia's War in Vietnam*, Allen & Unwin, Sydney, 1987, pp. 35–36.

24 Buttinger, *Vietnam*, p. 318, and see Edgar O'Ballance, *The Indo-China War, 1945–54: A Study in Guerilla Warfare*, Faber, London, 1964, pp. 89–90.

25 Phan Ngoc Danh, interview.

26 Gabriel Kolko, *Vietnam: Anatomy of a War, 1940–1975*, Allen & Unwin, London, 1986, pp. 59–61.

27 Jean Lacouture, *Vietnam: Between Two Truces*, Secker & Warburg, London, 1966, p. 244; Wilfred Burchett, *Vietnam: Inside Story of the Guerilla War*, International Publishers, New York, 1965, pp. 123–124; B.S.W. Murti, *Vietnam Divided: The Unfinished Struggle*, Asia Publishing House, London, 1964, p. 224, and Phan Ngoc Danh, *Lich Su*, p. 77.

28 'At worst', Denis Warner, *The Last Confucian: Vietnam, South-East Asia and the West*, Angus & Robertson, Sydney, 1964, p. 142; also based on Kolko, *Vietnam*, p. 99; Nguyen Van Kiem and Phan Ngoc Danh interviews.

29 'Binh Gia Ground Team Report, 25 Apr.–1 May 71 (incl)', in AWM, HS [1 Psyops U] R723–1–1. On numbers, see Lacouture, *Vietnam*, p. 104 and Alan Watt, *Vietnam: An Australian Analysis*, Cheshire, Melbourne, 1968, pp. 74, 82. American officials tended to round the figure of refugees from the North up to one million.

30 Lacouture, *Vietnam*, p. 74.

31 See Greg Lockhart, *Nation in Arms: The Origins of the People's Army of Vietnam*, Allen & Unwin, Sydney, 1989, for an analysis of the

crucial links between political conceptions of the nation and armed struggle.

Chapter 3

1   *The Age*, 10 & 13 May 1954; *News-Weekly*, 7 April 1954.
2   *The Age*, 7 & 25 May 1954; Millar (ed), *Australian Foreign Minister*, p. 82.
3   See Alan Renouf, *Let Justice be Done: The Foreign Policy of Dr. H.V. Evatt*, University of Queensland Press, St Lucia, 1983.
4   'Nations', Percy Spender, *Exercises in Diplomacy*, Sydney University Press, Sydney, 1969, pp. 201, 197; Hong Kong visit, P. Spender, interview 13 February 1968, de Berg tape 354, NLA Oral History Collection. p. 4218; 'Casey in Asia', A. Watt, interview 11 December 1974, by J.B.D. Millar, TRC 306, NLA, Oral History Collection, p. 3:1/8.
5   Percy Spender, *Politics and a Man*, Collins, Sydney, 1972; the ministerial statement is reproduced at pp. 307–329, quotations are from pp. 308–315.
6   CPD, vol. 206, House of Representatives, 16 March 1950, pp. 912–919.
7   'Cloud', Spender, *Politics*, pp. 325–326; A. Watt, *The Evolution of Australian Foreign Policy, 1938–1965*, Cambridge University Press, London, 1968, pp. 112–117 for Spender's policy on the UN; Acheson, in *The Age*, 6 February 1962.
8   CPD, vol. 206, House of Representatives, 16 March 1950, pp. 921–923.
9   Spender, *Politics*, p. 310.
10 *News-Weekly*, 28 July 1954.
11 CPD, vol. 206, House of Representatives, 16 March 1950, pp. 905, 913.
12 ibid. pp. 955–958.
13 Spender, *Exercises*, pp. 199, 207.
14 Millar (ed), *Australian Foreign Minister*, pp. 26–27, 126.
15 See Nicholas Brown, 'Possess the time: The formation and character of Australian intellectual conservatism in the 1950s', PhD, ANU, 1990.
16 'Saw communism', W.J. Hudson, *Casey*, Oxford University Press, Melbourne, 1986, pp. 231, 242–244; 'the local', Millar (ed), *Australian Foreign Minister*, p. 35, and Watt interview, NLA, pp. 2:1/10–19.
17 Peter Edwards, 'Some reflections on the Australian Government's commitment to the Vietnam War', in J. Grey and J. Doyle (eds), *Vietnam: War, Myth and Memory. Comparative perspectives on Australia's war in Vietnam*, Allen & Unwin, Sydney, 1992, p. 4; for a description of the policy on Malaya, see the first volume of the official history, Peter Edwards with Gregory Pemberton, *Crises and Commitments: The Politics and Diplomacy of Australia's Involvement in Southeast Asian Conflicts 1948–1965*, Allen & Unwin in association with the Australian War Memorial, Sydney, 1992, particularly chapters 2, 3, 10, 11.

18 CPD, vol. 206, House of Representatives, 21 March 1950. pp. 968–969, 970–971, 973.

19 W. Macmahon Ball, *Nationalism and Communism in East Asia*, Melbourne University Press, Melbourne, 1952, pp. 1, 62. See also J. D. Legge & H. Feith, 'Introduction' in R.J. May & W. O'Malley (eds), *Observing Change in Asia: Essays in Honour of J.A.C. Mackie*, Crawford House Press, Bathurst, 1989, pp. 2–3, which gives an indication of Macmahon Ball's effect on a generation of students.

20 John Burton, *The Alternative: A Dynamic Approach to our Relations with Asia*, Morgans Publications, Sydney, 1954, pp. 13–26, and A. Bevan, *In Place of Fear*, Heinemann, London, 1952, p. 135.

21 Spender, *Exercises in Diplomacy*, p. 32, and Watt, *The Evolution*, p. 112. On the supremacy of Menzies over Spender in 1950–51, see David Lowe, 'Robert Menzies and Australia's role in the next World War, 1950–52', paper delivered to Australian Historical Association Conference, Canberra, 1992, and David Lee, 'Australia, the British Commonwealth and the United States, 1950–1953', *Journal of Imperial and Commonwealth History*, vol. 20, no. 3, September 1992.

22 Spender's initiative, in close consultation with Watt, is described in Alan Watt, *Australian Diplomat: Memoirs of Sir Alan Watt*, Angus & Robertson, Sydney, 1972, pp. 173–176, and Spender, *Politics and a Man*, chapter 30.

23 See Gregory Pemberton, *All The Way: Australia's Road to Vietnam*. Allen & Unwin, Sydney, 1987.

24 Quote on Korea debates, Robert Murray, *The Split: Australian Labor in the Fifties*, Cheshire, Melbourne, 1972, p. 73; quote on CPA ban, Frank Cain and Frank Farrell, 'Menzies' war on the Communist Party, 1949–1951', in A. Curthoys and J. Merritt (eds) *Australia's First Cold War, 1945–1953, Vol. 1: Society, Communism and Culture*, Allen & Unwin, Sydney, 1984, p. 122 and passim. On the ALP and the Dissolution Bill, Murray, *The Split*, chapter 6, and Colm Kiernan, *Calwell: a Personal and Political Biography*, Thomas Nelson, Melbourne, 1978, chapter 7.

25 Bevan, *In Place*, p. 122.

26 Arthur Miller, *Timebends: A Life*, Methuen, London, 1987, p. 341, and see Stephen J. Whitfield, *The Culture of the Cold War*, Johns Hopkins University Press, Baltimore, 1991, pp. 46–51.

27 Hudson, *Casey*, pp. 249–254.

28 For example, Stan Keon, CPD, House of Representatives, vol. 4, 11 August, 1954, p. 187 and Gough Whitlam, 12 August, 1954, pp. 272–273.

29 Watt, *Australian Diplomat*, pp. 185–189, 202.

30 Alastair Davidson, *The Communist Party of Australia: A Short History*, Hoover Institution Press, Stanford, 1969, pp. 92, 103–104, 120 and chapter 6.

31 Quotations from Alec Robertson, 'CPA in the anti-war movement', *Australian Left Review*, 27, October–November, 1970, pp. 40–3, and see H. Colebatch, 'An examination of the sources, ideologies and political importance of peace movements in Australia from approximately 1950 to approximately 1965,' MA, U of WA, 1974, p. 130.

32 Julius Braunthal, *History of the International: World Socialism, 1943–1968*, Victor Gollancz, London, 1980, pp. 151, 549–551.
33 Jack Blake, *Communist Review*, May 1956, no. 173, p. 153.
34 Quote from Davidson, *Communist Party*, pp. 104–105. Also based on Bill Gollan, interview, 25 August 1990, Sydney. Gollan was on the CPA's central committee from 1943 to 1974.
35 Ian Turner, 'My Long March', in *Room for Manoeuvre: Writings on History, Politics, Ideas and Play*, Drummond, Richmond, 1982, p. 129.
36 On the relation of church and Communist Party activity in the peace movement, see Barbara Carter, 'The peace movement in the 1950s', in A. Curthoys & J. Merritt (eds), *Better Dead than Red: Australia's First Cold War, 1945–1959*, vol. 2, Allen & Unwin, Sydney, 1986, and Colebatch, 'An examination', chaps 2 & 3.
37 See File: 'PQF', [Peace Quest Forum] in Ralph Gibson Papers, UMA, and Carter, 'The peace movement', p. 64.
38 Colebatch, 'An examination', pp. 60–69, 96, 112–113.

Chapter 4

1 *News-Weekly*, 26 May 1954.
2 Based on cablegram, Australian Embassy, Washington to External Affairs, Canberra, 29 March 1954, in AA, A5954/17, Box 2299, 'Indo-China—Geneva Conference. Box 2', File: 'Geneva Conference: Indo-China; United States Proposals for United Action', and Cablegram, Australian Embassy, Washington to External Affairs, Canberra, 31 March 1954, in AA, A816/30, Item 11/301/924, 'Indo-China. Geneva'.
3 Churchill quote, Whitfield, *Culture*, p. 9, and see the caustic portrait of Dulles in Barbara Tuchman, *The March of Folly: From Troy to Vietnam*, Abacus, London, 1985, pp. 313–316. 'Rash', *The Age*, 10 May 1954, and Macmahon Ball in 'Geneva Conference, May 9th 1954', in NLA MS7851, Box 'Broadcasting, Journalism, Press', Folder 'Australia and the World'.
4 The letter was reprinted in *Tribune*, 13 April 1954, and—with further statements—republished as a pamphlet entitled 'Debate on Indo-China' [1954]. *News-Weekly*, 14 April 1954.
5 CPD, House of Representatives, 8 April 1954, pp. 244–245.
6 *Tribune*, 6 January 1954 [editorial].
7 Cablegram, 'For Menzies and Casey only from Spender', 26 March 1954, in AA, A5954/17, Box 2299, File: 'Geneva Conference—Indo-China', and George McT. Kahin, *Intervention: How America Became Involved in Vietnam*, Alfred Knopf, New York, 1986, chapter 2, esp. pp. 45–54. On 'united action' and Canberra's views, see also the detailed discussion in Edwards, *Crises*, chapter 8.
8 Cablegram, Spender to External Affairs, Canberra, 18 April 1954, in AA, A5954/17, Box 2299, File: 'Geneva Conference: Indo-China—United States Proposals for United Action', and see Kahin, *Intervention*, pp. 48–55.
9 Inwards message, Tange to Minister of Defence, 5 April 1954, and covering note, Tange to Casey, 5 April 1954, both in AA, A5954/17, Box 2299, File: 'Geneva Conference—Indo-China'.

10 Cablegram, Spender to Casey, 6 April 1954, and Watt to External Affairs, Canberra, 7 April 1954, both in AA, A5954/17, Box 2299, File 1.

11 Millar (ed), *Australian Foreign Minister*, p. 125 [12 April 1954].

12 Rear Admiral Harries, Washington to Shedden, Canberra, 22 April 1954, in AA, A816/1, Item 19/311/215, and 'Text of Personal Message dated 22 May [1954] from Mr. Eden in Geneva to Mr. Casey', in AA, A816/12, Item 11/301/922, 'Indo-China—Five Power Military Discussions'.

13 *Tribune*, 5 May 1954.

14 Millar (ed), *Australian Foreign Minister*, p. 12 [12 April 1954] (emphasis in original) and chapter 5.

15 'Minutes of Meeting of Cabinet, 6 April 1954', in AA, A4907/XMI, 'Cabinet Minutes', vol. 3.

16 Millar (ed), *Australian Foreign Minister*, p. 147 [2 May 1954], and Pemberton, *All the Way*, pp. 45–46.

17 *Daily Telegraph*, 23 April 1954 and AA, A1838/T184, Item 3004/13/3, Part 4: 'South East Asia Area—Geneva Conference on Indo-China 1954'.

18 Cablegram, Ambassador, Washington to Acting Minister and Secretary, Canberra, 6 May 1954, in AA, A5954/17, Box 2299, 'Geneva Conference, file 3'; cablegram: 'For Casey from Spender', 18 May 1954, in AA, A816/12, Item 11/301/922, 'Indo-China—Five Power Military Discussions', and Millar (ed), *Australian Foreign Minister*, p. 153 [10 June 1954].

19 *The Age*, 17 May and 23 July 1954.

20 Watt to Spender, 21 July 1954, in NLA, MS4875, Box 1, Folder 3.

21 'For Cabinet: Indo-China. Submission No. 686', in AA, A4905/XMI, 'Cabinet Submissions and Decisions', vol. 24; Millar (ed), *Australian Foreign Minister*, p. 152 [4 June 1954] and 'Minutes of Meeting of Cabinet, 4 June 1954, Decision No. 1026', in AA, A4907/XMI, 'Cabinet Minutes', vol. 3.

22 CPD, vol. 4, House of Representatives, 10 August 1954, p. 142. The latter comment was made by D.H. Drummond, a conservative member.

23 ibid, pp. 65–69.

24 ibid, p. 14.

25 ibid, pp. 128–136.

26 ibid, p. 188–190.

27 *News-Weekly*, 18 August 1954. The article was unsigned but—as he confirmed in an interview with the author—*News-Weekly*'s statements on foreign policy were invariably written by Santamaria.

28 Francis Stuart, *Towards Coming-of-Age: A Foreign Service Odyssey*, CSAAR, Nathan, 1989. p. 175.

29 Australian Labor Party, 'Labor's plan for world peace: Declarations and decisions of the Hobart Conference' [1955]; on Labor's relations with the peace movement up till 1959, see Colebatch, 'An Examination', pp. 122–126, and chapter 5.

30 Jack Blake, 'Report to the Central Committee', *Communist Review*, July 1956, no. 175, p. 219.

31 Davidson, *Communist Party*, p. 120, and Turner, 'My Long March', pp. 140–143.

Chapter 5

1 *The Age*, 3, 4 and 5 September, 1957.
2 *The Age*, 4 September 1957; *News-Weekly*, 11 September 1957, and *Tribune*, 28 August 1957.
3 'Cabinet Submission No. 18', 22 July 1954, in AA, A 4906/XM1, vol. 1, pp. 2–3.
4 Robert Shaplen, *The Lost Revolution: Vietnam, 1945–1965*, Andre Deutsch, London, 1966, W. Burchett, *Vietnam*, and *The Furtive War: The United States in Vietnam and Laos*, International Publishers, New York, 1963, and Ellen Hammer, *A Death in November: America in Vietnam, 1963*, Dutton, New York, 1987.
5 Based on Australian Military Attache, Saigon to Department of External Affairs, 28 May, 1955, AA, A 816/1, Item 19/311/211, 'Indo-China; File No. 6'; John Donnell, 'National Renovation Campaigns in Vietnam', *Pacific Affairs*, vol. 32, no. 1, April 1959, pp. 73–88; Warner, *Last Confucian*, chapter 5; Bernard Fall, 'The political-religious sects of Viet-Nam', *Pacific Affairs*, vol. 28, no. 3, September 1955, pp. 235–253; O'Ballance, *Indo-China War*, p. 195 and Buttinger, *Vietnam*, pp. 406–413.
6 'Troops Information Sheet, no. 44', in AWM, HS, HQ IATF CD, May 1967; Frost, *Australia's War*, p. 37 and Carlyle Thayer, *War by Other Means: National Liberation and Revolution in Viet-Nam, 1954–1960*, Allen & Unwin, Sydney, 1989. Chapters 3 & 7.
7 Watt, *Vietnam*, p. 82.
8 Based on Thayer, *War*.
9 Burchett, *Furtive War*, pp. 39–41, and on personalist ideology, see Donnell, 'National renovation'.
10 Quotations from Phan Ngoc Danh, *Lich Su*, p. 88, except 'atmosphere of death', from Ban Chap Hanh Dang Bo Cong San Viet Nam Tinh Dong Nai [Executive Board of the Party Branch of the Vietnamese Communist Party in Dong Nai Province], *Dong Nai: 30 Nam Chien Tranh Giai Phong (1945–1975)* [Dong Nai: 30 Years of the War of Liberation], Nha Xuat Ban Dong Nai, Bien Hoa, 1986, p. 146; also based on Phan Ngoc Danh interview.
11 Burchett, *Furtive War*, p. 43, and 'into', Hickey, *Village*, pp. 202–204.
12 Hickey, *Village*, p. 205.
13 Figures in Thayer, *War*, pp. 116–117, Kolko, *Vietnam*, pp. 99–101; see also Lacouture, *Vietnam*, pp. 29–31.
14 See Thayer, *War*, pp. 190–196, and Kolko, *Vietnam*, pp. 97–108 for a discussion of the debates within the Party. Also Truong Nhu Tang, *Journal of a Vietcong*, Jonathan Cape, London, 1986, especially chapter 7.
15 'To many' Warner, *Last Confucian*, p. 121, Watt, *Vietnam*, pp. 77–78; and Roy Jumper & Nguyen Thi Hue, *Notes on the Political and Administrative History of Viet Nam, 1802–1962*, Michigan State University, Viet Nam Advisory Group, 1962.
16 *The Pentagon Papers*, The Senator Gravel Edition, vol. 2, Beacon

Press, Boston [nd, 1971] p. 24, and Jumper and Nguyen Thi Hue, *Notes*, pp. 152–154.

17   Quoted in Thayer, *War*, p. 143; figures at p. 145.

18   Douglas Pike, *Viet Cong: The Organization and Techniques of the National Liberation Front of South Vietnam*, MIT Press, Cambridge, 1966, pp. 58–61.

19   William A. Smith, 'The strategic hamlet program in Vietnam', *Military Review*, vol. 44, no. 5, May 1964, pp. 17–23. See also chapter 2, 'The strategic hamlet program, 1961–1963', *Pentagon Papers*.

20   Milton Osborne, *Strategic Hamlets in South Viet-Nam: A Survey and Comparison*, Data Paper no. 55, Southeast Asia Program, Cornell University, Ithaca, 1965, p. 23; also Nguyen Long, 'Village government in Vietnam: Politics of infrastructure', PhD, University of California, Berkeley, 1974.

21   'Interview with Pham Van Toai, 18 February 68', in J. Race, *Vietnamese Materials* [microfilm], University of Chicago Library, Chicago, 1969. [Translation in original.] 'Patriotism', Kolko, *Vietnam*, p. 135, and Lacouture, *Vietnam*, pp. 87–91.

22   *Pentagon Papers*, p. 150; Ban Chap, *Dong Nai*, pp. 168–171, and Osborne, *Strategic Hamlets*, pp. 26–35.

23   Phan Ngoc Danh, *Lich Su*, p. 106–109; Ban Chap, *Dong Nai*, chapter 5, and Hickey, *Village*, pp. 53–54.

24   '*Chien Dau* (Struggle), Internal Journal of the Vietnamese Revolutionary People's Party: Provincial Committee of Baria', November 1962, in D. Pike (compiler), *Documents on the National Liberation Front of South Vietnam* [microfilm], MIT, Centre for International Studies, Cambridge, 1967. Item VCD 48. [Translation in original.] Also Phan Ngoc Danh, interview; Phan Ngoc Danh, *Lich Su*, p. 109.

25   'With the 1ATF in Vietnam, 1966', in AWM, HS, [ATF].

26   Ban Chap, *Dong Nai*, pp. 180, 209.

27   Burchett, *Vietnam*, pp. 43–45.

28   Based on Pike, *Viet Cong*, pp. 87, 391.

29   Based on ibid., pp. 119–26.

30   Burchett, *Vietnam*, p. 68; on Social Darwinism, Marr, *Vietnamese Tradition*, chapter 7.

31   'Vietnam Report', February & March 1964, Australian Services Attache, Australian Embassy, Saigon, in AWM, HS.

32   'M. Taylor to President, January 6, 1965', in P. Kesaris (ed), *The War in Vietnam: Classified Histories by the National Security Council*, University Microfilms of America, Frederick [nd], 'Deployment of Major U.S. Forces to Vietnam: July 1965', reel 1, vol. 1, frame 0022.

33   Quoted in Hammer, *Death*, pp. 309–310.

34   ibid., p. 279.

Chapter 6

1   For example, the *Sydney Morning Herald* quarterly index covering 1955 to September 1961 has the following number of items on Vietnam: 1955, 37 items (Diem's confrontation with Bao Dai);

1956, 14 items (the refusal to hold reunification elections); 1957, 18 items (Diem's Australian visit); 1958, 4 items; 1959, 4 items; 1960, 13 items (the November coup attempt); and to September 1961, 31 items (the escalation of American military aid).

2   *The Age*, November 4 1963 [editorial].

3   See Rodney Tiffen, 'News coverage of Vietnam', in P. King (ed), *Australia's Vietnam*, Allen & Unwin, Sydney, 1983, pp. 168–171; Michael Sexton, *War for the Asking: Australia's Vietnam Secrets*, Penguin, Ringwood, 1982, p. 124, and W. Macmahon Ball, 'Foreign news and the Australian community', p. 3, Paper given to A.J.A. School of Journalism Conference, Canberra, February 1966, in NLA MS7851, Box: 'Broadcasting, Journalism, Press', File: 'Miscellany, 1936–1966'.

4   'South Vietnam', date stamped 25 July 1956, in 'Vietnam—Economic and Political Information Reports', AA, CRS A463, Item 1956/448; 'Notes on policy matters to be discussed', 31 August, 1957, in 'Vietnam. Brief for President Diem's Visit to Australia. 1957', AA, CRS A1838/233, Item 383/11/1/1. and J. Plimsoll, Acting Secretary External Affairs to Acting Minister [Menzies], 2 September 1957, in AA, CRS A1838/233, Item 383/11/1/1.

5   Ministerial despatch, 28 January, 1958, [Blakeney to Casey], and Ministerial despatch No. 2, 19 September, 1958, [Blakeney to Casey], both in AA, A4231/2, NN, 'Australian Legation. Saigon. Ministerial Despatches', 1958 volume.

6   Alan Renouf, *The Frightened Country*, Macmillan, South Melbourne, 1979, p. 277, and Gregory Clark, 'Vietnam, China and the foreign affairs debate in Australia: A personal account', in King (ed), *Australia's Vietnam*, pp. 21–22.

7   Renouf, *Frightened Country*, p. 259; Watt, *Vietnam*, p. 112; 'In the Southeast', Clark, in King (ed), *Australia's Vietnam*, p. 24 and Peter Howson, *The Howson Diaries: The Life of Politics* (ed. D. Aitkin), Viking, Ringwood, 1984, p. 53 [27 August 1963].

8   Edwards, *Crises*, pp. 275, 318, 383–384 and E.G. Whitlam, *The Whitlam Government, 1972–1975*, Viking, Ringwood, 1985, p. 35; see Sexton, *War*, pp. 94–96 for the text of a number of cables to Anderson.

9   See Pemberton, *All the Way*, for the best statement of this argument.

10 'The strategic basis of Australian Defence policy', report by the Defence committee, October 1956, Submission no. 522, February 1957, in 'Cabinet Submissions', AA, A4926/XMI, vol. 21. The Defence committee, advisory to the minister, consisted of the secretaries of Defence and External Affairs, the chiefs of staff and the chairman of the chiefs of staff committee. In 1960, it was expanded to include Prime Minister's and Treasury.

11 'Visit of President Ngo Dinh Diem: Defence Questions' [nd. August 1957] in 'Vietnam. Brief for President Diem's Visit'.

12 'Strategic Basis of Australian Defence Policy', report by the Defence committee, January 1959, Annex B: 'Areas of Strategic Interest to Australia', p. 2, and Annex C: 'Nature of the Conflict', pp. 1–2, with Cabinet Submission no. 59, in AA, A5818/2, vol. 2.

13 Quoted from Paltridge's submission, in ibid, p. 2.

14 Cabinet minutes, 23 March and 9 November, 1959, Decisions no. 113 and 522, in ibid.
15 1962 comments, Edwards, *Crises*, pp. 247–248, and 1964 minute, Pemberton, *All the Way*, p. 205.
16 Howson, *Diaries*, p. 102 [11 July 1964], p. 115 [4 October 1964] and p. 105 [31 July 1964]. See Pemberton, *All the Way*, pp. 217–218 on Hasluck's views.
17 Spender to Casey, 6 April 1954, in AA, A5954/17, Box 2299, 'Indo-China. Geneva Conference. Box 2,' and Hasluck to Waller [April, 1965] quoted in Sexton, *War*, p. 141.
18 'Strategic Basis' (1959); on 'counterinsurgency', see R.B. Smith, *An International History of the Vietnam War*, vol. 2, *The Struggle for South-East Asia, 1961–65.* Macmillan, London, 1985.
19 *The Age*, 15 November, 1963.
20 'The Menace of Communism', Melbourne, 23 September 1960, in NLA, MS4936, Series 6, Box 269, folders 135 & 136 (draft notes).
21 'Opening speech, Melbourne, 15 November 1961', Folder 160, and 'Final Broadcast 6 December, 1961', Folder 161, both in NLA, MS 4936, Series 6, Box 273.
22 'No. 3 TV Recording: Talk to the Nation', 28 November 1961, Folder 161, ibid; Pemberton, *All the Way*, p. 128, and Edwards, *Crises*, pp. 216–27.
23 'Demonstrable', Pemberton, *All the Way*, p. 148, and *Australia's Military Commitment to Vietnam* [hereafter *AMCV*], Department of External Affairs, 1975, pp. 5–7.
24 'Statement by the Australian Minister for Defence, Mr. A. Townley, 24th May, 1962', in *Viet Nam since the 1954 Geneva Agreements*, Select Documents on International Affairs, no. 1 of 1964, Department of External Affairs, Canberra [1964], p. 36. See Edwards, *Crises*, chapter 13, and Pemberton, *All the Way*, pp. 160–61.
25 Quotations from 'Parliamentary Statement by the Australian Minister for External Affairs, Sir Garfield Barwick, 21 August, 1962', in *Viet Nam*, pp. 49–52; 'frontier' statement: Edwards, *Crises*, p. 246; infiltration figures: Australian Services Attache, 'Vietnam Report, July, 1964', in Australian Embassy, Saigon, AWM, HS.
26 David Marr, *Barwick*, Allen & Unwin, Sydney, 1980. pp. 179–180, 194; 'Statement by the Australian Minister for External Affairs, Sir Garfield Barwick, 8 November 1963', in *Viet Nam since*, p. 56.
27 Marr, *Barwick*, pp. 203–204.
28 Speech notes in NLA, MS4936, Series 6, Box 218, Folder 215; *The Age*, 11 November 1964, and see Pemberton, *All the Way*, p. 213.
29 Calwell, *The Age*, 16 November 1964; Fairbairn, *Nation*, no. 158, 28 November 1964; Pemberton, *All the Way*, pp. 214–216, and Edwards, *Crises*, pp. 329–31.
30 *Age*, 2, 11 & 12 November 1964, and *Australian*, 11 November 1964.
31 *Nation*, no. 158, 28 November 1964; Edwards, *Crises*, p. 304, and see Glen Withers, *Conscription: Necessity and Justice. The Case for an All Volunteer Army*, Angus & Robertson, Sydney, 1972. pp. 39–41.
32 Howson, *Diaries*, p. 50 [23 July 1963]; *The Age*, 9 November 1964.

33 Based on *Australian*, 7 November 1964, *The Age*, 5 November 1964, Howson, *Diaries*, pp. ix, 121, and Edwards, *Crises*, pp. 328–329.
34 Pemberton, *All the Way*, pp. 215–216.
35 M. Goot & R. Tiffen, 'Public opinion and the politics of the polls', in King (ed), *Australia's Vietnam*, p. 142; *The Age*, 13 & 'provoke' 17 November and 8 December 1964; 'resort', *Nation*, 14 November 1964; on the Catholic church, Val Noone, 'Melbourne Catholics and the Vietnam War: A participant's study of peace work in a pro-war church', PhD, LaTrobe University, 1991.
36 *The Age*, 13 & 16 November and 8 December 1964.
37 See *AMCV*, pp. 15–23.

Chapter 7

1 On the parliamentary debates, Colebatch, 'An Examination', pp. 140–157; Oliver Paul, 'Why they asked J.B. Priestley', *Nation*, November 7, 1959, p. 6, and W. Macmahon Ball, 'What's in a Peace Congress?', *Nation*, July 4, 1959, p. 6; on the congress in general, see R. Summy & M. Saunders, 'The Melbourne Peace Congress: Culmination of anti-communism in Australia in the 1950s', in Curthoys & Merritt (eds), *Better Dead*.
2 'Led by', *Outlook*, vol. 3, no. 6, December 1959; Macmahon Ball, 'I was no match for Madame', *Nation*, November 21, 1959, pp. 6–7, and 'Resolution of Artists and Writers Conference', UMA, CICD Papers.
3 'Net effect', *Outlook*, vol. 3, no. 6, December 1959, and 'one occasionally', vol. 8, no. 2, April 1964.
4 'Gambit', 'Towards a New Left', *Outlook*, vol. 2, no. 4, August 1958. See also Alan Barcan, *The Socialist Left in Australia, 1949–1959*, A.P.S.A. monograph, Sydney, 1960.
5 Jim Jupp, 'What happened to "the New Left": Melbourne socialists v. Sydney fellow-travellers', *Bulletin*, 15 September 1962, pp. 29–31.
6 CND notes in NLA, MS6206, Box 69, folder 3, and R. Summy, 'The Australian Peace Council and the anticommunist milieu, 1949–1965', in Charles Chatfield & Peter van den Dungen (eds), *Peace Movements and Political Culture*, Knoxville, University of Tennessee Press, 1988, pp. 251–252.
7 Quote in R. Summy, 'A reply to Fred Wells', in R. Forward & B. Reece (eds), *Conscription in Australia*, University of Queensland Press, St Lucia, 1968, p. 207, and see VCND newsletter, *Sanity* (1963), in NLA, MS6206, Box 69, folder 3.
8 *The Age*, 7 November 1963.
9 Ralph Summy, 'Australian peace movement 1960–67: A study in dissent', MA thesis, University of Sydney, 1971, pp. 170–173, at p. 173.
10 'General Information re Pledgers etc.: As at 18.11.61', in UMA, Hartley Papers, File: '1960–63, Victorian Peace Council Notes'.
11 Victor James, 'Vietnam for the Vietnamese', Victorian Peace Council, Melbourne [1961].
12 S. Murray-Smith, interview, 18 June 1982, conducted by Emma Quick, UMA; 'Report to Executive—by Mrs Dorothy Gibson, 22.2.1960' and Agenda, 'Victorian Peace Council Meeting,

22/10/62', both in '1960–63, Victorian Peace Council Notes', UMA, Hartley Papers.

13 Quotes from *Outlook*, vol. 8, no. 2, April, 1964; also based on Gollan, interview, and Summy, 'Australian peace movement', pp. 190–191.

14 Robertson, 'CPA', p. 46.

15 Notes in NLA, MS6206, Box 97, Folder 2, 'Peace Congress, 1964'; also *Outlook*, vol. 8, no. 2, April 1964.

16 *Tribune*, 12 September 1956; Summy, 'The Australian Peace Council', p. 242, and Gollan, interview.

17 Fred Daly, *From Curtin to Kerr*, Sun Books, Melbourne, 1977, p. 152.

18 Kim C. Beazley, 'Post-Evatt Australian Labor Party attitudes to the United States alliance', MA, University of WA, 1974, p. 129, and pp. 163–164.

19 G. Freudenberg, *A Certain Grandeur: Gough Whitlam in Politics*, Penguin, Ringwood, 1987, p. 55; Tom Uren, in G. Langley, *A Decade of Dissent*, Allen & Unwin, Sydney, 1992, p. 22. The ALP statement is reprinted as Appendix D in Beazley, 'Post-Evatt'.

20 Paul Ormonde, *A Foolish Passionate Man: A Biography of Jim Cairns*, Penguin, Ringwood, 1981, p. 82; Freudenberg, *Certain Grandeur*, pp. 50–51; Beazley, in King (ed), *Australia's Vietnam*, p. 45. Also based on interviews with Jim Cairns Melbourne, 23 September 1991 and Clem Lloyd Wollongong, 9 December 1991.

21 Maxwell Newton, 'The Vietnam Decision', *Nation*, May 15 1965, pp. 6–7; Howson, *Diaries*, p. 148 [25 March 1965] and p. 151 [22 April 1965], and Edwards, *Crises*, chapter 18, especially pp. 358–362.

22 Freudenberg, *Certain Grandeur*, p. 56.

23 J.F. Cairns, *The Eagle and the Lotus: Western Intervention in Vietnam, 1847–1971*, Lansdowne Press, Melbourne, 1971, pp. viii—ix.

24 J.F. Cairns, *Living with Asia*, Lansdowne Press, Melbourne, 1965. pp. 2, 23, 57–59, 94–95.

25 Cairns, *The Eagle*, pp. xi-xii; *Living with Asia*, p. 3, and Freudenberg, *Certain Grandeur*, p. 55.

26 Cairns, *Living with Asia*, pp. 4, 21–22, 111–112, 146, 169.

27 Tim Rowse, *Australian Liberalism and National Character*, Kibble, Malmsbury, 1978, chapter 5, and Allan Ashbolt, *An Australian Experience: Words from the Vietnam Years*, Australasian Book Society, Sydney, 1974, p. 77.

28 Craig McGregor, *People, Politics and Pop: Australians in the Sixties*, Ure Smith, Sydney, 1968, p. 183, and Ormonde, *Foolish Passionate Man*, p. 115.

Chapter 8

1 SOS Minute book, 17 June 1965; A. Pert to Secretary, New York SDS, 5 July 1967; M. Strickland to P. Ashcroft, 6 December 1965, and *Sanity*, vol. 4, no. 7, Christmas 1965, all in NLA, MS3821, Boxes 1 and 4.

2 J. McLean to P. Ashcroft, 5 July and 19 August 1965, in NLA, MS3821, Box 1, folder 4; Summy, 'A Reply', p. 203. See also Jean

McLean, 'Anti-Vietnam War activist', in Gloria Frydman, *Protesters*, Collins Dove, Blackburn, 1987.

3 Crew of *SS Lake Torrens* to SOS (NSW), 13 July 1965, and Minute book, 18 August 1966 and 9 November 1968, both in NLA, MS3821, Boxes 2 and 4. On the self-image of the Melbourne women, see Rosemary Francis, 'Women in protest movements: the Women's Peace Army and the Save Our Sons movement', MA Prelim., U. of Melbourne, 1984; on bohemianism, see Langley, *Decade*, p. 32.

4 Leaflet, 'Special Demonstration, December 2, 1966', and Minute book, 19 August 1965, in NLA, MS3821, Boxes 1 and 4.

5 Based on M. Hamel-Green, 'The resisters: A history of the anti-conscription movement, 1964–1972', in King (ed), *Australia's Vietnam*; Chris Guyatt, 'The anti-conscription movement, 1964–1966', and Summy, 'A reply', both in Forward & Reece (eds), *Conscription*, and the *Australian*, 21 March 1966.

6 Editorial,'The Coming Storm', *Sanity*, vol. 4, no. 6, October-November 1965, vol. 4, no. 3, June 1965, and vol. 4, no. 5, August-September 1965; *Viet Protest News*, vol. 1, no. 8 [1966]; Summy 'A reply'; and Guyatt, 'Anti-conscription movement'.

7 'The Coming Storm', and 'Speech made on 9th April, 1965, by Mr. Sam Goldbloom, Secretary, A.N.Z. Congress for International Co-operation and Disarmament', in CICD, *Vietnam Information Bulletin* [1965], in UMA, CICD Papers.

8 J. Burns to P. Ashcroft, 24 February, 11 and 21 March, 1966, NLA, MS3821, Box 2.

9 Goot & Tiffen, in King (ed), *Australia's Vietnam*, p. 135, and M. Hamel-Green, 'Conscription and legitimacy, 1964–1972', *Melbourne Journal of Politics*, no. 7, 1974–75, pp. 3–16. Tables I & II.

10 *Australian*, 9 June 1966, and Nadine Jensen, 'A confession of my crime', in NLA, MS3821, Box 1.

11 M. Myers to N. Hewitt, 3 May 1966, in NLA, MS3821, Box 1.

12 'Statement of the F.P.L.P. on the war in Vietnam, 12 May 1966', Appendix F in Beazley, 'Post-Evatt', p. 359.

13 Howson, *Diaries*, pp. 161 [22 June 1965], 166 [30 July 1965] and 213 [23 March 1966].

14 Liberal Reform, *The Justification for Intervention in Vietnam*, East St. Kilda [nd., 1966], p. 20.

15 Robert Cooksey, 'Foreign policy review', *Australian Quarterly*, vol. 38, no. 2, June 1966, p. 107.

16 Minister for External Affairs, *Viet Nam: Questions and Answers*, Commonwealth Government Printer, Canberra, 1966, pp. 10, 11, 13 & 31.

17 Hasluck and Whitlam, quoted in Robert Cooksey, 'Foreign policy review, November 1966-September 1967', *Australian Quarterly*, vol. 39, no. 4, December 1967, pp. 92–109, at pp. 96–99; Menzies, quoted in Minister for External Affairs, *Viet Nam: Recent Statements of Australian Policy*, November 1965, p. 3.

18 Robert Cooksey, 'Foreign policy review, May–October, 1966', *Australian Quarterly*, vol. 39, no. 1, March 1967, pp. 96–109, at p. 97.

19 Department of State, *Aggression from the North: The Record of North Viet-Nam's Campaign to Conquer South Viet-Nam*, Washington, DC,

1965, and Liberal Party, 'The Facts about South Vietnam' [1965?],
pp. 2, 3. Other conservative pamphlets at the time were: Minister
for External Affairs, *Viet Nam and SEATO* (1966); and two
produced by the Liberal Party, *Communist China's Objectives* [1966?]
and *The Stake is Freedom: the Aims of Australian Foreign Policy*
(1966).

20 *The Real Facts about S. Vietnam: A Reply to the Liberal Party* [CPA],
Sydney [1965], p. 13, and *Vietnam, the Answers: A Reply to the
Holt Government's pamphlet 'Vietnam, Questions and Answers'* [CPA],
Sydney [1966], p. 12.

21 *Vietnam: News-Weekly Viet Nam Supplement* [Melbourne], [1966],
p. 3; DSC, *Vietnam: Myth and Reality. An Appraisal of Western
Policy* [Melbourne], [1965]; *Fact and Vietnam*, ALP Victorian
Branch, Melbourne [1966] and J.F. Cairns, *Vietnam: Is it Truth we
Want?*, ALP Victorian Branch, Melbourne, 1965.

22 Cooksey, 'Foreign policy' [June 1966], p. 107.

23 Jim Killen, *Killen: Inside Australian Politics*, Methuen Haynes,
Sydney, 1985, p. 106, and *Things I Hear*, 15 July 1966.

24 'American Embassy, Canberra to Secretary of State, Washington',
3, 7 and 9 October 1966; 'E. Cronk to Rostow', 22 October 1966,
in P. Kesaris (ed), *The War*, 'Manila Conference and President's
Asian Trip', Reel 1, vol. 4, and *Things I Hear*, 14 and 21 October
1966.

25 Kiernan, *Calwell*, p. 260; Beazley, 'Post-Evatt', p. 144 and *Sanity*,
vol. 5, no. 5, Oct–Nov. 1966.

26 Calwell quote in Beazley, in King (ed), *Australia's Vietnam*, p. 49.
Based also on interviews with Clem Lloyd and Jim Cairns.

27 Leaflet: 'The Vote No Conscription Campaign', in NLA, MS6206,
Box 69; *Sanity*, vol. 5, no. 5, October–November 1966; also *Viet
Protest News*, vol. 1, no. 7 [1966], and A. Robertson, 'Foreign policy
and its distortion', *Australian Left Review*, no. 2, 1966, p. 4.

28 *The Age*, 22 and 23 November 1966.

29 Killen, *Killen*, p. 107; *The Age*, 24 November, 1966; Melbourne
Club opinion, Howson, *Diaries*, pp. 249 & 250 [16 & 22 November
1966], and Monash University SRC, 'Facts about the Anti-LBJ
Demonstration' [1966], in NLA, MS6206, Box 69, folder 2.

30 A. Calwell, *Be Just and Fear Not*, Lloyd O'Neil, Hawthorn, 1972,
pp. 77, 232.

31 *Australian*, 30 April 1965; Ian Turner 'An open letter to Douglas
Brass, 3 May 1967', in NLA, MS6202, Box 69, folder 3.

32 Rev. David Pope, 'The Moral Scourge of Vietnam', 27 January
1967, in NLA, MS6202, Box 69, folder 3.

Chapter 9

1 Australian Military Forces, *Pocketbook: South Vietnam*, Canberra,
1967, p. 7; on naivety, see Stuart Rintoul, *Ashes of Vietnam*,
Heinemann, Richmond, 1987, pp. 9, 15, 17, 22, 24 for examples.

2 'These are', Graham Walker, 'Like a card house in the wind', in
K. Maddock (ed), *Memories of Vietnam*, Random House, Sydney,
1991, pp. 190–191; on local villagers, see Rhys Pollard, *The Cream
Machine*, Angus & Robertson, Sydney, 1972, pp. 56–57, and

Rintoul, *Ashes*, p. 34. Also Robin Gerster 'Occidental tourists: The "Ugly Australian" in Vietnam War narratives', in P. Pierce, J. Doyle & J. Grey (eds), *Vietnam Days: Australia and the Impact of Vietnam*, Penguin, Ringwood, 1991, and John Murphy, ' "Like outlaws": Australian narratives from the Vietnam War', *Meanjin*, vol. 46, no. 2, June 1987, pp. 153–162.

3 Quoted from *The Division in Battle: Pamphlet no. 11: Counter-revolutionary warfare*, in Frost, *Australia's War*, p. 58.

4 Aims: quoted in Frost, *Australia's War*, p. 164; Hoa Long: 'Civil Affairs Plan', 9 July 1966, [HQAFV] 'Civilian General', R176-1-5 [Emphasis added], and phases: 'GS Instruction 8/67: Civil Affairs', HQ 1ATF CD, June 1967, both in AWM, HS.

5 'Annex G to 1 Aust CA Unit Monthly Report. Jan 70', [ATF] R723-1-12; also John Lybrand, 'Evaluation Report—Australian Task Force—Phuoc Tuy' [June 1967], [ATF] R723-1-16, both in AWM, HS, and Lt. Col. B.C. Milligan, 'Evaluating the Effectiveness of Civil Aid—a Feasibility Study' (Report no. 13/68), 1 Psychological Research Unit, Melbourne, 1968. p. 50.

6 'Civic Action: 1 Aust CA Unit Monthly Report, Oct 70', [ATF] R723-1-12, in AWM, HS.

7 Based on Message Log, 26 July 1969, HQ 1ATF CD, July 1969; 'Report by Maj. M.D. Currie on Psy[chological] Operations Phuoc Tuy Province, 5 Mar 69', [1 Psy Ops] R723-1-5, and 'Quarterly Summary Report, Implementation of the Combined Campaign Plan, Period 1 Jan 67–31 Mar 67', [ATF] R723-1-39 (part 1) in AWM, HS.

8 Kolko, *Vietnam*, chapters 17 & 18.

9 Based on Pat Burgess, 'The village of hidden hate', *Bulletin*, August 21, 1976, pp. 16–17; Terry Burstall, *A Soldier Returns*, University of Queensland Press, St Lucia, 1990; 'With the 1ATF in Vietnam, 1966', [ATF]; 'Civil Affairs Plan', 9 July 1966, [HQAFV] R 176-1-5, and 'Survey Report of Hoa Long Village', 25 February 1967, [1CA Unit] R176A-2-2, last three items in AWM, HS.

10 'Diary of Huynh Chien Dau', AWM, DR 3/7551. [Translation with original], and 'Annex B to 8RAR Ops 5', 6 April 1970, HQ AFV After Action Reports, R 723-1-196, in AWM, HS.

11 Based on 'Current Civil Affairs Policies', 14 June 1966, [HQ AFV] R 569-1-190; 'Annex B to 8RAR Ops 5', and 'Hoa Long Ground Team Report, 13-17 Apr. 1971', [1 Psyops U] R 723–1–2, 'Monthly Report, 4 Sep 71' [1 Psyops U] R 723-1-1, all in AWM, HS.

12 Cane: 'Survey Report of Hoa Long Village'; scroll: 'Civic Action WHAM Report, 14/66', 3 November 1966, in [AFV] R 176-1-7; bodies: 'Weekly Attitude Report: On the Public Display of Viet Cong Bodies in Hoa Long Village', March 17 1967, [1CAU] R694-1-1, all in AWM, HS; the atrocity allegations were made in Alex Carey, *Australian Atrocities in Vietnam*, Vietnam Action Campaign, Sydney [1968].

13 Based on 'Annex A, Intsum 239/70, 27 August 1970, HQ 1ATF, CD August 1970; 'Phoi Hop, 8RAR, 7–19 Apr 70', HQ AFV, After Action Reports, R723-1-196, and 'Hoa Long Ground Team Report', in AWM, HS.

14 ATF Press Release [nd, circa November 1967], [1ACAU] R176-1-9,

and 'After Action Report, Operation Ainslie', HQ 1ATF CD, November 1967, in AWM, HS.

15 Brig. Hughes to Maj. Nguyen Ba Truoc, Province Chief, 13 November 1967, HQ ATF, Operations—Particular—Securing of Rice Harvest, R569-2-55, in AWM, HS.

16 Based on 1 ACA Unit to Comd 1 ATF, 30 October 1968, [1ACAU] R176-1-9; 'Monthly Report, Nov 67', [1 ACAU] R176A-1-7; Boring (Assistant Province Adviser) to Gration (Commanding Officer, 1 ACAU), July 4 1969 [1 ACAU] R176-1-9; 'Civic Action: 1 Aust CA Unit Monthly Report, Oct 70', [ATF] R723-1-12 and 'CORDS III CTZ Rural Technical Team: Field Survey Report, 12 Oct 1969. Security in Suoi Nghe Refugee Hamlet, Phuoc Tuy', [1 ACAU] R176-1-9, in AWM, HS.

17 'CORDS III CTZ'; 'Survey Report of Hoa Long Village'; and Lt. Col. P.C. Gration to Deputy Commander [ATF], 10 April 1969, [1 ACAU] Civic Action, R176-1-9 in AWM, HS.

18 'Ap Suoi Nghe Ground Team Report, 5 Apr–9Apr', 8 May 1971, [1 Psyops U] R723-1-1, in AWM, HS.

Chapter 10

1 See for example, Phan Ngoc Danh, *Lich Su*, p. 124.

2 Frost, *Australia's War*, pp. 141, [deletions and insertions in original] and 38–52; and Intsum [Intelligence Summary] no. 207–69, 26 July 1969, HQ 1ATF CD, July 1969, in AWM, HS.

3 Security: After Action Report, Operation *Kings Cross*, HQ AFV, 'Combat Operations After Action Reports', 723-1-196; chief: NZV Force to External Affairs, Wellington, [no date, but April 1969], AAAGV Non-Registry file, both in AWM, HS. Also 'Vietnam Digest, no. 4, 11–17 August 1968', HQ1ATF CD August 1968, in AWM, HS and Frost, *Australia's War*, p. 99.

4 PSDF: Annex A to Intsum 262–69, 19 September 1969, HQ1ATF CD September 1969; proselytising: 'Annex A' HQ 1ATF CD, June 1969, both in AWM, HS.

5 See Frost, *Australia's War*, pp. 47–48 and 152–158, and Ian McNeill, *The Team: Australian Army Advisers in Vietnam 1962–1972*, Australian War Memorial, Canberra, 1984, at pp. 405–411. Both point to the ineffectiveness of the Phoenix Program in Phuoc Tuy.

6 Quote from 'Troops Information Sheet, no. 96, 19–25 May 1968', HQ 1ATF CD, June 1968; also based on 'Troops Information Sheet, no. 77, 31 December 1967–6 January 1968', HQ 1ATF CD, January 1968, and Annex F to Intsum 121/71, 1 May 1971, HQ 1ATF CD, May 1971, in AWM, HS.

7 Quote from 'Annex B, Intsum 134/71, 14 May 1971', HQ 1ATF CD, May 1971; also based on 'Area Study (Psyops) of Phuoc Tuy Province, [US] Department of Army, 17 March 1967', [1 AUST CA Unit] R694-1-1; 'Ap Suoi Nghe Ground Team Report, 5 April–9 April [1971]', 8 May 1971, [1 Psyops Unit] R723-1-1; 'Annex A, Intsum 235/70, 23 August 1970', HQ 1ATF CD, August 1970, and 'Intsum, 28/70, 28 January 1979', HQ 1ATF CD, January 1970, all in AWM, HS.

8 'Troops Information Sheet, no. 70, 12–18 November 1967', HQ

1ATF CD, November 1967, and Diary, HQ 1ATF CD, July 1970, both in AWM, HS.

9   'Translation of Judgement of Assassinated GVN Official', Annex B to 1ATF Monthly Psyops Report, June 1971, [ATF] Monthly Psyops Reports, in AWM, HS.

10 Access: 'Intelligence Annex to Operation Orders, Operation Leeton', HQ1ATF CD, March 1967; Lambretta: 'Operation Orders, Operation Forrest', HQ 1ATF CD, November 1967. Also based on 'Annex A to Operation Instruction 72/69', HQ 1ATF CD, August 1969; '5th VC Division', HQ 1ATF CD, April 1967 and 'Annex A to Operation Order, Operation Portsea', HQ 1ATF CD, March 1967, all in AWM, HS, and Phan Ngoc Danh, *Lich Su*, pp. 114–115.

11 'Diary of Huynh Chien Dau', p. 24 of translation; instruction: 'Supintrep 31/70', 12 August 1970, HQ 1ATF CD, August 1970. Also based on 'Enemy Situation—Phuoc Tuy Province', 13 September 1968, HQ 1ATF CD, September 1968; 'Intsum 86–70', 1ATF CD, March 1970, and 'After Action Report: Operation Bondi II', HQ AFV, R723-1-196, all in AWM, HS.

12 Frost, *Australia's War* pp. 141. [deletions and additions in original] and 149–152.

13 Error: Frost, *Australia's War*, p. 95; N.J. Clark to parents, 26 May 1967, AWM, PR 86/122; fence: 'Moneval Aug. 67', HQ 1ATF CD September 1967, and Brigadier Graham spelt out the rationale for the fence in 'Narrative', HQ 1ATF CD March 1967, both in AWM, HS.

14 Cable: AFV to Army Canberra, 27 July 1969, [AAAGV] Non-reg. Misc. Signals; Brig. Hughes to Maj. Nguyen Ba Truoc, 15 November 1967, HQ 1ATF Operation Leeton, R569-2-26; map: File note, no date, HQ 1ATF Operation Leeton, R569-2-26; mobilisation: 'Intsum 262-69, 17 Sep 69', HQ 1ATF CD, September 1969. Also based on 'Operation Instruction 13/68—Operation Cooktown Orchid', 1ATF CD March 1968, all in AWM, HS; Ban Chap Hanh Dang, *Dong Nai*, pp. 231–235, and Phan Ngoc Danh, *Lich Su*, pp. 132–142.

15 Quote from 'Order of the Day from HQ SVNLA to all VC/NVA military forces, captured 3 February', HQ 1ATF CD February 1968, in AWM, HS; also based on Kolko, *Vietnam*, chapter 23 & 24, and General Tran Cong Man interviews, Hanoi, 4 & 5 February 1988.

16 Cowardice: quoted in Frost, *Australia's War*, p. 112; based on Kolko, *Vietnam*, p. 308; Phan Ngoc Danh, *Lich Su*, pp. 144–149; 'Narrative' and 'Message Log', HQ 1ATF CD February 1968; 'Annex to Op Instr. Op Clayton', HQ 1ATF CD February 1968, and '1 Aust CA Unit—Monthly Report—Feb 68', [AFV] R176-1-10, in AWM, HS.

17 Kolko, *Vietnam*, p. 311 and pp. 397–398.

18 Westmoreland: Jonathan Mirsky, 'The war that will not end', *New York Review of Books*, 16 August 1990. p. 29. See Michael Maclear, *Vietnam: The Ten Thousand Day War*, Methuen, London, 1981, chapter 13 and in particular p. 295 and McNeill, *The Team*, p. 153. The classic statement of this argument, in relation to media coverage of Tet, is Peter Braestrup, *Big Story: How the American Press and*

Television Reported and Interpreted the Crisis of Tet 1968 in Vietnam and Washington, Anchor, New York, 1979; see also Tiffen, in King (ed), *Australia's Vietnam*, at pp. 175–178.

19 Quote: Kolko, *Vietnam*, p. 313 and chapter 25, and 'National Security Study Memorandum, no. 1, January 21, 1969', in Gareth Porter (ed), *Vietnam: A History in Documents*, Meridian, New York, 1981, at pp. 373–380.

Chapter 11

1 *Age*, 3 & 7 February 1968.

2 Based on Howson, *Diaries*, p. 319 [21 August 1967], p. 321 [25 August 1967] and p. 325 [6 September 1967]; *AMCV*, p. 34, and Freudenberg, *Certain Grandeur*, pp. 113–114.

3 Robert Cooksey, 'Foreign policy review: October–December, 1967', *Australian Quarterly*, vol. 40, no. 2, June 1968, pp. 99–110, and Minister for External Affairs, *Viet-Nam: Efforts for Peace. An Australian View* (November 1967).

4 Freudenberg, *Certain Grandeur*, p. 125, and *News-Weekly*, 19 February 1969, p. 16.

5 George Westbrook, 'Foreign policy review: January–June, 1968', *Australian Quarterly*, vol. 40, no. 3, September 1968, pp. 92–103 at pp. 99–100; Renouf, *Frightened Country*, p. 267 and Howson, *Diaries*, p. 415 [2 April 1968].

6 'Comment', *Australian Left Review*, June–July, 1968. pp. 1–5.

7 Howson, *Diaries*, p. 486 [10 February 1969] and p. 546 [10 September 1969]; *News-Weekly*, 15 January and 19 February 1969; and Robert Cooksey, 'Foreign policy review: July–December, 1968', *Australian Quarterly*, vol. 41, no. 1, March 1969, pp. 78–91.

8 Westbrook, 'Foreign policy', and B.A. Santamaria, 'Struggle on two fronts: The D.L.P. and the 1969 election', *Australian Quarterly*, vol. 41, no. 4, December 1969, pp. 33–42.

9 Howson, *Diaries*, p. 449 [14 August 1968] and *Australian*, 15 May 1968.

10 *Australian*, quoted in Philip Ayres, *Malcolm Fraser: A Biography*, Heinemann, Richmond, 1987, p. 148; John Lloyd, interview conducted by Patricia Donnelly, Melbourne, 11 June 1982, in UMA and Sir John Gorton interview, Canberra, 21 October 1991.

11 Based on B.A. Santamaria interview, Melbourne, 27 September 1991; Santamaria, 'Struggle'; *News-Weekly*, February 19 1969; Freudenberg, *Certain Grandeur*, p. 159; Ayres, *Fraser*, p. 143, and D.W. Rawson, 'The Vietnam War and the Australian party system', *Australian Outlook*, vol. 23, no. 1, April 1969, pp. 58–67.

12 *Age*, 16 May and 10 June 1969, and *News-Weekly*, 18 June 1969.

13 *Age*, 10 June 1969; Fairhall quoted in Hugh Smith, 'Foreign policy review: July–December, 1969', *Australian Quarterly*, vol. 42, no. 1, March 1970, pp. 108–116 at p. 111; see also D. Solomon, 'Gorton knew more than he told', *Australian*, 17 May 1969, and Robert Howard, 'Foreign policy review: January–June, 1969', *Australian Quarterly*, vol. 41, no. 3, September 1969, pp. 99–108.

14 Whitlam, *Whitlam Government*, pp. 6, 38; Beazley, 'Post-Evatt', pp. 204, 234–235, and Rawson, 'Vietnam War', pp. 63–64.

15 Beazley, 'Post-Evatt', pp. 192, 204 –206;

16 Beazley, 'Post-Evatt', pp. 199–200; also Robert Cooksey, 'Foreign policy review: November, 1966–September, 1967', *Australian Quarterly*, vol. 39, no. 4, December 1967, pp. 92–109.

17 Colbourne: *Australian*, 25 February 1967; NSW executive quoted in Ralph Summy, 'Militancy and the Australian peace movement, 1960–1967,' *Politics*, vol. 5, no. 2, Nov. 1970. pp. 148–162 at p. 157, and *Vietnam Action*, vol. 1, no. 1, April 1967 [Editorial].

18 Whitlam press conference: *The Age*, 3 February 1968; ambiguities: Rawson, 'Vietnam War', p. 65; see also Beazley, 'Post-Evatt', pp. 227, 232–233; Summy, 'Militancy' and Malcolm Saunders, 'The ALP's response to the anti-Vietnam war movement: 1965–73', *Labour History*, no. 44, May 1983, pp. 75–91.

19 Poll: *Herald*, 10 September 1969. Whitlam quoted in Smith, 'Foreign policy', p. 108, and 'agony': quoted in Rawson, 'Vietnam War', p. 67.

20 Summy, 'Militancy', p. 159.

21 A. Pert to V. Ward, 10 February 1967, in NLA, MS3821, Box 1, folder 5. Ky quoted in *Viet Protest News*, vol. 2, no. 2 [1967].

22 Howson, *Diaries*, p. 263 [20 January 1967], and Central Intelligence Agency, 'Intelligence Information Cable, August 2, 1967', in P. Kesaris (ed), *CIA Research Reports: Vietnam and Southeast Asia, 1946–1976*, University Publishers of America, Frederick, 1983. Reel VII, Item 0165.

23 Labor MPs: Don Aitkin, 'Political review', *Australian Quarterly*, vol. 39, no. 1, March 1967, pp. 92–93; Teichmann: speech on 22 January 1967, in *Viet Protest News*, vol. 2, no. 1.

24 Michael Hamel-Green, 'Vietnam: Beyond pity', *Australian Left Review*, no. 24, April–May, 1970, pp. 54–55.

25 Aitkin, 'Political Review', pp. 91–92; Bill White Conscientious Objectors Defence Committee, *News Sheet*, no. 1, April 1967, in NLA, MS3821, Box 2, folder 13, and Inter-Church Committee on Peace, 'Notes on the Conduct of Cases for Conscientious Objectors', Melbourne, July 1968.

26 SOS Minute Book, 11 March 1967, Box 4; Circular letters, Conscientious Objectors (Non-Pacifist), February and 10 April 1968, Box 1, folder 7; 'Statement by Executive Committee, Australian Council of Churches, "Conscientious Objection to Particular Wars" ', Sydney, April 1969, Box 2, folder 17, all in NLA, MS3821; A.J. Lloyd to D. Mowbray, 2 May 1969, in UMA, CICD Papers, 'A.J. Lloyd (Personal)' file, and *Viet Protest News*, no. 19, December 1968.

27 'R. v District Court: Ex parte Thompson', *Commonwealth Law Reports*, (1968), 118, pp. 488–503, at p. 493.

28 SOS Minute Book, 14 December 1968; CANSA leaflet [1968], Box 1, folder 7; Federal Pacifist Council, 'Press Release, no. 6/69, December 1, 1969', Box 1, folder 6, all in NLA, MS3821; 60 liable young men: Hamel-Green, in King (ed), *Australia's Vietnam*, p. 119; 'falsies': Langley, *Decade*, p. 88. See also Bob Scates, *'Draftmen Go Free': A History of the Anti-Conscription Movement in Australia*, [self-published], [1989], pp. 29–36.

29 Quote from Hamel-Green, 'Vietnam: Beyond pity', p. 64; see also Hamel-Green, in King (ed), *Australia's Vietnam*, p. 115.

30 Based on M. M. van Gelder, 'Australia's Selective National Service Training Scheme, 1965–72', *Defence Force Journal*, no. 19, November–December 1979, p. 50; Ann-Mari Jordens, 'Conscription and dissent: The genesis of anti-war protest', in G. Pemberton (ed), *Vietnam Remembered*, Weldon, Sydney, 1990, pp. 68–70, and Ann-Mari Jordens, 'Conscription', in G. Aplin, S. G. Foster & M. McKernan (eds), *Australia: A Historical Dictionary*, Fairfax Syme & Weldon, Sydney, 1987, pp. 88–89.

31 Ashbolt, *Australian Experience*, p. 210.

Chapter 12

1 On the New Left, see Chris Rootes, 'The development of radical student movements and their sequelae', *Australian Journal of Politics and History*, vol. 34, no. 2, 1988, pp. 173–186; Richard Gordon & Warren Osmond, 'An overview of the Australian New Left', in Richard Gordon (ed), *The Australian New Left: Critical Essays and Strategy*, Heinemann, Melbourne, 1970, and the chapters by O'Brien and Osmond; and Ian Carroll, 'The new radicals', *Arena*, no. 21, 1970, pp. 65–71.

2 Based on Rootes, 'Development'; Michael Hamel-Green, 'Dissent on the war to protest at the system', *Tribune*, 10 July 1968; Denis Freney, *A Map of Days: Life on the Left*, Heinemann, Melbourne, 1991, chapter 11; and Peter O'Brien, 'The Socialist alternative', *Tribune*, 5 July 1969.

3 'Student activism: Interviews with Kirsner, Hannan, Cahill, Aarons, Thompson, Duncan and O'Brien', *Australian Left Review*, no. 4, August–September, 1968, pp. 30–38, 43–53; Mark Taft, 'Confrontation: When and how?', *Tribune*, 11 March, 1970.

4 Intensive discussion: Warren Osmond, 'Towards self-awareness', in Gordon (ed), *Australian New Left*, p. 168, also Rex Mortimer, 'The socialist flux: Some shorthand comments', *Outlook*, June 1970, pp. 14–16, and Carroll, 'New radicals'; on women in the New Left, see Langley, *Decade*, pp. 96, 153.

5 Politics of display: Rootes, 'Development', p. 183, and Rex Mortimer, 'Student action—out of nihilism', *Australian Left Review*, no. 24, April–May, 1970, pp. 73–78; on the New Left in Britain and America, see Nigel Young, *An Infantile Disorder? The Crisis and Decline of the New Left*, Routledge & Kegan Paul, London, 1977.

6 Based on John Herouvim, 'Politics of the revolving door: The Communist Party of Australia (Marxist-Leninist)', *Melbourne Journal of Politics*, vol. 15, 1983–84, pp. 54–68; Barry York, *Student Revolt!: La Trobe University, 1967–1973*, Nicholas Press, Campbell, 1989, and Denis Freney, 'Ructions at Resistance', *Tribune*, June 17, 1970.

7 Posture: Michael Hamel-Green, 'Direct Action in a modern industrial society', Vietnam Co-ordinating Committee, *Conference Report* [Anti-War Conference, September 6–8, 1968], pp. 6–9; see also Harry van Moorst, 'Politics and Demonstrations', pp. 4–5, in the same report, both in UMA, CICD Papers; 'anti-bureaucratic':

Michael Hamel-Green, 'Theory and practice of the student New Left', *Tribune*, 12 March 1969.

8   Davidson, *Communist Party*, chapter 7; Rex Mortimer, 'Dilemmas of Australian Communism', in H. Mayer (ed), *Australian Politics: A Second Reader*, Cheshire, Melbourne, 1969, pp. 382–394; Keith McEwen, *Once a Jolly Comrade*, Jacaranda, Brisbane, 1966, and Bernie Taft, interview, Melbourne, 30 September 1991.

9   'The working class' & 'two sides': 'Serve the People: no. 1, 29/4/70', pp. 1–3, in NLA, MS 6206, Box 41, Folder: 'Students' Movement, 1970'; 'betrayal': Albert Langer, in *Viet Protest News*, no. 19, December 1968, pp. 6–7.

10 Jones, quoted in *Australian*, 26 February, 1968; Robertson, 'CPA in the anti-war movement', pp. 42–43, 47; Summy, 'Militancy', pp. 159–160; Humphrey McQueen, 'A Single Spark', *Arena*, no. 16, 1968; Freney, *Map*, p. 224, and Albert Langer, 'Revolutionaries and the Moratorium', in *Papers of the National Anti-War Conference*, February 1971, in UMA, Hartley Papers, 'Vietnam Peace Material' file.

11 'Militant high': quoted in York, *Student Revolt*, p. 68; also CICD Executive and Committee Minutes, 24 July 1968 and Executive Minutes, 30 April and 11 June 1969, in UMA, CICD Papers.

12 S. Goldbloom to J. Lloyd, 24 September 1969, and Lloyd: 'Secretary's Report—1968–69', 20 August 1969, both in UMA, CICD Papers.

13 Advertisement for the NSW Vietnam Moratorium Campaign, *Australian Left Review*, no. 24, April–May 1970, p. 52.

14 *Australian*, 4 December 1969. The paper repeated the message in a front-page editorial on the following day.

15 Malcolm Saunders, 'The trade unions in Australia and opposition to Vietnam and conscription, 1965–73', *Labour History*, no. 43, November 1982, pp. 69–70.

16 Davidson, *Communist Party*, p. 181, and chapter 8; Aarons's report: L. Aarons, 'Report of the Central Committee', 21st Congress, June 9, 1967, p. 14. See also Eric Aarons, 'As I saw the sixties', *Australian Left Review*, no. 27, October–November 1970, pp. 60–73, and Mortimer, 'Dilemmas'.

17 *Tribune*, 12 March 1969.

18 'Revitalise': Rootes, 'Development', p. 181; Freney, *Map*, p. 238; D. Kirsner & J. Playford, 'Left Action Defended', at p. 97, and D. White & G. Sharp, 'Reply', *Arena*, no. 19, 1969, at p. 99; *News-Weekly*, 9 April 1969.

19 Jack Lindsay, 'No Escape', in Shirley Cass, Ros Cheney, David Malouf & Michael Wilding (eds), *We Took Their Orders and Are Dead*, Ure Smith, Sydney, 1971, p. 140.

20 J.F. Cairns, *Silence Kills: Events Leading up to the Vietnam Moratorium on 8 May*, Vietnam Moratorium Committee, Richmond North, 1970.

21 See Tiffen, in King (ed), *Australia's Vietnam*, and Malcolm Saunders, 'The Vietnam Moratorium movement in Australia: 1969–73', PhD, Flinders University, 1977, pp. 78–88.

22 Carey, *Australian Atrocities*, p. 18 and 'The new Anzac legend', *Outlook*, February 1970, pp. 5–8. Ashbolt's leftist humanism was

another example, in 'The repressive society' (1969) and 'The socio-psychological causes of war' (1968) in Ashbolt, *Australian Experience*.

23 John Romeril, 'The fairy floss memorial', in Cass *et al* (eds), *We Took Their Orders*, p. 155.

24 Quotes from David Caute, *Sixty-Eight: The Year of the Barricades*, Hamish Hamilton, London, 1988, p. 32; see also Young, *Infantile*, chapter 9, and Freney, *Map*, p. 243.

Chapter 13

1 Quoted from AICD Committee Minutes, 20/5/1970, 'Minute Book, 1964–1970', in ML, MS4324, Box 'AICD Minutes'; and based on CICD Executive Minutes, October 22, 1969, in UMA, CICD Papers; Lloyd interview, and Saunders, 'Vietnam Moratorium', pp. 25–31.

2 See Fred Halstead, *Out Now!: A Participant's Account of the American Movement Against the Vietnam War*, New York, Monad Press, 1978, at pp. 491–521, and Charles DeBenedetti and Charles Chatfield, *An American Ordeal: The Antiwar Movement in the Vietnam Era*, Syracuse University Press, New York, 1990.

3 'Dressed': *The Age*, 17 December 1969; 'first': *Australian*, 17 December 1969; Howson, *Diaries*, p. 586 [14 December 1969] and p. 584 [30 November 1969], and Smith, 'Foreign policy', p. 112.

4 *The Age*, 17 December 1969; *Australian*, 17 December 1969 [editorial], and *News-Weekly*, 24 December 1969.

5 Based on Saunders, 'Vietnam Moratorium', pp. 26–32; CICD Committee minutes, December 3, 1969, CICD Executive, Minutes, February 3, 1970 and 'Secretary's Report, 1969/70, CICD Annual General Meeting, November 4, 1970', all in UMA, CICD Papers; Lloyd interview; VMC, 'Decisions of the NSW Sponsors' Meetings, 17/12/69 and 18/1/70' in NLA, MS3821, Box 1, folder 6; and AICD Committee Minutes, 25/3/70, 'Minute Book, 1964–1970', in ML MS4324, Box 'AICD Minutes'.

6 Saunders, 'Vietnam Moratorium', pp. 31–35.

7 ibid, p. 136. Saunders gives the more conservative estimates of the numbers involved as Melbourne 70 000, Sydney 25 000, Brisbane 5000, Adelaide 5000, Perth 3000, Hobart 2000, Newcastle 1500–2000, Wollongong 1000 and others in smaller towns such as Fremantle and Launceston. Cairns cited slightly higher figures, in *Silence Kills*, p. 9.

8 *The Age*, 9 May 1970.

9 Ian Turner, 'The Vietnam Moratorium', *Meanjin*, vol. 29, June 1970, pp. 243–244. The earlier reference to the Dylan lines was in 'The retreat from reason', *Meanjin*, June 1966.

10 *Herald*, 26 March 1970; Saunders, 'Vietnam Moratorium', p. 56.

11 CPD, House of Representatives, vol. 66, 14 April 1970, pp. 1066–1068.

12 Howson, *Diaries*, p. 631 [8 May 1970], and Snedden: CPD, House of Representatives, vol. 67, 7 May 1970, p. 1783.

13 N.E. Lauritz, *The Vietnam Moratorium*, Hawthorn Press, Melbourne, 1970.

14 Saunders, 'Vietnam Moratorium', pp. 141–143, 365–370.
15 ibid., pp. 364–365.
16 'CICD, Annual Meeting, November 4, 1970: Secretary's Report, 1969/1970', in UMA, CICD Papers; also John Lloyd, 'Restructuring the Moratorium in Victoria' [no date, but early to mid–1971], in NLA, MS4969, Box 1.
17 Geoff Anderson *et al*, 'The facts about AICD's role in the Moratorium' [no date, but mid–1970], [Moratorium series], Box 8, Folder 'Committee', and 'AICD Annual Report 1971' [Admin. series], Box 12, both in ML, MSS 4324.
18 Freudenberg, *Certain Grandeur*, p. 169, and Ormonde, *Foolish*, p. 110.
19 Ormonde, *Foolish*, p. 126; Saunders, 'Vietnam Moratorium', pp. 45–57; Whitlam: quoted in Freudenberg, *Certain Grandeur*, pp. 167–169.
20 'Broadly based': Anderson *et al*, 'The facts'; 'role of CICD': John Lloyd, 'Annual Report, September 1971', UMA, CICD Papers; 'many of those': Sam Goldbloom, 'The role of the peace movement', in *Papers of the National Anti-War Conference*, pp. 1–2.
21 Quotes from Bernie Taft, 'The debate in the anti-war movement', pp. 1–2 [no date, but early to mid–1971], [emphasis in original] in NLA, MS4969, Box 2; see also Laurie Aarons, 'Perspectives of the anti-war movement: A Communist view', in *Papers of the National Anti-War Conference*, p. 4.
22 Langer, 'Revolutionaries and the Moratorium', pp. 1–2.
23 Taft interview.
24 Langer, 'Revolutionaries and the Moratorium', p. 4; 'NSW Sponsoring Organisations for the Vietnam Moratorium Campaign; as at April 23, 1970', and 'NSW Vietnam Moratorium Action Groups (27.4.70)' both in UMA, CICD Papers; Vietnam Moratorium Campaign [NSW], Committee Minutes, 2 March 1970, in ML, MS4324, Moratorium Series, Box 8, File 'Committee'.
25 'Talks to': Saunders, 'Vietnam Moratorium', p. 122; CICD Committee Minutes, April 1 1970, and 'The Moratorium groups': John Lloyd, 'Paper for presentation to CICD Committee, June 3, 1970', both in UMA, CICD Papers.

Chapter 14

1 *The Age*, 23 April 1970.
2 'Upon arrival': 'Consolidated Vietnamese Communist Infrastructure Neutralization Report, Province Senior Adviser to Director, Phoenix Directorate, Saigon, 27 Feb 1970', R569-1-1 (2); 'can now operate': 'Correspondence—JIO—1MR's: JIO to Military Attache Saigon, 7 April 1971', Embassy File no. MA 237-5-3. Part 2, both in AWM, HS.
3 'Ineffectiveness': 'AFV Monthly Report, Aug 71', dated 15 September 1971 [ATF], R723-1-60, in AWM, HS; 'the grip': General Peter Gration, 'Speech at the launch of Frank Frost *Australia's War in Vietnam*', Australian War Memorial, Canberra, 7 July 1987.
4 'The people': 'Psyops Debriefing Report', dated 12 October 1970;

'the population': 'Psyop Debriefing Report', dated 12 August 1971, both in (1 Psy Ops Unit), R723-1-5, AWM, HS.

5 McMahon, quoted in A.C. Palfreeman, 'Foreign policy review', *Australian Quarterly*, vol. 44, no. 2, June 1972, pp. 112–121, at p. 116; reaction: 'Monthly Report, 4 Sep 71', [1 Psy Ops Unit] R723–1–1, AWM, HS.

6 Palfreeman, 'Foreign policy', p. 117; Frost, *Australia's War*, chap. 7; figures in Pemberton (ed), *Vietnam Remembered*, p. 198, except for the number of dead, which is recorded on the Vietnam National Memorial in Canberra.

7 Quoted in Frost, *Australia's War*, p. 162.

8 Saunders, 'Vietnam Moratorium', pp. 144–146.

9 'Dupes': *Tribune*, 24 June 1970; 'total waste': Langley, *Decade*, p. 122; also *Tribune*, 10 June and 1 July 1970, and Freney, *Map*, pp. 233–235.

10 R.F.I. Smith, 'Political Review', *Australian Quarterly*, vol. 42, no. 2, December 1970, pp. 111–119, at p. 112, and see also Malcolm Saunders, ' "Law and order" and the anti-Vietnam War movement: 1965–72', *Australian Journal of Politics and History*, vol. 28, no. 3, 1982, pp. 367–379.

11 Based on National Co-Ordinating Committee [VMC], Minutes October 3, 1970, in ML MSS4324, Box 8, File: 'NSW Co-Ordinating C'ee'; Smith, 'Political Review', pp. 114–116; Freney, *Map*, pp. 274–276; Ashbolt, *Australian Experience*, pp. 201–205, and Langley, *Decade*, pp. 163–164.

12 Quoted from AICD Committee Minutes, 19 April 1971, in Box: 'AICD Minutes', 'Minute Book, from 1st July, 1970—'; also 7 October 1970, in Moratorium series, Box 8, File: 'Committee', and both in ML, MSS4324; also Saunders, 'Vietnam Moratorium', p. 370.

13 'To keep': Joint motion by the Radical Action Movement and Draft Resisters' Union, VMC [Vic], Agenda, Public Meeting, 5 September 1971; 'virtually non-existent': VMC Executive [Vic], 'Moratorium Perspectives', 25 January 1972; see also VMC General Committee, Minutes, 27 September 1971, all three in UMA, CICD Papers, and Saunders, 'Vietnam Moratorium', chapter 9.

14 Robert Howard, 'Foreign Policy Review: January–June, 1970', *Australian Quarterly*, vol. 42, no. 3, September 1970, pp. 109–116, at pp. 109–110.

15 W. Macmahon Ball, 'Australia's role in Asia', 18th Roy Milne Lecture, Melbourne, 1967, p. 3, and Freudenberg, *Certain Grandeur*, p. 200.

16 Bob Howard, 'Foreign policy review: July–December, 1970', *Australian Quarterly*, vol. 43, no. 1, March 1971, pp. 115–121, at p. 121, and *The Age*, 2 June 1971.

17 *The Age*, 'amplified': 3 July, and Gair: 12 July 1971.

18 *Australian*, 13 July 1971.

19 'Tragic and dangerous': Robert Duffield, 'The China debate: back to the 1950s', *Australian*, 14 July 1971; 'China has always': quoted in Bob Howard, 'Foreign policy review: January–June, 1971', *Australian Quarterly*, vol. 43, no. 3, September 1971, pp. 97–108, at p. 103; 'at last': *The Age*, 17 July 1971.

20   Howson, *Diaries*, p. 751 [20 July 1971] and Freudenberg, *Certain Grandeur*, p. 211.
21   *Australian*, 17 July 1971 [editorial].

Conclusion

1   For example, the ABC Television documentary 'Hindsight: Power to the people', 6 May 1990, gave this impression, as well as suggesting that the Moratorium was fundamentally the expression of student radicalism.
2   See Brown, 'Possess the time', p. 19, and Gerster, 'Occidental tourists', pp. 209–211. Each is drawing on Edward Said, *Orientalism*, Pantheon, New York, 1978.
3   Neil Mathews, 'The obscure and the everyday', in Maddock (ed), *Memories*, pp. 117–150, at pp. 135, 139. See also J. Spriggs, 'Vietnam: So what?', in John J. Coe (ed), *Desperate Praise: The Australians in Vietnam*, Artlook Books, Perth, 1982, pp. 37–40, on the same theme.

Bibliography
and sources

1 Archival sources

Two main deposits of official records were used for the research on this book: government documents of the Commonwealth Cabinet and various departments, held in the Australian Archives, and army records of the Vietnam war, held in the Australian War Memorial.

Australian Archives, Canberra [AA]

The official records are covered by the rule which normally makes them unavailable for 30 years after they were created. This means that all the government documents on the Vietnam commitment will not be available to the public until 2002. The documents consulted for this history were concentrated in the 1950s; the most fruitful of the series used were those of Cabinet submissions, decisions and minutes from 1951 to 1960, and the files of the departments of External Affairs, Defence and the Prime Minister.

Australian War Memorial, Canberra [AWM]

The War Memorial holds a series of documents entitled the Herbicide Series (AWM—181), which were released for public access in 1982 as a result of the controversy over Agent Orange. The series is a fragment (some 30 metres on the shelves) of the defence force records created in Vietnam. The documents released all make some reference to herbicides or chemical spraying, but are also an invaluable resource for other aspects of the Australian intervention. In addition to these official records, the AWM holds donated and private records, including soldiers' letters and diaries, photographs and captured NLF documents.

National Library of Australia, Canberra [ANL]

The National Library holds a number of collections which were useful for this research. Those which proved most fruitful were the papers of W. Macmahon Ball (MS 7851), Percy Spender (MS 4875), Ian Turner (MS 6206) and the NSW branch of Save Our Sons (MS 3821). Useful on the radical left and student movement were the papers of Jill Jolliffe (MS 4969); in addition, I consulted the speeches in the voluminous collection of R.G. Menzies (MS 4936). Finally, the ANL also holds a large collection of oral history interviews, especially with prominent politicians and bureaucrats of this period; the most useful were interviews with Sir Alan Watt, Sir Paul Hasluck, Wilfred Burchett and Sir Percy Spender.

Some of the most comprehensive sources for the study of the peace and student movements—in addition to the collections of Turner, SOS and Jolliffe above—are the large collections of AICD and CICD.

Mitchell Library, State Library of NSW, Sydney [ML]

The Mitchell Library holds the papers of AICD (Association for International Co-operation and Disarmament) (ML MSS 4324 & 1808/79), which were particularly useful for the NSW Moratorium movement. It is a very large collection which was being relisted when consulted in 1990; series and box titles are identified as found at that time.

University of Melbourne Archives, Melbourne [UMA]

The papers of AICD's Melbourne equivalent CICD (Congress for International Co-operation and Disarmament) (LS 7/3/13) are deposited in the University of Melbourne Archives, and cover 1959 to 1976. When consulted in 1990, this collection had not yet been sorted, and was held in unnumbered boxes. The archives also hold the papers of CICD's forerunner, the Victorian Peace Council, (LS 7/3/5) a useful collection for the peace movement in the 1950s.

In addition to these very rich institutional collections, the archives have the papers of the three 'peace parsons', Alf Dickie, Frank Hartley and Victor James, which—due to those men's ubiquitous involvement in the peace movement since the late 1940s—provide an invaluable cross-section of the movement. Finally, the archives also hold a number of oral history interviews of relevance, in particular with Stephen Murray-Smith, Sam Goldbloom and John A. Lloyd.

2 Published sources

A number of published collections of French, American and Australian official or quasi-official documents are available on the colonial period and the war. The most important are:

Australian Military Forces, *Pocketbook: South Vietnam*, Canberra, 1967.

Commonwealth of Australia, *Parliamentary Debates* (Hansard), (Senate and House of Representatives), 1950–1971.

——*Viet Nam since the 1954 Geneva Agreements*, Select Documents on International Affairs, no. 1 of 1964, Department of External Affairs, Canberra, 1964.

——*Viet Nam: Recent Statements of Australian Policy*, Minister for External Affairs, Canberra, 1965.

——*Viet Nam: June 1965 to February 1966*, Select Documents on International Affairs, no. 7, Department of External Affairs, Canberra, 1966.

——*Viet Nam: Questions and Answers*, Department of External Affairs, Canberra, 1966.

——*Vietnam, Australia and Asia*, Department of External Affairs, Canberra, 1967.

——*Australia's Military Commitment to Vietnam* [*AMCV*], Paper tabled in accordance with the Prime Minister's statement to the House of Representatives, 13 May 1975. Department of Foreign Affairs [prepared by Prof. Neale, tabled 19 August 1975].

Gouvernement Général de l'Indochine, *Contribution à l'histoire des mouvements politiques de l'Indochine française*, Direction des Affaires Politiques et de la Sûreté Générale, Hanoi, 1933. 6 volumes.

Pike, Douglas (compiler), *Documents on the National Liberation Front of South Vietnam*, Massachusetts Institute of Technology, Centre for International Studies, Cambridge, 1967 (11 microfilm reels).

Kesaris, P. (ed), *CIA Research Reports: Vietnam and Southeast Asia, 1946–1976*, University Publishers of America, Frederick, 1983.

——*The War in Vietnam: Classified Histories by the National Security Council*, University Microfilms of America, Frederick [nd].

The Pentagon Papers: The Defense Department History of United States Decisionmaking on Vietnam, Senator Gravel Edition (5 volumes), Beacon Press, Boston, 1971.

Porter, Gareth (ed), *Vietnam: A History in Documents*, Meridian, New York, 1981.

Race, Jeffrey (ed), *Vietnamese Materials*, Chicago, Department of Photoduplication, University of Chicago Library, 1969 (3 microfilm reels).

3 Personal interviews granted to author

Brian Aarons	Sydney 10 December 1991
Wilfred Burchett	Paris 2 July 1982
Jim Cairns	Melbourne 23 September 1991
Bill Gollan	Sydney 25 August 1990
Robin Gollan	Canberra 9 January 1987
Sir John Gorton	Canberra 21 October 1991
Clem Lloyd	Wollongong 9 December 1991

Nguyen Van	Commander of Provincial NLF forces, Long Hai, 23 February 1988
Phan Ngoc Danh	historian, Bien Hoa, 22 February 1988
B.A. Santamaria	Melbourne 27 September 1991
Bernie Taft	Melbourne 30 September 1991
General Tran Cong Man	Editor *Quan Doi Nhan Dan* Hanoi, 4 & 5 February 1988

4 Newspapers and journals

The Age (Melbourne) 1950–1971
Australian Quarterly (Sydney) 1966–1972
Australian (Sydney-Melbourne) 1964–1971
Australian Left Review (Sydney) 1966–1971
Communist Review (Sydney) 1956–1958
Herald (Melbourne) parts only
Nation (Sydney) 1958–1966
News-Weekly (Melbourne) 1954–1970
Outlook [ed. Helen Palmer] (Sydney) 1957–1964
Sydney Morning Herald (Sydney) parts only
Things I Hear (Sydney) 1954–1966
Tribune (Sydney) 1954–1971

5 Unpublished theses

Some very good postgraduate work in Australia on the Vietnam involvement has remained unpublished. Two theses were particularly important for this book: Kim C. Beazley's 'Post-Evatt Australian Labor Party attitudes to the United States alliance: an analysis of the effects of selected Australian foreign policy and defence issues on the evolution of Australian Labor Party attitudes to the United States alliance, 1961–1972' (MA, University of Western Australia, 1974) is a well-informed analysis of ALP debates, including on Vietnam. And the best study on the Moratorium movement in all states is M. J. Saunders, 'The Vietnam Moratorium movement in Australia: 1969–73' (PhD, Flinders University, 1977).

Other unpublished theses consulted were Nicholas Brown, ' "Possess the time": The formation and character of Australian intellectual conservatism in the 1950s' (PhD, ANU, 1990), a stimulating analysis of intellectuals, though not of policy makers; Terry Burstall, 'Australian involvement in Vietnam: The credibility gap, rhetoric and reality, 1962–1972' (PhD, Griffith, 1991), a veteran's account of the gap between government statements and what soldiers were experiencing; Hal Colebatch, 'An examination of the sources, ideologies and political importance of peace movements in Australia from approximately 1950 to approximately 1965' (MA, University of Western Australia, 1974), which is detailed, though marked by a concern to hunt down and expose communists. Rosemary Francis, 'Women in protest movements: The Women's Peace Army and the Save Our Sons movement' (MA Prelim, University of Melbourne, History, 1984) has some useful insights on SOS in Melbourne, while Michael Hamel-Green's 'The legitimacy of the 1964–1972 Australian conscription scheme' (MA, University of

Melbourne, Political Science, 1976) is a solid account of the movement against conscription. Val Noone, 'Melbourne Catholics and the Vietnam War: A participant's study of peace work in a pro-war church' (PhD, LaTrobe University, Religious Studies, 1991) is the most detailed account available of debates inside the Catholic church, while Ralph Summy's '[The] Australian peace movement, 1960–67: A study in dissent' (MA, University of Sydney, 1971) remains the best study of the thinking of the peace movement in the early 1960s.

6 General: Works on Vietnamese history, colonialism and the Vietnam War

Books

Anderson, Benedict, *Imagined Communities: Reflections on the Origin and Spread of Nationalism*, Verso, London, 1983.

Aubaret, G., *Histoire et description de la Basse Cochinchine*, Imprimerie Impériale, Paris, 1863.

Ban Chap Hanh Dang Bo Dang Cong San Viet Nam Tinh Dong Nai, [Executive Board of the Party Branch of the Vietnamese Communist Party in Dong Nai Province], *Dong Nai: 30 Nam Chien Tranh Giai Phong 1945–1975)* [Dong Nai: 30 Years of the War of Liberation], Nha Xuat Ban Dong Nai, [Bien Hoa], 1986.

Bevan, Aneurin, *In Place of Fear*, Heinemann, London, 1952.

Braunthal, Julius, *History of the International: World Socialism, 1943–1968* [vol. 3], Gollancz, London, 1980.

Braestrup, Peter, *Big Story: How the American Press and Television Reported and Interpreted the Crisis of Tet 1968 in Vietnam and Washington*, Anchor, New York, 1979.

Burchett, Wilfred, *The Furtive War: The United States in Vietnam and Laos*, International Publishers, New York, 1963.

——*Vietnam: Inside Story of the Guerilla War*, International Publishers, New York, 1965.

——*Vietnam Will Win*, Monthly Review Press, New York, 1968.

——*Passport: An Autobiography*, Nelson, Melbourne, 1969.

——*Grasshoppers and Elephants: Why Viet Nam Fell*, Outback Press, Collingwood, 1977.

——*At the Barricades*, Macmillan, Melbourne, 1981.

Buttinger, Joseph, *Vietnam: A Political History*, Andre Deutsch, London, 1969.

Callis, Helmut, *Foreign Capital in Southeast Asia*, AMS Press, New York, 1978. (First published 1942.)

Caute, David, *Sixty-Eight: The Year of the Barricades*, Hamish Hamilton, London, 1988.

Chatterjee, Partha, *Nationalist Thought and the Colonial World: A Derivative Discourse*, Zed Books, London, 1986.

Chesneaux, Jean, *Contribution à l'histoire de la nation vietnamienne*, Editions Sociales, Paris, 1955.

Cortambert, E. & de Rosny, L., *Tableau de la Cochinchine: rédigé sous les auspices de la Société d'Ethnographie*, Armand le Chevalier, Paris, 1862.

Coulet, Georges, *Les sociétés secrètes en terre d'Annam*, Imprimerie Commerciale, C. Ardin, Saigon, 1926.

Dacy, Douglas, *Foreign Aid, War and Economic Development: South Vietnam, 1955–1975*, Cambridge University Press, Cambridge, 1986.

DeBenedetti, Charles, *An American Ordeal: The Antiwar Movement of the Vietnam Era*, Syracuse University Press, New York, 1990.

Devillers, Philippe, *Histoire du Viet-Nam de 1940 à 1952*, Editions du Seuil, Paris, 1952.

Devillers, Philippe & Lacouture, Jean, *End of a War: Indochina 1954*, Pall Mall, London, 1969.

Dunn, Peter M., *The First Vietnam War*, Hurst & Co, London, 1985.

Ennis, Thomas E., *French Policy and Development in Indochina*, University of Chicago Press, Chicago, 1936.

Evans, Grant & Rowley, Kelvin, *Red Brotherhood at War: Indochina since the Fall of Saigon*, Verso, London, 1984.

Fall, Bernard, *The Two Vietnams: A Political and Military Analysis*, Praeger, New York, 1963.

——*Street Without Joy*, Schocken, New York, 1972.

Gellner, Ernest, *Nations and Nationalism*, Blackwell, London, 1983.

Giap, Vo Nguyen, *People's War, People's Army*, Foreign Languages Publishing House, Hanoi, 1961.

Gourou, Pierre, *L'Utilisation du sol en Indochine française*, Centre d'Etudes de Politique Etrangère, Paris, 1939.

Guides Madrolle, *Indochine du Sud. De Marseille à Saigon*, Librairie Hachette, Paris, 1928.

Halstead, Fred, *Out Now!: A Participant's Account of the American Movement Against the Vietnam War*, Monad Press, New York, 1978.

Hammer, Ellen, *The Struggle for Indochina*, Stanford University Press, Stanford, 1954.

——*A Death in November: America in Vietnam, 1963*, Dutton, New York, 1987.

Hémery, Daniel, *Révolutionnaires vietnamiens et pouvoir colonial en Indochine: Communistes, trotskystes, nationalistes à Saigon de 1932 à 1937*, François Maspero, Paris, 1975.

Hickey, Gerald, *Village in Vietnam*, Yale University Press, New Haven, 1964.

Ho Chi Minh, *On Revolution: Selected Writings, 1920–66*, Bernard Fall, ed, Pall Mall, London, 1967.

Hunt, David, *Villagers at War: the National Liberation Front in My Tho, 1965–1967*, Special Issue of *Radical America*, vol. 8, no. 1–2, January–April 1974.

Huynh Kim Khanh, *Vietnamese Communism: 1925–1945*, Cornell University Press, Ithaca, 1982.

International Labour Office, *Labour Conditions in Indo-China*, ILO, Geneva, 1938.

Jumper, Roy & Nguyen Thi Hue, *Notes on the Political and Administrative History of Viet Nam, 1802–1962*, Viet Nam Advisory Group, Michigan State University, 1962.

Kahin, George McT., *Intervention: How America Became Involved in Vietnam*, Knopf, New York, 1986.

Kiernan, Ben (ed), *Burchett: Reporting the Other Side of the World 1939–1983*, Quartet Books, London, 1986.

Kiernan, Victor, *From Conquest to Collapse: European Empires from 1815 to 1960*, Pantheon, New York, 1982.

Kolko, Gabriel, *Vietnam: Anatomy of a War, 1940–1975*, Allen & Unwin, London, 1986.

Lacouture, Jean, *Vietnam: Between Two Truces*, Secker & Warburg, London, 1966.

Le Thanh Khoi, *Le Viet-Nam: Histoire et civilisation*, Les Editions de Minuit, Paris, 1955.

Le Thanh Tuong, *Monographie de la province de Ba Ria*, Publiée par Le Thanh Tuong—Chef de la Province [1950].

Lockhart, Greg, *Nation in Arms: The Origins of the People's Army of Vietnam*, Allen & Unwin, Sydney, 1989.

Loubet, J. & Taboulet, G., *L'Indochine Francaise*, Librairie Hachette, Paris, 1931.

Maclear, Michael, *Vietnam: The Ten Thousand Day War*, Methuen, London, 1981.

Marr, David G., *Vietnamese Anti-colonialism, 1885–1925*, University of California Press, Berkeley, 1971.

——*Vietnamese Tradition on Trial, 1920–1945*, University of California Press, Berkeley, 1981.

McAlister, John T., *Viet Nam: the Origins of Revolution*, Knopf, New York, 1970.

McCoy, Alfred (ed), *Southeast Asia under Japanese Occupation*, Yale Southeast Asia Council, New Haven, 1980.

McVey, Ruth (ed), *Southeast Asian Transitions: Approaches Through Social History*, Yale University Press, New Haven, 1978.

Miller, Arthur, *Timebends: A Life*, Methuen, London, 1987.

de Montaigut, Fernand, *La colonisation française dans l'Est de la Cochinchine*, Imprimerie de Perette, Limoges, 1929.

Murray, Martin, *The Development of Capitalism in Colonial Indochina, 1870–1940*, University of California Press, Berkeley, 1980.

Murti, B.S.W., *Vietnam Divided: The Unfinished Struggle*, Asia Publishing House, London, 1964.

Ngo Vinh Long, *Before the Revolution: The Vietnamese Peasants under the French*, MIT Press, Cambridge, 1973.

Nguyen Khac Vien, *Tradition and Revolution in Vietnam*, Indochina Resource Centre, Berkeley, 1974.

Nores, Georges, *Itinéraires automobiles en Indochine: Guide du Touriste, II. Cochinchine, Cambodge*, Imprimerie d'Extrême-Orient, Hanoi, 1930.

O'Ballance, Edgar, *The Indo-China War, 1945–54: A Study in Guerilla Warfare*, Faber, London, 1964.

O'Neill, Robert J., *General Giap: Politician and Strategist*, Cassell, Melbourne, 1969.

Osborne, Milton, *Strategic Hamlets in South Viet-Nam: A Survey and Comparison*, Data Paper No. 55, Southeast Asia Program, Cornell University, Ithaca, 1965.

——*The French Presence in Cochinchina and Cambodia: Rule and Response (1859–1905)*, Cornell University Press, Ithaca & London, 1969.

Pasquier, Pierre, *L'Annam d'autrefois: Essai sur le constitution de l'Annam avant l'intervention française*, Société d'Editions Géographiques, Maritimes et Coloniales, Paris, 1929.

Pham Cao Duong, *Vietnamese Peasants under French Domination: 1861– 1945*, University Press of America, Lanham, 1985.

Phan Ngoc Danh & Tran Quang Toai, *Lich Su Dau Tranh Cach Mang cua Huyen Long Dat*, [History of the Revolutionary Struggle in Long Dat District], Nha Xuat Ban Dong Nai [Bien Hoa], 1986.

Pike, Douglas, *Viet Cong: The Organisation and Techniques of the National Liberation Front of South Vietnam*, Massachusetts Institute of Technology, Cambridge, 1966.

Popkin, Samuel, *The Rational Peasant: The Political Economy of Rural Society in Vietnam*, University of California Press, Berkeley, 1979.

Race, Jeffrey, *War Comes to Long An: Revolutionary Conflict in a Vietnamese Province*, University of California Press, Berkeley, 1972.

Robequain, Charles, *The Economic Development of French Indo-China*, Oxford University Press, London, 1944.

Rosie, George, *The British in Vietnam: How the Twenty-five Year War Began*, Panther, London, 1970.

Rousset, Pierre, *Communisme et nationalisme vietnamien: le Vietnam entre les deux guerres mondiales*, Editions Galilée, Paris, 1978.

Scigliano, Robert, *South Vietnam: Nation under stress*, Houghton Mifflin, Boston, 1964.

Schriener, A., *Les institutions annamites en Basse Cochinchine avant la conquête française*, Claude & Cie, Saigon, vol 1: 1900, vol. 2: 1901.

Scott, James C., *The Moral Economy of the Peasant: Rebellion and Subversion in Southeast Asia*, Yale University Press, New Haven, 1976.

Shaplen, Robert, *The Lost Revolution: Vietnam, 1945–65*, Andre Deutsch, London, 1966.

Smith, R.B., *An International History of the Vietnam War*, Macmillan, London, vol. 1: 1983, vol. 2: 1985.

Société des Etudes Indo-Chinoises, *Geographie physique, economique et historique de la Cochinchine: V^e fascicule. Monographie de la province de Ba-Ria et de la Ville du Cap Saint-Jacques*, Imprimerie L. Ménard, Saigon, 1902.

Société des Etudes Indochinoises, *La Cochinchine*, P. Gastaldy, Saigon, 1931.

Stanford Research Institute, *Land Reform in Vietnam: Prepared for the Republic of Vietnam and the United States Agency for International Development*, Stanford, Menlo Park, 1968.

Thayer, Carlyle, *War by Other Means: National Liberation and Revolution in Viet-Nam, 1954–60*, Allen & Unwin, Sydney, 1989.

Thomazi, Auguste, *La Conquête de l'Indochine*, Payot, Paris, 1934.

Thompson, Virginia, *French Indo-China*, Octagon, New York, 1968.

Truong Nhu Tang, *Journal of a Vietcong*, Jonathan Cape, London, 1986.

Tuchman, Barbara, *The March of Folly: From Troy to Vietnam*, Abacus, London, 1985.

United States, Dept. of State, *Aggression from the North: The Record of North Viet-Nam's Campaign to Conquer South Viet-Nam*, Department of State, Washington, 1965.

——*A Threat to the Peace: North Viet-Nam's Effort to Conquer South Viet-Nam*, Department of State, Washington, 1961.

Vial, Paulin, *Les premières années de la Cochinchine, colonie française,* Challamel Aimé, Paris, 1874.

Viet-Nam, République du, *Recensemente pilote de la province de Phuoc-Tuy,* Institut National de la Statistique, Saigon [1960].

Viet-Nam, Republic of, *Report on the Agricultural Census of Viet-Nam, 1960–1961,* Department of Rural Affairs, Cholon, 1962.

Viet-Nam, Cong-Hoa, *Dan-So Viet-Nam: Theo Don-Vi Hanh-Chanh Trong Nam 1965,* [Population of Vietnam; according to administrative units in 1965], Vien Quoc-Gia Thong-Ke [National Institute of Statistics], [Saigon], [nd. 1965].

Warner, Denis, *The Last Confucian: Vietnam, South-East Asia and the West,* Angus & Robertson, Sydney, 1964.

——*Not With Guns Alone,* Hutchinson, Richmond, 1977.

Weinstein, Franklin, *Vietnam's Unheld Elections,* Cornell University Data Papers, no. 60, New York, 1966.

White, John, *A Voyage to Cochin China,* Oxford University Press, London, 1972.

Whitfield, Stephen, *The Culture of the Cold War,* Johns Hopkins University Press, Baltimore, 1991.

Woodside, Alexander, *Community and Revolution in Modern Vietnam,* Houghton Mifflin, Boston, 1976.

Young, Nigel, *An Infantile Disorder?: The Crisis and Decline of the New Left,* Routledge & Kegan Paul, London, 1977.

Zasloff, J.J., *Origins of the Insurgency in South Vietnam: 1954–1960. The role of the southern Vietminh cadres,* Rand Corporation, Santa Monica, 1967.

Articles & chapters

Bertrand, Trent J., 'An evaluation of U.S. economic aid to Vietnam, 1955–59', *France Asie/Asia,* vol. 21, no. 188, 1966–67, pp. 207–228.

Brocheux, Pierre, 'Le prolétariat des plantations d'hévéas au Vietnam Méridional: Aspects sociaux et politiques (1927–1937)', *Le mouvement sociale,* Janvier–Mars 1975, no. 90, pp. 55–86.

——'Moral economy or political economy?: The peasants are always rational', *Journal of Asian Studies,* vol. 42, no. 4, August 1983, pp. 791–803.

Cadière, Leopold, 'La famille et la religion au Viêt-Nam', *France-Asie,* vol. 15, no. 145, 1958, pp. 260–271.

Chesneaux, Jean, 'Stages in the development of the Vietnam national movement 1862–1940', *Past and Present,* Issue 7, 1955, pp. 63–75.

Cotter, Michael G., 'Towards a social history of the Vietnamese southward movement', *Journal of Southeast Asian History,* vol. 9, no. 1, March 1968, pp. 12–24.

Donnell, John C., 'National renovation campaigns in Vietnam', *Pacific Affairs,* vol. 32, no. 1, April 1959, pp. 73–88.

Dorsey, John T., 'The bureaucracy and political development in Viet Nam', in Joseph La Palombara (ed), *Bureaucracy and Political Development,* Princeton University Press, New Jersey, 1967.

Fall, Bernard, 'The political-religious sects of Viet-Nam', *Pacific Affairs,* vol. 28, Issue 3, Sept. 1955, pp. 235–253.

Girard, M., 'Le labourage des plantations', *Bulletin Economique de l'Indochine*, no. 103, Juil.–Août, 1913, pp. 762–765.

——'L'Hévéa en Cochinchine', *Bulletin Economique de l'Indochine*, no. 106, 1914, pp. 46–53.

Homberg, Octave, 'Rubber in Indo-China', *The Asiatic Review* (London), July 1936, vol. 32, pp. 583–588.

Hunt, David, 'From the millennial to the everyday: James Scott's search for the essence of peasant politics', *Radical History Review*, no. 42, 1988, pp. 155–172.

——'Peasant routes in France and Vietnam', paper to the American Historical Association Convention, December 1989.

Le Van Hoang & Truong Nhu Hien, 'La stratification et la mobilité sociale au Viet-Nam', *East Asian Cultural Studies*, vol. 4, March 1965, pp. 205–226.

Mai-Tho-Truyen, 'Le Bouddhisme au Viet-Nam', *France-Asie*, vol. 16, 1958–59.

McCoy, Alfred W., 'U.S. foreign policy and the tenant farmers of Asia', *France Asie/Asia*, vol. 24, no. 200, 1970, pp. 41–77.

Mus, Paul, 'The role of the village in Vietnamese politics', *Pacific Affairs*, no. 22, 1949, pp. 265–272.

Nguyen T., 'Les catholiques vietnamiens et les perspectives de paix au Vietnam', *France Asie/Asia*, vol. 20, no. 193, 1968, pp. 221–232.

Smith, William A., 'The strategic hamlet program in Vietnam', *Military Review*, vol. 44, no. 5, May, 1964, pp. 17–23.

7 *Australian works on politics, foreign policy and the Vietnam intervention*

Books

Albinski, Henry S., *Politics and Foreign Policy in Australia: The Impact of Vietnam and Conscription*, Duke University Press, Durham, 1970.

Alexander, David, *When the Buffalo Fight*, Hutchinson, Richmond, 1980.

Ashbolt, Allan, *An Australian Experience: Words from the Vietnam Years*, Australasian Book Society, Sydney, 1974.

Australian Broadcasting Commission, *Vietnam: A Reporter's War*, ABC, Sydney, 1975.

Australian Council of Churches, *Vietnam*, ACC, Sydney, 1966.

——*Conscientious Objection to Military Service: Report of a Special Committee of the Australian Council of Churches*, ACC, Sydney, 1968.

Ayres, Philip, *Malcolm Fraser: A Biography*, Heinemann, Richmond, 1987.

Ball, W. Macmahon, *Nationalism and Communism in East Asia*, Melbourne University Press, Melbourne, 1952.

——*Australia's Role in Asia*, 18th Roy Milne Memorial Lecture, Australian Institute of International Affairs, Melbourne [1967].

Barcan, Alan, *The Socialist Left in Australia, 1949–1959*, Australian Political Studies Association, Occasional Monograph, no. 2, Sydney, 1960.

Barclay, Glen St J., *A Very Small Insurance Policy: The Politics of Australian Involvement in Vietnam, 1954–1967*, University of Queensland Press, St Lucia, 1988.

Burgess, Pat, *Warco: Australian Reporters at War*, Heinemann, Richmond, 1986.

Burstall, Terry, *The Soldiers' Story: The Battle of Xa Long Tan Vietnam, 18 August 1966*, University of Queensland Press, St Lucia, 1986.

——*A Soldier Returns: A Long Tan Veteran Discovers the Other Side of Vietnam*, University of Queensland Press, St Lucia, 1990.

Burton, John, *The Alternative: A Dynamic Approach to our Relations with Asia*, Morgans Publications, Sydney, 1954.

Cairns, J.F., *Living With Asia*, Lansdowne Press, Melbourne, 1965.

——*Silence Kills: Events Leading up to the Vietnam Moratorium on 8 May*, Vietnam Moratorium Committee, Richmond North, 1970.

——*The Eagle and the Lotus: Western Intervention in Vietnam, 1847–1971*, Lansdowne Press, Melbourne, 2nd ed., 1971.

Calwell, A.A., *Be Just and Fear Not*, Lloyd O'Neil, Hawthorn, 1972.

Carroll, John, *Token Soldiers*, Wildgrass Books, Boronia, 1983.

Cass, Shirley; Cheney, Ros; Malouf, David & Wilding, Michael (eds), *We Took Their Orders and Are Dead: An Anti-War Anthology*, Ure Smith, North Sydney, 1971.

Clark, Gregory, *In Fear of China*, Lansdowne Press, Melbourne, 1967.

Coe, John J., (ed), *Desperate Praise: The Australians in Vietnam*, Artlook Books, Perth, 1982.

Connell, R.W., *The Child's Construction of Politics*, Melbourne University Press, Carlton, 1971.

Curthoys, Ann & Merritt, John (eds), *Australia's First Cold War, 1945–1953: Vol. 1: Society, Communism and Culture*, Allen & Unwin, Sydney, 1984.

——*Better Dead than Red: Australia's First Cold War: 1945–1959*, vol. 2. Allen & Unwin, Sydney, 1986.

Dalziel, Allan, *Evatt the Enigma*, Lansdowne Press, Melbourne, 1967.

Daly, Fred, *From Curtin to Kerr*, Sun Books, Melbourne, 1977.

Davidson, Alastair, *The Communist Party of Australia: A Short History*, Hoover Institution Press, Stanford, 1969.

Edwards, Peter, with Pemberton, Gregory, *Crises and Commitments: The Politics and Diplomacy of Australia's Involvement in Southeast Asian Conflicts, 1948–1965*, Allen & Unwin, Sydney, 1992.

Eggleston, F.W., *Reflections on Australian Foreign Policy*, Cheshire, Melbourne, 1957.

Fairbairn, Geoffrey, *Revolutionary Warfare and Communist Strategy: The Threat to South-East Asia*, Faber, London, 1968.

Findlay, P.T., *Protest Politics and Psychological Warfare: The Communist Role in the Anti-Vietnam War and Anti-Conscription Movement in Australia*, Hawthorn Press, Melbourne, 1968.

Forward, Roy & Reece, Bob (eds), *Conscription in Australia*, University of Queensland Press, St Lucia, 1968.

Frazer, Michael, *Nasho*, Aries Imprint, West Melbourne, 1984.

Freney, Denis, *A Map of Days: Life on the Left*, Heinemann, Melbourne, 1991.

Freudenberg, Graham, *A Certain Grandeur: Gough Whitlam in Politics*, Penguin, Ringwood, 1987.

Frost, Frank, *Australia's War in Vietnam*, Allen & Unwin, Sydney, 1987.

Frydman, Gloria, *Protesters*, Collins Dove, Blackburn, 1987.

Gollan, Bill, *Bond or Free: The Peace and Disarmament Movement and an Independent Australian Foreign Policy for Peace and Security*, NSW Teachers Federation [Sydney], 1987.

Gollan, Robin, *Revolutionaries and Reformists: Communism and the Australian Labour Movement, 1920–1950*, Allen & Unwin, Sydney, 1975.

Gordon, Richard (ed), *The Australian New Left: Critical Essays and Strategy*, Heinemann, Melbourne, 1970.

Grant, Bruce, *The Crisis of Loyalty: A Study of Australian Foreign Policy*, Angus & Robertson, in association with the Australian Institute of International Affairs, Sydney, 1972.

Greenwood, G. & Harper, N. (eds), *Australia in World Affairs, 1950–55*, Cheshire, Melbourne, 1957.

——*Australia in World Affairs, 1956–60*, Cheshire, Melbourne, 1963.

——*Australia in World Affairs, 1961–1965*, Cheshire, Melbourne, 1968

Grey, J. & Doyle, J. (eds), *Vietnam: War, Myth and Memory*, Allen & Unwin, Sydney, 1992.

Hartley, Marion, *The Truth Shall Prevail: The Rev. Cr Francis John Hartley, B.A., B.D.*, Spectrum Publications, Melbourne, 1982.

Hasluck, Paul *Diplomatic Witness: Australian Foreign Affairs, 1941–1947*, Melbourne University Press, Melbourne, 1980.

Haylen, Leslie, *Twenty Years' Hard Labor*, Macmillan, Melbourne, 1969.

Henderson, Gerard, *The Vietnam Moratorium: An Interpretation Based on Left-Wing Sources* [no publisher], Melbourne, 1970.

Howson, Peter, *The Howson Diaries: The Life of Politics*, Don Aitkin, ed., Viking, Ringwood, 1984.

Hudson, W.J., *Casey*, Oxford University Press, Melbourne, 1986.

James, Victor, *Windows on the Years* [self-published], [nd].

Kane, Jack, *Exploding the Myths: The Political Memoirs of Jack Kane*, Angus & Robertson, Sydney, 1989.

Kiernan, Colm, *Calwell: A Personal and Political Biography*, Nelson, Melbourne, 1978.

Killen, D.J., *Killen: Inside Australian Politics*, Methuen Haynes, Sydney, 1985.

King, Peter (ed), *Australia's Vietnam*, Allen & Unwin, Sydney, 1983.

Langley, Greg, *A Decade of Dissent: Vietnam and the Conflict on the Australian Home Front*, Allen & Unwin, Sydney, 1992.

Lauritz, N.E., *The Vietnam Moratorium*, Hawthorn Press, Melbourne, 1970.

Lunn, Hugh, *Vietnam: A Reporter's War*, University of Queensland Press, 1985.

Mackay, Ian, *Australians in Vietnam*, Rigby, Sydney, 1968.

Maddock, Kenneth (ed), *Memories of Vietnam*, Random House, Sydney, 1991.

Maddock, Kenneth & Wright, Barry (eds), *War: Australia and Vietnam*, Harper & Row, Sydney, 1987.

Main, J.M. (ed), *Conscription: The Australian Debate, 1901–1970*, Cassell, Melbourne, 1970.

Marr, David, *Barwick*, Allen & Unwin, Sydney, 1980.

May, R.J. & O'Malley, W.J. (eds), *Observing Change in Asia: Essays in Honour of J.A.C. Mackie*, Crawford House, Bathurst, 1989.

Menzies, R.G., *The Measure of the Years*, Cassell, Melbourne, 1970.

McAulay, Lex, *The Battle of Long Tan: The Legend of ANZAC Upheld*, Hutchinson, Melbourne, 1986.

McCormack, Gavan, *Cold War, Hot War: An Australian Perspective on the Korean War*, Hale & Iremonger, Sydney, 1983.

McCulloch, Jock, *The Politics of Agent Orange: The Australian Experience*, Heinemann, Melbourne, 1984.

McEwen, Keith, *Once a Jolly Comrade*, Jacaranda, Brisbane, 1966.

McGregor, Craig, *People, Politics and Pop: Australians in the Sixties*, Ure Smith, Sydney, 1968.

McKay, Gary, *In Good Company: One Man's War in Vietnam*, Allen & Unwin, Sydney, 1987.

——*Vietnam Fragments: An oral history of Australians at war*, Allen & Unwin, Sydney, 1992.

McMullin, Ross, *The Light on the Hill: The Australian Labor Party, 1891–1991*, Oxford University Press, Melbourne, 1991.

McNeill, Ian, *The Team: Australian Army Advisers in Vietnam, 1962–1972*, Australian War Memorial, Canberra, 1984.

Millar, T.B., *Australia's Foreign Policy*, Angus & Robertson, Sydney, 1968.

——(ed), *Australian Foreign Minister: The Diaries of R.G. Casey*, Collins, London, 1972.

Munster, George, *A Paper Prince*, Penguin, Ringwood, 1987.

Murray, Robert *The Split: Australian Labor in the Fifties*, Cheshire, Melbourne, 1972.

Nagle, William, *The Odd Angry Shot*, Angus & Robertson, Sydney, 1975.

Oakes, Laurie, *Whitlam PM: a Biography*, Angus & Robertson, Sydney, 1973.

O'Neill, R.J., *Vietnam Task*, Cassell, Melbourne, 1967.

——*Australia in the Korean War, 1950–53* (2 vols), Australian War Memorial and AGPS, Canberra, 1981.

Ormonde, Paul, *The Movement*, Nelson, Melbourne, 1972.

——*A Foolish, Passionate Man: A Biography of Jim Cairns*, Penguin, Ringwood, 1981.

Pemberton, Gregory, *All The Way: Australia's Road to Vietnam*, Allen & Unwin, Sydney, 1987.

——(ed), *Vietnam Remembered*, Weldon, Sydney, 1990.

Pierce, Peter, Doyle, Jeff & Grey, Jeffrey (eds), *Vietnam Days: Australia and the Impact of Vietnam*, Penguin, Ringwood, 1991.

Pollard, Rhys, *The Cream Machine*, Angus & Robertson, Sydney, 1972.

Reid, Alan, *The Whitlam Venture*, Hill of Content, Melbourne, 1976.

Renouf, Alan, *The Frightened Country*, Macmillan, Melbourne, 1979.

——*Let Justice Be Done: The Foreign Policy of Dr H.V. Evatt*, University of Queensland Press, St Lucia, 1983.

Rintoul, Stuart (ed), *Ashes of Vietnam: Australian Voices*, Heinemann, Richmond, 1987.

Rix, Alan, *W. Macmahon Ball—a Pioneer in Australian Asian Policy*, Centre for the Study of Australian–Asian Relations, Australians in Asia Series No. 3, Nathan, 1988.

Rowse, Tim, *Australian Liberalism and National Character*, Kibble, Malmsbury, 1978.

Santamaria, B.A., *The Price of Freedom: The Movement—After Ten Years*, Hawthorn Press, Melbourne, 1966.

Saunders, Malcolm & Summy, Ralph, *The Australian Peace Movement: A Short History*, Peace Research Centre, Canberra, 1986.

Scates, Bob, *'Draftmen Go Free': A History of the Anti-Conscription Movement in Australia*, [self-published], Melbourne [1989].

Sexton, Michael, *War for the Asking: Australia's Vietnam Secrets*, Penguin, Ringwood, 1981.

Spender, Percy, *Exercises in Diplomacy: The ANZUS Treaty and the Colombo Plan*, Sydney University Press, Sydney, 1969.

——*Politics and a Man*, Collins, Sydney, 1972.

Spratt, Elwyn, *Eddie Ward: Firebrand of East Sydney*, Rigby, Adelaide, 1965.

Stone, Gerald L., *War without Honour*, Jacaranda Press, Brisbane, 1966.

Stuart, Francis, *Towards Coming-Of-Age: A Foreign Service Odyssey*, Centre for the Study of Australian–Asian Relations, Australians in Asia Series No. 2, Nathan, 1989.

Turner, Ian, *Room for Manoeuvre: Writings on History, Politics, Ideas and Play*, selected and edited by Leonie Sandercock and Stephen Murray-Smith, Drummond, Richmond, 1982.

University Study Group, *Vietnam and Australia: History, Documents, Interpretations*, University Study Group on Vietnam, Gladesville, 1966.

Walter, James, *The Leader: A Political Biography of Gough Whitlam*, University of Queensland Press, St Lucia, 1980.

Watt, Alan, *Vietnam: An Australian Analysis*, Cheshire, Melbourne, 1968.

——*The Evolution of Australian Foreign Policy, 1938–1965*, Cambridge University Press, London, 1968.

——*Australian Diplomat: Memoirs of Sir Alan Watt*, Angus & Robertson in association with the Australian Institute of International Affairs, Sydney, 1972.

Whitlam, E.G., *Beyond Vietnam: Australia's Regional Responsibility*, Victorian Fabian Society Pamphlet no. 17, Fabian Society, Melbourne, 1968.

——*The Whitlam Government, 1972–1975*, Viking, Ringwood, 1985.

Wilkes, John (ed), *Communism in Asia: A Threat to Australia?*, Angus & Robertson for the Australian Institute of Political Science, Melbourne, 1967.

Withers, Glenn *Conscription: Necessity and Justice. The Case for an All Volunteer Army*, Angus & Robertson, Sydney, 1972.

York, Barry, *Student Revolt!: La Trobe University, 1967–73*, Nicholas Press, Campbell, 1989.

Articles & chapters

Aarons, Brian, 'History of the student left movement at Sydney University', *Left Forum*, March 1966, pp. 3–10.

Aarons, Eric, 'As I saw the Sixties', *Australian Left Review*, no. 27, Oct.–Nov. 1970, pp. 60–73.

Altman, Denis, 'Foreign policy and the elections', *Politics*, vol. 2, no. 1, May 1967, pp. 57–66.

Anon, 'Between Moscow and Peking—the C.P. of Australia', *Current Affairs Bulletin*, vol. 34, no. 3, June 22, 1964.

——'Commitment in Vietnam', *Current Affairs Bulletin*, vol. 36, no. 10, September 27, 1965.

Barcan, Alan, 'The New Left in Australia', *Outlook*, vol. 4, no. 3, June 1960, pp. 8–10.

Beilharz, Peter, 'Australia', *International Yearbook of Communist Affairs*, Hoover Institution, Stanford, 1976, pp. 231–238.

Berry, J.W., 'Who are the marchers?', *Politics*, vol. 3, no. 2, Nov. 1968, pp. 163–175.

Carroll, Ian, 'The new radicals', *Arena*, no. 21, 1970. pp. 65–71.

Freudenberg, Graham, 'The Australian Labor Party and Vietnam', *Australian Outlook*, vol. 33, no. 2, 1979, pp. 157–165.

Frost, Frank, 'Australia and Vietnam, 1950–1980: Part I, 1950–1972', *Dyason House Papers*, vol. 6, no. 3, March 1980, pp. 1–5.

Goot, Murray, 'Party dominance and partisan division, 1941–1972', in Cameron Hazlehurst (ed), *Australian Conservatism: Essays in Twentieth Century Political History*, Australian National University Press, Canberra, 1979.

Gration, P.C., 'A brief history of Baria Province', *Australian Army Journal*, no. 290, July 1973, pp. 36–42.

Hamel-Green, Michael, 'Vietnam: Beyond pity', *Australian Left Review*, no. 24, April–May, 1970.

——'Conscription and legitimacy: 1964–1972', *Melbourne Journal of Politics*, no. 7, 1974–75, pp. 3–16.

Herouvim, John, 'Politics of the revolving door: The Communist Party of Australia (Marxist-Leninist)', *Melbourne Journal of Politics*, vol. 15, 1983–84, pp. 54–68.

Hughes, C.A., 'The rational voter and Australian foreign policy: 1961–69', *Australian Outlook*, vol. 24, no. 1, April 1970, pp. 5–16.

Jackson, Andra & Wieneke, Diane, 'Student power—an alternative view', *Arena*, no. 19, 1969, pp. 85–91.

Jupp, James, 'What happened to the New Left?: Melbourne socialists v. Sydney fellow-travellers', *Bulletin*, 15 September 1962, pp. 29–31.

Kirsner, Douglas *et al*, 'Student activism', *Australian Left Review*, Aug–Sept. 1968, no. 4, pp. 30–38 and 43–53. [Interviews with Douglas Kirsner, Grant Hannan, Rowan Cahill, Brian Aarons, Mitch Thompson, Peter Duncan and Peter O'Brien]

'Lacordaire', 'The Movement downhill', *Nation*, January 30, 1960, pp. 8–10.

Laver, Brian, 'Behind student power', *Australian Left Review*, June–July, 1968, pp. 22–25.

McDougall, Derek, 'The Australian press coverage of the Vietnam War in 1965', *Australian Outlook*, vol. 20, no. 3, December 1966, pp. 303–310.

McNeill, Ian, 'An outline of the Australian military involvement in Vietnam: July 1962–December 1972', *Defence Force Journal*, no. 24, Sept./Oct. 1980, pp. 42–53.

McQueen, Humphrey, 'A single spark', *Arena*, no. 16, 1968, pp. 50–56.

Mortimer, Rex, 'The New Left', *Arena*, no. 13, Winter 1967, pp. 16–28.

——'Dilemmas of Australian Communism', in Henry Mayer (ed), *Australian Politics: A Second Reader*, Cheshire, Melbourne, 1969, pp. 382–394.

——'Student activism—Out of nihilism', *Australian Left Review*, no. 24, April–May, 1970, pp. 73–78.

Murphy, John, ' "Like outlaws": Australian narratives from the Vietnam War', *Meanjin*, vol. 46, no. 2, June 1987, pp. 153–162.

Osmond, Warren, 'Student revolutionary left', *Arena*, no. 19, 1969, pp. 22–27.

——'Marxists and the changing Communist Party', *Arena*, no. 20, 1969, pp. 62–64.

Rawson, D.W., 'The Vietnam War and the Australian party system', *Australian Outlook*, vol. 23, no. 1, April 1969, pp. 58–67.

Robertson, Alec, 'CPA in the anti-war movement', *Australian Left Review*, no. 27, Oct.–Nov., 1970.

Robertson, Mavis, 'Conscription', *Australian Left Review*, no. 1, 1966, pp. 11–15.

Rootes, C.A., 'The development of radical student movements and their sequelae', *Australian Journal of Politics and History*, vol. 34, no. 2, 1988, pp. 173–186.

Santamaria, B.A., 'Struggle on two fronts: The D.L.P. and the 1969 election', *Australian Quarterly*, vol. 41, no. 4, December 1969, pp. 33–42.

Saunders, M.J., 'The trade unions in Australia and opposition to Vietnam and conscription: 1965–73', *Labour History*, no. 43, November 1982, pp. 64–82.

——' "Law and order" and the anti-Vietnam War movement: 1965–72', *Australian Journal of Politics and History*, vol. 28, no. 3, 1982, pp. 367–379.

——'The ALP's response to the anti-Vietnam War movement: 1965–73', *Labour History*, no. 44, May 1983, pp. 75–91.

Saunders, Malcolm & Summy, Ralph, 'Salient themes of the Australian peace movement: An historical perspective', *Social Alternatives*, vol. 3, no. 1, 1982, pp. 23–32.

Summy, Ralph, 'Militancy and the Australian peace movement, 1960–67', *Politics*, vol. 5, no. 2, Nov. 1970, pp. 148–162.

——'The Australian Peace Council and the anticommunist milieu, 1949–1965', in Charles Chatfield and Peter van den Dungen (eds), *Peace Movements and Political Culture*, University of Tennessee Press, Knoxville, 1988.

Turner, Ian, 'The Vietnam Moratorium', *Meanjin*, vol. 29, June 1970, pp. 243–244.

van Gelder, M.M., 'Australia's selective National Service training scheme, 1965–72', *Defence Force Journal*, no. 19, Nov./Dec. 1979. pp. 49–55.

Western, J.S. & Wilson, P.R., 'Attitudes to Conscription', *Politics*, vol. 2, no. 1, May, 1967, pp. 48–56.

Index

Harvest of fear

movement, *see* peace
movement; role in Moratorium
campaign, *see* Vietnam
Moratorium Campaign; *see
also* Aarons; Blake; Gollan;
Taft
Communist Party of Australia
(Marxist–Leninist) (CPA
(M–L)), 220, 245; analysis of
Vietnam war, 225–6; split
from CPA, 224–5; *see also*
Maoism
Communist Party in Vietnam,
37, 85, 94, 193; and
anti-colonial movement, 26–8;
cadres, 28, 31, 37, 181–2,
184–5; 'dual power' strategy,
181–7; early activity in Baria,
24–6, 28–31, 32–3; front
strategy, 32; military strategy
in Tet Offensive, 192–3;
military units in Baria, 34, 85;
in Phuoc Tuy in 1960s, 94–6,
260–1; relation to patriotism
and nationalism, 8–9, 28,
37–8, 153; repression of,
(1954–59), 85–90; *see also*
NLF; Viet Minh
confrontation
(Indonesia–Malaysia), 103,
114–15
Confucianism, 6, 16, 26, 29, 32
Congress for International
Co-Operation and
Disarmament (CICD), 124,
142, 144, 204, 310; formation
(1959), 121–3; role in peace
movement, 125, 127–8,
227–9; role in Moratorium
campaign, 244–5, 250–1,
253–4; *see also* peace
movement
conscientious objectors, 144,
213–15; *see also* conscription
in Australia
Conscientious Objectors
(Non-Pacifist), 214
conscription in Australia, 147,
155, 156–7, 264–5, 267–8;
and civil liberties, 144, 202,
213–14, 216, 217; and draft
resistance, 215–17, 228;

introduction (1964), 114–18;
statistics, 216, 217; *see also*
Australian Labor Party (ALP),
attitudes to conscription
counter-revolutionary warfare;
Australian doctrine of, xx,
165–9, 180, 260–3, 275; *see
also* civic action and civil
affairs
CPA *see* Communist Party of
Australia (CPA)
Cultural Revolution, Chinese, 223
Curtin, John, 157

Dat Do; minefield, 189–92;
village, 15, 29, 92, 182, 188,
194
death, Vietnamese cultural
attitudes to, 6, 175
Defence committee, 103, 108,
200, 202
Defence, department of, 51, 66,
117, 243, 260
defoliation, *see* chemical agents
Democratic Labor Party (DLP),
76–7, 118, 204–05, 259; *see
also* Santamaria, B.A.
Democratic Socialist Club
(Melbourne university), 142,
154
detente, 152, 204
Dickie, Rev. Alf, 58, 122, 242,
310; (illus.), 76
Diem, Ngo Dinh, 36, 99–102,
112–13, 126, 275;
assassination, 93, 97, 114;
consolidation of power, 84–5;
ideology, 84, 86, 90;
repression of Communists by,
85–90; visit to Australia,
81–4, 100, 104, 212; (illus.),
82
Dien Bien Phu, battle (1954),
xvii, 36, 39, 61–2
Draft Resistance Movement
(DRM), 215
Draft Resisters' Union (DRU),
254–5
Dulles, John Foster, 61–3, 64–5,
67, 68, 74; (illus.), 45
Duong Bach Mai, 23–4
Dylan, Bob, 222, 223, 236, 246